3rd edition

Learning
& Behavior

Paul Chance
Salisbury State University

Brooks/Cole Publishing Company
Pacific Grove, California

For Arno H. Luker

Brooks/Cole Publishing Company
A Division of Wadsworth, Inc.

Printed in the United States of America
10   9   8   7   6   5   4   3   2   1

Library of Congress Cataloging-in-Publication Data

Chance, Paul.
    Learning and behavior / Paul Chance. — 3rd ed.
        p.   cm.
    Includes bibliographical references and index.
        ISBN 0-534-17394-2
        1. Conditioned response.   2. Learning, Psychology of.   3. Nature and nurture.   I. Title.
BF319.C45   1993
153.1'5—dc20   93-2435
                                                                         CIP

Sponsoring Editor: *Ken King, Marianne Taflinger*
Editorial Assistant: *Gay Meixel, Virge Pirelli-Minetti*
Production Editor: *Laurel Jackson*
Manuscript Editor: *Joanne Tenenbaum*
Permissions Editor: *Karen Wootten*
Interior and Cover Design: *Terri Wright*
Cover Photo: *Ken Bohn; Sea World, Inc.*
Art Coordinator: *Lisa Torri*
Interior Illustration: *Accurate AA, Inc.*
Indexer: *Wm. J. Richardson Associates*
Typesetting: *Kachina Typesetting, Inc.*
Cover Printing: *Phoenix Color Corporation*
Printing and Binding: *Arcata Graphics/Fairfield*

Brief Contents

This topic is closely and emphatically relevant to the problem of the Evolution of Civilization. . . . Civilization is, indeed, the chief product of human learning.

—E. L. Thorndike

Contents

three   **Pavlovian Learning: Principles   57**

four   **Pavlovian Learning:**
Applications   85

five   # Operant Learning: Principles   101

six   # Operant Learning: Applications   135

seven   ## Observational Learning   163

eight   ## Generalization
                ## and Discrimination   185

nine   # Schedules of Reinforcement   **215**

ten   # Aversive Control   **251**

Preface

THIS THIRD EDITION OF *LEARNING AND BEHAVIOR* IS ALMOST AS DIFFERENT from the second as the second was from the first. One obvious difference is that there are now 12 chapters rather than 10. Three chapters have been added: one each on the application of Pavlovian and operant learning, and one on aversive control. The chapter on thinking is gone, but most of the material covered in it has been incorporated into other chapters.

Most chapters have been heavily revised. Chapter Two's discussion of research design has been expanded and now includes material on anecdotal and case study methods. The discussion on the use of animals in behavioral research has also been enlarged. Extinction, previously discussed in conjunction with forgetting, is covered in the chapter on reinforcement schedules. Forgetting is now a chapter unto itself and includes a section on improving recall. (Instructors may want to encourage students to read the latter section early on so that they can apply it throughout the course.)

The chapter on observational learning is somewhat shorter than in the second edition, due primarily to the deletion of material on vicarious Pavlovian learning. This topic is problematic because it is extremely difficult to distinguish between vicarious Pavlovian conditioning and ordinary Pavlovian conditioning.

The new chapter on aversive control includes a discussion of noncontingent aversives, followed by negative reinforcement and punishment. Considerable space is devoted to problems associated with aversive control and to its alternatives, including response prevention and functional communication training. I believe the latter may be the most promising alternative to aversives yet developed.

Each chapter of the new edition begins with one or two quotations. These are meant to set the stage for what is to come in the chapter. Presumably, the students will have a different understanding of the quotations after reading the chapter than they had before. The quotations might also be useful as a springboard for class discussion or as the basis for essay exam questions.

The third edition includes questions that appear throughout the text. Most of these queries ask simple, straightforward questions about the material just read. The idea is for the student to read the query, attempt to answer it without looking at the preceding text, and then turn to the end of the chapter and read the answer given there. It is hoped that this activity will not only help the student assess his or her progress, but add to the reinforcers for reading the text.

The queries are fairly straightforward; the chapter review questions are another matter. Many of the latter are quite challenging (some students would say annoying) and require considerable thought. The questions ask the students to apply what they have learned by, for example, designing an experiment, setting up a treatment program, or providing an example that does not come from the text. I believe that grappling with such questions can help students master principles. In any case, the questions have proved useful in stimulating discussion. In hopes of increasing their usefulness, I have provided guidelines concerning points that might be made in answering them in an instructor's guide. (The guide also includes test items for each chapter, text commentaries, and other material.)

Several things about the text remain essentially unchanged. The theme that learning is a biologically evolved mechanism for coping with an ever-changing environment runs through every chapter, if not every paragraph. The book continues to supplement research studies with "real-world" examples and applications. (The working assumption is that laboratory research has a lasting impact on the typical student only if it is shown to have some relevance outside of the laboratory.) As in the past, I have tried to write in a style that is simple, clear, and engaging without trivializing the material. To avoid giving students the impression that learning is something only rats and pigeons do, I have included many studies and examples involving humans. And humorous remarks (such as the one in the previous sentence) continue to appear here and there, intended not so much to enlighten the reader as to reinforce the act of reading.

Although this text is longer than the previous edition, the difference has less to do with additional concepts than with additional examples and illustrations meant to increase understanding. The text makes no attempt to be encyclopedic. It is not meant to expose students to the vast variety of topics in learning research, but to help them master the fundamental principles of learning.

This notion of what an introductory science text should do has gained some support in recent years. The American Association for the Advancement of Science (1989), in its report, *Science for All Americans*, argues that what is needed to improve science instruction is not more course content, but less. Students, the report argues, need to embroil themselves in a relatively small number of concepts and skills for a prolonged period, rather than memorize long lists of terms, facts, and figures. Others are hearkening to this message (for example, Dempster, 1993). Whether the AAAS philosophy is sound is subject to debate; instructors should know, however, that it is the philosophy upon which this text is based.

As in the past, I had a good deal of help in preparing this edition. Nothing is so useful to a textbook author as honest criticism. I therefore offer my sincere thanks to Carl D. Cheney, Utah State University; R. H. Defran, San Diego State University; William E. Gibson, Northern Arizona University; Robert J. Grissom, San Francisco State University; Charles O. Hopkins, University of Illinois at Urbana-Champaign; Mike Knight, University of Central Oklahoma; John Lutz, East Carolina University; Brady Phelps, Utah State University; David Paul Ribbe, Medical University of South Carolina; Ronald R. Ulm, Salisbury State University; and Jerry Venn, Mary Baldwin College. I must single out Carl Cheney and Jerry Venn for special thanks. They not only put this and previous editions under their microscopes, but offered constant support for my efforts. They have been good friends and colleagues.

The first two editions of *Learning and Behavior* were published under the Wadsworth imprint. During the preparation of the present edition, Wadsworth Publishing Company made certain organizational changes. One of these was a decision to place all psychology texts with Brooks/Cole, a part of the parent company. I am grateful to Ken King and others at Wadsworth for making this transition smooth and painless. I also want to thank my new friends at Brooks/Cole, including Carline Haga; Laurel Jackson; Marianne Taflinger; and manuscript editor Joanne Tenenbaum. I especially want to thank Marianne Taflinger for helpful advice and criticism and Laurel Jackson for guiding the book through production.

If the book pleases, much of the credit goes to those just mentioned and to those who have used earlier editions and offered feedback. If the book disappoints in one way or another, the complaints belong on my doorstep.

Either way, I hope you will give me the benefit of your reaction. Feedback from instructors is very helpful in revising a text, and I hope you will let me know how the book might be improved. You can write to me in care of Brooks/Cole or via e-mail. My Compuserve address is 72134,1263. If you are on BITNET, use INTERNET:72134.1263@CompuServe.Com. I look forward to hearing from you.

—Paul Chance
Salisbury State University

Note to the Student

Before you begin reading the text, please consider the following points:

Queries.   The queries that appear here and there in the text are meant to assist you in learning about learning. Most of them ask you to recall something you have just read. To get the most out of the queries, attempt to answer each one when you encounter it—without rereading the preceding section. Write down your answer on a scrap of paper, and then immediately compare your answer with the answer at the end of the chapter. (The reasons for this procedure should become clear when you read Chapter Five.) If your answer is incorrect, reread the section involved. Once you have finished a chapter, you may use the queries in reviewing. However, keep in mind that the queries touch on only a few topics in each chapter.

Review questions.   The questions that appear at the end of each chapter are meant to help you review the chapter content. Many of these questions require something more than merely recalling points made in the chapter; they require you to use principles in the chapter (and perhaps in previous chapters) to solve new problems. Wrestling with the review questions should help you understand the chapter content better.

Both the queries and review questions should prove useful in preparing for exams, particularly if you compare your answers with those of other students. Ask your instructor about questions that you and your classmates are unable to answer satisfactorily.

Learning to remember.   Chapter Eleven, "Forgetting," contains a section on learning to remember. This material includes practical advice, derived from research on learning and forgetting, that should improve your ability to recall the content of this text. *Do not read this* *material until directed to do so by your instructor.* Reading this material before it is assigned could give you an unfair advantage over students who do not read it. And you wouldn't want that to happen.

Feedback.   Please let me know what you think of this text. There is a reply card enclosed for that purpose, or if the reply card is missing, you can write to me in care of Brooks/Cole, 511 Forest Lodge Road, Pacific Grove, CA 93950-5098. You can also reach me through e-mail at Compuserve; my address is 72134,1263. If you enclose a return address, I will try to reply to your remarks. I am not fishing for compliments, and I hope you will not hesitate to tell me of improvements you think need to be made. Your comments (positive or negative) will be appreciated and will be used when preparing the next edition of *Learning and Behavior.*

  You are about to begin studying what I believe is the most fascinating and important subject in the behavioral sciences. Very likely your instructor feels the same way. I hope some of our enthusiasm for learning and behavior will rub off on you.

one

Introduction: Nature, Nurture, and Behavior

Blood will tell.
—AUTHOR UNKNOWN

Just as the twig is bent, so the tree's inclin'd.
—ALEXANDER POPE

BACKGROUND

Change, said the Roman philosopher Lucretius 2,000 years ago, is the only constant. Yet we tend to regard change as an aberration, a brief disruption in a normally constant world. When a great volcano such as Mount Saint Helens in Washington erupts, as it did in 1980, knocking over thousands of trees and covering the earth for miles around with a blanket of volcanic ash, we think how strange it is that nature should misbehave so. It is, we tell ourselves, a momentary lapse, a kind of geological tantrum; soon our old planet will regain its composure, its sameness.

But the truth is that only our short tenure on earth deludes us into seeing sameness. In the course of an individual human's lifetime, volcanic eruptions, earthquakes, and the like are rare, but in the life of the earth, they are the very stuff of existence. Our time here is too brief to see continents crash together and tear apart, mountains rise and fall, vast deserts replace oceans; too brief to see thousands of animal and plant species come and go, like the ever-changing, varicolored crystalline shapes of a kaleidoscope.

Change is not the exception to the rule, then, but the rule itself. Throughout nature, the struggle to prevail is a struggle against change: food supplies dwindle, prey animals become faster, predators become more formidable. Some changes, such as the movement of continents, take place over eons; others, such as the advance of glaciers, take thousands of years; still others, such as the rising and setting of the sun or the appearance and disappearance of hungry predators, occur daily. The one constant is change. Any individual or species must be able to cope with change if it is to survive. But how? By what mechanisms can we and other organisms deal with such a fickle world?

NATURE: ADAPTATION THROUGH EVOLUTION

One mechanism for coping with change is evolution. In *On the Origin of Species*, published in 1859, the English naturalist Charles Darwin proposed that species arise through the process of natural selection. There is, he argued, tremendous variation among the members of any species. Some of these variations are relevant to features in the environment; others are not. Relevant features may be either beneficial to the species or harmful. Not only are individuals with favorable variations more likely to survive, and hence to reproduce, but their offspring are more likely to show this helpful variation. Characteristics that contribute to survival are selected by the environment, so future generations will increasingly display these characteristics. Evolution is therefore the inevitable product of variation and natural selection.

Query: Why is variation important in evolution?[1]

Although Darwin did not understand the genetic basis for variation (the work of Gregor Mendel was not then widely known), he knew from direct observation that variation among the members of a species was common. He also knew that selective breeding of farm animals with a specific variation often resulted in offspring that resembled their parents in that characteristic. And he knew that selective breeding of individuals with a given characteristic would, over several generations, result in a high proportion of animals with that characteristic.

Darwin went beyond the animal breeders, however, by proposing that this same sort of selection process takes place throughout nature.

---

[1] Try answering each query as it appears, and immediately check the answers at the end of the chapter.

A characteristic such as the thickness of a mammal's fur varies widely among the members of the species. If the climate turns gradually colder, individuals with thicker coats will have an advantage over those with thinner coats, so they will live longer and produce more thick-coated offspring. With each succeeding generation, there will be proportionally more animals with thick coats.

Darwin's theory does not require the involvement of any intelligent agent; we need not, for example, imagine God as animal husbandry expert. The slow-witted and the slow afoot are culled by natural predators. Those that are not suited to a change in climate, a change in the food supply, a change in predators, perish. The environment selects desirable characteristics, and selects out undesirable characteristics.

It is often difficult for people to see how natural selection could produce the complex systems we call plants and animals. Richard Dawkins (1986), in a book called *The Blind Watchmaker*, offers this analogy:

> If you walk up and down a pebbly beach, you will notice that the pebbles are not arranged at random. The smaller pebbles typically tend to be found in segregated zones running along the length of the beach, the larger ones in different zones or stripes. The pebbles have been sorted, arranged, selected. (p. 43)

What has sorted, arranged, and selected the stones, Dawkins notes, is the mechanical, unthinking force of the waves. Big stones are affected differently by the waves than small stones, so they end up in different places. Order has evolved from disorder as the inevitable product of natural forces.

Another analogy is the sieve. If you pour gravel into a sieve, the finer material will pass through while the larger material will not. The sieve selects objects of a certain size, and selects out objects of a different size. The characteristics selected depend upon the characteristics of the sieve, yet we do not attribute intelligence to the sieve.

Research on *Biston betularia*, one of the many large moths found on the British Isles, illustrates natural selection nicely. *Betularia* feeds at night and rests during the day on the trunks and limbs of trees. Its survival depends in large part on its ability to escape detection by the birds that find it an appetizing food. Several decades ago, nearly all *betularia* were a mottled light gray color, closely resembling the lichen-covered trees on which they rested. A rare black variation of the moth stood out against this background like coal against snow. But when pollutants in certain industrial areas killed the lichen and darkened the bark, the light-colored moths increasingly fell prey to birds, while the dark moths tended to survive and reproduce. An examination of *betularia* collections reveals that in forests near industrial centers, where pollution is common, the black *betularia* has increased and the light-colored variety has declined. In some areas, 90% of the *betularia* are of the once-rare black variety (Kettlewell, 1959).

It is possible that the same sort of process that affected the coloration of *betularia* has affected the skin color of humans living in very different climates. A natural substance in the skin, melanin, screens out the sun's rays. The more melanin, the darker the skin, and the more sunlight is screened out. The people of Scandinavia and Northern Europe, where there is relatively little sunlight, are characteristically fair-skinned, which allows them to absorb the sunlight needed to produce vitamin D. People who live near the equator, where there is an abundance of sunlight, are characteristically dark-skinned, which provides them with protection against the hazards of too much sun. Like *betularia,* the human species takes on the coloration that survival in a given environment requires.

Genetic variation and natural selection account for most of the differences within a species from one geographic region to another and from one time to another. However, genetic diversity is also affected by abrupt changes in the genes. These **mutations,**[2] as they are called, can occur in any of the body's cells and are sometimes the cause of life-threatening diseases. If a mutation occurs in the genes of reproductive cells (sperm or ova), the mutation will be passed along to the next generation.

Offspring with mutated genes may or may not display a new characteristic, just as a person who carries the gene for blue eyes may or may not have blue eyes. But the mutated gene will be passed on, unseen or not, to future generations.

Most mutations produce changes that are not helpful to survival. Many of these changes are simply of no consequence. People who have alligator green or navy blue eyes as a result of a mutation may experience some ostracism (or, given the fickleness of fashion, increased popularity) but their chances of surviving and reproducing are not likely to be strongly affected. Other mutations put the individual at risk. Gene mutations can result in two-headed snakes, for example. Since two heads are not, in fact, better than one, such animals seldom live long enough to reproduce their kind. Thus, harmful mutations are selected out.

On very rare occasions, mutations result in adaptive changes. A mutation might, for instance, provide an animal with a horn that proves useful in defense. Or it might provide resistance against certain diseases. When mutations are useful, they can mean rapid changes in the defining characteristics of a species because the offspring of individuals carrying the useful gene will be more likely to survive and reproduce.

---

[2] Glossary terms appear in boldface when introduced.

Query: How do mutations affect variation?

Evolution would be of limited importance to the study of behavior if it applied only to physical characteristics such as eye color, fur thickness, and susceptibility to disease. But the principles of variation and natural selection also apply to certain forms of behavior; as the environment changes, individuals that behave in adaptive ways are favored. Variations in behavior and the process of natural selection produce a repertoire of innate adaptive behavior. Such genetically based forms of behavior can be classified as reflexes, fixed action patterns, and inherited behavior traits.

■ Reflexes

A **reflex** is a simple relation between an event and an involuntary reaction to that event (see "The Reflex Arc"). Reflexes are either present at birth or appear at predictable stages in development. They are part of the inherited adaptive equipment of the organism. All animals, from protozoa to professors, have reflexes.

Many reflexes protect the organism from injury. The amoeba is an irregularly shaped, one-celled animal that travels by extending a part of its perimeter forward and then pulling the rest along after. When the amoeba encounters a toxic substance, it immediately withdraws from it; this reflex minimizes the harmful effects of the noxious substance. Larger animals do much the same thing when they withdraw a limb from a painful object. The professor who picks up a very hot skillet will immediately release it and withdraw the injured hand. Other protective reflexes in humans include the eye blink, in which the eye closes when any object approaches it; the pupillary reflex, in which the iris contracts or relaxes in response to changes in light; the sneeze, by which irritants such as dust and pollen are expelled from the nose and lungs; the patellar reflex, or knee jerk, which keeps us on our feet when something trips us up; and the vomit reflex, which removes harmful substances from the stomach in an efficient, if indelicate, manner.

Other reflexes are important in food consumption. When an amoeba encounters some edible object, such as a dead bacterium, it immediately responds to the object by engulfing it and making a meal of it. Humans have a number of such consummatory reflexes: Touch a baby's face and she will turn toward what touched her; this rooting reflex, as it is called, is useful in finding the mother's nipple. When the nipple touches the baby's lips, this evokes the sucking reflex, which brings milk into the baby's mouth. Food in the mouth elicits the salivary reflex, the flow of saliva that begins the process of digestion. The presence of saliva triggers swallowing. Swallowing triggers peristalsis, the rhythmic motion of the lining of the esophagus that carries food to the stomach. Food in the stomach prompts yet another

The Reflex Arc

A reflex is a relation between a specific event and a specific response to that event. Reflexes are mediated by (carried out by means of) a relatively simple set of interconnected units called the **reflex arc.** Take, for example, the patellar reflex. A sharp blow to the patellar tendon, just beneath the kneecap, causes the foot to swing forward. What happens is this: The blow excites receptors at the tendon. This electrochemical excitation is transferred to nearby sensory neurons (nerve cells), which carry the impulse to the spinal cord, where connecting interneurons are activated. The interneurons carry the impulse to motor neurons, which convey the excitation to muscles in the leg. The muscles contract, pulling the leg forward. In other reflexes, the sequence ends with the excitation of glands rather than muscles, so the reflex arc is said to consist of receptors, sensory neurons, interneurons, motor neurons, and effectors (muscles or glands).

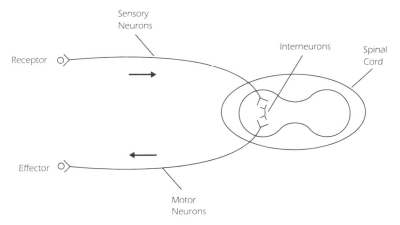

Reflex arc

Notice that the reflex arc does not require higher brain centers. We do not have to think about jerking our leg when rapped on the knee. We are ordinarily aware that the knee has been struck because sensory nerves in the spinal cord carry impulses to the brain. The impulse that reaches the leg muscles does not emanate from the brain, however, but from the spinal cord. Thus, we become aware that we have been hit at about the same time our leg jerks forward.

reflex, the flow of digestive juices. Thus, the simple act of eating is, in large measure, a chain of innate reflexes.

We tend not to notice our own reflexes until they fail to function properly. When we swallow, for example, a flap of cartilage called the epiglottis closes over the windpipe, thus preventing food from entering

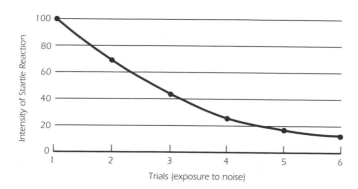

FIGURE 1-1 Habituation of the startle reflex. The intensity of the startle response declines with each exposure to the noise. (Hypothetical data.)

the lungs. After the swallowed material passes, the epiglottis, which works rather like a hatch, opens again so that we can breathe. Occasionally, the hatch gets stuck after it closes, and we are unable to inhale. We gasp for air until the hatch opens. It is a frightening experience. For some people, such problems are fairly common; fortunately, most of us are blissfully unaware that we even have an epiglottis until, once in a great while, it malfunctions.

Reflexes are highly stereotypic; that is, they are remarkably invariant in form, frequency, strength, and time of appearance during development. This is not to say, however, that they do not vary at all. The rooting reflex, for example, may first appear in one infant at the age of seven days, but may not show up in a second infant for another week.

There is also some variation in the form a reflex takes. A tap below the knee may produce a barely detectable patellar reflex in one person, while in another the same light blow may result in a kick that looks like an attempt to make a field goal.

Evoking a reflex response once can make it more likely to occur a second time. This is called **sensitization.** If, for example, you jump when startled by a loud noise, you are then more likely to jump if you hear a soft noise. The loud noise sensitizes you to the soft noise.

Repeatedly evoking a given reflex response will result in a reduction in the strength of the response. This phenomenon, which is actually a primitive sort of learning, is known as **habituation** (see Figure 1-1). S. Sharpless and H. Jasper (1956) noted the effects of loud noises on cats by recording their brain waves on an electroencephalograph (EEG). The EEG showed marked arousal at first, but the reaction declined steadily with each repetition of a given sound, until the noise had hardly any effect.

Wagner Bridger (1961) studied habituation in infants. You know that a sudden loud noise will make you jump; another part of this startle reflex is the quickening of the heartbeat. Bridger found that when babies first heard a noise, they responded with an increase in heart rate, but with repetition of the noise at regular intervals, the change in heart rate became less and less pronounced until, in some cases, the noise had no measurable effect at all.

Although habituation is a relatively simple phenomenon, it is not so simple as this discussion implies. Repeated exposure to a loud sound will produce habituation of the startle reflex; but the degree of habituation and the rate at which it occurs depend upon the loudness of the sound, variations in the quality of the sound, the number of times the sound occurs in a minute, the time interval between repeated exposures to the sound, and so on. (For more information, see Thompson & Spencer, 1966.)

> Query: What is the difference between habituation and sensitization?

Though reflexes are more complex and variable than most people imagine, they nevertheless represent the simplest and most uniform kind of innate behavior. Other forms of inborn behavior are more complex and more variable.

■ Fixed Action Patterns

Fixed action patterns are series of interrelated acts. They resemble reflexes in that they are innate; display little variability from individual to individual, or from day to day in the same individual; and often are reliably elicited by a particular kind of event. They differ from reflexes in that they involve the entire organism rather than a few muscles or glands; are more complex, often consisting of long series of reflexlike acts; are more variable, though still very stereotypic; and are less likely to be evident at or soon after birth. Fixed action patterns used to be called *instincts*, but this term has fallen out of favor, partly because it has come to refer to any more or less automatic behavior (as in, "He heard a shot and instinctively drew his weapon").

> Query: How are fixed action patterns different from reflexes?

Some fixed action patterns protect the animal from predators. When confronted by a threatening dog, the house cat arches its back, hisses, growls, and flicks its tail. These acts make the cat appear larger and more formidable than it really is and may therefore serve to put off an attacker. The opossum responds quite differently to predators: It plays dead. Most of the opossum's predators are reluctant to eat dead animals they encounter, so a "dead" opossum has a good chance of surviving.

Other fixed action patterns provide protection against the elements. Geese and many other birds migrate to warmer climates in the fall. When geese migrate, they typically fly in flocks in V formation. It has been suggested that this practice allows all but the lead bird to benefit from reduced wind resistance. The lead bird drops back after a time, so that the burden is spread throughout the flock. The theory is that the V formation substantially reduces the amount of energy required for flying and thereby increases each bird's chances of reaching its destination (Ruppell, 1975).

Some fixed action patterns help creatures procure food. Pigs root for worms, larvae, and truffles buried in the ground; some spiders build webs with which to capture their prey; and woodpeckers tap holes in tree bark to get at the insects that live there.

Many fixed action patterns involve courtship and mating. The male western grebe, a water bird, attracts a mate by running on the water; the male bighorn sheep wins a partner by bashing its head against that of its rival. In most animals, the mating act itself involves characteristically stereotyped behavior. When the female chimpanzee is capable of conceiving, she approaches an adult male and presents her swollen and inflamed genitals; the male responds to this display by mounting her. The act may be repeated numerous times while the female is receptive, but each performance is nearly identical to the last.

Fixed action patterns also govern the care and rearing of the young. After mating, the female of certain species of wasp builds a nest, places a paralyzed spider into it, lays an egg on top of the spider, closes the nest, and goes on its way, leaving the young wasp to fend for itself after it has hatched and eaten its first meal. The newborn of many higher species of animals require more nurturing, for which task their parents are genetically equipped. Birds work slavishly to feed their ever-hungry young. The brown-headed cowbird cares for its young by depositing its eggs in another bird's nest, often tricking an unsuspecting sparrow into making a heroic effort to feed a youngster twice its own size.

We saw that reflexes are reliably elicited by specific kinds of events. Fixed action patterns are also initiated by certain events, called **releasers.** For instance, the male rat ordinarily will mate only with females that are in estrus (that is, in heat). The estrous female produces odorous chemicals, called pheromones, that act as releasers for sexual behavior in the male. In the absence of these pheromones, the male will not usually attempt to mate. Similarly, a nesting gray lag goose responds to an egg that has rolled out of the nest by "stretching the neck towards it, bringing the bill behind the egg and with careful balancing movements rolling it back into the nest" (Tinbergen, 1951,

p. 84). A ball, an oval stone, or almost any more or less egg-shaped object near the nest will release this fixed action pattern.

Because of their complexity and their utility, many fixed action patterns appear to be thoughtful acts. In fact, they are probably no more thoughtful than is the behavior of a person who responds to a rap on the knee by jerking a leg. Take, for instance, the brown-headed cowbird's practice of placing its own eggs into another bird's nest and throwing out one or more of the nesting bird's eggs. The cowbird seems to do this in order to save itself the trouble of rearing its young. Further, the casual observer might infer that the bird knows what it is about, that it understands the logic in what it does. But there is, in reality, no reason to believe that this behavior reveals avian cleverness. The fact that the behavior occurs throughout the species, but not among other, equally intelligent birds, indicates that it is a fixed action pattern, as much a product of evolution as the color of the cowbird's feathers.

Another illustration of the unthinking nature of fixed action patterns is provided by the tropical army ant. Entire colonies of these ants charge across the forests in what appears to be a highly organized, intelligently directed campaign. In fact, the ants are merely following a chemical trail laid down by the ants ahead of them. T. C. Schneirla (1944) demonstrated that on a flat surface, such as a road, where no obstacles direct the course of the march, the lead ants tend to move toward the ants beside them. The column then turns in on itself, and the ants soon march round and round in a circle. This is not very thoughtful behavior.

Despite such evidence, some people persist in believing that fixed action patterns are learned behavior. They argue that the behavior is so complex that it could not possibly be the product of evolution. How, for example, could genetic variation and selection account for the fact that a cowbird removes eggs from another bird's nest and replaces them with its own? How could genes for such a complex behavior suddenly emerge? The answer is that their emergence is probably not sudden.

What we see in fixed action patterns may well be the product of thousands, perhaps millions, of years of evolution. B. F. Skinner (1975, 1984; see also Carr, 1967) has theorized that complex fixed action patterns may be selected by gradual changes in the environment, changes that take place over eons. Take, Skinner suggests, the salmon's migration upstream to breed. This act often requires the fish to ascend steep cliffs and swim against rushing currents. How could such complex and difficult behavior be the product of evolution? Skinner notes that at one time, returning to the breeding grounds might have constituted a relatively easy swim up a gently rising stream. As geological changes gradually increased the steepness of the slope, fish that could make the trip bred successfully and reproduced their kind, while those not up to the challenge failed to reproduce. As geological changes continued to increase the difficulty of the task, the process of natural selection produced salmon capable of mastering it. Skinner suggests that other complex fixed action patterns (such as migration) may have been molded by the environment in much the same way.

Query: How can the sieve analogy, presented earlier in this chapter, be used to illustrate the evolution of fixed action patterns?

Are there any fixed action patterns in human beings? It is hard to say. Several decades ago, textbooks listed dozens of human instincts, including the sex instinct, the social instinct, the maternal instinct, and the territorial instinct (see, for example, McDougall, 1908). But the list has shrunk in recent years. Some researchers today maintain that there are no fixed action patterns in human beings, that the supposed instincts lacked the monotonous character of, say, nesting birds and foraging ants. People, like chimpanzees, approach prospective sexual partners from time to time, but among humans the method of approach varies tremendously from culture to culture, from individual to individual, and even within the same individual from time to time. Humans have invented marriage, dating services, prostitution, singles bars, personals columns, and all sorts of rules and customs for defining how, when, where, and with whom sexual acts may be performed. There are even scripts (often called *lines*) that some people follow in approaching an individual of the opposite sex. ("Hi. Do you come here often?") The complexity and variability of mating rituals among humans does not closely resemble the stereotypic mating behavior of lower animals.

Much the same case can be made against the so-called maternal instinct. True, many women do desire to have children and to protect and nurture them, as do many men. But again, there is tremendous variation in how mothers perform these tasks. In some societies, for example, young children are fondled and held constantly, and their slightest need is met immediately; in other societies, the same children would be left pretty much to their own resources. Moreover, women in Western societies increasingly delay or forgo altogether the traditional maternal role. True fixed action patterns are not so readily discarded.

Perhaps the best case for a fixed action pattern in humans is the incest taboo. E. O. Wilson (1978) argues that people have an innate aversion to mating with members of their own families. In support of this, he cites research showing that children reared in Israeli kibbutzim (large, family-like communal groups) almost never marry within the kibbutz (Shepher, 1971).

Even the instinct against incest is, however, suspect. Sigmund Freud (1913/1918) pointed out that if there were a natural aversion to incest, there would be no need for an incest taboo. The taboo, he argued, was a cultural invention designed to avoid problems caused by incest. Further doubt about Wilson's view has been raised by recent studies showing that incestuous behavior is much more common than had been thought (Russell, 1986a, 1986b). If the incest taboo were a fixed action pattern, incest would be quite rare.

But even if we accept the view that incest, territoriality, and perhaps a few other patterns of behavior have genetic bases, it is clear that they are not nearly as stereotypic as the fixed action patterns of so many other animals. In humans, the role of genetics in behavior is generally more subtle and takes the form of inherited behavior traits.

■ Inherited Behavior Traits

Over the past few decades, a great deal of research has been done on the role genes play in determining general behavioral tendencies, or traits. Many of these traits fall under the heading of personality characteristics: activity level, aggressivity, neuroticism (that is, the tendency toward deviant behavior), and so forth. Others are more narrowly defined: taste preference, hoarding (of food, for instance), and sexual preference. Such tendencies, referred to here as **inherited behavior traits,** were once classified as instincts, but they differ from fixed action patterns in important ways.

As already noted, fixed action patterns are elicited by fairly specific kinds of environmental events, called releasers. The gaping mouth of a fledgling induces the parent bird to provide food, while a closed mouth does not. Inherited behavior traits, on the other hand, are elicited by a wider variety of events. For instance, under certain circumstances, aversive (painful or unpleasant) events reliably elicit aggressive behavior in many animals and in humans[3] (Berkowitz, 1983; Oliver et al., 1974; Ulrich, 1966; Ulrich & Azrin, 1962). But the term *aversive event* covers a lot of territory: It can refer to an electric shock, a pinprick, a spray of cold water, an air temperature above 80 degrees, insults, cross words, and so on. All can elicit aggressive behavior. Fixed action patterns are not released by so many different kinds of events.

Another difference between fixed action patterns and inherited behavior traits concerns the degree of fixedness of the behavior. Compare the fixed action pattern of the web spinning spider with the aggressiveness of a shocked rat. Each web-spinning spider spins a web with a genetically dictated pattern, and it goes about the task with a remarkable sameness, like someone living a recurrent dream. More-

---

[3] Humans are, of course, animals. The distinction is made here and elsewhere to avoid the impression that we are concerned only with "lower" species.

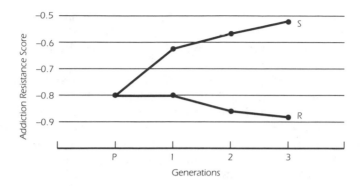

FIGURE 1-2 Inherited behavior trait. There is no instinct for addiction, but heredity plays a role in its development. From an unselected population of rats (P), rats susceptible (S) or resistant (R) to morphine addiction were interbred for three generations. Susceptible rats became increasingly susceptible, while resistant rats became increasingly resistant, to addiction. SOURCE: From "Addiction Liability of Albino Rats: Breeding for Quantitative Differences in Morphine Drinking" by J. R. Nichols and S. Hsiao. In *Science, 157*, pp. 561–563. Copyright © 1967 by the American Association for the Advancement of Science.

over, the web-spinning of one spider is remarkably like that of other members of the same species (Savory, 1974). But the rat that attacks its neighbor goes about it in a far less stereotypic manner, and there may be considerable difference between the attack of one rat and that of another.

While inherited behavior traits are more elusive than fixed action patterns, there is no doubt about their heritability. Selective breeding can, for example, produce strains of animals differing in fearfulness (Hall, 1937), aggressiveness (Fuller & Scott, 1954), activeness (Rundquist, 1933), and addiction proneness (Nichols & Hsiao, 1967; see Figure 1-2).

Recent research on the reproductive habits of certain snakes offers evidence of the way evolution shapes behavioral tendencies (Madsen et al., 1992). Researchers in Sweden compared adders (a kind of poisonous snake) that had had several sexual partners with those that had not. They found that the more promiscuous snakes produced more offspring than the others. It turned out that some male snakes were better at fertilizing the female's eggs, perhaps because they had more active sperm. Female snakes that had more partners had a better chance of copulating with the more effective males. To the extent that the tendency to copulate with several partners is inherited, these snakes will pass on this behavior to their young.

Humans also inherit many behavior traits. Studies of identical twins separated soon after birth suggest that they often have much in common as adults (Farber, 1981). They may have similar career interests, wear the same styles of clothes, enjoy the same kinds of art, music, entertainment, hobbies, and so on. Although this research is controversial, it supports the popular view that certain behavioral tendencies can run in families.

Studies comparing different racial groups also show the role of heredity in behavior traits. Daniel Freedman (1974; reported in Wilson, 1978) compared Chinese American infants with white American infants and found marked differences in disposition. The babies with Asian ancestry were less disturbed by noise, less irritable, and less likely to object to being restrained than were those with European backgrounds (see also Rushton, 1988).

Numerous studies have suggested that genes play an important role in some forms of troublesome behavior. Certain behavioral abnormalities, such as depression (Kallmann, 1953) and anxiety (Kendler et al., 1992), tend to run in families. Other researchers have found evidence that even criminality may be influenced indirectly by genes (Raine & Dunkin, 1990).

Similarly, although people do not have a social instinct (in the strict sense of fixed action patterns), they do have a strong, apparently innate tendency toward affiliating with other people. True hermits are rare, if not nonexistent. A sense of group membership seems to be an inevitable consequence of this trait. The famous psychoanalyst Erik Erikson (1968) was among those who observed that group members tend to demean outsiders. Groups, he said, engage in *pseudospeciation:* Members of other groups are considered inferior, as though they were subhuman species. Certain hunter-gatherer tribal groups refer to themselves by a word that in their language means merely *human being.* The implication is that members of other tribes are something less than human beings. Members of sophisticated Western societies have by no means outgrown this tendency (Bandura, 1973; Keen, 1986).

It is easy to see how inherited behavior traits might be products of natural selection. Rabbits are not well equipped for fighting, so the more combative among them are apt to be shortlived. The rabbit that flees the fox may escape, while the rabbit that stands and fights is unlikely to mate again. The same evolutionary forces no doubt have influenced human behavior: Individuals who preferred isolation to the security of the group, for example, were probably more likely to become some predator's meal.

> Query: Are inherited behavior traits more like fixed action patterns
> or more like reflexes? Explain.

Thanks to genetic variation and the process of natural selection, then, adaptive forms of behavior—reflexes, fixed action patterns, and inherited behavior traits—evolve. As the environment changes, new adaptive forms of behavior appear in the species, and old forms of behavior that are no longer adaptive disappear. In a sense, the environment selects what is needed for the species to survive. Evolution is therefore a marvelous invention for coping with a variable environment, but it has its limits.

■ Limits of Evolution

The chief problem with evolution as a way of coping with change is that it is slow. Changes in the environment do not produce changes in the genes that are helpful to individuals now living; they merely give a reproductive advantage to individuals with adaptive characteristics.

Suppose, for example, that the winters became gradually more severe in North America's Rocky Mountains. The bears that live in this region would have to adapt to colder winters to survive. Contrary to popular belief, bears are not true hibernators. They spend much of their winters sleeping in dens, but they awaken periodically and even emerge occasionally from their dwellings to feed. If the winters grew colder, such forays might be too expensive in terms of calories expended. Bears that were genetically inclined to sleep for long periods and to stay within their lairs would therefore have an advantage over those that stirred about more frequently. The sleepers would be more likely to survive and reproduce, so over a period of many generations, the bears in this region might evolve into true hibernators.

But the evolution of adaptive behavior is measured not in hours or days but in generations. Evolution is therefore of no value in helping individuals adapt either to cataclysmic changes or to the minor variations in daily life. Evolution will do nothing to help the current generation of bears meet the challenge of colder winters. And if a bear is able to endure the cold, but finds in the spring that its traditional food supply has been destroyed by the lower temperatures, evolution does not give it an appetite for another kind of food, or the skill to obtain it. Genetic variation and natural selection make it possible for the *species* to adapt to change, but they do not help the living *individual* to adapt.

Query: Why is evolution helpful to species but not to individuals?

As a consequence, evolutionary change is always "behind the times." Individuals are born with particular characteristics not because those characteristics will help them survive, but because in the past they helped that individual's ancestors to survive. As the environment changes, what was for one generation a very adaptive characteristic may become irrelevant or even injurious for the next.

Lee Cronk (1992) provides several examples of this phenomenon in a delightful article called *Old Dogs, Old Tricks.* "Behavioral and physical adaptations that seem to make no sense in an organism's current environment," Cronk writes, "can be traced to the legacy of an earlier, different environment in which those traits were favored" (p. 13). He cites the example of the rabbit that dodges back and forth when pursued by foxes, bobcats, and coyotes. This practice is still helpful in eluding these predators, but it is not effective when the rabbit finds itself on a highway "pursued" by a truck. Similarly, Cronk notes, armadillos befuddled approaching predators for thousands of years by springing into the air. Once again, however, this behavior is not adaptive on modern highways. As Cronk puts it, "Leap two feet high in front of a Buick, and you're buzzard bait" (p. 13).

B. F. Skinner (1983b) has pointed out that human beings also can become hostages to their genetic history. He notes, for example, that humans evolved in a world in which salt and sugar were not readily available. Individuals who had a natural preference for these foods were more likely to get the sodium and the calories needed for survival. We have, as a consequence, evolved into a species with strong likings for both salty and sweet foods. But our world has changed. In industrial societies, salt and sugar are abundant, and we consume too much of them, endangering our health in the process. Similarly, Skinner notes, a strong appetite for sexual contact favored the survival of our species during most of its evolution. Until recently (in evolutionary terms), diseases killed most children before they reached reproductive maturity; others died in early adulthood from starvation, childbearing, or the routine hazards of an untamed world. Consequently, those individuals who were most virile and most fertile were favored. But in the last 200 years, advances in medicine, sanitation, and food production have so greatly reduced the mortality rate of our young that we no longer need to be so virile and fertile for our species to survive. Yet we retain our antiquated sexual appetite, with the result that we are overpopulating the planet.

This is not to say that evolution is intrinsically self-destructive, nor that it is unimportant to survival. But evolution is limited by its sluggishness. Fortunately, another mechanism for adapting to changes in the environment is available, the mechanism of learning.

NURTURE: ADAPTATION THROUGH LEARNING

A second way of adapting to a variable environment is through learning. Of course, learning is itself a genetically evolved biological mechanism. It is an inborn ability to adapt to changes in the environment, an "inherited modifiability" (Skinner, 1953).

Learning takes up where reflexes, fixed action patterns, and inherited behavior traits leave off. Learning enables the organism to adapt to situations for which its innate behavior is inadequate. Consider, for example, how animals come to avoid eating poisonous foods. To some extent, poisonous foods may be avoided because of an animal's inherited tendency to avoid certain tastes, such as bitter or sour. But the inborn taste preferences are not perfect; some items that taste good are deadly. How then does an animal or a person survive this danger? The answer is by learning to avoid eating the harmful items. A rat that becomes ill after eating a plant with a particular taste is likely to avoid eating that plant the next time it encounters it. We do exactly the same thing when we avoid eating foods that "don't agree" with us.

Query: What is the chief advantage of learning over evolution?

Poisonous foods are not the only hazards, of course, and learning plays an important role in protecting humans and other animals from such dangers as fire, water, storms, and natural predators. There is evidence that learning may even play an important role in fighting off diseases. Some research suggests, for example, that learning experiences can modify the behavior of the body's immune system (Ader & Cohen, 1975; Bovbjerg et al., 1990).

But learning is not merely a defense mechanism. Especially among the higher species (that is, the better learners), learning is a means of fulfilling both the needs of survival and of "the good life." An intriguing study by anthropologist Shirley Strum (1987) shows how success among baboons may depend upon learned strategies.

Strum studied a troop of baboons in Kenya. She noted, as others had before her, that the highest-ranking males were the most aggressive. These animals took what they wanted, be it sexual favors or food; low-ranking males were passive. This is just as Tennyson would have it: "Nature, red in tooth and claw." But Strum began taking careful note of which animals actually benefitted most from life in the troop. It wasn't, she discovered, the aggressive, dominant males that had the greatest success with females or got the best foods; it was the lowest-ranking, least aggressive ones. She found, for instance, that only one out of four successful attempts to mate with females involved aggression. The less aggressive animals used a kinder, gentler approach to getting what they wanted, and it worked.

Strum found that the most aggressive males were usually newcomers, while the least aggressive were long-term members of the troop. She speculates that when males first join a troop, they are very aggres-

The Superior Animal

Humans spend an amazing amount of time trying to prove their superiority over other species. Part of this effort has been devoted to finding some uniquely human characteristic, some quality that sets our species apart from lower organisms. We used to say, for example, that *Homo sapiens* was the only animal that reasoned, but studies of animal learning raised serious doubts about that. We said we were the only creature to make and use tools, but then we discovered that chimpanzees make and use tools all the time. We said humans were the only animals capable of learning language, but then we taught apes and porpoises to communicate.

One by one, the characteristics we have held to be uniquely human have proved to be shared by other species. The ultimate futility of proving our superiority was pointed out by the British philosopher Bertrand Russell: "Organic life, we are told, has developed gradually from the protozoan to the philosopher; and this development, we are assured, is indubitably an advance. Unfortunately, it is the philosopher, not the protozoan, who gives us this assurance" (quoted in Durant, 1926, p. 523).

Perhaps the only uniquely human characteristic is this: So far as we know, we are the only creature that spends time trying to prove its superiority over other creatures. The rest of the animal kingdom treats the matter with indifference.

sive. With time, however, most learn to use other, more effective techniques. Those who do not change their ways eventually leave the troop. "Real power," writes Strum, "resided with those who were 'wise' rather than those who were 'strong' " (p. 151).

Learning also provides the power to modify the physical environment. This is most clearly evident in the case of humans; their extraordinary learning ability has enabled them to reshape their world. They are, as one writer puts it, "the only animals living in a world almost entirely of their own making. They cocoon themselves in synthetic materials, create their own daylight, breathe climate-controlled air, transform their food by cooking and chemistry, and spend much of their time sending and responding to electronic messages" (Marschall, 1992, p. 52). None of these changes in the natural environment is the result of inherited behavior; all are products of learning.

Learning, like evolution, is an adaptive mechanism, a way of coping with the challenges of a changing environment. In a sense, learning *is* a kind of evolution; through it, adaptive behavior is selected and nonadaptive behavior is selected out (Skinner, 1981, 1984). Evolution and learning are merely two different ways of dealing with a changing world. Typically, the two processes work together, as we shall now see.

THE NATURE-NURTURE DEBATE

One of the longest-running arguments in the study of behavior concerns the roles of nature and nurture in behavior. Basically, the issue is whether behavior is inherited or learned. Do we, as individuals, behave a certain way because we were born that way, or do we behave a certain way because we are products of our past?

The debate is evidenced in aphorisms people use every day, often without thinking about their larger significance. Is it true, for instance, that "blood will tell," or is it more accurate to say that "as the twig is bent, so the tree is inclined"? Are leaders born, or are they made? Can a person "turn over a new leaf," or is the leopard stuck with its spots?

The questions raised by such aphorisms apply to other species as well. Is the gorilla naturally very gentle, or is it gentle because life in the jungle (or zoo) has taught it gentleness? Is the chimpanzee largely vegetarian by nature, or does its diet merely reflect its food supply?

Of course, no advocate of the genetic view denies that learning is important, at least in higher animals, and no one who leans toward the role of learning completely ignores heredity. Nevertheless, for centuries people have lined up on one side or the other of this debate, according to what they believed was the more important determinant of behavior.

The trouble with the nature-nurture debate is that it creates an artificial division between the adaptive mechanisms of evolution and learning. The question wrongly implies that the answer must be one or the other (Cheney, 1991). Stephen Jay Gould (1987) suggests that we should view the origins of behavior on a continuum from inherited to learned, with most behavior falling somewhere in between. A reflex response, for example, is a relatively inflexible, genetically based behavior, while marriage customs are more dependent upon experience.

Query: In what sense is learning ability an evolutionary mechanism?

Heredity and learning are best seen as two great forces that interact in a synergistic way to produce behavior. In this view, evolution and learning work together to increase the organism's chances of survival. Consider, for example, aggression among rats. Researchers have found that rats can be induced to attack their peers if they are given an electric shock. Even if the rats are in different parts of a cage, the shocked rat will run over to its roommate and attack it (Ulrich, 1966; Ulrich & Azrin, 1962). This response to pain seems to be innate, but aggression is not an inevitable response to pain. In one early study, Nathan Azrin and his colleagues (1966) found that if rats learned how to escape from a situation in which they were shocked, they were far less likely to attack their fellows. In another study, researchers found that when rats were first taught to be aggressive toward other rats, they were far more aggressive when shocked than were rats that had not had this training (Baenninger & Ulm, 1969). Other studies showed that animals rarely fought when shocked unless they had had fighting experience (Powell & Creer, 1969). Thus, the likelihood that aversive stimulation (such as electric shock) will induce aggressive behavior depends on both the rat's genetic history and its learning history.

The interplay of nature and nurture is equally apparent when we examine human aggression. Wilson (1978) notes that among the !Kung San, the aboriginal people of Australia, violence against their fellows is now almost unknown. But Wilson points out that several decades ago, when the population density among these people was greater and when there was less governmental control over their behavior, their per capita murder rate rivaled that of America's most dangerous cities.

Wilson (1978) notes that the Semai of Malaya also have demonstrated the capacity for both gentleness and violence. Murder is unknown among these people; they do not even have a word in their language for the concept of killing. Yet when the British colonial government trained Semai men to fight against Communist guerrillas in the 1950s, the Semai became fierce warriors. One anthropologist wrote that "they seem to have been swept up in a sort of insanity which they call 'blood drunkenness' " (Dentan, 1968; quoted in Wilson, 1978, p. 100). Wilson (1978) concludes from such evidence that "the more violent forms of human aggression are not the manifestations of inborn drives . . . [but are] based on the interaction of genetic potential and learning" (p. 105).

What is true of aggression is true of other kinds of behavior. Harry and Margaret Harlow (1962a, 1962b) reared infant monkeys in isolation to see how their development would be affected. They found, among other things, that as adults these monkeys were sexually incompetent. When given the opportunity to mate with a normally reared monkey, they sometimes showed an interest, but were at a loss as to how to proceed. Isolation had evidently deprived them of learning experiences important to normal sexual functioning.

Again, the same phenomenon can be seen in the human animal. The mistaken ideas that children and some uneducated adults have about sex and reproduction make it clear that learning is also very important in the development of human sexual behavior. But human sexuality is not entirely the product of learning. Numerous studies have suggested that heredity may play an important part, for instance, in determining the frequency of adult sexual activity, the number of sexual partners a person has in a lifetime, and even the kinds of sexual practices an individual finds acceptable (Eysenck, 1976). As in the case of aggressive behavior, sexual behavior is not entirely a matter of doing what comes naturally; it is the product of both heredity and learning.

Child-rearing practices follow a similar pattern. In their studies of monkeys, the Harlows (1962a, 1962b) found that when female monkeys reared in isolation had offspring, they later became poor mothers. They showed little interest in their young, seldom petted or fondled them, and even neglected to nurse them. There are no comparable studies of humans reared in isolation, but studies do show that many child abusers were neglected or abused themselves as children (Widom, 1989; Wiehe, 1992). We speak of a maternal instinct (and, less often, of a paternal instinct), but if such instincts exist, they are clearly insufficient to account for parental behavior.

Even neurotic and psychotic behavior is the product of the interaction of heredity and learning. Studies have shown that animals that are selectively bred for signs of deviance produce successively more deviant offspring (Broadhurst, 1973). But other studies show that certain experiences can produce a "nervous breakdown" in otherwise healthy animals (Pavlov, 1927; see Chapter Four). And the Harlows (1962a, 1962b) found that their isolated monkeys, though genetically normal, grew up to be neurotic adults.

A similar picture emerges from a study of deviant behavior in humans. There is evidence that humans can inherit a tendency toward anxiety, bizarre thinking, and other forms of abnormal behavior (Carter, 1933; Pedersen et al., 1988). Phobias, for example, are more common among those who have phobic relatives than among those who do not (Fyer et al., 1990). Criminal behavior also appears to be influenced by heredity (Shields, 1973). But experience also plays an important role in aberrant behavior. Henry P. David and his colleagues (1988) report, for instance, that unwanted babies are more likely than others to show signs of maladjustment later on, which suggests that early learning experiences play an important role in adult adjustment.

Almost any form of behavior reflects the same sort of interaction between nature and nurture. Take the nocturnal habits of certain animals. Animals that once hunted by day, such as the North American puma and the bobcat, now hunt mainly by night. Perhaps this shift to a nocturnal lifestyle first occurred because animals learned to avoid humans by staying hidden during the day. But evolution also might have played a part: Animals with a strong innate tendency to roam about during the day are more likely to be killed by people than are those that prefer to hunt at night.

Evolution and learning, nature and nurture, both play a part in adaptation. They are merely different ways of adapting to the environment, different ways of coping with life's one constant—change.

SUMMARY

Change is the only constant, and the ceaseless struggle for existence is the struggle to adapt to an ever-changing world. Adaptation is accomplished by two mechanisms, evolution and learning.

Charles Darwin's theory of evolution states that genetic adaptation depends upon variation and natural selection. A given characteristic varies within a species, and variations that are adaptive are selected because they contribute to the survival of individuals with that characteristic. Mutations can be passed on to progeny, thereby affecting evolution. Inherited characteristics include physical attributes, such as size and weight, and certain kinds of behavior: reflexes, fixed action patterns, and inherited behavior traits.

Reflexes are simple responses to specific events; they are involuntary and largely invariable. Examples include the startle response, eye blink, and knee jerk. Reflexes are mediated by a set of interconnected units called a reflex arc. Evoking a reflex tends to sensitize the organism to other stimuli; when a reflex is evoked repeatedly, it tends to habituate.

Fixed action patterns, which used to be called instincts, are series of reflexlike acts in response to a particular event. Like reflexes, fixed action patterns are involuntary and relatively invariable. Unlike reflexes, fixed action patterns usually involve the entire organism rather than a few muscles or glands, and they may be fairly complex. The event that sets a fixed action pattern into motion is called a releaser. Examples of fixed action patterns include the oppossum's habit of playing dead when attacked, web spinning in certain spiders, and the migration of salmon. It is uncertain whether there are true fixed action patterns in humans.

Inherited behavior traits are general behavioral tendencies. They differ from reflexes and fixed action patterns in that they are far more variable and are elicited by a wider variety of events. Examples include activity level, aggressivity, and fearfulness.

The evolution of adaptive forms of behavior plays an important role in the survival of a species. But evolution is a slow process that does nothing to aid the individual organism faced with a new challenge. A mechanism by which the individual organism can adapt to change is learning.

The capacity for learning is a biological characteristic of the species and is itself the product of evolution. Through learning, an organism can cope with aspects of its environment for which its innate behavior is inadequate.

The argument over the relative importance of genetics and learning in determining behavior—the nature-nurture debate—tends to obscure the underlying fact that both evolution and learning typically contribute to the survival of the species. They are merely different ways of adapting to change.

REVIEW QUESTIONS

Note: Many of the questions that appear here (and in subsequent chapters) cannot be answered merely by searching through the chapter and copying a line or two from the text. The answers to such questions are not to be found in the text in this literal sense. To answer these questions properly, you may have to apply information in the text in imaginative ways.

1. Define the following terms. Give an example or illustration of each that does *not* appear in the text.

evolution	*natural selection*
fixed action pattern	*nature-nurture debate*
genetic variation	*reflex*
inherited behavior trait	*releaser*

2. What are the twin mechanisms of evolution?

3. Is the process of evolution still going on today? Explain.

4. Why has the field mouse not evolved into an animal as large and ferocious as the grizzly bear?

5. In what sense is evolution the product of experience?

6. How are reflexes and fixed action patterns like the ROM (read-only memory) of a computer?

7. A man is asked to blink his eyes and does so. Is this a reflex act? Justify your answer.

8. Invent a new reflex, one that would be helpful to humans.

9. One learning specialist (Rachlin, 1976) refers to fixed action patterns as complex reflexes. Do you favor this idea? Explain.

10. Speculate on whether, as their learning ability evolved, humans lost fixed action patterns they once had, or whether their learning ability evolved because they lacked adaptive fixed action patterns.

11. Do you think the human tendency to believe in some sort of religion is an inherited behavior trait? Why or why not?

12. During wars, some soldiers sacrifice themselves to save their comrades. Some researchers believe such altruistic

behavior is the product of natural selection. How can this be, when the altruistic act ends the person's opportunities for reproduction?

13. How are reflexes, fixed action patterns, and inherited behavior traits alike? How do they differ?

14. How would the length of a species' life span affect its chances of adapting to change through evolution?

15. Explain how the cowbird's parenting behavior could be the result of evolution. *Hint:* Consider the salmon.

16. Why are most mutations unhelpful?

17. In an unchanging world, would an organism with appropriate innate behavior need to learn?

18. Under what circumstances might learning be *non*adaptive?

19. Caged animals behave very differently from animals in the wild. In which circumstance is their true nature revealed? Where should one look to see true human nature?

20. Suppose a dozen young children were placed on an island and provided with food and shelter but no opportunities to learn from adult human beings. What would they be like as adults? Would they have a language? Laws? Marriage customs? A religion? Government?

Suggested Readings

It is hoped that reading this chapter has left you wanting to know more about the roles of nature and nurture in human (not to mention animal) behavior. If it has, you may want to read one or more of the following works. You will find even the more technical among them surprisingly readable.

The classic work on biological adaptation through evolution is Darwin's *On the Origin of Species*, originally published in 1859. Several very entertaining contemporary works on evolution are also available, including *The Blind Watchmaker* by biologist Richard Dawkins. (Dawkins is also author of *The Blind Watchmaker Evolution Simulation*, software that allows us to see evolution take place; see Dawkins's book for ordering information.) *The Origins* by novelist Irving Stone is a fictional account of Darwin's life and work.

Reflexes were first described by the 17th-century French philosopher René Descartes in *Treatise of Man*. Fixed action patterns are discussed in E. O. Wilson's *Sociobiology: The New Synthesis*.

The interaction of nature and nurture in behavior is the subject of an excellent article by B. F. Skinner, "Selection by Consequences."

And, although sociobiologist E. O. Wilson is often accused of neglecting the role of experience in behavior, readers of *On Human Nature* will see that he fully appreciates its importance.

Answers to Queries

Page 2: Without variation there could be no evolution because there would be no basis for selection.

Page 5: Mutations can produce new variations.

Page 8: In habituation, response strength decreases; in sensitization, it increases.

Page 8: Fixed action patterns involve whole organisms and are more complex, more variable, and less likely to be present at birth.

Page 11: Fixed action patterns that aid survival are "caught" by the sieve of evolution. Over time, the characteristics of the sieve will change, as will the fixed action patterns captured by it.

Page 14: They are more like fixed action patterns because, like fixed action patterns, they involve the entire organism, are complex, and are not necessarily present at birth.

Page 15: Evolution changes the characteristics of future generations but does not change the living organism.

Page 17: Learning is faster.

Page 19: Learning ability evolved because it had survival value.

two

The Study of Learning and Behavior

Science is more than the mere description of events as they occur. It is an attempt to discover order, to show that certain events stand in lawful relations to other events.
—B. F. SKINNER

If I ask an engineer how a steam engine works, I have a pretty fair idea of the general kind of answer that would satisfy me. Like Julian Huxley I should definitely not be impressed if the engineer said it was propelled by *"force locomotif."* And if he started boring on about the whole being greater than the sum of its parts, I would interrupt him: "Never mind about that, tell me how it *works*." What I would want to hear is something about how the parts of an engine interact with each other to produce the behavior of the whole engine.
—RICHARD DAWKINS

BACKGROUND

We have seen that learning is an adaptive mechanism, a way of coping with a changing world. The study of learning, then, is the study of the relation between an organism's behavior and changes in its environment.

An organism constantly interacts with its surroundings: A rat wanders down an alley in a maze; the alley divides; the rat turns to the right; the alley leads to a dead end; the rat returns to the choice point and takes the alternate alley; the alley leads to another choice point; and so on. Or, on a somewhat higher level: A freshman exploring social life on campus runs through a maze of cliques, clubs, and fraternities, occasionally enters a dead end, backtracks, and moves on to a new alley. The question to be considered in this chapter is, How is this process of adaptation to be studied?

Learning is a difficult subject for scientific analysis. B. F. Skinner (1953), an eminent figure in the field, notes that the difficulty stems partly from the fact that learning is a process rather than a thing. (To draw an analogy to chemistry, learning is rather like combustion.) Processes are like moving targets, and moving targets are harder to hit than stationary ones.

Undoubtedly, another source of difficulty is that most of us grow up with the idea that behavior is immune to scientific analysis. The notion that changes in behavior, especially important kinds of human behavior, can be studied in a truly scientific manner is completely foreign to most people. The result is that students of learning often have a lot to *un*learn.

Because of these problems, some of what follows might be difficult to grasp. The natural science approach to behavior set forth in this text is foreign not only to most students, but to some psychologists (Schneider, 1992). Once you have mastered the concepts presented here, however, subsequent concepts should fall readily into place. Let us begin by defining our subject.

DEFINING LEARNING

Learning is often defined very simply as a change in behavior due to experience. The apparent simplicity of this definition is, however, illusory.

Consider, for example, the word *change.* Why should learning be said to be a change in behavior? Why not say, for example, that learning is the acquisition of behavior?

The word *change* is preferred over *acquisition* because learning does not always appear to involve acquiring something (at least, not in the usual sense), but it does always involve some sort of change. Consider this example: Domesticated hens have a tendency to establish a pecking order, or rank. When a new bird joins a flock, it fights with the other birds until it establishes its proper position in the hierarchy of feathered society. It will then dominate those birds beneath it in rank and defer to those above it. Although the tendency to establish a pecking order is innate, learning appears to be involved in determining an individual's rank. Learning in this case means that the bird continues to peck certain birds but *gives up* pecking others. In this instance, learning seems to mean that something is lost rather than gained.

Similarly, learning among humans sometimes means giving up something: Joan would like to quit smoking; Bill wants to stop biting his nails; Richard would like to be less nervous when meeting people; and Mary and Harry would like to quarrel less when they go out together. All of these reductions in behavior, if they occur, are examples of learning.

The word *behavior* must also be explained. We say that learning is a change in behavior, not that it is a change in knowledge, perceptions, expectations, or other cognitive attributes. Why?

This word choice is troublesome, even to some psychologists. They point out that the fact that a rat does not run a maze does not necessarily mean that it cannot run the maze. Nor can we assume that a girl is unable to read merely because she does not read when asked to do so. There is a difference between what an organism *can* do and what it *does*, between learning a response and performing it. Because of this, some psychologists (for example, Kimble, 1961) have argued that learning means a change in the *potential* for behavior, rather than an actual change in behavior.

One problem with this approach is that potential cannot be measured. We cannot remove a section of a rat's skull and determine from a study of its brain whether it has learned to run a maze. Nor can we attach electrodes to a man's head and determine, from a reading of the electrical impulses obtained, what he knows. We can ask people whether they have learned to read, but until they actually do read, we cannot be sure that their answers are accurate. An example illustrates the difficulty. Once a teacher asked a student if he could type. He said he could, so the teacher had him sit at a computer to enter some data. It became immediately apparent that to the student, knowing how to type meant being able to find and depress the appropriate keys in the proper order given an unlimited amount of time to "hunt and peck." It was not until he actually began typing, however, that his level of learning—or lack thereof—became clear. Ultimately, then, we must define learning in terms of behavior.

> Query: What is the objection to defining learning as a change in potential for behavior?

Our definition of learning says learning is "due to experience." This phrase is necessary because, while all learning involves changes in behavior, not all changes in behavior involve learning. Fatigue, injury, drugs, disease, and maturation can change behavior, but these changes are not considered learning. Learning refers only to changes in behavior due to experience.

An experience is "an event or series of events participated in or lived through" (*American Heritage Dictionary*, 1971). Events are *physical* occurrences: They are the changes in air pressure we call sound, the light waves we call sights, the tactile pressures we call touch. The delicate fragrance of a rose derives from just so many molecules of "rose matter" arising from the flower. Even the gentle caress and softly whispered words of a lover are, in scientific terms, merely physical events. This does not mean the events we call experience do not have significance beyond their physical properties; but this greater significance is usually itself the product of learning.

Query: What is learning?

Having examined the terms used to define learning, we can see that learning involves the interaction between two kinds of events— what the organism does (response events) and what the environment does (stimulus events). We must take a closer look at these two kinds of events, for they are at the very essence of our subject.

■ Response Events

Learning experts use the term **response** to mean a specific instance of behavior observed under prescribed circumstances. This means that a response is defined by its measurement.

In ordinary conversation, we might talk about how certain experiences, such as sitting down to a meal after a long period without food, make our mouths water. To study this phenomenon, however, we must define mouth watering in some precise way. A person's mouth waters when the salivary glands secrete saliva, so we might measure the excretion from these glands by putting cotton balls in either side of a person's mouth. After a time, we would collect these cotton balls and weigh them; this would give us a precise measure of salivation. The salivary response is then defined, in this instance, as the number of milligrams of saliva absorbed by cotton balls of uniform size placed at particular points in the mouth.

Similarly, we might be interested in teaching a pigeon to peck a small disk. But what is a disk peck? If the bird makes a pecking motion in the direction of the disk, is that a disk peck? If it strikes the area near the disk, does that count? What if it touches the disk very lightly with its beak? If three people observed a pigeon and counted disk pecks, we might easily get three different counts. For this reason, the researcher typically defines the disk-pecking response by setting up a recording apparatus that will be activated when a certain amount of pressure is exerted on the disk. If the bird strikes the disk hard enough to activate the recorder, it has made a disk-pecking response; otherwise, it has not.

Notice that our definition of a response does not require that each performance of a response be precisely the same as the last. The researcher might require a certain minimum of saliva for the salivary response, but otherwise the saliva produced might differ substantially from time to time and from person to person. A pigeon might peck a disk hundreds of times in the course of an experiment, but that does not mean every pecking response is exactly the same. In fact, it may be that among those hundreds of disk pecks, no two are exactly alike. A bird may strike a disk a glancing blow from the right, then from the left, then head on. It may peck the disk with varying amounts of force. It may peck the center of the disk, the top, the bottom, or either side. It may peck while arching its neck or standing on one foot or flapping its wings. Yet each of these variations in behavior counts as a disk-pecking response if it activates the recording device.

Responses can be very complex. In the laboratory, a researcher may train a rat to run a maze. The maze may be quite complex, and running it may require making correct turns at dozens of choice points, but reaching the end of the maze may be considered one maze-running response. Outside the laboratory, the teacher of a computer literacy course may want students to learn how to start, or boot, a computer. Booting may consist of inserting a disk in the appropriate drive, closing the drive door, turning on the power, and entering the date and time at the appropriate prompts. The booting response would require the performance of all these steps.

All of the foregoing examples of responses involve overt behavior, behavior that is publicly observable. Does this mean that thoughts and feelings are off limits to learning researchers? The point is debated, but most psychologists would probably say that if a thought or feeling can be defined in some measurable way, it can be studied.

If we want to study fear of spiders, for example, we might define fear as a rise in heart rate, an increase in the rate of respiration, an increase in the electrical activity of certain muscles, an increase in the electrical conductivity of the skin, a verbal expression of fear, or as some combination of these or other actions in the presence of spiders. Some psychologists would say that fear *is* these reactions, while others would argue that they merely indicate the presence of fear. But even if sweating and breathing faster are not the same thing as feeling afraid, they are reliably found in people who are judged to be afraid, and so they make convenient definitions of the fear response.

Query: *How else might you define fear?*

Thoughts are more difficult. They include experiencing things that are not present (we can close our eyes and "see" the home in which we grew up), and they include the things we say silently to ourselves while working through a problem. Sometimes, however, thoughts spill over into overt behavior. For instance, when students study for an exam or try to solve a difficult problem, they use the same vocal muscles they use in speech even though they remain silent. By electronically monitoring their speech apparatus, we can observe these subtle forms of thought. Even the thoughts of a person who is unable to speak can be monitored if that person is proficient in sign language. Mute people who use sign language to communicate with others think with their fingers (see, for example, Max, 1935). We can also study thoughts by asking people to report them. We can, for example, ask a woman to solve a division problem without pencil and paper and ask her to "think out loud" as she works toward the answer.

Some responses have a strong genetic component; others do not. Some are simple; others, complex. Some are easy to define and study; others are more difficult. All are defined by the way they are measured. They are all also affected by stimulus events.

■ Stimulus Events

All organisms live in changing environments, but some changes are more important than others. We are exposed daily to ultraviolet light, radio waves, radon gas, neutrinos, and many other kinds of physical events. Some of these events have important effects upon our bodies, yet they do not noticeably affect behavior. For our purposes, the term *experience* refers only to events that affect, or are capable of affecting, behavior. Such events may be said to stimulate behavior, so they are called stimulus events, or **stimuli.**

It is impossible to determine whether an event is a stimulus for an individual without determining its effect upon that individual's behavior. The sonic boom of a jet plane flying overhead may seem a clear example of a stimulus, but it may not be a stimulus for snakes, which are deaf, or for a person who has suffered auditory nerve damage. Similarly, a mouse hiding in the grass a hundred yards away may not be a stimulus for a person, but it may be for a falcon. Exposure to low levels of x-radiation may have no effect upon a rat's behavior, in which case the radiation is not a stimulus, but slightly higher doses of x-radiation may make the rat stop eating, in which case it is a stimulus.

Query: What is a stimulus?

Various characteristics determine the effectiveness of a stimulus. Two are particularly important: intensity and duration. In general, the more intense a stimulus is, the more likely it is to evoke some sort of response. Clapping your hands is apt to evoke the startle response (see Chapter One); bursting a balloon is even more likely to evoke this response. Often, it is not the absolute intensity of a stimulus that matters so much as its relative intensity—the intensity of that stimulus compared with other stimuli. For instance, you may answer when someone calls your name on a quiet street, but on a noisy subway car the same greeting may go unnoticed.

The power of a stimulus to affect behavior is also related to how long the stimulus lasts. If its duration is very short (say, a very brief flash of light), the organism may behave as if the event never occurred. If, on the other hand, it continues indefinitely, as in the case of the background hum of an air conditioner, it may cease to have any impact on behavior.

When we speak of the impact of a stimulus, we usually mean the stimulus's ability to evoke a particular response. A rap just beneath a person's knee evokes the knee-jerk response. The pupils of our eyes enlarge as the light falling on them diminishes; the change in light is a stimulus that evokes the pupillary response. These examples are consistent with the everyday use of the word *stimulus* as something that evokes a response. But not all stimuli affect behavior in this way.

If you use a knife to retrieve bread from a toaster and get a shock, the shock is a stimulus that will make you less likely to retrieve bread that way again. The shock does not, however, evoke the "not getting bread from a toaster with a metal knife" response. Similarly, if a student spells a word and the teacher pronounces the effort correct, the word *correct* is a stimulus, but it does not induce the student to begin spelling the word again. Stimuli do not always have the effect of inducing reflex or reflexlike responses.

The effects of a stimulus on behavior depend not only upon the characteristics of the stimulus, then, but upon the relationship of the stimulus to other events, including responses. These relationships among stimulus and response events are at the heart of the experiences that produce learning. These relationships differ in the extent to which they are contiguous and contingent.

Contiguity concerns the nearness of events to one another. **Temporal contiguity** refers to the extent to which events occur near each other in time. Thunder and lightning are temporally contiguous: We hear thunder soon after we see lightning. Similarly, the dinner bell and the appearance of food on the table occur close together, if not simultaneously. These are examples of close temporal contiguity among stimuli. Contiguity between responses and stimuli is also important. We put money into a vending machine and immediately receive the selected item; if there were a delay of several hours between inserting money (a response) and receiving our selection (a stimulus), we might be less inclined to use the machine. Or imagine how difficult using a computer would be if there were a delay of five minutes between the time you typed a word and the time the word appeared on the screen. The degree of temporal contiguity between stimuli or between responses and stimuli is an important factor in how much learning takes place.

Temporal contiguity has long been an important topic in the study of learning, and when psychologists speak of contiguity, they usually mean temporal contiguity. It is clear, however, that **spatial contiguity,** or the nearness of events in space, also is important to learning. A world in which lightning appeared in the north and thunder came from some other direction (sometimes the south, sometimes the west, sometimes the east) might be a difficult world in which to learn about lightning.

A **contingency** is said to exist between events when one depends upon the other. A contingency is a kind of if-then statement: If X occurs, then Y will occur. An event that is **stimulus contingent** is one that occurs if and only if a particular stimulus occurs; the event is dependent upon the stimulus. In the laboratory, we can arrange a rat's environment so that food appears in a tray if and only if a buzzer has sounded. Outside the laboratory, traffic lights are designed so that the red light comes on if and only if the yellow light has gone off.

An event that is **response contingent** is one that occurs if and only if a particular response occurs; in this case, the event is dependent upon the response. In the laboratory, we can arrange a rat's environment so that food will appear in a tray if and only if the rat has pressed a lever. Outside the laboratory, a driver receives a speeding ticket if and only if he exceeds the posted limit.

> Query: Can one event be contingent upon another without the two events being temporally or spatially contiguous? Explain.

When we say that learning is *due to experience*, we mean learning is produced by the relation of stimuli to each other and to behavior. And when we say that learning is a *change in behavior*, we mean the individual under study responds differently than it once did. How are we to measure these changes in behavior, these response differences, that comprise learning?

MEASURING LEARNING

Perhaps the most obvious way to measure learning is to look for a change in the *topography* of a response—that is, a change in the form a response takes. (You might think of a topographic map, which shows the shape of the earth's surface.) In the laboratory, researchers usually look for changes in the topography of simple responses. When a rat

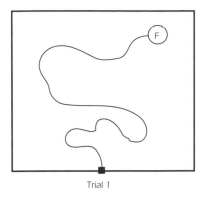
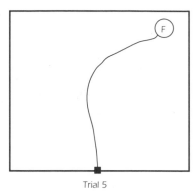

Trial 1   Trial 5

FIGURE 2-1 Topography as a measure of learning. On the first trial, a cat wanders around the cage until it finally discovers the food (F); by the fifth trial, the cat goes immediately to the food. (Hypothetical data.)

learns to press a lever, the topography of its behavior with respect to the lever changes. At first, it may press the lever in a variety of ways: standing on it with both front legs, sitting on it, depressing it with its nose, and so on. But typically, after a while we see changes in the character of its lever pressing. The rat's behavior becomes simpler, smoother, more efficient, less variable. Eventually, the rat sits before the lever and presses it with one paw. This transformation is what is meant by a change in the topography of a response (see Figure 2-1).

We can observe the same phenomenon outside the laboratory. One difference between novice ice skaters and experts is the forms their behavior take. Both may move across the ice without incident, but while the expert glides with ease and grace, the novice's movements are halting and clumsy. As the novice becomes more graceful and efficient, we say that he or she has learned. Such changes in the topography of behavior provide one measure of learning.

Another measure of learning is a reduction in the number of *errors* (see Figure 2-2). A rat can be said to have learned to run a maze to the extent that it goes from start to finish without taking a wrong turn. As training progresses, the rat makes fewer and fewer errors. Similarly, a student is said to have learned a spelling list when she can spell all the words without error. A reduction in the number of errors is often a convenient measure of learning.

We can also measure learning by noting changes in the *strength* of a response (see Figure 2-3). Laboratory rats are often taught to press a lever. If the resistance of the lever is then increased, so that greater force is required to depress the lever, the rat will learn to increase the pressure it exerts. The increase in pressure is a change in the strength of the lever press response and is one measure of learning. The same sort of process occurs outside of the laboratory. Having taught a dog to bark on command, we can then teach it to bark softly.

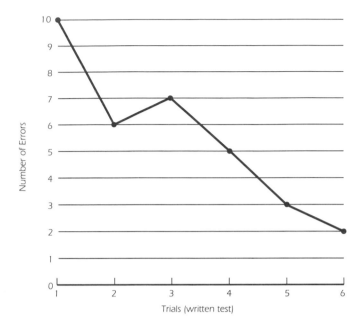

FIGURE 2-2 Errors as a measure of learning. The first time a driver takes the written test, he or she makes a number of errors. On succeeding tests, the driver makes fewer and fewer errors. The reduction in errors reflects learning. (Hypothetical data.)

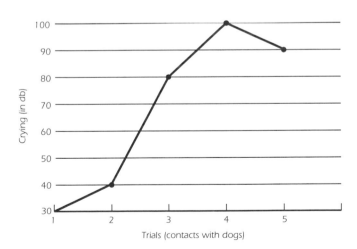

FIGURE 2-3 Response strength as a measure of learning. The increase in the strength of a child's cries (expressed in decibels, db) indicates that the child has acquired a fear of dogs. (Hypothetical data.)

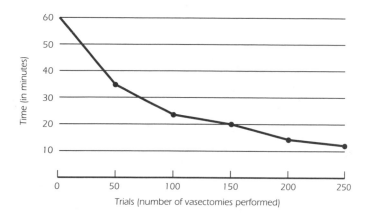

FIGURE 2-4 Speed as a measure of learning. The decrease in the time it takes a surgeon to perform an operation reflects (we all hope) learning. (Hypothetical data.)

> Query: Give an example of human learning measured as a
> decrease in response strength.

A change in the *speed* of a response also indicates learning (see Figure 2-4). The rat that has learned to run a maze reaches the goal faster than an untrained rat. In the same way, a first-grader takes a long time to recite the alphabet at the beginning of the year, but later runs through it with the speed of an auctioneer. Likewise, the novice typist takes a long time to type a sentence, while the expert does it quickly. As these examples illustrate, learning is usually associated with an increase in response speed. It is possible, however, for a slower pace to reflect learning. When children are very hungry, they are inclined to eat quickly; learning good table manners means learning to slow down.

A similar measure of learning is a change in response *latency*, the time that passes before a response occurs. We will see in the next chapter that a dog can be taught to salivate at the sound of a bell. As the training proceeds, the interval between the bell and the first drop of saliva shortens, indicating that learning has occurred (see Figure 2-5). Similarly, a student beginning to learn the multiplication table pauses before answering a question such as "How much is 5 times 7?" With practice, the pauses become shorter, and eventually the student responds without hesitation. This decrease in hesitation, or latency, is a measure of learning.

In the laboratory, learning is often measured as a change in the *rate* at which a response occurs. A pigeon can be trained to peck a colored disk at a steady rate—that is, a certain number of times a minute. The experimenter may then attempt to increase or decrease

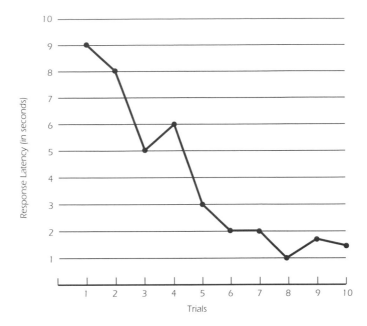

FIGURE 2-5 Latency as a measure of learning. The decrease in the time elapsed before a response begins indicates learning. (Hypothetical data.)

the rate of disk pecking. The resulting change in response rate indicates learning. Similarly, students who want to break the habit of biting their fingernails learn when they reduce the rate at which nail biting occurs, while students who want to become more outgoing learn when they increase the rate at which they interact with people. Response rate has proved to be an especially useful measure of learning, partly because it allows us to see subtle changes in behavior.

The simplest way to record a change in response rate is to tally the number of times a response occurs in a given period. In the laboratory, we can do this by means of a **cumulative recorder** (see Figure 2-6). With this device, every occurrence of the response under study is recorded by the movement of a pen on a sheet of paper, which moves under the pen at a steady pace. So long as the response in question does not occur, the pen makes a straight line along the length of the paper. When a response occurs, the pen moves a short distance across the paper. The faster the response rate, the more the pen moves and the steeper the slope of the ink line; the slower the response rate, the flatter the line. A point on the line indicates the total number of responses to that point, so the graph provides a cumulative record.

Outside of the laboratory, recording response rate is often more difficult. Suppose, for instance, we want to determine the effect of a teacher's efforts to reduce the number of times students are off task for

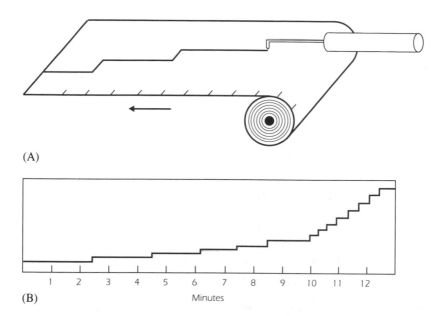

(A)

(B) Minutes

FIGURE 2-6 Rate as a measure of learning. If a sheet of paper moves under a needle at a steady rate, and if the needle moves at a right angle to the direction of movement each time an organism responds (A), the sheet will provide a cumulative record of the responses (B). A change in the rate at which a behavior occurs suggests learning.

ten seconds or more. (*Off task* means not engaging in academic work. Studies have shown that the amount of time spent off task is a good predictor of classroom learning; see Merrett and Wheldall, 1978, and Stallings, 1980.) We might measure a change in the rate of off-task behavior by sitting in a classroom and keeping a running count of the number of times students appear to be off task (staring out the window, passing notes, doodling, reading comic books, and the like). But with 25 or 30 students in a class, it might be difficult to make accurate observations, and it might be impractical to record data throughout the school day for several weeks. One solution is to observe the behavior of a few randomly selected students for periods of, say, 20 minutes, perhaps twice each day at randomly selected times. This procedure is called **response sampling.** Assuming that the students and the time intervals selected are representative of the behavior of the entire class throughout the day, such sampling should yield results similar to those that would be obtained by recording the responses of all the students throughout the school day.

The importance of measuring learning is clear: We cannot study learning unless we can measure it in some precise way. But there is more to studying learning than measuring it; there is also the problem of designing research.

RESEARCH DESIGNS

There are various ways of arriving at generalizations about learning and behavior. Let us consider the major kinds of evidence available to those who study learning.

■ Anecdotal Evidence

All of us have experiences that shape our views of behavior. Such **anecdotal evidence** is often identified by phrases such as "In my experience" and "I've found that." Sometimes anecdotal evidence takes on the character of common wisdom: "They say that," "It's common knowledge that," and "Everybody knows that."

Unfortunately, what everybody knows is not always correct. Bloodletting persisted as a treatment for medical disorders for generations because "everybody knew" that it worked. People can point to anecdotal evidence to support all kinds of principles and practices, and it is hard to sort out which anecdotes to believe.

Consider the problem of determining the effects of smoking tobacco on learning. Ask a number of people about this, and some are likely to say, "I always smoke whenever I study for a test. I know it helps me learn." But how do we know that smoking facilitates learning? The anecdotes describe what people *say* about the effects of tobacco, not the effects themselves.

Despite its limitations, anecdotal evidence is not to be summarily dismissed. Anecdotes can provide useful leads, and they keep us in contact with popular wisdom, which is not always wrong. Still, more concrete evidence is required for a science of learning.

■ Case Studies

We obtain a better grade of data with the case study. While anecdotal evidence consists of casual observations of behavior, a case study examines a particular individual in considerable detail.

The case study method is often used in medicine. A patient with a disease or symptom may be studied with great care in an attempt to understand his illness more clearly. Economists also do case studies. They may study a company to find out why it failed or succeeded. Similarly, educational researchers might do a detailed study of a teacher or school that gets particularly good results.

One problem with the case study is that it takes a good deal of time. Because of this, it is not possible to do many case studies. This means we must make generalizations based upon a few subjects. If those few subjects are not typical of the group they represent, our conclusions will be incorrect. Moreover, the case study is not applicable to many questions about behavior. How, for example, could we use the case study to determine the effects of using tobacco on learning?

> Query: What is the difference between an anecdote and a case study?

When appropriate, the case study is more useful than the anecdote because at least the data are obtained in a fairly systematic way. But a sound science of behavior cannot be built upon the sandy soil of the case study. More control is required.

■ Descriptive Studies

More control is provided by the **descriptive study** (also called a statistical or correlational study). Instead of examining a few cases in great detail, the descriptive study examines many cases—sometimes hundreds or thousands—in far less detail. To devoted advocates of the case study, the descriptive study seems superficial. But by examining many cases, or subjects, and analyzing the data statistically, the descriptive study lessens the risk that a few unrepresentative subjects will distort the findings.

In a typical descriptive study, we might ask people (in interviews or by means of a questionnaire) questions about smoking. We might then compare the academic records of those who smoke with those who do not. Statistical analysis would then reveal whether there were any reliable (that is, statistically significant) differences between the two groups. We might find, for example, that people who smoke have lower grades, on average, than people who do not.

Descriptive studies represent a vast improvement over case studies, but they have their faults. One limitation of descriptive research is that although it can provide hypotheses about phenomena, it cannot prove those hypotheses. We may find that smokers usually get lower grades, but this does not prove that they get lower grades because they smoke. It could be, for example, that smokers are less intelligent than nonsmokers. Even if we replicate (repeat) a descriptive study and obtain the same findings, we cannot be sure that the findings are due to the features we have identified. The only way to do that is to perform an experiment.

■ Experimental Studies

In an **experiment,** two kinds of variables (literally, things that vary), must be identified. The **independent variable** is the one that we believe may be a factor in producing the phenomenon under study. The **dependent variable** is the variable that we believe will be affected by

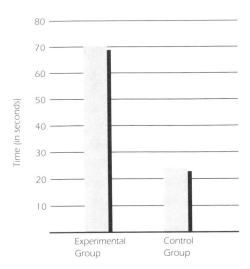

FIGURE 2-7 *Group design data. Average time to solve anagrams in the experimental (smoking) group and in the control (nonsmoking) group. (Hypothetical data.)*

the independent variable. In learning experiments, the independent variable is usually some sort of experience (a stimulus contingent or response contingent event), and the dependent variable is usually a response, or a change in a response. The independent variable is controlled (made to vary) by the experimenter; the dependent variable is allowed to vary freely. The dependent variable depends upon the independent variable, hence its name. There are many different kinds of experimental studies, but all true experiments fall into one of two types, group designs and single subject designs.

In **group design** experiments, the researcher typically identifies two groups of subjects. The independent variable is then made to differ across these groups. If we wanted to study the effects of smoking on learning, we might have some subjects smoke while solving a series of anagrams; others would work without smoking. The subjects who smoke are called the **experimental group,** while those who do not are called the **control group.** (The subjects need not work in groups; here, the term *group* refers only to assignment to experimental or control conditions.) If experimental subjects learn more slowly than control subjects, we might conclude that the difference is due to smoking (see Figure 2-7).

> Query: Identify the independent and dependent variables in the tobacco study just described.

Although experiments involving two groups are common, it is quite possible to conduct studies with many groups. In an experiment

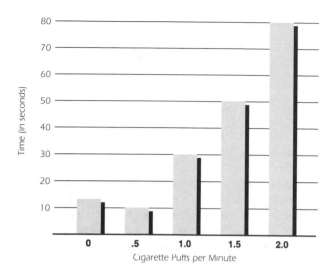

FIGURE 2-8 Group design data with multiple experimental groups. Average time to solve anagrams in groups varying from 0 puffs (control) to 2 puffs per minute. (Hypothetical data.)

on smoking, for example, we might have several experimental groups that differ in the amount of tobacco inhaled. We would then compare each of these groups not only with the control group, but with every other experimental group (see Figure 2-8).

The essential element of a group design is that subjects that have been exposed to some experience are compared to other subjects that have not had that experience. Any differences in their behavior are then attributable to differences in their respective experiences.

Group designs rest upon the assumption that the subjects being compared are similar and that any differences in their behavior are therefore attributable to differences in the independent variable. In a study on the effects of smoking tobacco on learning, for example, we must be able to assume that the subjects are nearly identical in all respects except the experimental treatment. If one group were brighter than the other, any differences in the results might be due to differences in their intelligence rather than to differences in their exposure to tobacco. Likewise, the two groups should not differ in health, age, weight, aggressiveness, or a host of other variables.

To minimize such differences, each subject is randomly assigned to one of the groups. (This can be done, for example, by flipping a coin: If the coin comes up heads, the subject goes into the experimental group; if it comes up tails, the subject is assigned to the control group.) Through such random assignment, any differences among the subjects should be distributed more or less equally among the groups.

With small groups, even random assignment leaves open the possibility of initial differences among the groups, so group design studies usually include at least ten subjects in each group.

Query: Why is it best to have a large number of subjects in a group design experiment?

One way to keep the number of subjects down (which is desirable because it saves both time and money) is to reduce the differences among the subjects through a procedure known as **matched sampling.** In matched sampling, subjects are assigned randomly to the experimental or control group after they have been matched on variables that are likely to affect the results. Animals can be matched for age and sex quite easily. Human subjects can be matched for these variables, and also for IQ, educational level, and socioeconomic background. Genetic differences can be matched by using litter mates (in the case of animals) and identical twins (in the case of humans).

Once the results of a group experiment are collected, they are usually submitted to statistical analysis. This estimates how much of the difference between the groups is attributable to the independent variable rather than to extraneous variables. The more subjects involved in the study, the less likely it is that uncontrolled variables have affected the outcome. However, even with large numbers of subjects it is possible that unintended differences among the groups have distorted the results. To rule out this possibility, researchers must replicate the experiment with new subjects.

An alternative to the group design is the **single subject design.** In this case, a single subject's behavior is observed before the experimental treatment, and then during or after it. To study the effects of tobacco on learning, we might give a student a number of anagrams to solve. After, say, 20 minutes, we might then have the student smoke while tackling additional anagrams for 20 minutes. By comparing the subject's performance in the two sessions, we could see whether the experimental treatment had any effect on the rate of learning. The resulting data are often plotted on a cumulative record (see Figure 2-9).

The pretreatment observation is known as the **baseline period** because it provides a baseline for comparison. It is usually labeled A. The treatment period is usually labeled B. If the A and B periods yield different results (for example, different response rates), we can attribute those differences to the treatment.

Because the same organism is used in both conditions, the results of a single subject experiment are unlikely to be due to differences in the subject. However, it is conceivable that some extraneous variable coincidental to the experimental manipulation is responsible for the results. A subject could become ill during the experiment, for example, for reasons having nothing to do with the experiment. This would give

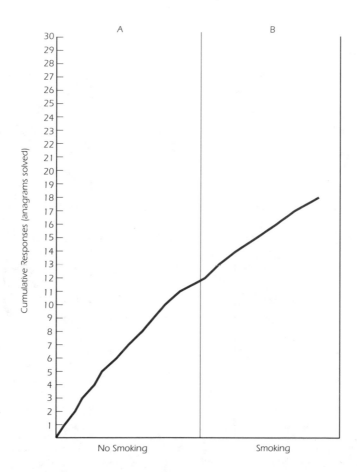

FIGURE 2-9 Single subject design data on cumulative record. Rate of anagram solutions when not smoking (A) and when smoking (B). Note that the rate of problem solving slows during smoking. (Hypothetical data.)

the illusion that the experimental treatment had changed the subject's behavior when, in fact, it had not. To rule out such possibilities, the experimenter may reinstate the baseline (A) condition, in what is known as an **ABA design** (see Figure 2-10). If the behavior returns to the previous baseline pattern, then the results have been replicated within the same experiment. The researcher can provide clear evidence that the behavior is a function of the independent variable by repeatedly alternating between A and B conditions.

Using an ABA design is a little like turning a light switch on and off to see whether it controls a light. By switching back and forth between A and B conditions, researchers can demonstrate the extent to which a response is controlled by the independent variable under study. The data are all the more convincing if they are obtained with more than

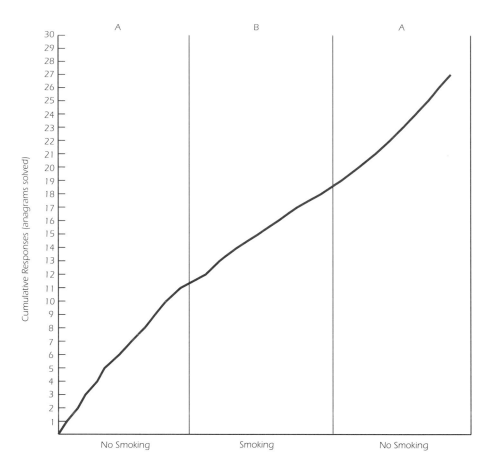

FIGURE 2-10 ABA reversal design data on cumulative record. Reversal (return to nonsmoking condition) confirms that the rate of anagram solutions is affected by smoking. (Hypothetical data.)

one subject. Consequently, researchers usually repeat a single subject experiment with at least a few subjects. Large numbers of subjects are, however, usually unnecessary.

> **Query:** Why is random assignment of subjects unnecessary in ABA studies?

Although single subject design studies usually involve only a handful of subjects, while group designs often involve dozens, size is not the essential difference between them. The important difference is that in single subject designs, each subject is in both the experimental and the control condition; in group design studies, each subject is in only one condition.

Both single subject and group design experiments allow us, within limits, to see the effects of independent variables on dependent variables. Not even experimental studies are perfect, however.

The great power of the experiment comes from its control over variables. However, this very control has led to the criticism that experiments create an artificial world from which the researcher derives an artificial view of animal and human nature.

In many learning experiments the dependent variable is an extremely simple response: a rat presses a lever; a pigeon pecks a disk; a person presses a button. The independent variable is also likely to be simple: a light may go on or off; a few grains of food may fall into a tray; a person may receive a nickel or hear the word *correct*. The experiment may also occur in an extremely sterile, artificial environment: a small cage, for example, or (in the case of human subjects) a room with little in it besides a table, a chair, and a toggle switch. Many people have a hard time believing that the artificial world of the experiment can tell us anything interesting about rats and pigeons, much less about people.

To some extent the criticism is fair. Experiments do create artificial conditions, and what we find under those artificial conditions may not always tell us something interesting about more natural conditions. But the control that makes the experiment seem artificial is necessary to isolate the effects of independent variables. Similarly, while we are not particularly interested in lever pressing, disk pecking, and button pushing, using such simple responses as dependent variables allows us to see more clearly the impact of the independent variable. More complicated behavior would be more realistic, but less revealing. (For more on this point, see Berkowitz and Donnerstein, 1982.)

The artificiality of experiments is the inevitable result of control. When we create more realistic experiments and study more complicated behavior, we almost inevitably lose control over important variables and produce data that are hard to interpret. One solution to the problem is to do two kinds of experiments: Laboratory experiments offer the control that allows the researcher to derive clear-cut principles of behavior. Field experiments allow the researcher to test laboratory-derived principles in more natural settings. For instance, we might study learning in the laboratory by having rats run mazes, and then test the principles derived in field experiments of squirrels foraging in the wild. Or we might test the effects of different lecture rates on student learning in carefully controlled laboratory experiments, and then perform an analogous experiment in a classroom.

Despite their limitations, experiments provide a kind of power that is not available through other means. Consequently, most of the evidence considered in the pages that follow is the result of experimental research. Much of that research involves animals.

ANIMAL OR HUMAN SUBJECTS?

If learning researchers are interested primarily in understanding how people adapt to changes in the environment (and most of them are), why do they so often study animals? If the goal is to understand people, why study rats and pigeons? There are several reasons.

First, since experimental animals are purchased from research supply companies, their genetic histories are fairly well known. This means that genetic differences from one subject to another, an important source of variability in behavior, can be reduced. It is, of course, difficult to obtain the same sort of control over genetic variability in humans.

Second, animals can be housed in environments that are far less variable than their natural environments, thus essentially ruling out the influence of unintended learning experiences. Once again, this sort of control cannot be achieved with human subjects.

Third, it is possible to do research with animals that cannot be done with human beings. It might be interesting and useful to know whether a certain kind of experience would make people depressed, give them ulcers, or induce them to attack their neighbors, but such research raises serious ethical problems.

Because of these advantages, many researchers rely exclusively upon animals. In experiments on learning, by far the most popular subjects are rats and pigeons. This preference has largely to do with economics and convenience: Rats and pigeons are inexpensive to purchase and maintain, and they take up little space. Many lower species, such as sponges and fish, share these advantages but are less desirable because they are less adept at learning. Higher animals, particularly monkeys and apes, would be preferable to rats and pigeons because they more closely resemble humans in learning ability, but they are more expensive to purchase and house and more difficult to care for properly.

Despite the advantages of animals as research subjects, their use has been criticized. Ethical problems also exist in the use of animals, particularly if the experiment causes discomfort. The issue is controversial (Balster et al., 1992; Burdick, 1991; Miller, 1985; Shapiro, 1991a, 1991b). But most people probably believe that animal research is justified *if* it might lead to discoveries that will alleviate human suffering (see the box entitled "Animal Rights and Human Suffering").

This is not to say that researchers are free to practice animal cruelty in the name of science. The American Psychological Association (1992) and other organizations have established guidelines for the conduct of animal research. These guidelines require that certain standards be met in the care and handling of animals. Animals may,

Animal Rights and Human Suffering

Autism is a devastating disease of uncertain origin that strikes humans at or soon after birth. Its symptoms include all sorts of bizarre behavior: endless rocking back and forth, hand flapping, avoidance of eye contact, severe tantrums, little or no normal speech, and, in about 10% of cases, self-mutilation.

The treatment of such children used to consist of little more than warehousing them in institutions. Those who tried to injure themselves or others were often restrained with straitjackets or bindings. The worst cases were tied spread-eagle to their beds; that way they couldn't hurt themselves or anyone else. It wasn't that no one cared; the problem was that no one knew what else to do.

There is still no known cure for autism, but today most autistic children can be helped, and many can reach normal or near-normal levels of functioning (Lovaas, 1987; for a summary, see Chance, 1987).

Even though the disorder almost certainly has an organic cause, the treatment techniques that have proved most effective are based on learning principles described in this book. The same principles have helped those who suffer from phobias, hypertension, ulcers, depression, schizophrenia, and countless other disorders. (For more on this, see Miller, 1985.) They have also found application in education, business, energy conservation, and other areas.

These principles were discovered largely through research with animals. Some of that research involved exposing animals to shocks or other unpleasant experiences. Some animal rights advocates have been critical of this research, arguing that humans have no right to profit from animal suffering.

It can be argued that animals have also benefitted from animal research. Animal training, for instance, used to rely very heavily upon the whip; learning research showed how animals could be trained more quickly without such abuse. Some of this research was done on human subjects. Yet it has to be admitted that humans have benefitted far more from animal suffering than animals have benefitted from human suffering.

Ultimately, we must decide what the improvement of the human condition is worth. We could decide that our obligation to animal welfare means that we should end all animal research, or at least all research that causes discomfort to animals. It is important to remember, however, that had we taken that step 30 years ago, we might still be tying autistic children spread-eagle to their beds.

for instance, be made to work for their food; but the amount of work is typically far less than that required of animals in the wild. The guidelines also set standards for the use of aversive procedures. If a question can be answered without the use of aversives, for example, they are not to be used. When aversives are deemed necessary, they must be no more severe than is required by the nature of the research. Usually this means, for example, a shock that, while painful, causes no tissue damage. The use of aversives must also be justified by the probable benefits to be gained from the research. The result is that laboratory animals live more comfortably than many household pets. They are not, for example, beaten, left unfed, subjected to inclement weather, or abandoned. Even so, the use of aversives in animal research is not to be treated lightly.

Another complaint about animal research is that the results obtained may not provide information relevant to people. People, after all, are not rats or birds. While we cannot assume that a finding from animal research applies equally to humans, we cannot assume the opposite, either. As you will see in the chapters that follow, many studies conducted with animals are then replicated with human subjects. In most cases, these studies yield results similar to those obtained with animals. Since study after study has produced comparable results for humans and other species, we have little reason to believe that animal research is irrelevant to human behavior. Where differences do appear, they often provide valuable insights into the differential roles of evolution and learning in the adaptation of humans.

Nevertheless, some people resist the notion that animal studies reveal useful insights into human behavior. "Just because pigeons behave that way," they complain, "doesn't mean that I behave that way." For this reason, you will find many studies involving human subjects in the pages that follow. Usually, a principle is illustrated with one or more animal studies first (since animal studies typically offer the greatest control of variables), followed by similar research with people. The purpose is to demonstrate, wherever possible and practical, that the principle under discussion *does* apply to people as well as to animals.

Some readers will not be persuaded even by this evidence. Often this is because they wrongly assume that if a principle applies to both people and animals, they must conclude that people are just furless rats or featherless pigeons. This is an error.

The similarities between humans and other creatures are sometimes extraordinary, but this does not in any way lessen the significance of their differences. If rats and humans both learn from the same essential experiences, this does nothing to lessen the fact that the remarkable learning ability of humans has enabled them to learn far more from such experiences than rats. If a pigeon can, thanks to the diligent application of learning principles, learn to spell *Mississippi*, this does not reveal human inadequacy; rather, it reveals human potential. For if rats and pigeons, given the proper experiences, can surprise us with their accomplishments, how much greater are the accomplishments of humans likely to be if we provide them with the "proper conditions"?

Both animal and human research is aimed at answering certain key questions about learning and behavior. Since the bulk of this book deals with those questions, it may be useful to summarize them here.

QUESTIONS ABOUT LEARNING

The study of learning and behavior may be viewed as primarily an effort to answer certain key questions. The remaining chapters introduce these questions and summarize the efforts of researchers to answer them. It might be helpful to review these questions here so that you will better understand the course upon which we are set.

1. *What kinds of experiences produce changes in behavior?* As you have seen, learning researchers define experience in terms of stimulus contingent and response contingent events in an organism's environment. In the natural environment, these contingencies occur as the result of physical or biological forces; in the laboratory, they are arranged by the researcher. Three kinds of experiences will be dealt with; they are the subjects of Chapters Three through Seven.

2. *How does an experience that changes behavior in one environment affect behavior in other environments?* Suppose that a child learns to ride a bicycle. Will the child then be able to ride a motorcycle? If an animal trainer teaches your dog to heel, will the dog then heel for *you?* We take up this question in Chapter Eight.

3. *What are the effects of the various reinforcement schedules?* Certain response contingent events have powerful effects on behavior. The pattern of these events is called a reinforcement schedule. Their distinctive effects on behavior are considered in Chapter Nine.

4. *What are the effects of aversive stimuli on behavior?* The natural environment teaches painful as well as pleasant lessons. Aversive stimuli teach us to escape or avoid certain kinds of behavior. Such aversive control is explored in Chapter Ten.

5. *Must we forget?* Once learning has occurred, it is appropriate to ask under what circumstances the effects of learning are lost. Chapter Eleven attempts to account for forgetting.

6. *What are the limits of learning as an adaptive mechanism?* Learning is a marvelous invention for coping with environmental change, but it has its limitations. We discuss these limitations in Chapter Twelve.

These are the principal questions that fascinate learning researchers. The following chapters offer insight into why researchers find these questions so absorbing. It is hoped that in reading these chapters, you will come to share some of the researcher's enthusiasm for the adaptive mechanism called learning.

SUMMARY

Before beginning the study of learning, it is necessary to have a clear understanding of certain key terms. Learning is defined as a change in behavior due to experience. A response is an instance of behavior measured by certain effects upon the environment. Changes in behavior can be measured in terms of changes in topography, number of errors, or changes in the strength, speed, latency, or rate (often recorded on a cumulative recorder) of a response.

To say that learning is due to experience means that it is brought about by changes in the environment called stimuli. The intensity and duration of a stimulus, as well as the pattern of stimulus events, are important determinants of its effects. In particular, temporal and spatial contiguity are important, as is the degree to which stimuli are stimulus contingent or response contingent.

An understanding of learning can be arrived at in various ways. Anecdotes, case studies, and descriptive studies are problematic. Because of this, learning is usually studied by means of experiments; these allow us to see the effects of an independent variable on a dependent variable.

Group experiments involve relatively large numbers of subjects assigned to experimental or control groups. The effects of the independent variable are judged by statistical comparison of the dependent measure in the groups. Extraneous differences between groups can be reduced through random assignment or by matched sampling.

Single subject experiments involve relatively small numbers of subjects. Their behavior is observed before and after some change in the environment, and the effects of this experience are judged by noting changes in the subject's behavior. Often the original condition is reinstated, in which case the experiment is an ABA design.

Both animals and people can serve as subjects for experiments on learning. Both have certain limitations. Animals make greater control possible but leave open the possibility that the results do not apply to humans. Often, basic research is done on animals, and the principles derived from this research are tested on humans in applied settings. Ethical problems are raised by research on animals and humans; researchers have set guidelines to minimize harm.

The remainder of this book attempts to provide insight into the answers currently available to certain fundamental questions about learning and behavior. These questions involve the kinds of experiences that produce learning; the circumstances under which learning in one situation carries over to another situation; the effects of different reinforcement schedules; the effects of aversive stimuli; the durability of learned behavior; and the limitations of learning.

If you are typical of students taking a first course in learning, much of the material in this chapter is new to you. The following chapters are based on the assumption that you have mastered the content of this chapter. The scientific approach to behavior is very different from the commonsense approach to which most students are accustomed. Learning this new approach will give you a new perspective on learning and behavior.

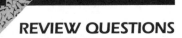

REVIEW QUESTIONS

1. Define the following terms in your own words. Give an example or illustration of each that is not provided in the text.

   baseline   response rate
   cumulative recorder   response sampling
   random assignment   stimulus
   response   topography

2. In what sense can an organism's interactions with its environment be said to constitute a kind of communication?

3. What are the principal *similarities* between single subject and group designs?

4. When would it not be possible to use an ABA design in the study of behavior?

5. Consider two worlds. In one world, related events (such as the movement of a man's lips and the sound of his voice) are temporally contiguous but not spatially contiguous. In the second world, the opposite condition prevails. In which world would it be more difficult to learn? Why?

6. Explain why psychologists often speak of *responses* rather than *behavior.*

7. How are the quotations from Skinner and Dawkins that begin this chapter related?

8. A psychologist studies maze learning in rats by running 50 rats through a maze, 1 at a time. He does this 10 times. Then he computes the average time for all rats on each run and plots this on a graph. Is this a group or single subject design?

9. A hawk appears outside my window (a very unusual event), and within seconds, the phone rings. Is there a contin-

gency between the appearance of the bird and the ringing of the phone?

10. Explain how response rate is reflected on a cumulative record.

11. What is the chief virtue of response sampling?

12. Give an example not provided by the text of an event that would be a stimulus for one person but not for another.

13. A woman says she has a toothache. Does the term *toothache* refer to a stimulus? If so, what is it?

14. What is wrong with defining learning as the acquisition of new behavior?

15. You have 20 rats in a large cage, and you want to assign them to two groups. You put the first rat you catch in the experimental group, the second into the control group, and so on. Why is this bad science?

16. An animal rights activist criticizes your animal research. Defend your choice of subject.

17. You are attempting to discover learning principles by studying the effects of experience on the eye blink. A friend says that eye blinking is a trivial kind of behavior, not worth studying. Defend your work.

18. A teacher says that psychology relies too much upon animal studies and adds that "you can't tell anything about people from research on rats." How could you defend "rat psychology" against this criticism?

19. How many groups are there in an ABA experiment?

20. Some psychologists argue that learning is a change in the potential for behavior. Discuss the virtues and weaknesses of this definition.

Suggested Readings

An interesting and highly readable little book on research methods is *Psychological Research: An Introduction* by Arthur Bachrach. The author provides an insider's view of behavioral research. For a comparison of case study and experimental approaches, read "Little Hans or Little Albert?" (Chapter Three) in *Fact and Fiction in Psychology* by Hans Eysenck. Richard Dawkins's book, *The Blind Watchmaker*, recommended in Chapter One for its discussion of evolution, is also worth reading for its elucidation of scientific reasoning. But if you read only one work on behavioral research, let it be B. F. Skinner's 1956 article, "A Case History in Scientific Method."

Answers to Queries

Page 29: We cannot measure potential behavior.

Page 30: A change in behavior due to experience. (Some psychologists add that the change is "relatively enduring." But it is difficult to get consensus about what that phrase means.)

Page 31: Answers will vary. Examples include movement away from an object; refusal to approach or touch an object; and emotional reactions, such as sobbing.

Page 32: A stimulus is an event that affects or is capable of affecting behavior.

Page 34: Yes. For example, if a company in New York suffers a setback in January, a stockholder in New Mexico might receive a smaller dividend check in June.

Page 37: Answers will vary. Examples include the following: A child learns to eat with his or her mouth closed (chewing movements become smaller); a lover becomes more gentle in his or her caresses; a neophyte cook learns to break eggs without splattering them all over the kitchen.

Page 41: Anecdotes involve casual, everyday observation. Case studies involve careful, often intense study of an individual.

Page 42: The independent variable is smoking tobacco; the dependent variable is performance on anagrams.

Page 44: Large numbers of subjects reduce the effects of unintended and uncontrolled differences among subjects, differences that might affect the dependent variable.

Page 46: Each subject acts as its own control. That is, each subject is compared with itself, not with other subjects.

three

Pavlovian Learning: Principles

The normal animal must respond not only to stimuli
which themselves bring immediate benefit or harm,
but also to [those that] only signal the approach of
these stimuli; though it is not the sight and sound
of the beast of prey which is in itself harmful . . .
but its teeth and claws.
—IVAN PAVLOV

BACKGROUND

Around the turn of the century, a Russian scientist reached a turning point in his career. He had spent several years doing research on the physiology of digestion, important research that would one day win him a Nobel prize. But at middle age, still relatively unknown, he wrestled with one of the most difficult decisions of his career: Should he continue his present line of work or take up a new problem, one that might lead nowhere and that some of his colleagues might regard as an unfit subject for a respectable scientist? The safe thing to do, the easy thing to do, would have been to continue the work he had started. But if he had, psychology would have suffered an immeasurable loss, and the chances are that neither you nor I would ever have heard of Ivan Petrovich Pavlov.

The problem Pavlov decided to study was called the *psychic reflex.* To understand why he found this phenomenon so intriguing, we have to look at his earlier work. Pavlov started his career with research on the circulatory system and then moved on to the physiology of digestion. He developed special surgical procedures that enabled him to study the digestive processes of animals over long periods of time by

FIGURE 3-1   Surgical preparation for studying the salivary reflex. When the dog salivated, the saliva would collect in a glass tube attached to the dog's cheek. This way the strength of the salivary response could be precisely measured.

redirecting an animal's digestive fluids outside of the body, where they could be measured. He used this technique to study the salivary glands, stomach, liver, pancreas, and parts of the intestine. In the case of the salivary glands, the procedure was a relatively simple operation. The salivary duct of an animal, often a dog, was detached from its usual place inside the mouth and directed through an incision in the cheek. When the dog salivated, the saliva would flow through the duct and be collected in a small glass tube. With animals prepared in this way, Pavlov could make precise observations of the actions of the glands under various conditions (see Figure 3-1).

One of Pavlov's goals was to understand how the body breaks down food into chemicals that can be absorbed into the blood. This process starts with the salivary reflex: When food is taken into the mouth, it triggers the flow of saliva. The saliva dilutes the food and produces substances that start breaking the food down chemically. In a typical experiment on the salivary reflex, Pavlov would bring a dog into the laboratory, put food into its mouth, and observe the result.

Pavlov was fascinated by the adaptability of the glands. He found, for instance, that if he gave a dog dry, hard food, there was a heavy flow of saliva; if he gave the animal watery food, there was very little saliva. And if he put an inedible substance into the dog's mouth, the amount of saliva generated depended upon the amount needed to eject the substance: A marble evoked very little saliva, while sand resulted in a large supply. So the reflex action of the gland depended upon the nature of the stimulus. Each time, the gland responded according to the need. "It is as if," said Pavlov, "the glands possessed a 'kind of intelligence' " (quoted in Cuny, 1962, p. 26).

The cleverness of the glands did not end there, however. When an animal had been fed a number of times, it began to salivate *before* anything was put into its mouth. In fact, it might start salivating as

Ivan Pavlov: An Experimenter from Head to Foot

George Bernard Shaw said he was the biggest fool he knew. H. G. Wells thought he was one of the greatest geniuses of all time. But Ivan Pavlov described himself as "an experimenter from head to foot" (in Wells, 1956, p. 38).

Of the three characterizations, Pavlov's was probably the most accurate. His discoveries were much more important, and much less commonsensical, than Shaw believed, but they also failed to bring the utopia that Wells anticipated. There is, however, no denying that Pavlov was a brilliant experimenter, a zealot fiercely committed to science.

Pavlov was born in Ryazan, a small peasant village in Russia, in September, 1849, ten years before the publication of Darwin's *On the Origin of Species*. His father was a poor priest who had to keep a garden to ensure that his family would eat.

As a boy, Pavlov showed little promise of later greatness. His academic performance was mediocre, and probably few people in his community expected him to become a famous scientist—or a famous anything else, for that matter.

He grew up to be slim, agile, athletic, and incredibly energetic, with blue eyes, curly hair, a long beard, and the fire of genius. As Professor Pavlov, he was sometimes an impatient, stubborn, and eccentric man who waved his hands excitedly when he spoke to others. If one of his assistants botched an experiment, he might explode in anger; half an hour later, he would have forgotten all about it. But of all the things one might say about Pavlov, surely the most important is this: He was an experimenter. Nothing was so important, nothing so precious, as his experiments. "Remember," he once wrote, "science requires your whole life. And even if you had two lives they would not be enough. Science demands . . . the utmost effort and supreme passion" (quoted in Cuny, 1962, p. 160).

Pavlov's passion for science stayed with him throughout his long life. Age slowed him, of course, but not the way it slows others. Ever the experimenter, he observed the toll that time had taken and noted it with objective interest. On his deathbed, he was the observer, as well as the subject, of a final experiment. As life slowly left him, he described his sensations to a neuropathologist so these data might be recorded for the benefit of science. Somehow he kept this up almost until the end. One report of Pavlov's death (in Gantt, 1941) relates that in those last moments he slept a bit, then awoke, raised himself on his elbows, and said, "It is time to get up! Help me, I must get dressed!" (p. 35). Then it was over; he was dead.

The effort was understandable. He had been away from his laboratory, from his science, for nearly six whole days.

soon as it entered the laboratory. Pavlov, like others of his day, assumed that these "psychic secretions" were caused by the thoughts, memories, or wishes of the animal. The ancient Greeks had noticed that merely talking about food often made a person's mouth water. What fascinated Pavlov was that such psychic reflexes did not occur when the animals were first brought into the laboratory, but only after

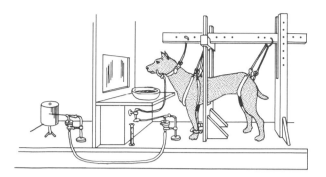

FIGURE 3-2 *Pavlov's conditioning stand. Once a dog was strapped into a stand as shown, an experimenter could begin testing the effects of various stimuli on the salivary response. Saliva could be collected in a glass tube at the fistula (as shown in Figure 3-1), or it could be directed by a tube to a graduated vial. In addition, a cumulative record of the total amount of saliva could be recorded by the movement of a needle on a revolving drum. See Pavlov, 1927, pp. 18–19. Source: From Yerkes & Morgulis, 1909.*

they had been fed there repeatedly. How could this be? How could experience alter the action of a gland?

This question preoccupied Pavlov to the point of making him shift his attention to psychic reflexes. It was not an easy decision. It was extremely important to Pavlov to retain his identity as a physiologist. And if psychic reflexes really were the products of the mind, of the inner life of the animal, then they were not a fit subject for a physiologist. On the other hand, if psychic reflexes involved glands, then why should a physiologist not study them? Pavlov argued with himself along these lines, back and forth; finally, he could no longer resist the challenge. He had to understand these psychic reflexes.

BASIC PROCEDURES

Pavlov (1927) began by observing: "I started to record all the external stimuli falling on the animal at the time its reflex reaction was manifested . . . at the same time recording all changes in the reaction of the animal" (p. 6). At first, the only reaction was the ordinary salivary reflex: When food was put into a dog's mouth, it salivated. But after a while, the animal would salivate before receiving food. By observing the "external stimuli falling on the animal," Pavlov was able to see what triggered these psychic secretions (see Figure 3-2). He noticed, for instance, that the sight or smell of food would cause the dog to salivate. "Even the vessel from which the food has been given is sufficient . . . and, further, the secretions may be provoked even by the sight of the person who brought the vessel, or by the sound of his footsteps" (1927, p. 13).

There are, Pavlov concluded, two distinct kinds of reflexes. One kind is the inborn, unlearned, and usually permanent reflex that is found in virtually all members of a species and that varies little from individual to individual. The dog that salivates when food is put into its mouth manifests this type of reflex. Pavlov called these **unconditional reflexes** because they occur more or less unconditionally.

The second type of reflex is not present at birth; it must be acquired through experience and is relatively impermanent. Because these psychic reflexes depend upon experience, they vary considerably from individual to individual. The dog that salivates to the sound of a particular person's footsteps manifests this type of reflex. Pavlov called these **conditional reflexes** because they "actually do depend on very many conditions" (Pavlov, 1927, p. 25).

Pavlov admitted that other terms would have served as well: Unconditional reflexes might have been referred to as *inborn, unlearned,* or *species reflexes;* conditional reflexes could have been called *acquired, learned,* or *individual reflexes.* But the terms *conditional* and *unconditional* caught on and are still used today."[1]

An unconditional reflex consists of an **unconditional stimulus (US)** and the response it evokes, the **unconditional response (UR).** Meat powder is an unconditional stimulus that reliably evokes the unconditional response of salivation:

$$US \rightarrow UR$$
$$\text{meat powder} \rightarrow \text{salivation}$$

A conditional reflex consists of a **conditional stimulus (CS)** and the response it reliably evokes, the **conditional response (CR).** When the sight of a food dish regularly evokes salivation, the food dish is a CS, and salivating is a CR:

$$CS \rightarrow CR$$
$$\text{food dish} \rightarrow \text{salivation}$$

Pavlov's next question was, How does a neutral stimulus—one that does not naturally evoke a reflex response—come to do so? How, for example, does a food dish become a CS for salivating? Pavlov had noticed that stimuli that were associated with food, such as the food dish and the handler who fed the dog, became conditional stimuli for salivating. He began conducting experiments to better understand how this association led to salivating.

---

[1] Most authors use the terms *conditioned* and *unconditioned.* The words *conditional* and *unconditional* are, however, closer to Pavlov's meaning (Gantt, 1966; Thorndike, 1931/1968).

Query: What is the major difference between conditional and unconditional reflexes?

In some experiments, Pavlov paired food with the sound of a metronome. At first, the ticking had no effect on salivation; but after the sound of the metronome had been repeatedly associated with food, the ticking began to elicit the salivary response. Pavlov found that virtually any stimulus could become a conditional stimulus if it were regularly paired with an unconditional stimulus.

An example will illustrate the point. If you clap your hands near a dog, it might respond in a number of ways, but salivating is not likely to be one of them. As far as the salivary reflex is concerned, clapping is a neutral stimulus. But a few bread crumbs placed on the tongue is an unconditional stimulus that elicits salivation:

$$US \rightarrow UR$$
$$bread \rightarrow salivate$$

Now clap your hands and immediately put bread crumbs into the dog's mouth:

$$CS \rightarrow \quad US \quad \rightarrow UR$$
$$clap \rightarrow bread \rightarrow salivate$$

Repeat this procedure several times, and the dog will begin salivating when you clap your hands:

$$CS \rightarrow CR$$
$$clap \rightarrow salivate$$

Each pairing of CS[2] and US is one **trial,** and the procedure is known as **Pavlovian, or classical, conditioning.**

It is important to note two things about the Pavlovian procedure. First, the presentation of the two stimuli is independent of the behavior of the organism; the CS and US are presented *regardless of what the animal does.* Second, the behavior involved is nearly always some sort of reflex response, such as salivating, blinking an eye, or jumping in response to a loud noise.

■ Measuring Pavlovian Learning

In most studies of Pavlovian learning, the CS and US are presented close together. Since the US is by definition capable of evoking the UR,

---

[2] Technically, the stimulus that is paired with the US is not a CS until it is capable of eliciting a CR, but it is customary to refer to a stimulus as a CS from its first pairing with a US.

how is it possible to tell when learning has occurred? Suppose, for example, that you sound a tone for two seconds and then, two seconds after the tone stops, you put food into a dog's mouth. How can you tell when the dog is salivating to the tone as well as to the food?

One answer is to note when salivation begins. If the dog begins salivating after the CS begins but before the presentation of the US, conditioning has occurred. In this case, the amount of learning can be measured in terms of the latency of the response—the interval between the onset of the CS and the first appearance of saliva. As the number of CS-US pairings increases, the response latency diminishes; the dog might begin salivating even before the tone has stopped sounding.

In some conditioning studies, the interval between CS onset and the appearance of the US is so short that it is very difficult to use response latency as a measure of learning. One way to test for conditioning in these situations is to use **test trials.** This involves presenting the CS alone (that is, without the US) every now and then, perhaps on every fifth trial. If the dog salivates even when it gets no food, the salivation is a CR to the tone. Sometimes test trials are presented at random intervals, with the CS presented alone, perhaps on the 3rd trial, then on the 7th, the 12th, the 13th, the 20th, and so (Rescorla, 1967). When test trials are used, the number of CRs in blocks of, say, ten test trials is plotted on a curve. Learning is thus represented as an increase in the frequency of a CR.

Another way to measure Pavlovian learning is to measure the strength or amplitude of the CR. Pavlov noted, for example, that the first CRs were apt to be very weak—a drop or two of saliva. But with repeated trials, the saliva flow in response to the CS increased rapidly.

One problem in attempting to measure Pavlovian learning is a phenomenon known as **pseudoconditioning** (Grether, 1938). Suppose a nurse coughs just before he gives you a painful injection. Now suppose he coughs again. Very likely you will jump, just as you did when you received the injection. You might think conditioning has occurred—the cough appears to have become a CS for jumping. But you might be mistaken. A strong stimulus, such as a loud noise, an electric shock, or a needle jab, can sensitize you to other stimuli so that you react to them more or less as you would react to the strong stimulus. If a nurse jabs you with a needle, you may then jump when he coughs, even if he did not cough before jabbing you. You jump because the needle jab has sensitized you to other stimuli (see Chapter One). In this instance, we can see clearly that the cough is not a CS, since it was never paired with the US. A problem arises, however, when a stimulus *has* been paired with a strong US. Is the response a CR, or is it the result of the earlier exposure to a strong stimulus?

Pseudoconditioning is important because it is a nuisance to researchers studying Pavlovian conditioning. Pseudoconditioning can be ruled out, however, by presenting the CS and US to control group subjects in a random manner so that the stimuli sometimes appear alone and sometimes appear together (Rescorla, 1967). The performance of these subjects is then compared with experimental subjects for which the CS and US always (or at least usually) appear together. If subjects in the experimental group perform differently from subjects in the control group, the difference in behavior can be attributed to conditioning.

HIGHER-ORDER CONDITIONING

The basic Pavlovian procedure, as you have seen, consists of pairing a neutral stimulus with an unconditional stimulus. It is easy to see how such a procedure might modify reflexive behavior in the natural environment. Anyone who has owned a dog has seen how stimuli regularly associated with food come to elicit salivation. But the pairing of neutral and unconditional stimuli is not the only Pavlovian procedure that is effective.

If a neutral stimulus is paired with a well-established CS, the effect is much the same as if the stimulus had been paired with a US. This was demonstrated in Pavlov's laboratory by G. P. Frolov (in Pavlov, 1927). Frolov trained a dog to salivate at the sound of a ticking metronome. When the metronome was well established as a CS for salivating, Frolov paired it with another stimulus, the sight of a black square. Frolov would hold up the black square where the animal could see it and then start the metronome:

$$CS \rightarrow \quad CS \quad \rightarrow CR$$
$$\text{black square} \rightarrow \text{metronome} \rightarrow \text{salivation}$$

At first, the dog salivated at the sound of the metronome, but not at the sight of the black square. After several pairings of the black square and the metronome, however, the dog began salivating when it saw the square. The black square had become a CS for salivating *even though it had never been associated with food:*

$$CS \rightarrow CR$$
$$\text{black square} \rightarrow \text{salivation}$$

This procedure of pairing a stimulus with a well-established CS is called **higher-order conditioning.** Some researchers (for example, Foursikov, in Pavlov, 1927) have attempted to carry the idea one step further by pairing a stimulus with a CS that has never been paired with a US. For example, if the pairing of the black square and the metronome results in the black square becoming an effective CS, we might then pair a bright light with the black square. Note that in this case, we are attempting to establish a CS (the bright light) by pairing it with a CS (the black square) that has never been paired with food. Such efforts usually meet with limited success. Nevertheless, it is clear that Pavlovian learning can be achieved by pairing stimuli with well-established conditional stimuli. This greatly increases the importance of Pavlovian conditioning because it means that many more stimuli can be effective in establishing conditional responses.

> Query: How is higher-order conditioning different from ordinary conditioning?

Since Pavlovian learning consists of pairing two stimuli, it is often spoken of as the simplest form of learning. The apparent simplicity is, however, misleading, as we shall now see.

VARIABLES AFFECTING PAVLOVIAN LEARNING

The course of Pavlovian conditioning depends upon a number of variables. Perhaps the most important of these is the manner in which the CS and US are paired.

■ Pairing CS and US

Pavlovian learning involves the association, or pairing, of stimuli. The amount of learning that occurs depends to a large extent upon how stimuli are paired or associated. There are four basic ways of pairing stimuli:

In **trace conditioning**, the CS begins and ends before the US is presented (see Figure 3-3). In the laboratory, trace conditioning is often used to study eyelid conditioning in the rabbit. Typically, a buzzer sounds for, say, five seconds, and then, perhaps a half second later, a puff of air is blown into the animal's eye, causing it to blink. After several such pairings of the buzzer and air, the rabbit blinks at the sound of the buzzer.

Trace conditioning also occurs outside the laboratory: We see the flash of lightning and, an instant later, we hear the crash of thunder; the dog barks and then lunges at our leg; the mother talks to her baby before offering the nipple. The identifying feature of trace conditioning is that the CS begins and ends *before* the US appears.

> Query: What are the CSs and USs in the examples just given involving lightning, barking, and nursing?

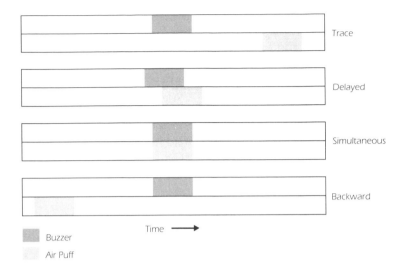

FIGURE 3-3 Pairing CS and US. A CS (such as the sound of a buzzer) may precede, overlap with, occur simultaneously with, or follow a US (such as a puff of air). See text for explanation.

In **delayed conditioning,** the CS and US overlap. That is, the US appears before the CS has disappeared. To apply the delayed procedure to eyelid conditioning, we might sound a buzzer for five seconds and, sometime during the last two seconds that the buzzer is sounding, we might blow a puff of air into the rabbit's eye.

Like trace conditioning, delayed conditioning often occurs outside the laboratory: We often hear the thunder before the lightning has faded from the sky; the dog might continue to snarl even as it bites; the mother might continue to talk softly as she nurses her baby. The defining characteristic of delayed conditioning is that the CS and US overlap.

Some researchers distinguish between short-delay procedures and long-delay procedures. The difference refers to the length of time the CS is present before the US appears. In the short-delay procedure, the CS may be present for anywhere from a few milliseconds (a millisecond is .001 second) to a few seconds before the US appears. A light might come on a tenth of a second before an electric current is applied to the grid floor of a rat's cage. In the long-delay procedure, the CS might persist for several seconds or minutes before the US appears. A light might come on and remain on for five minutes before the current is applied to the cage floor.

Initially, short- and long-delay procedures produce similar results: A conditional response begins to appear soon after the CS appears. But in the case of long-delay conditioning, the CR latency (the interval between the CS onset and the CR) gradually increases. Eventually, the

CR does not appear until just before the onset of the US. Apparently, what happens in long-delay conditioning is that the CS is not the stimulus presented by the experimenter but the combination of that stimulus and a given time interval. The animal learns to respond after the light has appeared *and* a certain amount of time has elapsed.

Query: What is the difference between short- and long-delay
procedures?

Both trace and delay procedures can produce CRs, and most studies of Pavlovian conditioning involve one of these two procedures. However, their effectiveness varies with the length of the interval between the stimuli being paired. In general, the shorter the delay, the more likely it is that learning will occur (see "CS-US Contiguity").

In **simultaneous conditioning,** the CS and US coincide exactly. We might, for instance, ring a bell and blow a puff of air into a rabbit's eye at the same instant. Both stimuli would begin and end at precisely the same instant. The simultaneous appearance of CS and US also takes place in the natural environment: Thunder and lightning occur together if the storm is nearby; the dog might snarl and bite at the same instant and stop snarling the moment it releases its grasp; the mother might provide the nipple at the very same time she talks to her baby, and she might stop talking the instant she withdraws the nipple. Simultaneous conditioning is a weak procedure for establishing a CR (Bitterman, 1964; Heth, 1976). In fact, if lightning always accompanied thunder but never preceded it, a sudden flash of lightning might not make us flinch in the least.

Finally, it is possible to arrange things so that the CS follows the US, a procedure called **backward conditioning.** For instance, a puff of air directed at a rabbit's eye could be followed by the sound of a buzzer. The US-CS sequence can also occur outside the laboratory, as when a person sits on a splinter and then (having jumped up from the uncomfortable resting spot) sees the offending object.

There is considerable debate about whether backward conditioning produces conditional responses. Pavlov (1927) described some of the attempts made at backward conditioning in his laboratory. In one experiment, one of his assistants exposed a dog to the odor of vanilla after putting a mild acid into the dog's mouth. (The acid was a US that elicited salivation.) The assistant paired acid and vanilla, in that order, 427 times, yet the odor of vanilla did not become a CS for salivating. However, when another odor was presented *before* the acid, it became a CS after only 20 pairings. These results are typical of those obtained by others who have attempted backward conditioning (Gormezano & Moore, 1969). Nevertheless, some researchers have argued that backward conditioning is sometimes effective in establishing a CR (for example, Keith-Lucas & Guttman, 1975; Spetch et al., 1981). We can say, however, that backward conditioning is, at best, a very inefficient procedure for producing a conditional response.

Because of the ineffectiveness of simultaneous and backward procedures, they are seldom used in studies of Pavlovian conditioning.

■ CS-US Contingency

You will recall from Chapter Two that a contingency is a kind of if-then statement. A contingency exists between two events, A and B, when it can be said that B occurs if and only if A occurs.

Various experiments have suggested that Pavlovian learning varies with the degree of contingency between CS and US. In one study, Robert Rescorla (1968) exposed rats to a tone followed by a mild shock. While all the rats received the same number of CS-US pairings, in additional trials the US sometimes appeared alone. In one group, the shock occurred in the absence of the CS in 10% of the additional trials; in a second group, the US appeared alone in 20% of the trials; and in a third group, the US appeared alone in 40% of the trials. The results showed that the amount of learning depended upon the degree to which the CS predicted shock. When the CS was nearly always followed by the US, conditioning occurred. When a shock was about as likely to occur in the absence of a CS as in its presence (the 40% group), little or no learning took place.

Rescorla concluded that contingency was essential to Pavlovian learning, but later work raised doubts about this. Some studies, for example, have found Pavlovian learning even when there was no contingency between CS and US (see Papini & Bitterman, 1990, and Wasserman, 1989, for discussions of this issue). Nevertheless, we can say that, other things being equal, the rate of Pavlovian learning will vary with the degree of CS-US contingency.

In the laboratory, it is a simple matter to ensure rapid learning by presenting the CS and US together on every trial. Outside the laboratory, however, the rate of learning is seldom optimal because a given stimulus will sometimes be paired with a US and other times will appear alone. Imagine that you take a job in the stockroom of a department store. A telephone in the stockroom is connected to a switchboard, and the operator has instructions that you are to receive outside calls only in cases of emergency. Thus, all the calls you receive will be either important (probably frightening or depressing) outside calls or routine calls from people within the company requesting supplies. Suppose that during your first week on the job, you get three outside calls: The first is from your fiancé (or fiancée), who calls to tell you he (or she) has decided to elope with the local mail carrier; the second is from the police, who tell you that your new car was stolen and wrecked; the third is from your landlord, who wants you to know that a burst water pipe has ruined all your personal belongings. The question is, What effect will the ring of the telephone now have on your behavior?

The answer probably depends upon the degree of contingency between the ringing phone and bad news. If those three calls were the only ones you received, then you will probably jump out of your skin the next time the phone rings. If, however, the 3 unpleasant calls were distributed randomly among 50 or 100 calls for supplies, so that the telephone's ring often preceded neutral stimuli, then you will be far less likely to be upset by a ringing phone. In the natural environment, such variations are quite common and may account for the fact that some people dread answering the phone, while others are delighted to receive a call.

■ CS-US Contiguity

Another important variable in Pavlovian learning is contiguity (see Chapter Two). In Pavlovian conditioning, contiguity refers to the length of the interval between the CS and the US. In trace conditioning, this means the interval between the termination of the CS and the onset of the US; in delayed conditioning, where the two stimuli overlap, it means the interval between the onset of the CS and the onset of the US.

In general, the more contiguous the CS and US (the shorter the interval between them), the more quickly a CR will appear (Mackintosh, 1974; Wasserman, 1989). However, the optimum interval depends, in turn, upon a number of variables.

One important factor is the kind of response being conditioned. For instance, it is possible to obtain very good results with long CS-US intervals in studies of taste aversion (see Chapter Four). Some researchers have produced taste aversions with CS-US intervals of several hours (Revusky & Garcia, 1970; Wallace, 1976). On the other hand, in establishing a conditioned eye-blink response in rabbits, long intervals are unlikely to be effective. Indeed, in this case, an interval of one-half second may be best.

The optimum CS-US interval also varies according to the type of conditioning procedure used, with short intervals generally being less important in delayed conditioning than in trace conditioning. However, even in trace conditioning, extremely short intervals may not work well, as a study by Gregory Kimble (1947) demonstrates. Kimble trained college students to blink in response to a light. The gap between the light and a puff of air was short, from one-tenth of a second to four-tenths of a second. On every tenth trial, Kimble with-

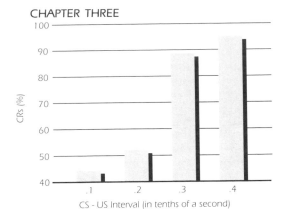

FIGURE 3-4 CS-US interval. The average percentage of conditional responses on test trials revealed improved conditioning with longer CS-US intervals up to .4 seconds. SOURCE: Compiled from data in Kimble, 1947.

held the US to see whether or not the students would blink. At the end of the experiment, he compared the response rates and found that the group with the longest CS-US intervals produced conditional responses on 95% of the test trials. Groups with shorter intervals responded less frequently; the shortest intervals produced CRs on an average of only 45% of the test trials (see Figure 3-4).

It is difficult to generalize about the role of contiguity in Pavlovian learning. We cannot say, for example, that short CS-US intervals are essential to learning, or even that they are always helpful. The ideal interval varies in complex ways from situation to situation. However, the contiguity of CS and US cannot be ignored, since it affects the success of any conditioning procedure.

■ Stimulus Features

It might seem that one neutral stimulus would serve as a CS as well as another. But while nearly any stimulus can become an effective CS, some stimuli serve the purpose more readily than others.

This is illustrated by experiments in which the CS consists of two or more stimuli (for example, a red light and a buzzer) presented simultaneously. Such a **compound stimulus** is paired with a US for one or more trials, after which the experimenter tests for conditioning by presenting the compound stimulus and each component of the CS alone.

In one of the first studies of compound stimuli, one of Pavlov's assistants (in Pavlov, 1927) simultaneously presented cold and tactile stimulation to a dog, followed by a few drops of mild acid in the mouth (a US for salivation). Then the experimenter tested the dog with the tactile stimulus alone, the thermal stimulus alone, and the compound stimulus. The results revealed that while both the tactile stimulus and the compound stimulus were effective conditional stimuli, the thermal stimulus alone was utterly ineffective.

Other studies consistently reveal that neutral stimuli that are quite capable of becoming conditional stimuli when paired with a US may be ineffective when they are part of a compound stimulus. This phenomenon is known as **overshadowing** because, as Pavlov (1927) noted, "the effect of one [stimulus] was found very commonly to overshadow the effect of the others almost completely" (p. 141). The overshadowed stimulus does not go entirely unnoticed; it simply is not an effective CS (Rescorla, 1973).

Perhaps the chief distinguishing characteristic of an effective CS is its intensity: Strong stimuli overshadow weak ones. Leon Kamin (1969) used a compound stimulus consisting of a strong light and a weak tone and found that the light alone produced a stronger CR than the tone. Other studies demonstrate that a loud noise makes a better CS than a soft noise, that a bright light is more effective than a soft light, that a distinct flavor or odor works better than a bland one, and so on.

The intensity of the US also is very important; in general, stronger stimuli produce better results than weaker ones. This was demonstrated by Kenneth Spence (1953) in a study of eyelid conditioning. The US was a puff of air exerting either ¼ pound of pressure per square inch (psi) or 5 pounds psi. In a 20-trial test period, college students trained with the weak US produced an average of fewer than 6 conditional responses to the CS, while those trained with the stronger US made an average of 13 CRs. In a more recent experiment, Brett Polenchar and his colleagues (1984) used four levels of mild shock (from 1 to 4 milliamps) as the US. They sounded a tone and then delivered a shock to the hind leg of a cat, causing it to flex its leg. The rate of CR acquisition increased with the intensity of the shock (see Figure 3-5).

It is possible, however, for a CS or US to be too intense. In eyelid conditioning, a bright light may make a better CS than a dim one, but if the light is very strong, it may be an unconditional stimulus for blinking and will therefore interfere with learning. Likewise, while a very weak electric shock makes a poor US, so may a very strong one.

Query: How would you determine the optimum intensity of a CS for eyelid conditioning?

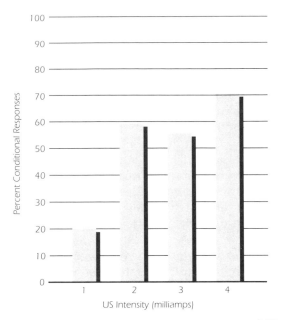

FIGURE 3-5 Conditioning and US intensity. Average percentage of CRs on seventh day of training for cats exposed to four levels of shock. Generally, the more intense the US, the more effective the training. Source: Compiled from data in Polenchar et al., 1984.

■ Prior Experience with CS and US

The effects of conditioning depend partly upon the organism's previous exposure to the stimuli that serve as CS and US. Suppose, for example, that before a conditioning experiment begins, a dog hears a bell that is sounded repeatedly but is never paired with food. If the experimenter then begins pairing the bell with food, how will the dog's previous experience with the bell affect learning?

What happens is that it takes longer for the bell to become a CS than it would have had the dog never heard the bell by itself. Being exposed to a stimulus in the absence of a US interferes with the ability of that stimulus to become a CS (see Figure 3-6). This phenomenon is called **latent inhibition** (Lubow & Moore, 1959).

Latent inhibition suggests that novel stimuli (stimuli with which the organism has had little experience) are more likely to become conditional stimuli than are familiar stimuli that have not been paired with the US. But what if the novel stimulus is part of a compound stimulus that includes an effective CS? Suppose, for example, that a researcher conducts an experiment on Pavlovian learning in rats, first by repeatedly pairing a tone and electric shock, then by repeatedly pairing a compound stimulus consisting of the tone and a novel stimulus—light—with the shock. What will happen if the researcher now presents the light alone? Leon Kamin (1969) performed this experi-

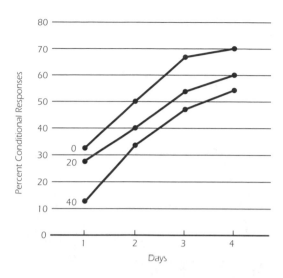

FIGURE 3-6 Latent inhibition. Percentage of CRs (leg flexion) in sheep and goats on four days following 0, 20, or 40 pre-exposures to the CS. SOURCE: R. E. Lubow, "Latent Inhibition: Effects of Frequency of Nonreinforced Preexposure of the CS," *Journal of Comparative and Physiological Psychology,* 1965, *60,* p. 456, figure 2. Copyright 1965 by the American Psychological Association. Reprinted by permission.

ment and found that the light did not become a CS. This phenomenon, called **blocking,** resembles overshadowing in that one stimulus interferes with the ability of another stimulus to become a CS. In overshadowing, however, the effect is due to differences between the stimuli in characteristics such as intensity or similarity; in blocking, the effect is due to prior experience with one part of the compound stimulus.

There is another way experience with a neutral stimulus can affect later conditioning. Suppose that two neutral stimuli, such as a bell and a light, are repeatedly presented together but are not paired with a US. Then one of these stimuli, perhaps the bell, is paired with an unconditional stimulus so that it becomes a CS. What effect will this procedure have on the capacity of the light to become a CS? Wilfred Brogden (1939), using dogs as subjects, paired a light and a bell for 2 seconds, 20 times a day for 10 days. Then, for some of the dogs, he repeatedly paired the bell with a mild shock to one of the animal's front legs to elicit a reflex movement. Next, Brogden presented the light to see what would happen. He found that this stimulus often elicited a CR even though it had never been paired with the US, a phenomenon Brogden called **sensory preconditioning.** Control animals, dogs that had not been exposed to the bell-light pairing, did not respond to the light in this way. In general, then, a stimulus will become a CS more

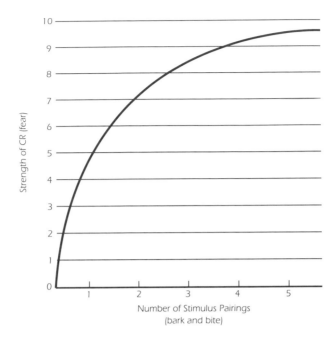

FIGURE 3-7 Number of stimulus pairings and conditioning. The more often a dog barks and then bites you, the stronger your fear. However, the first few stimulus pairings are more important than later pairings. (Hypothetical data.)

rapidly if it has been paired with another stimulus that has sub-sequently become a CS.

◼ Number of CS-US Pairings

Unless a neutral stimulus is paired with an unconditional stimulus (or a well-established CS), it will not become a CS. It seems only logical, then, that the more often the neutral and unconditional stimulus appear together, the more efficiently learning will occur. In general, nature accepts this logic.

However, the relationship between the number of stimulus pair-ings and the amount of learning is not linear; the first few associations are more important than later ones (see, for example, Hovland, 1937b). Thus, Pavlovian learning usually follows a decelerating curve (see Fig-ure 3-7). Often the first pairing of conditional and unconditional stim-uli produces marked changes in behavior, while later pairings have little additional effect (Rescorla & Wagner, 1972; Wagner & Rescorla, 1972).

From a survival standpoint, this makes excellent sense. If impor-tant stimuli are reliably associated, the sooner the organism adapts, the better. If, for instance, the sight of a poisonous snake is associated with a painful bite, it is important that we acquire a healthy fear of the snake without being bitten several times. Individuals who require several CS-US pairings for learning in this kind of situation are obviously at a disadvantage.

■ Intertrial Interval

We saw earlier that the CS-US interval was important to learning. Another time interval that affects the rate of Pavlovian learning is the gap between successive trials. (Recall that each pairing of the CS and US is one trial.) Obviously, the rest period between trials can vary from less than a second to several years. Let's say that you want to train a dog to salivate when you clap your hands. You decide that you will pair the hand clap with food ten times. How much time should you allow between each of the ten trials?

In general, experiments comparing various intertrial intervals yield results showing that longer intervals are more effective than shorter ones. Whereas the best interstimulus interval is often a second or less, the optimum intertrial interval may be 20 or 30 seconds or more (see, for example, Prokasy & Whaley, 1963).

> Query: Name four variables that affect the rate of Pavlovian learning.

■ Other Variables

The variables discussed thus far are perhaps the most important, but many others affect the course of Pavlovian learning.

For instance, Harry Braun and Richard Geiselhart (1959) found that Pavlovian learning varied as a function of age. These researchers investigated eyelid conditioning in children, young adults, and senior citizens. As Figure 3-8 shows, learning was closely related to age; in fact, the procedure was not effective in establishing a conditional eye blink in the oldest subjects.

Temperament can also affect conditioning. Pavlov (1927) noticed that some dogs are highly excitable, while others are much more sedate. He found that these differences in temperament, which may be largely due to heredity, affected the rate of learning.

The emotional state of the subject also affects the rate of learning. Janet Taylor (1951) found, for example, that anxious students acquired conditional responses more quickly than those who were more relaxed (see Figure 3-9).

Many other variables affect the course of Pavlovian learning. The present discussion is meant only to give some flavor of the complexity of what is usually thought of as a simple form of learning. Pavlovian learning is far more complicated than most people imagine. Its com-

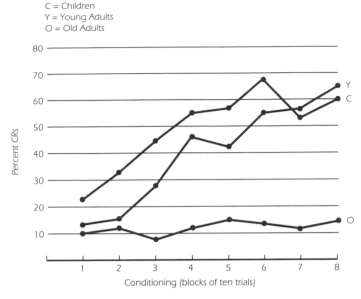

FIGURE 3-8 Conditioning and age. Eyelid conditioning proceeded more rapidly among younger subjects. SOURCE: After Braun & Geiselhart, 1959.

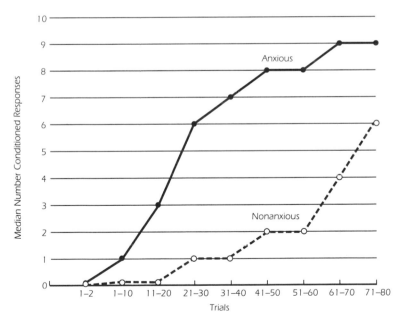

FIGURE 3-9 Conditioning as a function of anxiety. Eyelid conditioning proceeded more rapidly among anxious college students than among relaxed ones. SOURCE: From Taylor, 1951.

plexity is further revealed by the difficulty of answering a very simple question: What is learned in Pavlovian conditioning?

WHAT IS LEARNED IN PAVLOVIAN CONDITIONING?

When a dog salivates at the sound of a bell or a baby cries at the sight of a white rat, learning clearly has taken place, but what exactly has been learned?

■ Stimulus Substitution Theory

Pavlov believed that conditioning involved the formation of a new neurological connection between a new stimulus (the CS) and a reflex response (the UR). The CR and UR, he said, are one and the same; the CS merely substitutes for the US in evoking the response. According to Pavlov, then, conditioning does not involve the acquisition of any new behavior, but rather the tendency to respond in old ways to new stimuli.

Pavlov used the telephone as a convenient analogy. "My residence," he wrote, "may be connected directly with the laboratory by a private line, and I may call up the laboratory whenever it pleases me to do so; or on the other hand, a connection may have to be made through the central exchange. But the result in both cases is the same" (1927, p. 25).

This **stimulus substitution theory,** as it is called, says that the CR and UR are the same, but evidence indicates that they are not. As a rule, the conditional response is weaker, occurs less reliably, and appears more slowly than the UR. In addition, there are often qualitative differences between conditional and unconditional responses. For instance, Karl Zener (1937) trained dogs to salivate and then watched their spontaneous responses to food and to the conditional stimulus. Like Pavlov, Zener found that both the CS and the US elicited salivation, but Zener noticed that the two stimuli also elicited other behavior as well. When the dog received food, it made chewing movements but otherwise remained still; when the CS appeared, the dog became active but did not chew. Sometimes, the CR may even be the opposite of the UR (Hilgard, 1936). The unconditional response to electric shock, for example, is an increase in heart rate, while a CS that has been paired with shock elicits a *decrease* in heart rate.

Query: In stimulus substitution theory, what is substituted for what?

■ Preparatory Response Theory

The discovery of differences between CR and UR undermined Pavlov's stimulus substitution theory but led gradually to the **preparatory response theory.** This theory suggests that what is learned during Pavlovian conditioning is a response that prepares the organism for the appearance of the US. Sometimes the response required is nearly identical to the UR. On other occasions, the CR is quite different. In both cases, the CR helps the organism prepare for what is about to happen.

When a dog responds to a bell by salivating, for instance, this prepares the animal for the food that is about to come. By beginning to salivate before food arrives, the dog prepares to digest the food it will receive. In the same way, responding with fear at the sight of a dog that bit us on a previous occasion prepares us to fight or flee the danger.

Shepard Siegel (1983) has suggested that in certain cases, notably those involving addictive drugs, the CR prepares for the US by compensating for the effects of the US. The unconditional response to morphine, for instance, includes decreased sensitivity to pain, but the CR to stimuli associated with morphine is *increased* sensitivity to pain (Siegel, 1975). In this case, the organism prepares for the drug by suppressing the body's response to it.

This means that when people habitually take a drug in a particular setting, aspects of the setting become CSs for reduced responses to the drug. Thus, the preparatory response theory accounts for the phenomenon of drug tolerance. It also predicts that drug tolerance will not occur if drugs are taken in the absence of the conditional stimuli.

This prediction has been supported by research. In one study, L. O. Lightfoot (1980) had male college students drink a substantial amount of beer in a 30-minute period on each of 5 consecutive days. The first four drinking sessions took place in the same location. On the fifth day, some students drank beer in the familiar setting, while others imbibed in a new place. All the students then took tests of intellectual and perceptual-motor skills after drinking. Those who drank in the familiar setting scored higher on the tests, indicating they were less inebriated, though they had had the same amount of alcohol. Evidently, stimuli previously associated with drinking (CSs) had muted the effects of the alcohol. The novel setting lacked these CSs, so there was no preparatory CR, and the alcohol hit with full force.

> Query: In preparatory response theory, for what does the CS prepare the organism?

Preparatory response theory might also account for certain cases of sudden death following drug use. Such deaths are commonly attributed to an accidental overdose, but sometimes they occur following a dose that, given the person's history of drug use, should not have been fatal (Reed, 1980; Siegel, 1984). Anecdotal evidence suggests that the deaths are sometimes due to the absence of stimuli usually present during drug use. Siegel (1984) asked ten former heroin addicts who had nearly died following drug use about the circumstances surrounding their close calls. In seven cases, there was something unusual about the near-fatal event. Two addicts had used different injection preocedures, two had taken the drug in unusual locations, and so on. A woman who usually required two or more attempts at penetrating a vein nearly died after she injected herself successfully on the first try. Apparently, the unsuccessful attempts had become a CS that evoked a preparatory response. The absence of the CS meant a stronger, nearly fatal, reaction to the drug.

Laboratory research with animals supports the anecdotal data. Siegel and his colleagues (1982) gave three groups of rats, some of which had never received heroin before, a strong dose of the drug. The heroin-experienced rats received the test dose either in the same place they had received previous doses or in a novel setting. The results were clear-cut: The dose was lethal for 96% of the inexperienced rats, but for experienced rats, mortality depended upon the cues present. Of those injected in a strange environment, 64% died; of those injected in a familiar environment, only 32% died.

These studies are interesting in their own right, but they are also important to an understanding of what is learned during Pavlovian conditioning. When the US is food, the CR is salivation. When the US is an addictive drug, the CR is a reaction that subdues the effects of the drug. In each case, and in other instances of Pavlovian learning, the CR prepares the organism for the US that is about to appear.

Such studies hint at the adaptive value of Pavlovian learning. Yet many students come away from this topic convinced that Pavlov taught us little more than how to make dogs slobber. Chapter Four may dissuade you from that view.

SUMMARY

For centuries, we have known that people and certain animals salivate at the sight of food, but no one had given serious attention to these "psychic reflexes" until the Russian physiologist Ivan Pavlov took up the problem around the beginning of this century. By carefully controlling the environment of a dog, Pavlov was able to identify the conditions under which it salivated.

This research convinced Pavlov that there are two kinds of reflexes, unconditional and conditional. An unconditional reflex consists of an unconditional stimulus (US) and an unconditional response (UR); a conditional reflex consists of a conditional stimulus (CS) and a conditional response (CR). Unconditional reflexes are inborn; conditional reflexes are acquired. The procedure by which a conditional reflex is acquired is called Pavlovian or classical conditioning.

Various techniques are used to measure the effectiveness of Pavlovian procedures. One method is to continue pairing CS and US and observe whether the reflex response occurs before the presentation of the US. Another technique is to present the CS alone on certain trials and see whether a CR occurs. In testing for learning, it is important to control for the phenomenon of pseudoconditioning, in which a stimulus may elicit a CR even though it has not become an effective CS.

In most conditioning experiments, a CS is paired with a US, such as food. In higher-order conditioning, a CS is paired with a well-established CS. This procedure is less effective in establishing a CR than CS-US pairings.

Although Pavlovian conditioning appears to be quite simple, it is affected by a number of complicating variables. Chief among these is the manner in which CS and US are paired; these include trace, delayed, simultaneous, and backward procedures. The length of the CS-US interval and the degree to which the US is contingent upon the CS also affect the rate of learning. Characteristics of the stimuli involved can be important as well. When a compound stimulus is used as the CS, one aspect of the stimulus may overshadow another. Prior experience with the CS and US can affect learning; exposure to a stimulus before conditioning can cause latent inhibition and blocking. Other important variables include the number of CS-US pairings and the interstimulus and intertrial intervals. Often, these and other variables interact in complex ways, thus complicating this "simple" form of learning even further.

Pavlov believed that what an organism learned during conditioning was to respond to the CS in the same way as to the US. He believed the CR and UR were the same and that the CS merely substituted for the US. Subsequent research showed that the CR and UR are often quite different, and this led to the idea that Pavlovian learning involves the formation of a response that prepares the organism for the US.

Pavlov began by attempting to understand why dogs salivated at certain sights and sounds. He ended up discovering one of the basic forms of learning. We shall see that "simple Pavlovian conditioning" plays a major role in our complex lives.

REVIEW QUESTIONS

1. Define the following terms:

compound stimulus   *latent inhibition*
conditional response   *psychic reflex*
higher-order conditioning   *stimulus substitution*

2. What did Pavlov mean when he said that glands seemed to possess intelligence?

3. One of Pavlov's most important discoveries was that salivation could be attributed to events occurring in the dog's environment. Why is this important?

4. Why do you suppose Pavlovian conditioning is also called classical conditioning?

5. Explain the use of test trials in the measurement of Pavlovian learning.

6. Why is pseudoconditioning a problem for researchers?

7. Give an example of higher-order conditioning from your own experience.

8. If you wanted to establish a conditional eyeblink in response to a light, which procedure (trace, delayed, simultaneous, or backward) is least likely to be successful?

9. Give an example of overshadowing.

10. How is overshadowing different from blocking?

11. Why is it a mistake to speak of *simple* Pavlovian conditioning?

12. Explain the differences among trace, delay, simultaneous, and backward conditioning procedures. Illustrate each procedure with an example not given in the text.

13. What is the principal flaw in Pavlov's stimulus substitution theory?

14. In what sense is a CR a preparatory response?

15. A smug student intends to show off his conditioning skills by training a dog to salivate at the sound of a bell. A classmate wants to render these efforts ineffective and comes to you for help. What do you advise? (*Hint:* See *latent inhibition.*)

16. Peggy Noonan, a political speech writer, reports that soon after she had a baby she returned to the campaign trail. One day she saw something in a crowd and began lactating. What did she see?

17. Some dentists ask their patients to listen to music through headphones while having their teeth worked on. The idea is to help the patient relax, thereby reducing the painfulness of the procedure. Should people who do this listen to music they like, or music they dislike?

18. Some victims of insomnia sleep better at strange hotels than they do in their own bedrooms. Explain why.

19. In 1957, an amateur psychologist named James Vicary flashed imperceptible messages on a screen during show-

ings of the film *Picnic*. The messages were "Hungry? Eat popcorn" and "Drink Coca-Cola." Although Vicary claimed these "subliminal ads" increased sales of popcorn and Coke, research proved him wrong. However, the ads did have the effect of arousing hostility toward Pavlovian conditioning. Was Vicary's amateur experiment really a study of Pavlovian conditioning?

20. How has the study of Pavlovian conditioning altered your view of human nature?

Suggested Readings

Pavlov's *Conditioned Reflexes* (1927) is unquestionably the most important text on this subject, and it is also well worth reading as a study in scientific method. Textbooks leave out much of the process of scientific discovery; Pavlov lets us look over his shoulder as he works. Fortunately, he writes well enough that we can enjoy the view.

Other works by Pavlov are also well worth perusing. His article "Reply of a Physiologist to Psychologists" is seldom read today, but it discusses fundamental, and still relevant, issues on the nature of behavior science.

Answers to Queries

Page 62: Conditional reflexes depend upon conditions; that is, they depend upon learning experiences. Unconditional reflexes are innate; they do not depend upon experience.

Page 65: In ordinary conditioning, the CS is paired with a US; in higher-order conditioning, the CS is paired with a well-established CS.

Page 65: In the lightning example, the CS is lightning, and the US is thunder (a loud noise evokes the startle reflex). In the dog example, the CS is the bark, and the US is the bite. In the mother example, the CS is talking, and the US is food.

Page 67: Time. In short-delay procedures, the US appears within a few seconds after CS onset. In long-delay procedures, the US does not appear for at least several seconds after CS onset.

Page 69: The shorter the CS-US interval, the greater the contiguity.

Page 71: Answers will vary. One way would be to use a group design experiment with each group trained using a CS of a different intensity. The mean learning curves for each group would then be compared. This should yield an approximate answer. A more precise answer could be obtained by repeating the experiment with new subjects, this time using the best stimulus from the first study and stimuli that are slightly more and less intense than that best stimulus.

Page 75: Answers should include any four of the variables discussed in the text. These include method of pairing CS and US; CS-US contingency; CS-US contiguity; stimulus features; prior experience with CS and US; number of CS-US pairings; length of the intertrial interval.

Page 77: In stimulus substitution theory, the CS becomes a substitute for the US.

Page 78: It prepares the organism for the US.

four

Pavlovian Learning: Applications

Pavlov is a star which lights the world, shining
above a vista hitherto unexplored.
—H. G. WELLS

BACKGROUND

The fact that Pavlovian conditioning usually involves simple reflexive behavior has led many people to dismiss it as
unimportant. Pavlov, these people say, provides no insight into human
nature except to show us how to make people drool and twitch. Even
some psychologists have said that Pavlovian conditioning is merely of
historical interest, a dead subject in the morgue of behavior science.

Nothing could be further from the truth. Although thousands of
studies of Pavlovian conditioning have been carried out since Pavlov's
day, Pavlovian conditioning remains a rich lode that psychologists
continue to mine for insights into learning and behavior (Turkkan,
1989). Many of these studies have shed light on the role Pavlovian
conditioning plays in the adaptation (and sometimes maladaptation)
of organisms to their environments. Unfortunately, space does not
permit more than a glimpse at this work. Let us take that glimpse by
looking at the way Pavlovian research has changed our views of three
phenomena: taste aversions, emotions, and psychosomatic illness.

TASTE AVERSIONS

While eating is essential to survival, it is also dangerous. Some edible
substances are quite nutritious, but others are poisonous. It would be

very helpful if we had an innate tendency to seek nutritious foods and avoid dangerous substances, but it appears that, for the most part, such behavior is learned. But how?

Let us take the problem of learning to avoid eating harmful substances. Our current understanding of this problem, called **taste aversion,** owes much to the work of John Garcia and his colleagues. When Garcia was 10 years old, he had his first taste of licorice. Several hours later, he came down with the flu. After he recovered, he found he could no longer tolerate licorice (see Nisbett, 1990). Of course, the licorice had had nothing to do with making Garcia sick, but he had formed an aversion to licorice all the same.

There was nothing new about Garcia's experience. Many people had acquired taste aversions in much the same way. What was different about Garcia was that it occurred to him that this common phenomenon required an explanation. Years later, when Garcia turned to research, he attempted to find one.

In one of his first studies, Garcia and his colleagues (1955) gave rats a choice between ordinary tap water and saccharin-flavored water. The rats preferred the sweet-tasting water. Then Garcia exposed some of the rats to gamma radiation while they drank saccharin-flavored water. Several minutes later, the irradiated rats became nauseated. These rats later avoided saccharin-flavored water. Moreover, the higher the radiation level to which the rats were exposed, the stronger their aversion to sweet water (see Figure 4-1). Presumably, sweet water had become a CS for nausea; in other words, it made the animals sick.

Query: Identify the CS and US in the experiment conducted by Garcia and his colleagues.

This study differs from Pavlov's work, and from most other research on Pavlovian learning, in two important ways. First, the CS and US were paired only once, whereas most studies of Pavlovian conditioning involve dozens of pairings. Second, the interval between the CS and US was several minutes, whereas in most studies successful conditioning requires an interval of no more than several seconds. The situation was, however, analogous to Garcia's boyhood experience with licorice: One exposure to licorice followed much later by illness resulted in an aversion to licorice.

The fact that Garcia's experiment produced learning has important implications. Foods that can make an animal ill might also kill it or make it vulnerable to attack or disease, so one-trial learning can mean the difference between life and death. The animal that has a narrow escape and thereafter avoids eating that food is more likely to survive than one that must have 10 or 15 narrow escapes before it learns the lesson. Further, the effects of poisonous foods are often delayed, sometimes for several hours. The animal that acquires an aversion to a toxic food despite such delayed effects has a distinct advantage over an animal that learns only if it becomes ill immediately after eating. Thus, the ability to acquire taste aversions quickly and in

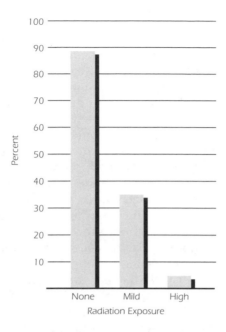

FIGURE 4-1   Taste aversion. Saccharin-flavored water consumed as a percentage of total water consumption. Exposure to radiation while drinking saccharin-flavored water produced an aversion to sweet-tasting water. SOURCE: Compiled from data in Garcia et al., 1955.

spite of long delays between eating and illness would seem to have considerable survival value.

Numerous studies support this view. Lincoln Brower (1971) studied taste aversion in the blue jay, which feeds on all sorts of insects, including butterflies. In the larval stage, the monarch butterfly sometimes feeds upon a kind of milkweed that is harmless to the monarch but renders it poisonous to other animals; it retains its poison in the butterfly stage. Wild blue jays generally refuse to eat monarch butterflies, but this tendency is not innate. If deprived of food for some time, the blue jay will eat a monarch, and if the insect is not poisonous, the bird will continue eating them. The jay quickly recovers its aversion, however, as soon as it eats a poisonous monarch. Sometimes, such jays later vomit at the sight of a monarch butterfly.

There have long been reports of taste aversions in humans. The English philosopher John Locke (1690/1975; cited in Garcia, 1981) noted a person who eats too much honey can feel ill merely at the mention of the word. Contemporary authors have reported that many people avoid eating certain foods that make them ill and are able to recall the incident that led to this aversion (Logue et al., 1981; Logue et al., 1983).

The phenomenon of latent inhibition (see Chapter Three) suggests that we should be more likely to develop aversions to novel foods than to familiar foods. This seems to be the case. Alexandra Logue and her colleagues (1983) found that many people have conditioned taste aversions, most of them traceable to illnesses following eating. But the researchers found that these aversions usually involved foods with which the person had had relatively little experience before becoming ill. An alcoholic whose preferred intoxicant is beer might, for instance, acquire an aversion to whisky, but not to beer. Or a person who rarely eats Mexican food might develop a distaste for it, but not for the Italian menu eaten daily. Thus, becoming ill after eating a kind of food we have eaten many times before is not likely to result in a taste aversion.

Conditioned taste aversions are sometimes the by-products of certain types of medical treatment. Many forms of cancer are treated with radiation or chemotherapy, each of which often causes severe nausea (Burish & Carey, 1986). Ilene Bernstein (1978) wondered whether such experiences produced conditioned taste aversions. To find out, she studied children undergoing treatment for cancer. She asked the children about their diets and found that those who were undergoing chemotherapy were more likely to report taste aversions than those who were not undergoing chemotherapy.

Bernstein also performed an experiment. She divided the children into three groups. One group ate a novel-flavored ice cream, a combination of maple and black walnut flavors, before their regular chemotherapy treatment. The second group had chemotherapy without first having ice cream. The third group had ice cream but no chemotherapy. Two to four weeks later, the children were given a choice between eating the maple-walnut ice cream and playing a game. Of those who ate ice cream before chemotherapy, only 21% chose the ice cream; of those who had ice cream but no chemotherapy, 73% chose the dessert. It seems clear that eating habits are likely to be affected by chemotherapy.

Since good nutrition is especially important for cancer patients, taste aversions may pose a serious problem for patients undergoing chemotherapy or radiation therapy. As the result of Pavlovian conditioning, such patients might experience nausea in response to many foods accidentally paired with radiation or chemotherapy. Thus, the learning that is so beneficial under ordinary circumstances is a hindrance under these special circumstances. However, an understanding of the role of conditioning in taste aversions may help reduce the problem. It might be wise, for example, for people who are undergoing chemotherapy to eat something with a distinct taste, a food that does not make up an important part of the patient's diet, shortly before each treatment. An aversion to that particular food would develop, but the patient's appetite for other foods might remain intact.

EMOTIONS

The first person to study emotions systematically was John B. Watson. Watson and his colleagues observed the behavior of babies and discovered that a relatively small number of stimuli would evoke emotional reactions. Stroking a baby's skin, for example, is an unconditional stimulus for smiling, cooing, and gurgling. This behavior can be referred to by the terms *joy, happiness, contentment,* or, more generally, *love.* We say that the baby is contented, or that he or she loves being stroked. Similarly, Watson found that a sudden loud noise is an unconditional stimulus for crying and other reactions commonly called *fear.*

But adults react emotionally to many stimuli that have little or no effect on the infant. For example, babies will put nearly anything into their mouths, including objects that adults do not willingly touch, such as insects and feces. How is it that previously neutral stimuli come to elicit disgust, fear, love, and anger? Watson's answer: through Pavlovian conditioning.

Emotional reactions, said Watson, are acquired in the same way that Pavlov's dogs learned to salivate at the sound of a tickling metronome. To test this idea, Watson and graduate student Rosalie Rayner (Watson & Rayner, 1920; see Watson, 1930/1970) conducted a series of experiments. First, they tested a number of infants to see their reactions to fire, dogs, cats, laboratory rats, and other stimuli. It was then commonly thought that infants were instinctively afraid of such items, but the experimenters found no evidence of any such instincts.

Next, the researchers attempted to establish a fear reaction through classical conditioning. Their subject was Albert B., a healthy, 11-month-old boy who showed no signs of fearing a white rat, a pigeon, a rabbit, a dog, a monkey, cotton wool, or a burning newspaper. He appeared to be a happy, normal baby who rarely cried. The researchers established that a loud noise was a US for fear. When they struck a steel bar with a hammer behind Albert's head, he would jump suddenly. Using this loud noise as an unconditional stimulus, it took little time to establish a conditional fear response to a white rat. Watson and Rayner presented Albert with the rat, and then one of the experimenters hit the steel bar with a hammer. After a few pairings of this sort, Albert began to cry and show other signs of fear as soon as he saw the rat. He had learned, through Pavlovian conditioning, to fear white rats.

We can readily come up with examples of fearful reactions that very likely were established in the same way that Little Albert learned to fear white rats. Most people, for example, are made uneasy (at the least) by visits to the dentist. This is hardly surprising when one considers that dental visits frequently entail some discomfort. The whine of the dentist's drill is all too often associated with pain, so the sound of the drill soon arouses anxiety. We may even come to fear anything associated with the painful drill, such as the dentist and the dentist's assistant (Ost & Hugdahl, 1985).

Very likely, the same sort of process accounts for the fear people sometimes feel in a doctor's examining room, the school principal's office, or a particular classroom. A person who struggles with a

Thank You, Albert

The experiment with Little Albert has been harshly criticized on ethical grounds (Harris, 1979). Today, most people find the idea of deliberately causing a phobia in a baby outrageous, and a similar experiment would no longer be sanctioned by psychologists. We should perhaps remember, however, that the ethical standards of Watson's day were different.

In any case, Albert's sacrifice completely changed our understanding of fear and immediately suggested effective treatments for phobias and other problems. These treatments have since relieved the suffering of thousands of people.

Mary Cover Jones (1924a, 1924b), another of Watson's colleagues, was the first to show that Pavlovian conditioning could help people overcome fears as well as acquire them. Jones's subject was Peter, a 3-year-old with a fear of rabbits. Peter's fear was "home grown," as Watson phrased it, not the result of experimentation. The experiment with Albert showed how Peter's fear may have been acquired; more importantly, it suggested how it might be removed.

Jones started by bringing a rabbit in view but keeping it far enough away that it did not disturb Peter as he ate a snack of crackers and milk. In this way, Jones paired a CS (the sight of the rabbit) with a positive US (crackers and milk). The next day, Jones brought the rabbit closer but was careful not to bring it close enough to make the child uneasy. On each succeeding day the experimenter brought the rabbit closer, until Peter showed no fear even when Jones put the rabbit into his lap. "Finally," wrote Watson (1930/1970), "he would eat with one hand and play with the rabbit with the other." (p. 174).

This use of Pavlovian procedures to undo the effects of accidental conditioning is called **counterconditioning.** Unfortunately, Little Albert was taken away soon after his encounter with the white rat, so his fear was never counterconditioned. If Albert is alive today, he is in his seventies and may yet have an unreasonable fear of white rats and similar objects. He has, however, contributed in a very important way to the alleviation of human suffering. He showed the way to therapies that have helped thousands of people overcome fears and other debilitating problems. Albert made a contribution in infancy far in excess of anything most of us accomplish in a lifetime.

Thank you, Albert, wherever you are.

mathematics course, for example, may feel ill at ease in his mathematics classroom even when class is not in session.

Watson suggested that the same sort of experiences account not only for fear but for other emotional reactions. Babies enjoy being stroked, he argued, so any stimulus that is regularly paired with stroking will come to be enjoyable. Thus, the mother or father who cuddles a baby becomes a conditional stimulus for the emotional response of love, and we say that the baby loves his or her parents.

Hostility is another reaction that can be established through Pavlovian conditioning. Leonard Berkowitz (1964) found that people who received electric shocks in the company of another person later showed hostility toward that person, even though the object of their wrath had not delivered the shocks (see also Berkowitz, 1983; Riordan & Tedeschi, 1983).

Such research shows that through Pavlovian conditioning, neutral events can become conditional stimuli for positive and negative emotions. But how is it that stimuli that seem to be naturally unpleasant sometimes arouse positive emotional reactions? Consider, for example, the masochist—a person who enjoys being treated in ways that others would consider unpleasant. One masochistic man wrote in his diary, "Debbie spanked me so hard I was burning. My skin was blistered in certain parts . . . *I need Debbie*" (Pipitone, 1985; emphasis added). Nor can such behavior be attributed to stupidity and dismissed. The 16th-century mathematical genius, Girolamo Cardano, "enjoyed poor health," according to his biographer (Muir, 1961), and admitted he took some delight in biting his lips, twisting his fingers, and pinching his arm "until the tears started in my eyes" (quoted in Muir, 1961, p. 50).

How does a person come to enjoy pain? Pavlov's work seems to provide an answer. In one experiment, he paired an electric current with food. Incredibly, the dog soon salivated in response to the shock, just as it might have salivated in response to a bell. In other words, the shock became a CS for salivating. Other dogs learned to salivate in response to other painful stimuli, such as pinpricks. What is even more astonishing is that these stimuli seemed to lose their noxious qualities. Pavlov (1927) wrote that "not even the tiniest and most subtle objective phenomenon usually exhibited by animals under the influence of strong injurious stimuli can be observed in these dogs. No appreciable changes in the pulse or in the respiration occur in these animals, whereas such changes are always most prominent when the noxious stimulus has not been converted into [a CS for salivating]" (p. 30). Pavlov's dogs actually behaved as if they enjoyed pain! After witnessing one of these demonstrations, the famous British physiologist Sir Charles Sherrington remarked, "At last I understand the psychology of the martyrs!" (in Cuny, 1962, p. 75).

Query: How does Pavlov's work account for martyrs?

In the same way, stimuli that are ordinarily conditional stimuli for fear may come to arouse other emotions. This is nicely illustrated by the story of the young socialite who began using drugs in boarding schools and eventually developed a $300-a-day habit that forced her into the kinds of neighborhoods generally associated with violent crime. "At first," she reported, "I was scared. But then it became a part of it that I really liked, going into a really bad neighborhood" (quoted in Anderson, 1983, p. 27). Evidently, what had been frightening stimuli (that is, a dangerous neighborhood) came to elicit good feelings

Bite Your Tongue!

Harper's Magazine (1992) "Chickens of the Sea," published an excerpt from a training manual used by tour guides at Sea World in Orlando, Florida. The manual warns that certain words and phrases have negative connotations. It advises guides to avoid these words and offers substitutes:

SUSPECT WORD	RECOMMENDED WORD
sick	ill
hurt	injured
captured	acquired
cage	enclosure
tank	aquarium
captivity	controlled environment
sex	courtship behavior
kill	eat, prey upon

The negative connotations Sea World is eager to avoid were probably acquired along the lines suggested by Staats and Staats. The word *captured* is more likely to be associated with negative words, such as *kill, enslave,* and *torture;* people are captured and killed, captured and enslaved, captured and tortured. The word *acquired,* on the other hand, is paired with all sorts of positive words; we acquire wealth, we acquire learning, we acquire prestige.

This notion might be tested by reading the words aloud and having people say the first word that comes to mind. Chances are, the words Sea World wants its guides to avoid will produce more negative associations.

because those sights and sounds were associated with the drugs that relieved her withdrawal symptoms.

Clearly, stimuli that are paired with emotion-arousing unconditional stimuli soon come to arouse emotions themselves. But not everything we react to emotionally has been paired with unconditional stimuli. In fact, people fear, love, hate, and are disgusted by stimuli with which they have had no direct contact. How is this possible?

Part of the answer seems to be higher-order Pavlovian conditioning (see Chapter Three). The names for objects are often paired with conditional stimuli that arouse emotions, so the names in turn become conditional stimuli for those emotions. This notion is supported by a series of brilliant experiments by Carolyn and Arthur Staats. Their basic strategy was to pair a neutral stimulus with one that was presumably a CS for some emotional response.

In one experiment (Staats & Staats, 1957), the researchers had college students look at nonsense syllables, such as *yof, laj,* and *qug,* as they were flashed on a screen. At the same time, the students

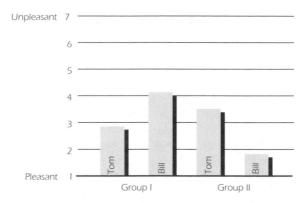

FIGURE 4-2 Conditioned emotional response to names. In Group I, *Tom* was paired with pleasant words and became pleasant, while *Bill* was paired with unpleasant words and became unpleasant. In Group II, the procedure was reversed, with corresponding results. SOURCE: Compiled from data in Staats & Staats, 1958.

repeated words spoken by the experimenters. For some students, the experimenters paired the syllable *yof* with positive words, such as *beauty, gift,* and *win,* and the syllable *xeh* with negative words such as *thief, sad,* and *enemy.* For other students, the associations were reversed: *xeh* was paired with positive words, *yof* with negative ones. (Notice that no US was ever presented.) After this, the students rated each nonsense syllable on a seven-point scale ranging from unpleasant to pleasant. The results indicated that the nonsense syllables acquired emotional meanings similar to the emotional value of the words with which they had been paired. When a nonsense syllable was regularly associated with pleasant words, it became pleasant; when it was paired with unpleasant words, it became unpleasant. In other words, *yof* came to elicit good feelings in some students and bad feelings in others, depending upon the words associated with it.

Can such higher-order conditioning account for the feelings we have about people we have never met? Staats and Staats (1958) performed an experiment in which they paired the names *Tom* and *Bill* with either pleasant or unpleasant words. As in the previous experiment, the pleasantness or unpleasantness of these names depended upon the kinds of words with which they had been associated (see Figure 4-2). When you first meet someone and they tell you, "Your reputation precedes you," they speak the literal truth.

Staats and Staats (1958) conducted an experiment that suggests that the same sort of higher-order conditioning may play an important role in racial and ethnic prejudice. In this study, college students watched as the words *German, Italian, French,* and so on flashed on a screen while they repeated words spoken by the experimenter. The experimenters paired most of the nationalities with unemotional words such as *chair, with,* and *twelve;* they paired the words *Swedish*

Pavlov Sells!

It's a long way from Pavlov's lab to Madison Avenue, but advertising agencies are very interested in the emotional reactions people have to objects. They are particularly interested in making objects arouse feelings of fondness, on the reasonable assumption that people are apt to buy objects they like.

Although they may not always be aware that they are using Pavlovian conditioning, ad writers regularly pair products with stimuli that reliably evoke positive emotions. In television commercials, for example, a particular brand of beer will be associated with attractive people having a good time. There will be no mention of alcoholism or fetal damage caused by alcohol consumption, no scenes of fatal car accidents, no photographs of children battered by parents who have had too much to drink; just young, healthy, beautiful people drinking beer and having a good time.

Can such ads induce us to like the advertised item? To find out, Gerald Gorn (1982) conducted an experiment in which college students listened either to a tune from the film *Grease* or to classical Indian music. (It was expected that the students would enjoy the popular American music more than the unfamiliar Eastern variety.) While listening to the music, the students viewed a slide showing either a beige or a blue pen. Later, the students were allowed to have one of the pens. Of the students who had listened to the popular music, 79% chose a pen of the same color they had seen while listening to the music, while 70% of those who had listened to the Indian music chose a pen *different* in color from the one they had seen on the slide.

Similar experiments have not always shown conditioning effects (Allen & Madden, 1985). But evidence does suggest that ad agencies are correct in believing that they can induce people to feel good about, and want, a product by pairing that product with stimuli (pleasant music, attractive people, and the like) that make them feel good (Stuart et al., 1987).

Of course, Pavlov did not invent this technique; people with something to sell have used it for centuries. What Pavlov and other researchers have done is to help us understand the role learning plays in consumer behavior. Armed with such understanding, we may be better equipped to protect ourselves.

and *Dutch*, however, with more potent words. For some students, they paired *Dutch* with *gift*, *sacred*, *happy*, and other positive words, while they associated *Swedish* with negative words such as *bitter*, *ugly*, and *failure*. For other students, this procedure was reversed: The researchers paired *Swedish* with pleasant words and *Dutch* with unpleasant ones. Afterwards, the students rated each nationality on a scale. These ratings showed that learning had indeed taken place: The feelings associated with the words *Swedish* and *Dutch* depended upon the emotional value of the words with which they had been associated.

Further support for the idea that higher-order conditioning may be involved in prejudice is offered by social psychologist Roger Brown (1965). Brown notes that adjectival forms of ethnic and national terms do not seem to arouse the same degree of emotional reaction as the noun forms of these words. *Swede, Turk,* and *Jew* sound worse than *Swedish, Turkish,* and *Jewish.* "In view of the Staats's experiment," he writes, "it seems probable that this is because the noun form has been accompanied by such disagreeable modifiers as dirty, whereas the adjective form has not" (p. 180).

It does not seem too farfetched to suppose that much of the prejudice directed toward certain ethnic, racial, and religious groups is due to the procedures that made some of the Staatses' subjects dislike *yof.* It can be argued that the Staatses established certain *words* as conditional stimuli, not the things those words represent. But there is evidence (for example, Williams, 1966; Williams & Edwards, 1969) that the two are related, that if the word *Arab* is paired with words like *dirty,* this will affect how we react toward Arabs as well as toward the word *Arab.* Similarly, if the words *Negro, Republican, black, Irish,* and *communist* are paired with negative words, we apparently acquire negative emotional reactions not only to the words, but to the people the words represent. The power of Pavlovian conditioning to affect how we feel about people and objects has not gone unnoticed by propagandists or advertisers (see the box entitled "Pavlov Sells!").

> Query: How might you use the work of the Staatses in designing an ad for a political candidate?

PSYCHOSOMATIC ILLNESS

The word *psychosomatic* is formed from the Greek words *psyche,* meaning mind or soul, and *soma,* meaning body. Hence, a psychosomatic illness is, traditionally, a disease of the body caused by the mind. This view is now largely rejected in scientific circles, though many health workers of the "old school" still cling to it.

The more modern view replaces the concept of mind with that of experience, so that **psychosomatic illnesses** are defined as organic disorders or symptoms due in whole or in part to experience. Common examples include allergic reactions, asthma, fainting, ulcers, and hypertension (high blood pressure). There is evidence that Pavlovian conditioning is one kind of experience involved in these and some other psychosomatic complaints.

For the sake of illustration, let us look at an experimental demonstration of the role of Pavlovian conditioning in allergic reactions. An allergic reaction involves the release of histamines by the immune system in response to certain kinds of substances known as allergens. The histamines serve to rid the body of allergens by, among other things, inducing sneezing and coughing.

Can Pavlov's Salivating Dogs Help Fight Cancer?

Pavlovian conditioning may one day form part of the armament in the battle against cancer.

It has been found that chemotherapy suppresses the immune system, the body's natural defenses against disease. Pavlovian conditioning suggests that stimuli associated with chemotherapy would, in time, also suppress the immune system. There is evidence that this is the case. Dana Bovbjerg and her colleagues (1990) found that women receiving chemotherapy for ovarian cancer showed decreased immune functioning when they returned to the hospital for treatment. Apparently, the hospital itself had become a CS for conditioned immunosuppression (that is, suppression of the immune system). This could mean that, because of conditioning, the treatment that is meant to help patients also hurts them (see also Ader & Cohen, 1975).

Such work also raises the possibility that Pavlovian procedures can be used to *boost* the immune system. If a neutral stimulus can be paired with a drug or procedure that accelerates immune functioning, that stimulus might then become a CS for conditioned immunofacilitation. Thus, Pavlov's efforts to teach dogs to salivate to the sound of a bell, so often trivialized by critics of behavioral research, may one day provide new forms of treatment for cancer and other organic diseases.

It has long been known that allergic reactions are not always due entirely to genetically based reactions to allergens. A hundred years ago, J. MacKinzie (reported in Russell et al., 1984) described the case of a patient who had an allergic reaction when presented with an *artificial* rose.

As a result of such reports, some scientists have wondered whether some allergic reactions might be partly the result of learning. Michael Russell and his colleagues (1984) exposed guinea pigs to the protein BSA so that they would be allergic to it. Next, the researchers paired BSA (now a US for an allergic response) with the odor of fish or sulfur. After several pairings, the guinea pigs were tested with the odors alone. The animals reacted with an immediate rise in blood histamine, a sure sign of allergic reaction. The odors had become conditional stimuli that elicited a conditional allergic response. In other words, the animals had become allergic to odors through Pavlovian conditioning. Russell suggests that, in the same way, a person who is allergic to a substance may become allergic to things frequently associated with it. Thus, the person who is allergic to tomatoes may break out in hives upon eating something that has the taste, smell, or look of tomatoes, even though there are no tomatoes in it. Similarly, a person who is allergic to rose pollen may sneeze at the sight of a rose—even an artificial one.

It is popularly assumed that psychosomatic disorders are "all in the head." This is usually said (sometimes by physicians, unfortunately) with a certain disdain for the suffering patient. The implication is that if an illness is psychosomatic, the symptoms are less real than those that can be attributed to viruses, tumors, injuries, and the like. But Russell and his colleagues note that the histamine levels produced in response to conditional stimuli in their experiment were nearly as high as those elicited by BSA. Thus, the person whose sneezing, wheezing, and headache are due to a CS is not necessarily less miserable than the person whose symptoms are caused by exposure to an allergen. Similarly, the person whose stomach cramp, ulcer, hypertension, or fatigue is due in whole or part to Pavlovian conditioning is not necessarily suffering less than the person whose symptoms are the result of an organic disease.

We have seen that Pavlovian conditioning provides insights into taste aversion, emotion, and psychosomatic illness. The analysis of these phenomena illustrates how important Pavlovian learning is to our daily lives, and to the lives of most creatures. "The inborn reflexes by themselves," wrote Pavlov (1927), "are inadequate to ensure the continued existence of the organism, especially of the more highly organized animals. . . . The complex conditions of everyday existence require a much more detailed and specialized correlation between the animal and its environment than is afforded by the inborn reflexes alone" (p. 16).

Indeed, were it not for the ability to learn through Pavlovian procedures, our lives would be far more precarious. As a result of Pavlovian conditioning, people withdraw their hands *before* they are seriously injured by the fire; they become ready to fend off the snarling dog when they see it, not just when it bites them.

Our ability to be modified by the association of stimuli also contributes in important ways to our individuality. Do you, for example, prefer jazz to classical music? Are you more comfortable alone than in large crowds? Does your blood boil when you see Ku Klux Klansmen marching in a parade? Do you feel a shiver up your spine when the national anthem is played? Does reading *Romeo and Juliet* move you to tears, or put you to sleep? When you hear rap music, do you sway in rhythm with the beat, or do you plug up your ears with cotton? All such reactions, and thousands of others that we think of as embedded in the very fiber of our being, are at least partly attributable to Pavlovian learning.

Pavlov and his successors helped create a new image of human nature. They began to move the causes of human behavior from inside the person (where they had existed in the form of qualities such as cowardice, bravery, honesty, and patience) to outside the person, where they existed in the form of specific kinds of observable events. Thus, Little Albert was not afraid of the white rat because he lacked courage; he was afraid because of the experiences he had had with the rat. Likewise, people do not hate the members of a particular ethnic group because of qualities in themselves or in those they hate, but rather because they have learned, largely through Pavlovian conditioning, to hate them.

This radical new image of human (and animal) nature is still not widely accepted. Radical new ideas, even those supported by decades of solid research, are usually slow to catch on. When they finally do, they are called common sense.

SUMMARY

Salivary conditioning is a prototype for studying Pavlovian learning, but the same procedures have enhanced our understanding of a number of areas of human and animal behavior.

Conditioned taste aversions are now known to be the product of the pairing of distinctive flavors and aversive (especially nausea-inducing) stimuli. Whereas normally CS and US must appear close together, taste aversions can occur even if the US is delayed for some time. Research in this field has not only helped us understand taste preferences, but may be useful in helping cancer patients maintain a good diet.

Studies of conditioned emotional responses have demonstrated how likes and dislikes, fears and hatreds, can be produced by pairing neutral stimuli with those that elicit positive or negative emotions. The analysis of emotion in terms of Pavlovian learning has also helped us understand puzzling behavior, such as masochism and ethnic prejudice.

Pavlovian learning has provided a new understanding of psychosomatic illnesses. Through conditioning, neutral stimuli can come to elicit physiological responses that mimic or produce disease processes. This work, in turn, has led to discoveries that may one day enable us to boost the immune reaction to help people fight off diseases such as cancer.

Many kinds of behavior are not due to Pavlovian conditioning. But it cannot be denied that Pavlovian learning plays a profound role in determining many of our most basic and common experiences. Pavlov made discoveries that have helped us understand many of the extraordinary events of our ordinary lives. In the process, he helped change our definition of what it means to be a human being.

REVIEW QUESTIONS

1. Define the following terms:

    counterconditioning   *psychosomatic illness*
    fear   *taste aversion*

2. Suppose that your doctor advises you to eat liver, which you despise. How might you overcome your aversion to liver?

3. You are the dietitian in charge of cancer patients at a hospital. How do you apply your knowledge of taste aversions to improve the health of your patients?

4. Pavlovian learning usually requires CS-US intervals of no more than a few seconds. Taste aversion conditioning is an exception. Explain this exception.

5. A man of about 70, named Albert, walks into a psychologist's office asking for help in overcoming an irrational fear of white, furry creatures. What can the psychologist do to help him?

6. How can you increase the likelihood that your child will share your devotion to jazz music?

7. You are in charge of rehabilitating criminals convicted of various hate crimes. Can Pavlovian learning help?

8. What do salivating dogs have to do with martyrs?

9. It has been said that people who have amorous encounters under clandestine conditions are sometimes later unable to enjoy amorous experiences under more ordinary conditions. Explain why.

10. What does the work of Staats and Staats lead you to predict about the backgrounds of Ku Klux Klan members?

11. In what sense are psychosomatic illnesses caused by events outside the patient's body?

12. Invent a better term for the disorders known as psychosomatic illnesses.

13. Why is it a mistake to speak of simple Pavlovian conditioning?

14. What sort of procedure (trace, backward, delayed, or simultaneous) did Garcia use in his experiments on taste aversion?

15. Why are people more likely to develop aversions to foods they do not often eat?

16. How is Pavlovian conditioning used to sell cars?

17. What is the essential difference between the way Peter and Albert acquired their fears?

18. What is a euphemism? Why are they used?

19. Many people hate groups of people with whom they have had no direct experience. How can Pavlovian learning account for these emotions?

20. How has reading this chapter changed your response to the term *Pavlovian conditioning*?

Suggested Readings

In his later years, Pavlov turned to the analysis of psychiatric problems. *Conditioned Reflexes and Psychiatry* (Volume 2 of his *Lectures on Conditioned Reflexes*) describes his views on this subject. For more recent work on the applications of Pavlovian procedures, see journals such as the *Journal of Behavior Therapy* and the *Journal of Behavior Therapy and Experimental Psychiatry*.

Answers to Queries

Page 86: The CS is saccharin; the US is radiation.

Page 91: Pavlov's work shows that noxious stimuli, if regularly paired with stimuli that elicit positive emotions, will come to elicit pleasant emotions. If martyrs enjoy suffering, conditioning might explain why. However, Sherrington might have been wiser to have substituted the term *masochist* for *martyr*.

Page 95: Answers will vary, but the essence is to pair the candidate's name and image with words and images that are apt to arouse positive emotions. One might also pair an opponent's name and image with words and images that arouse negative emotions. A famous instance of this involved a U.S. presidential election in which one candidate's name was paired with images of a convicted felon. Such ads have probably always been a part of elections.

five

Operant Learning: Principles

[People] act on the world, and change it, and are changed in turn by the consequences of their actions.
—B. F. SKINNER

BACKGROUND

At about the same time that Pavlov was trying to solve the riddle of the psychic reflex, a young American graduate student named Edward Lee Thorndike was tackling another problem, animal intelligence.

In the late 19th century, most people believed that higher animals learned through reasoning. Anyone who owned a dog or cat believed they could see the animal think through a problem and come to a logical conclusion, and stories of the incredible talents of animals abounded. Taken together, these stories painted a picture of animal abilities that made some pets little less than furry Albert Einsteins. Thorndike recognized the impossibility of estimating animal abilities from this sort of anecdotal evidence: "Such testimony is by no means on a par with testimony about the size of a fish or the migration of birds," he wrote, "for here one has to deal not merely with ignorant or inaccurate testimony, but also with prejudiced testimony. Human folk are as a matter of fact eager to find intelligence in animals" (1898, p. 4).

This bias led people to report remarkable feats, but not more ordinary, unintelligent acts. As Thorndike (1898) observed:

> Dogs get lost hundreds of times and no one ever notices it or
> sends an account of it to ascientific magazine, but let one

find his way from Brooklyn to Yonkers and the fact immediately becomes a circulating anecdote. Thousands of cats on thousands of occasions sit helplessly yowling, and no one takes thought of it or writes to his friend, the professor; but let one cat claw at the knob of a door supposedly as a signal to be let out, and straightway this cat becomes the representative of the cat-mind in all the books. . . . In short, the anecdotes give really the . . . *supernormal* psychology of animals. (pp. 4–5)

But how could one go about studying the *normal*, or ordinary, psychology of animals? How could one study animal intelligence scientifically? Thorndike's answer was to present an animal with a problem. Then he would give the animal the problem again and see if its performance improved, test it again, and so on. He would, in other words, study animal intelligence by studying animal learning.

In one series of experiments, Thorndike put a chick into a maze (see Figure 5-1). If the chick took the correct route, it would find its way to a pen containing food and other chicks. When Thorndike first put the animal into the maze, it tried to jump out of the enclosure and then wandered down one blind alley after another, peeping loudly all the while, until it finally found its way out. With succeeding trials, the chick became more and more efficient; finally, when placed in the maze, it would go directly down the appropriate path. Thorndike recorded the time it took the chick to reach its destination on each succeeding trial and plotted the time to produce a learning curve (see Figure 5-2).

Thorndike's most famous experiments were done with cats. He would place a hungry cat in a box and put food in plain view but out of reach (see Figure 5-3). The box had a door that could be opened by some simple act, such as pulling a wire loop or stepping on a treadle. Like the chicks, the cat began by making a number of ineffective responses. Thorndike (1898) wrote that the cat typically "tries to squeeze through any opening; it claws and bites at the bars or wire; it thrusts its paws out through any opening and claws at everything it reaches; it continues its efforts when it strikes anything loose and shakey; it may claw at things within the box" (p. 13). Eventually, the cat would pull on the loop or step on the treadle, the door would fall open, and the cat would make its way to freedom and food. When Thorndike returned the cat to the box for another trial, it went through the same sort of activity until it again made the correct response. With each succeeding trial, the animal made fewer ineffective movements until, after many trials, it would immediately pull on the loop or step on the treadle and escape (see Figure 5-4).

In experiment after experiment, with chicks, cats, dogs, and, later on, with fish and monkeys, Thorndike saw little evidence of the kind of reasoning that seemed to proliferate in the literature on animal intelligence. Instead, he observed a great deal of more or less random activity that eventually included the appropriate behavior. Over a series of trials, this response became more and more likely to occur,

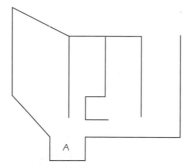

FIGURE 5-1 One of the mazes used by Thorndike. A chick was placed at A and would find other chicks and food in another pen when it reached the exit. The walls of this maze were made of books stood up on end. Thorndike referred to these structures as pens, but they were probably the first mazes ever used to study learning. SOURCE: From Thorndike, 1898.

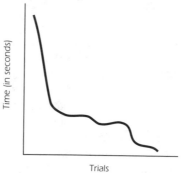

FIGURE 5-2 Learning curve showing the decrease in time one chick took to escape a maze similar to the one shown in Figure 5-1. SOURCE: After Thorndike, 1898.

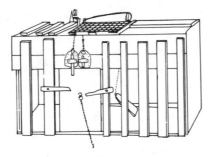

FIGURE 5-3 This is box K, typical of the boxes Thorndike used in his experiments with cats. Stepping on the treadle released the door bolt. A weight attached to the door then pulled open the door and allowed the cat to escape. SOURCE: From Thorndike, 1898.

while other, useless acts tended to disappear. Animal learning seemed to result <u>not from abstract intellectual activity</u> but from "<u>trial and accidental success</u>" (1911, p. 174).[1]

---

[1] Thorndike is often said to have studied "trial-and-error learning." In fact, he opposed the term, emphasizing that it is trial and *success*, not failure, that typically produces learning.

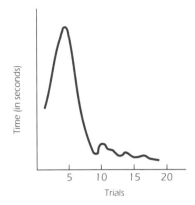

FIGURE 5-4   Learning curve showing how the time one cat took to escape from a puzzle box decreased. SOURCE: After Thorndike, 1898.

When an animal is placed in a particular situation, such as a maze or a box, it reacts by making a number of responses. A response typically has one of two kinds of consequences or effects. Thorndike called one kind of consequence a "satisfying state of affairs" and the other an "annoying state of affairs." If, for instance, a chick goes down a wrong alley, this response is followed by continued hunger and separation from other chicks—an annoying state of affairs. If the chick goes down the correct alley, this response leads to food and contact with other chicks—a satisfying state of affairs. When a hungry cat tries to squeeze through the bars of its cage, it stays hungry—an annoying consequence; when it pulls at a wire loop, the door opens and it gets food—a satisfying consequence.

Thorndike found that when a response is followed by a satisfying state of affairs, it tends to be repeated; when a response is followed by an annoying state of affairs, it tends to disappear. In other words, the probability of a response depends upon its effect on the environment, a principle that Thorndike called the **Law of Effect.** Another way of saying the same thing is, "Behavior is a function[2] of its consequences."

Later on, Thorndike (1931/1968) studied the Law of Effect as it applied to human learning. In one experiment, he asked college students to learn the meanings of a number of uncommon English words. Students would read one of the strange words, then examine a series of possible synonyms and guess which was the right one. Thorndike would tell the students whether they had guessed correctly, then give them the next item. By repeatedly going through the list of words in this way, the students eventually learned their meanings. Once again, learning depended upon the effects of behavior: Answers that produced desirable effects (hearing that the answer was correct) tended to

---

[2] The phrase *is a function of* means "depends upon" or "varies with."

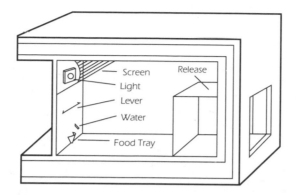

FIGURE 5-5   One of Skinner's original experimental boxes, now generally referred to as a Skinner box. One wall has been cut away to show the inside of the box. The food magazine and other apparatus were contained in the space outside of the left panel. Each time a rat pressed the lever, it activated the food magazine, which dropped a few pellets of food into the tray. SOURCE: B. F. Skinner, *The Behavior of Organisms: An Experimental Analysis.* Copyright 1938, renewed 1966, p. 49. Reprinted by permission of B. F. Skinner.

be repeated, while those that produced unfavorable effects (being told the answer was wrong) tended to die out.

Building on the foundation laid by Thorndike, B. F. Skinner (1938) began a series of studies in the 1930s that would greatly advance our understanding of learning and behavior. Skinner designed an experimental chamber now commonly called a Skinner box (see Figure 5-5). The box, now a standard feature of behavioral laboratories, was designed so that a food magazine could automatically drop a few pellets of food into a tray. After a rat became accustomed to the noise of the action of the food magazine and readily ate from the tray, Skinner installed a lever and observed the animal's behavior. As the hungry rat explored its environment, it would occasionally depress the lever. Skinner's next step was to connect the lever to the food magazine so that when the rat pressed the lever, food would fall into the tray. In other words, if the rat pressed the lever, this response would have a positive effect. Under these conditions, the rate of lever pressing increased dramatically (see Figure 5-6).

After a rat had learned to press the lever, Skinner modified the experimental chamber. Now lever pressing no longer produced food; instead, each time the rat pressed the lever, a mechanism slapped its paw; that is, if the rat pressed the lever, an aversive (painful or unpleasant) effect would result. For ten minutes, all lever presses resulted in slaps. Under these conditions, the rate of lever pressing (which had been high) declined dramatically (see Figure 5-7).

These procedures, whereby behavior is either strengthened or weakened by its consequences, became known as **operant learning** because the behavior can be said to operate on the environment. The behavior is typically instrumental in producing those consequences, so this type of learning is also called **instrumental learning.**

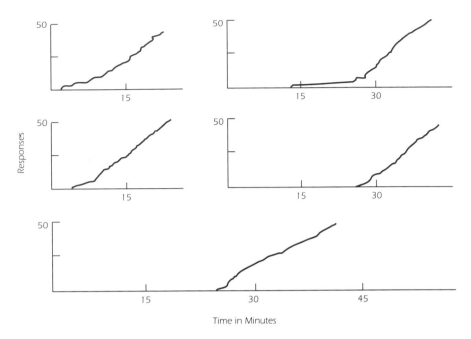

Time in Minutes

FIGURE 5-6 Lever pressing and reinforcement. The cumulative records above show that when each lever press was followed by food, the rate of pressing increased rapidly. SOURCE: B. F. Skinner, *The Behavior of Organisms: An Experimental Analysis.* Copyright 1938, renewed 1966, p. 68. Reprinted by permission of B. F. Skinner.

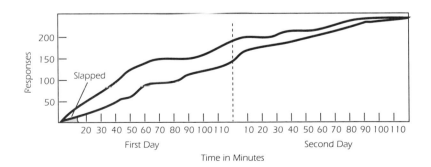

Time in Minutes

FIGURE 5-7 Lever pressing and punishment. When lever pressing no longer produced food, the rate of responding decreased. In addition, for some rats (lower curve) all lever presses were punished for ten minutes. This suppressed the rate of lever pressing for some time afterward. SOURCE: B. F. Skinner, *The Behavior of Organisms: An Experimental Analysis.* Copyright 1938, renewed 1966, p. 154. Reprinted by permission of B. F. Skinner.

E. L. Thorndike: What the Occasion Demanded

E. L. Thorndike started life on August 31, 1874, the son of an itinerant Methodist minister. His parents, who were bright and idealistic, ran a tight ship—so tight, in fact, that someone once said of the family, "There is no music in the Thorndikes." Thorndike's biographer, Geraldine Joncich (1968), wrote that there was "a smothering of lightheartedness and carefree gaiety . . . with Victorian culture and fundamentalist religion" (p. 39). This homelife produced a boy who was well mannered, industrious, and studious, but also shy, serious, and moderate to excess. Thorndike himself hinted that he lacked spontaneity and humor when he said, "I think I was always grown-up" (in Joncich, 1968, p. 31).

In 1893, the young grown-up went off to Wesleyan University, where he developed an interest in literature. As a graduate student at Harvard, he shifted from English to psychology and took up the problem of animal intelligence. There being no laboratory space for his subjects, he kept the animals in his room and conducted the experiments there "until the landlady's protests were imperative" (Thorndike, 1936, p. 264). Finally, William James (one of the founders of modern psychology) offered Thorndike the use of his cellar, and this became Thorndike's new laboratory. The work in James's basement went well, but Thorndike had little money, and when the offer of a fellowship at Columbia University came along, Thorndike packed up his "two most educated chickens" and moved to New York. It was at Columbia that Thorndike wrote the dissertation on animal intelligence that started him off on a brilliant career.

Toward the end of that career, Thorndike must have thought about these and other events in his life as he prepared a short autobiographical article. In it, he argued that his accomplishments were not the result of any deliberate plan or "inner needs." Instead, he seemed to compare his own behavior with the trial-and-success activity of his experimental animals. "I did," he explained, "what the occasion seemed to demand" (1936, p. 266).

The occasions seemed to have demanded a great deal. Thorndike's bibliography lists more than 500 items, including 78 books. In addition to his work in learning, he made important contributions to educational psychology (a field he practically invented) and to psychological testing. If, as Thorndike seemed to suggest, his behavior was simply the product of a fortuitous environment, then we are lucky indeed that Thorndike had such a splendid environment.

BASIC PROCEDURES

Skinner (1938, 1953) identified four operant procedures, two of which strengthen (increase the rate of) behavior and two of which weaken (decrease the rate of) behavior. He called procedures that strengthen behavior **reinforcement**, and those that weaken behavior **punishment**.

There are two kinds of reinforcement procedures. In **positive**

reinforcement, a response is followed by the appearance of, or an increase in the intensity of, a stimulus. This stimulus, called a **positive reinforcer**, is ordinarily something the organism seeks out. However, Skinner (1953) noted that "the only defining characteristic of a reinforcing stimulus is that it reinforces" (p. 72). In other words, a reinforcer is defined by its effect on behavior.

The effect of a positive reinforcer is to strengthen the behavior that precedes it. For instance, if a dog happens to bark and someone then gives it a bit of food, the dog is likely to bark again. In positive reinforcement, the occurrence of a response (R) is followed by a reinforcing stimulus (S^R):

$$R \rightarrow S^R$$
$$\text{bark} \rightarrow \text{receive food}$$

The procedure is not, of course, limited to animals. If you put money into a vending machine, and the machine then gives you candy, you are likely to put money into that machine in the future. The act of putting money into vending machines has been reinforced. Similarly, the saxophone playing of the novice may be reinforced by the notes he produces, even if, to other ears, the result is marvelously unmelodic.

In **negative reinforcement**, a response is followed by the removal of, or a decrease in the intensity of, a stimulus. This stimulus, called a **negative reinforcer**, is ordinarily something the organism tries to avoid or escape. For instance, if a dog is caught outdoors in a hailstorm, it can escape being pelted with hailstones by stepping under some sort of canopy. If it does so, it is likely to seek out a canopy the next time it begins to hail. Its behavior has been reinforced. In negative reinforcement, as in positive reinforcement, a response is followed by a reinforcing event—an event that strengthens behavior:

$$R \rightarrow S^R$$
$$\text{take shelter} \rightarrow \text{escape hailstones}$$

People who are caught in hailstorms also seek shelter under canopies because they, too, are in that way able to escape being hit on the head. Similarly, if your neighbor's amateurish saxophone playing is as irritating as fingernails scraped across a blackboard, you might pound on the wall separating your apartments. If the screeching noise then stops, you are apt to pound on the wall the next time a neighbor makes screeching noises. Pounding on the wall has been reinforced.

Query: What do positive and negative reinforcement procedures have in common?

Punishment procedures weaken (reduce the rate of) behavior. There are two kinds of punishment procedures. In **Type 1 punishment**, a response is followed by the appearance of an aversive stimulus. A dog that wanders onto a stranger's porch might, for example, be kicked by the person that resides there. The trespassing dog is less likely to visit that porch again. That behavior has been punished. In this form of punishment, a response (R) is followed by an aversive event (S^P):

$$R \rightarrow S^P$$
step on porch → receive kick

People likewise avoid repeating acts that have noxious consequences. If you go for a walk in the park and are mugged, you will be less likely to walk in that park in the future. That behavior has been punished.

In **Type 2 punishment**, behavior is followed by the *removal* of a positive reinforcer. A dog that is chewing on its master's shoe might come when its master calls. If the shoe is then taken away, the dog will be less inclined to answer its master's call the next time it has some plaything. The misbehavior is followed by removal of a positive reinforcer:

$$R \rightarrow S^P$$
answer call → toy is taken away

People encounter this sort of punishment when they are made to pay a fine for speeding or when they are docked for damaging merchandise at work. (In each case, money is taken away.) Parents and teachers also use this sort of punishment when they take away privileges, such as eating dessert, watching television, playing a game, or using a computer. Since the behavior "has a price," Type 2 punishment is often called **response cost**.[3]   *negative punishment*

Students typically have a good deal of difficulty keeping the four operant procedures straight. They are especially likely to confuse negative reinforcement with punishment. (Students are not alone in this; even some psychologists get the two procedures confused.) In distinguishing between negative reinforcement and punishment, try to remember that reinforcement procedures, including negative reinforcement, make the behavior *more* likely to occur, while both punishment procedures make the behavior *less* likely to occur.

■ Operant and Pavlovian Procedures Compared

Because operant and Pavlovian procedures are sometimes confused, it may be useful to point out the differences between them.

The most important difference is that Pavlovian conditioning

---

[3] Response cost might not seem like punishment at first. However, if the procedure has the effect of reducing the rate of the response, then it is, by definition, a form of punishment.

B. F. Skinner: The Darwin of Behavior Science

Burrhus Frederick Skinner was born in Susquehanna, Pennsylvania, in 1904. His mother kept house, and his father earned a living as a lawyer. As a boy, Skinner spent much of his free time building things and once tried his hand at a perpetual motion machine.

He went off to Hamilton College, in New York, for a classical education and continued to enjoy literature, history, music, and the arts throughout his life. After Hamilton, he lived in New York's Greenwich Village for a time and tried to become a novelist. The attempt failed and, after reading the work of Pavlov and Watson, he went to graduate school at Harvard to become a behaviorist. He found himself practically alone in that endeavor.

After Harvard, Skinner began the research that would eventually be published, in 1938, as *The Behavior of Organisms*. His views of behavior offended many, and Skinner was thereafter attacked and misrepresented. It was the misrepresentation that bothered him more. People said that he denied the existence of thoughts and feelings; that he denied a role for biology in behavior; that he believed people were robotic machines; that he rejected freedom and dignity. What Skinner actually said can scarcely be recognized from the writings of his critics (Todd & Morris, 1992).

Even Skinner's critics grudgingly acknowledge, however, that he made many important contributions to our understanding of behavior. He made changes in response rate a standard measure of learning; invented the cumulative recorder; made the individual, rather than the group, the object of study; practically invented the ABA research design; replaced Thorndike's subjective terminology with the more technical language we use today; replaced speculation about the mind with functional relations between behavior and physical events; and suggested ways that a natural science of behavior could be applied to medicine, work, child rearing, and education. Along the way he won practically every award ever given to a psychologist.

In January 1990, Skinner was diagnosed as having leukemia. It was, he said, not a bad way to go. There would not be much suffering, just an increasing vulnerability to the infectious diseases which would, sooner or later, carry him off.

On August 10, 1990, at its annual convention, the American Psychological Association awarded Skinner a special citation for a lifetime of outstanding contributions, the first such award ever granted by the association. Skinner was quite frail, but he approached the podium unassisted and spoke for 15 minutes without notes. His thesis was a familiar one: Psychologists should embrace the natural science approach to behavior.

It was to be Skinner's last public appearance. He left the auditorium to return to his home where, in his private study, he continued rising early in the morning to write, answer his mail, and greet visitors. Five days later he was admitted to the hospital. On August 19, while in the hospital, he worked on the final draft of an article. The next day he slipped into a coma and died.

It is now more than a hundred years since the death of Charles Darwin, and creationism is still taught in our schools. Yet the basic principles of evolution are understood and taken for granted by most educated people. A hundred years from now traditional ideas about behavior may still prevail, but perhaps the basic principles of behavior science will be understood and taken for granted by educated people. If so, much of the credit will have to be given to the Darwin of behavior science, B. F. Skinner.

involves pairing stimuli (the CS and US), while operant learning in- volves pairing responses and stimuli. In Pavlovian conditioning, one stimulus (the US) follows another stimulus (the CS); in operant learn- ing, a stimulus (the reinforcing or punishing event) follows a response. Because of this difference in procedure, Pavlovian and operant learn- ing are often called S-S and R-S learning, respectively.

Query: Why is operant learning sometimes called R-S learning?

A related difference has to do with the role of antecedent stimuli. In Pavlovian learning, an antecedent stimulus (the CS) evokes a re- sponse. In operant learning, antecedent stimuli merely set the occa- sion for a response. For instance, suppose the sound of a bell is paired with shock. If the shock makes you jump reflexively, then you will soon jump in response to the bell. Now consider the sound of a telephone. If your phone rings, you will probably pick up the receiver and say "Hello." But picking up a telephone receiver and saying "Hello" is not evoked in the same automatic way as jumping at the sound of a bell paired with shock. Or, suppose that you go into a restaurant to dine and the waiter says, "May I take your order?" This stimulus indicates that ordering will be reinforced, but it does not cause a recital of your food selection. In Pavlovian conditioning, then, an antecedent stimu- lus evokes a response; in operant learning, an antecedent stimulus merely indicates the likelihood that a response will be reinforced.

One reason antecedent stimuli play different roles in Pavlovian and operant learning is that different kinds of behavior are usually in- volved. Pavlovian learning usually involves involuntary or reflexive be- havior, such as the blink of an eye or the secretion of digestive juices; operant learning involves voluntary (nonreflexive) behavior, such as the wink of an eye or the purchase of food. It is possible (as we shall soon see) to apply operant procedures to reflexive behavior. We can, for example, attempt to increase salivation by following salivation with a reinforcing stimulus. But Pavlovian procedures work best with reflex- ive behavior, while operant procedures work best with voluntary be- havior.

A similar difference has to do with the biological systems involved in each procedure. Pavlovian conditioning involves behavior mediated by the autonomic (involuntary) nervous system and smooth muscles and glands, while operant learning involves behavior mediated by the voluntary nervous system and skeletal muscles.

While these differences are real, Pavlovian and operant learning often occur together. Consider the case of Little Albert, discussed in Chapter Four. Albert learned to fear a white rat when the rat was paired with a loud noise. This would appear to be a simple case of Pavlovian learning, and so it is. But read Rayner and Watson's labora- tory notes about the experiment: "White rat which he had played with for weeks was suddenly taken from the basket (the usual routine) and presented to Albert. He began to reach for rat with left hand. Just as his hand touched the animal the bar was struck immediately behind his head" (quoted in Watson, 1930/1970, p. 160). Note that the loud noise occurred just as Albert *reached for the rat*. Thus, an aversive stimulus followed a response. That is an operant procedure. Pavlovian conditioning was involved, since the rat and the noise were paired; but operant learning was also involved, since the loud noise followed a response.

Pavlovian and operant learning often, perhaps always, occur together, but our concern here is with operant learning. The four basic operant procedures are very effective ways of changing the rate of existing behavior. But do they account for the appearance of new forms of behavior? Dogs can learn to beg, "shake hands," climb a ladder, dance on their hind legs, and do all sorts of things they would rarely, if ever, do spontaneously. People learn to read, drive automobiles, use a telephone, and do all sorts of things they never did before. How is this possible? If operant learning depends upon the consequences of behavior, how can *new* behavior appear? The answer is a pair of procedures first described by Skinner: shaping and chaining.

SHAPING

One of the things that laboratory rats spend a good deal of time doing is pressing levers. We saw earlier that if lever pressing resulted in food falling into a tray, rats would learn to press the lever. But merely arranging the environment in this way and leaving the rat to itself results in relatively slow learning. How could we train the rat more quickly?

One answer is to reinforce successive approximations to the desired response. We might begin by dropping a bit of food into the food tray whenever the rat approached the lever. The result will be that the rat will spend more of its time in the vicinity of the lever. Next we might provide food only when the rat touches the lever in some way. The rat will then spend a good deal of its time mouthing, pawing, and otherwise manipulating the lever and will occasionally press it. Now we might provide food only when the rat presses the lever. The rat will soon remain at the lever, pressing it steadily. This procedure, in which successive approximations of a desired response are systematically reinforced, is called **shaping**.

Query: What are successive approximations?

Lever pressing is a very simple response to learn, so simple that shaping is not even necessary. Rats naturally explore their environments, and if that environment includes a lever they will sooner or later press it. If lever pressing is reinforced, it will be repeated. The real value of shaping is that it can be used to produce behavior that might not otherwise occur.

Suppose, for example, that you have trained a rat to press a lever at a steady rate, but you want the rat to exert great force when pressing it. You notice that the rat exerts the minimum amount of effort necessary to depress the lever, a force of about 35 to 40 grams. How could you train the rat to use greater force, say 60 grams, when pressing the lever?

Skinner's (1938) answer to this question was to reinforce lever pressing only when the rat applied a force of *at least* 40 grams. In response, the rat began applying more pressure to the lever, perhaps 40 to 45 grams. At this point, Skinner reinforced lever pressing only when the rat exerted at least 45 grams of pressure. This produced an additional increase in the average effort exerted, so that the rat typically applied a force of 45 to 50 grams. Skinner continued increasing the amount of force required for reinforcement until the rat reached the desired level. Skinner was able to train the rat to make a response it had never made before, and might never have made—pressing the lever with a force of 60 grams. Instead of waiting for the desired behavior to occur spontaneously, Skinner reinforced any behavior that approximated the desired act. In this way, he shaped a new response.

Skinner shaped all sorts of behavior in rats and pigeons. On one occasion, he accepted a challenge to train a dog for *Look* magazine (see Skinner, 1983a). The goal was to train the dog to jump. First Skinner provided reinforcement when the dog raised its nose slightly. Skinner gradually increased the height requirement until the dog had to raise up on its hind legs slightly to reach the height requirement. Then the dog had to jump slightly to earn a reinforcer. Finally, Skinner provided reinforcement only when the dog leapt high off the floor.

Query: How could you use shaping to get pigeons to turn in clockwise circles?

Shaping is not restricted to animal behavior. In an autobiographical volume, *The Shaping of a Behaviorist*, Skinner describes how he shaped the behavior of his daughter, Deborah, when she was less than a year old. Skinner held Deborah on his lap, and when the room grew dark he turned on a nearby table lamp. Deborah smiled at this, so Skinner decided to test the light as a reinforcer. He turned off the light and waited until Deborah lifted her left hand slightly, then turned the light on and off quickly. She moved her hand again, and Skinner turned the light on and off. Gradually, Skinner required bigger and bigger arm movements for reinforcement until Deborah was moving her arm in a wide arc "to turn on the light" (p. 179).

Query: Did Skinner shape up Deborah's arm movements, or did Deborah shape up Skinner's light switching?

The shaping procedure can be put to more practical use. A teacher can praise a student's first efforts at printing the alphabet even though the letters are barely recognizable. Once the student can easily make these crude approximations, the teacher can require something better for reinforcement. In this way, the teacher gradually "ups the ante" until the student prints the letters clearly. Similarly, a rehabilitation therapist may place relatively mild demands upon a patient at first and congratulate the patient for achieving them. When the patient becomes comfortable with the required task, the therapist can raise the standard.

Often behavior is shaped unknowingly and unintentionally. One family, for example, inadvertently shaped persistent barking in their dog. Usually, they kept the dog in the house, but sometimes they put the dog in a pen. When they first did so, the dog began to bark. After a few minutes of this noise, the dog's owners released it so it would stop barking. The next time they put the dog into the pen, it immediately began barking. This time its owners ignored it for several minutes before giving in, thereby reinforcing continuous barking. (Clearly this was not the intention, but it is what they reinforced.) The owners continued to try to outwait the dog but always ended by giving in, thereby reinforcing prolonged barking. Finally the dog would bark unceasingly for several hours, and the entire neighborhood was up in arms over "that stupid dog." The dog was not stupid; in fact, it learned quite well.

Children learn even faster than dogs, and you may observe parents shaping annoying behavior in their children in any grocery store. It is normal for young children to be unhappy when denied something they want. It is not, however, inevitable that under such circumstances children should throw themselves upon the floor, attack it with hands and feet, and scream like rock stars.

Such tantrums are the products of shaping. A tired parent may give in to a child's repeated requests "to shut him up," just as the dog owners did. On the next occasion, the parent may resist giving in to the child's usual demands. The child responds by becoming louder or crying. The parent yields to avoid causing a scene. On a subsequent occasion, determined to regain control, the parent may refuse to comply when the child cries or shouts, but gives in when the child produces bugle-like wails. And so it goes: The parent gradually demands more and more outrageous behavior for reinforcement, and the child obliges, eventually engaging in full-fledged tantrums. The parent has shaped tantrum-throwing.

Often the parents and other adults attribute tantrums and other annoying behavior to character flaws. "He's so immature!" they may say, or "What a willful child!" The children themselves seldom understand the shaping process any better than their parents. In fact, they often grow up attributing their misbehavior to immaturity, willfulness, or other internal traits, just as their parents had. But, like the barking dog, the child has merely done what was required for reinforcement.

What works for animals and children also works for adults. You may speak with your elderly aunt in a normal voice while her hearing is good, but when it begins to fail you will need to speak more loudly to receive the same reinforcers. (These reinforcers may consist of smiles, answers to your questions, entertaining stories about family members, and insights into historical events, among other things.) The worse your aunt's hearing gets, the more loudly you will have to speak to obtain these reinforcers. She will shape up speaking loudly by providing reinforcement only when you speak loudly. If she is able to provide powerful reinforcers, she will have you shouting yourself hoarse; if she is unable to provide strong reinforcers, she will become one of the many people who have become socially isolated by hearing loss.

It is reasonable to suppose that the same sort of shaping process contributes in important ways to survival. The goats of Africa's Serengeti Plain usually graze upon grass, but during prolonged droughts they must turn to the leaves of trees. As the lower leaves are devoured, the goats are forced to go after those higher up. Presumably, it was this shaping of behavior that resulted in goats actually climbing into trees to feed during the drought of 1984.

Some animals seem to use a kind of shaping procedure in the training of their young. Otters, for example, first feed their young on prey that they have already killed. As the otters mature, the parents bring animals that are dying; the young otters find the prey easy to kill. After this, the parents bring injured prey; their young must finish the job in order to eat. Finally, the adults take their young to the hunting area and bring them uninjured prey. Thus, the young otters build upon past skills until they master the art of hunting and killing prey on their own.

The behavior of human youngsters is shaped in much the same way. As children get older, more and more is required of them for reinforcement. This means not only that they are better able to survive on their own, but that they contribute to the survival of the group at the earliest possible age.

Shaping goes a long way toward explaining the appearance of new forms of behavior. Such behavior is, in a sense, constructed out of old behavior. But shaping alone is not sufficient to account for all forms of new behavior; to understand them, we must turn to chaining.

CHAINING

Women gymnasts compete on something called a balance beam. Basically this competition requires walking across a narrow plank and, along the way, doing somersaults, handstands, back flips, and other impossible stunts without landing on one's head. Competing on the balance beam consists of performing a number of acts in a particular sequence. Such a connected sequence of behavior is called a **response chain**.

Among more ordinary (and less hazardous) response chains, we may consider making a telephone call: One picks up the receiver, listens for a dial tone, dials a set of numbers, and holds the receiver to one's ear. Dining in a restaurant consists of sitting at a table, studying the menu, placing an order, eating the meal, paying the bill, and leaving. Booting a computer may consist of turning it on, inserting the startup disk, and typing a particular sequence of letters, such as a:bat. A good deal of animal behavior consists of learned response chains. Predators, for example, search for prey, stalk it, pursue it, attack and kill it, and eat it.

Usually the segments of a chain must be completed in a particular order. In using a telephone, if we dial the number before we pick up the receiver, we will not get through. Similarly, dining out may not go well if we attempt to order a meal before being seated. In booting a computer, we get nowhere if we type in the code before inserting the disk.

Query: What are the parts of the chain known as brushing one's teeth?

Training an animal or person to perform a response chain is called **chaining**. Skinner (1938) trained a rat to pull a string that released a marble from a rack, pick up the marble with its forepaws, carry it to a tube projecting two inches above the floor of its cage, lift the marble to the top of the tube, and drop it inside. Each response in the chain had to be shaped.

Other psychologists have since trained laboratory animals to perform even more complex response chains. Carl Cheney (1978) built the long chain of complex activities shown in Figure 5-8. The chain began with the rat at the foot of a ramp. The rat climbed the ramp, crossed a drawbridge, climbed a ladder, walked across a tightrope, climbed another ladder, crawled through a tunnel, stepped into an elevator that carried it back down to its starting point, pressed a lever, and received a few pellets of food.

Some response chains depend upon the behavior of others. A bucket brigade provides a simple example: The task is to take a bucket of water handed to you by someone on, say, your right, and hand it to someone on your left. This is a very short, simple chain, but executing it depends upon the performance of the people on your right and left. A more common example is the family meal in which the diners serve themselves from bowls passed around the table. Each person repeatedly executes a short chain in which he or she receives serving bowls from one side, takes some food, and passes the bowl along to the next person. Each person's execution of the chain depends upon the per-

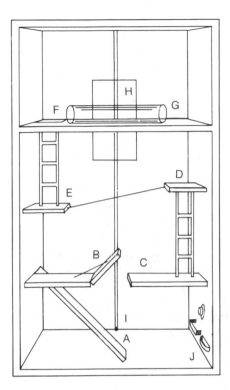

FIGURE 5-8 Chaining. Starting at A, rat climbs ramp to B, crosses drawbridge to C, climbs ladder to D, crosses tightrope to E, climbs ladder to F, crawls through tunnel to G, enters elevator at H, descends to I, presses lever at J, and receives food.

formance of other people. Indeed, the entire process can be considered a chain of chains.

It may seem logical to begin building a chain by shaping the first link. In training his rat, for example, Skinner might have started by shaping up string pulling, perhaps by providing a bit of food whenever the rat touched the string, then when it bit the string, then when it pulled it. Next he might have shaped up lifting a marble, and so on. But this is not always the most efficient way of developing a chain; it is sometimes better to begin with the *last* response in the chain. In the case of Skinner's rat, we would first train the animal to drop the marble down the tube. Once the rat had learned the last response, we could begin shaping the next to last response, lifting the marble to the top of the tube. Then we would begin training the response that precedes lifting the marble, and so on, backward to the starting point. The procedure is called **backward chaining**.

Note that in backward chaining, the chain is never *performed* backward. Skinner's rat does not drop the marble into the tube and then carry a marble to the tube. The parts of the chain are always performed in their proper order; training is backward only in the sense that links in the chain are added from back to front. So, once a rat has learned to perform the last response in a chain, it then learns to perform the last two responses in the chain. After that it learns to perform the last three responses in the chain, and so on.

> Query: How would you use backward chaining to train a rat to run a maze?

Each link in the chain is reinforced, at least in part, by the opportunity to perform the next step in the chain. Each step in baking a cake, for example, is reinforced by access to the next step in the baking process: Getting the ingredients together is reinforced by being able to mix them; mixing the ingredients is reinforced by being able to put the batter into the cake pans; filling the cake pans is reinforced by being able to put the pans into the oven; putting the pans in the oven is reinforced by seeing the batter rise and turn brown, and so on. Similarly, each link in the predator's chain is reinforced by the subsequent link: Searching for prey is reinforced by the opportunity to stalk it; stalking prey is reinforced by the opportunity to chase it; chasing prey is reinforced by the opportunity to attack it, and so on.

Chaining makes it clear just how important reinforcement is in operant learning. Yet reinforcement is not the only variable that affects the rate of learning.

VARIABLES AFFECTING OPERANT LEARNING

Operant learning, as we have seen, refers to a set of fairly simple experiences. But while the experiences are, in themselves, relatively simple, what we learn from them depends upon the complex interactions of many variables. We will consider just a few of these variables.

■ R-S Contingency

In the laboratory, researchers usually create a reliable contingency between a particular response and a particular consequence. They may arrange a rat's environment so that each time it presses a lever it receives a bit of food, but otherwise it receives nothing. In this case there is a clear contingency between lever pressing and food. If, on the other hand, lever pressing sometimes is followed by food and sometimes is not, the contingency between lever pressing and food is weaker. Other things being equal, the greater the degree of contingency between a response and a reinforcer, the faster learning proceeds. The same may be said of punishment: Consistent punishment of a response leads to a more rapid decline in response rate than occasional punishment.

It is easy to see the importance of contingency in ordinary learning. Suppose you are learning to use a new word processing program. You have a list of commands to control various type characteristics. To underline a word, for example, you press the ALT, OPT, and U keys simultaneously; to italicize a word you press ALT-OPT-I; and so on. Each and every time you press ALT-OPT-U, you get underlining. You do not get underlining if you press ALT-U or OPT-U, or type *please computer underline*. You get underlining only if you press ALT-OPT-U. And you *always* get underlining when you press that particular combination of keys. Under these circumstances, learning proceeds quickly.

Now imagine that there is a glitch in the program. Sometimes when you press ALT-OPT-U you get underlining; sometimes you do not. Sometimes when you press ALT-OPT-I you get italics; other times you do not. In these circumstances, learning is apt to proceed much more slowly.

The very term *operant learning* implies, to some extent, a contingency between a response and an event. Even a high level of R-S contingency might not produce much learning, however, if the interval between response and consequence is overly long, as we shall now see.

■ R-S Contiguity

The gap between a response and its consequences (whether reinforcing or punishing) has a powerful effect upon the rate of operant learning. In general, the shorter this interval, the faster learning occurs (see Hunter, 1913; Thomas et al., 1983).

A study by Ann Abramowitz and Susan O'Leary (1990) will illustrate. These researchers studied the effects of punishment on the off-task behavior of students. (Being off task means doing things other than the assigned work.) In their study, students were reprimanded whenever they got off task. Some reprimands occurred immediately; others were delayed. The results showed that immediate punishment was more effective than delayed punishment in suppressing the rate of off-task behavior.

Some studies of contiguity have raised doubts about its importance in learning (for example, Azzi et al., 1964; Arbuckle & Lattal, 1988). Part of the confusion stems from the fact that contiguity is sometimes entangled with other variables. Jeffrey Weil (1984), for example, notes that most studies of delayed reinforcement are confounded by the number of times the response is reinforced. To illustrate, let us compare two experiments: In one, lever pressing is reinforced immediately; in the second, the response is reinforced after a five-second delay. If we run animals under both conditions for one hour, we are likely to find that immediate reinforcement results in faster learning. But a problem arises in interpreting the results because immediate reinforcement means that the response is reinforced more often in an hour's time than is the case with delayed reinforcement. Weil dealt with this problem by making the number of reinforcers constant. The results showed that reinforcement delay *did* make a difference: the shorter the interval between response and reinforcer, the more rapidly learning occurred.

Query: *What is the point of Weil's study?*

Reviews of the literature on contiguity have found that operant learning varies fairly consistently with contiguity. Susan Schneider (1990), for instance, in an examination of one subset of this literature, found that "no clear exceptions to support for contiguity exist as yet." (p. 247).

One reason that immediate consequences produce better results is that a delay allows time for other behavior to occur. This behavior, and not the appropriate response, is then reinforced or punished. Imagine, for example, that you are learning to pilot an oil tanker. Big ships change direction slowly, so there is a delay between turning the ship's wheel and a change in the ship's direction. You might turn the wheel appropriately, but by the time the ship finally responds, you might have made some other, inappropriate, response. This inappropriate response is then reinforced by the desired change in direction. This delay is no doubt one thing that makes learning to steer great ships difficult.

■ Response Features

Certain qualities of the behavior to be modified affect the course of learning. It is fairly obvious that learning to walk a balance beam is easier than learning to walk a tightrope. It is somewhat less obvious that behavior that depends upon smooth muscles and glands is harder to modify through operant procedures than is behavior that depends upon striated muscles.

It used to be assumed that reflexive or involuntary behavior (mediated by smooth muscles and glands) could be altered only through Pavlovian procedures. It seemed absurd, for example, to think that people might learn to regulate their heart rate if changes in their heart rate were reinforced. But in the 1960s, Neal Miller and Alfredo Carmona (1967) used operant learning to train a dog to salivate, something that was not supposed to be possible.

Then Miller and Leo DiCara (1967) took on the problem of teaching rats to control their heart rates. To ensure that changes in heart rate were not due to the animal learning to tense and relax certain voluntary muscles (and thereby indirectly changing heart rate), they gave the rats a derivative of the drug curare, which temporarily paralyzed their voluntary muscles. Miller and DiCara then reinforced changes in heart rate by electrically stimulating a "pleasure center" in the rat's brain. (Stimulation of this part of the brain had been shown to be reinforcing.) At first, the researchers reinforced small changes in heart rate that were in the desired direction; then they required greater and greater deviations from the normal rate. During a 90-minute training period, the rats learned to increase or decrease their heart rates by an average of about 20%.

These astonishing results led people to envision the treatment of medical problems such as high blood pressure and irregular heartbeat through operant procedures. Unfortunately, researchers were not always able to replicate the early findings. Miller (1978) himself began to express doubts, and he and collaborator Barry Dworkin (Dworkin & Miller, 1986) finally concluded that "the existence of visceral learning remains unproven" (p. 299).

Today, the extent to which reflexive behavior can be modified by operant procedures remains uncertain. What is certain is that operant learning proceeds much more rapidly and predictably when applied to voluntary behavior (mediated by striated muscles) than when applied to involuntary behavior (mediated by smooth muscles and glands). Even with the best of reinforcers, learning to lower your blood pressure is more difficult than learning to lower your voice.

■ Distributed versus Massed Practice

The way learning trials are distributed over time affects the rate of learning. Suppose you want to learn how to touch-type over the summer vacation, and you want to spend the least amount of time on this activity so you can spend the rest of your vacation in more entertaining activities. How should you go about it?

One possibility is to condense the practice time in a short period; you might practice at the keyboard four hours a day, five days a week. Another alternative is to spread the practice sessions out; you might practice at the keyboard one hour a day, five days a week. Which plan would result in the fastest rate of learning and allow you to spend the greatest amount of time relaxing at the lake?

Alan Baddeley and D. J. A. Longman (1978) conducted a study very much like this. The British Post Office asked for their advice on devising a program to teach a large number of postal workers how to type. Naturally, the amount of time spent in training was important because the more time it took, the more it would cost. The researchers had the workers spend different amounts of time practicing each day. Some practiced only an hour a day; some practiced two hours a day; and some spent four hours a day at the keyboard.

The results showed that the rate of learning varied inversely with the amount of time spent practicing each day. Those who practiced less each day learned more from each hour than those who practiced in larger blocks. In fact, the ones who practiced an hour a day had learned as much in 55 hours of practice as those who practiced 4 hours a day learned in 80 hours of practice. Similar findings have been obtained in other studies (Lorge, 1930).

Spreading learning trials over a long period is called **distributed**

Octopi Individuality

Peter Dews (1959) discovered that individual differences in learners affect the course of learning, even when the learners are octopi.

Dews wanted to see if lever pulling could be shaped in three octopi, Albert, Bertram, and Charles. Each octopus lived in a tank filled with salt water, with a lever mechanism attached to the tank during training sessions. The basic procedure consisted of shaping lever pulling by providing the octopus with food when it approached the lever, then when it touched it, and finally only when it pulled it.

Learning proceeded by the book with both Albert and Bertram. Charles also learned to pull the lever, but things did not go as smoothly with him. Instead of pulling the lever while floating, Charles anchored several tentacles to the sides of his tank, wrapped his other tentacles around the lever, and pulled with great force. He bent the lever a number of times and finally broke it, which led to the unplanned termination of the experiment.

Charles also displayed unusual interest in a light suspended over the water. He repeatedly grasped the light with his tentacles and pulled it toward the water. This behavior, as Dews observed, was incompatible with lever pulling.

Perhaps Charles's most interesting behavior was a tendency to squirt water out of the tank, usually in the direction of the experimenter. Dews reports that Charles "spent much time with eyes above the surface of the water, directing a jet of water at any individual who approached the tank. This behavior interfered materially with the smooth conduct of the experiments, and is, again, clearly incompatible with lever pulling" (p. 62).

Charles's behavior demonstrates that individual differences exist, even among octopi. The differences may be due to previous learning, heredity, or other factors. Whatever their source, such individual differences play an important role in the course of operant learning.

practice; condensing learning trials into a short period is called **massed practice**. Thus, distributed practice is more efficient than massed practice. This finding has obvious implications for student learning.

> Query: What is the implication of the value of distributed practice for the way you study?

■ Deprivation Level

The effectiveness of food, water, and warmth as reinforcers varies with the extent to which an organism has been deprived of food, water, and warmth. In general, the greater the level of deprivation (for example, the longer the interval since eating), the more effective the reinforcer (Cotton, 1953; Reynolds & Pavlik, 1960).

At least, this is the case with reinforcers (such as those just mentioned) that satisfy a physiological need. Water, for instance, reinforces the behavior of a thirsty rat because it replaces water lost through bodily functions. This implies that such reinforcers will lose their effectiveness over the course of a training trial, and this is, in fact, what happens.

Not all reinforcers meet physiological needs, however. Money is often a powerful reinforcer, but it does not alleviate a physiological condition induced by depriving an organism of money. Moreover, money is not always less reinforcing for those who are rich than it is for those who are "money deprived" (college students, for example). Similarly, praise is a reinforcer, but praise does not necessarily become less reinforcing with each compliment. Deprivation level is important, then, mainly when the reinforcer alters some physiological condition.

■ Other Variables

The variables just reviewed are among the most important in determining the effectiveness of operant procedures, but other variables also play a part (see the box entitled "Octopi Individuality"). There are differences between and within species that suggest genetic differences in learning ability. There are also differences due to previous learning experiences. There is even evidence that much of the difference between fast- and slow-learning schoolchildren disappears when both have similar learning histories (Greenwood, 1991). And there are other variables. Operant learning is far more complicated than is usually supposed by those who incorrectly refer to it as trial-and-error learning.

THEORIES OF REINFORCEMENT

It is often said that "practice makes perfect," as though merely performing a skill repeatedly leads inevitably to mastery. Thorndike (1931/1968) showed, however, that this popular idea is in error.

Thorndike conducted several experiments intended to separate the influence of practice from that of reinforcement. In one experiment, he tried to draw a 4-inch line with his eyes closed. He drew the line over and over again for a total of 3,000 responses, yet there was no improvement. On the first day of practice, the lines varied from 4.5 to 6.2 inches; on the last day, they varied from 4.1 to 5.7 inches. The medians for each day also reveal no evidence of learning (see Figure 5-9). Thorndike concluded that practice is important mainly insofar as it provides the opportunity for reinforcement.

Reinforcers produce learning because they select certain responses. We saw this with Thorndike's cats, and we can see that Thorndike's failure to improve in drawing a 4-inch line was the result

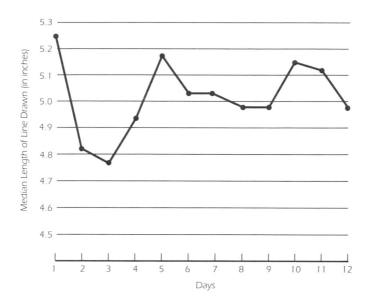

FIGURE 5-9 The effect of practice without reinforcement. Attempts to draw a 4-inch line while blindfolded showed little improvement. Source: Compiled from data in Thorndike, 1931/1968.

of the absence of events that would reinforce, or select, appropriate responses. *Why* do reinforcers strengthen behavior? Many psychologists have attempted to solve the riddle; we will consider the efforts of Hull, Premack, and Timberlake and Allison.

■ Drive-Reduction Theory

Clark Hull (1943, 1951, 1952) believed that animals and people behave because of motivational states called **drives**. For him, all behavior is literally driven. An animal deprived of food, for example, is driven to obtain food. Other drives are associated with deprivation of water, sleep, oxygen, and sexual stimulation. A reinforcer is a stimulus that reduces one or more drives. To an animal that has been deprived of food, food is an effective reinforcer because it reduces the drive known as hunger. An animal that is sated on food, in contrast, learns slowly when food is the reinforcer.

Hull's **drive-reduction theory** works reasonably well with reinforcers such as food and water because these reinforcers alter a physiological state. But, as noted earlier, many reinforcers do not seem to reduce physiological needs. Parents and teachers more often reinforce behavior with positive feedback (for example, "Mmm-hmm," "OK," "That's right") and praise than with food and water. Employers are more likely to strengthen desirable employee behavior with bonuses and commendations than with food or sleep. Yet there is no evidence that feedback, praise, money, and commendations satisfy physiological needs. How, then, can reinforcement be explained in terms of drive reduction?

Hull answered this criticism by suggesting that there are two kinds of reinforcers. **Primary reinforcers** reduce physiological needs found in all members of a species; examples include food and water. **Secondary reinforcers** do not reduce physiological needs; examples include money and praise. Secondary reinforcers, said Hull, derive their reinforcing powers from their association with primary reinforcers through Pavlovian conditioning. (For this reason, secondary reinforcers are sometimes called **conditioned reinforcers**.)

A good deal of research supports this notion. In one study with rats, W. Marvin Davis and Stanley Smith (1976) paired a buzzer with intravenous injections of morphine and then used the buzzer as a reinforcer for lever pressing. Not only was the buzzer an effective reinforcer, but its effectiveness was directly related to the amount of morphine with which it had been paired (see also Goldberg et al., 1981). It is easy to see how other secondary reinforcers might acquire their powers. Food reduces hunger, and since one needs money to buy food, money is regularly associated with food. Thus, money acquires its reinforcing properties by being paired with the things it buys.

Query: What are the two kinds of reinforcers Hull identified?

The distinction between primary and secondary reinforcers is widely accepted by behavior scientists today, but Hull's critics were not satisfied that this distinction saved his theory. They pointed out that some reinforcers seemed to be neither primary reinforcers nor secondary reinforcers. It has been demonstrated, for instance, that bringing an image into focus will reinforce the behavior of a baby (Siqueland & Delucia, 1969). This reinforcer does not reduce any known physiological need, nor does it seem to depend upon associations with primary reinforcers. Other secondary reinforcers are equally troubling. Because of this problem, most psychologists today find Hull's drive-reduction theory an unsatisfactory explanation of why reinforcers work. There are just too many reinforcers that neither reduce drives nor acquire their reinforcing properties from association with primary reinforcers. Hull is not without his defenders (see Smith, 1984), but most psychologists find other theories of reinforcement more attractive.

■ Relative Value Theory and the Premack Principle

David Premack (1959, 1965) took an altogether different approach to the problem of reinforcement. Whereas reinforcers are ordinarily viewed as stimuli, Premack noticed that they could be thought of as behavior. Take the case of reinforcing lever pressing with food. The

reinforcers = reinforcing behavior

reinforcer is usually said to be the food itself, but it can just as easily be considered to be the act of eating.

Now, said Premack, it is clear that in any situation, some kinds of behavior are more likely to occur than others. A rat is typically more likely to eat, given the opportunity to do so, than it is to press a lever. Thus, different kinds of behavior have different values, relative to one another, at any given instance. It is these relative values, said Premack, that determine the reinforcing properties of behavior. This theory, which may be called the **relative value theory**, makes no use of assumed physiological drives. Nor does it depend upon the distinction between primary and secondary reinforcers. To determine whether one activity will reinforce another, we need know only the relative values of the activities.

As a measure of the relative values of two activities, Premack suggested measuring the amount of time a subject engaged in both activities, given a choice between them. According to Premack, "reinforcement involves a *relation*, typically between two responses, one that is being reinforced and another that is responsible for the reinforcement. This leads to the following generalization: Of any two responses, the more probable response will reinforce the less probable one" (1965, p. 132). This generalization, known as the **Premack Principle**, is usually stated somewhat more simply: High probability behavior reinforces low probability behavior.

> Query: What is the relation between responses to which Premack refers?

The Premack Principle suggests that if a rat shows a stronger inclination to drink than to run in an exercise wheel, drinking can be used to reinforce running. Premack (1962) tested this idea by conducting an experiment in which he deprived rats of water so that they were inclined to drink, and then made drinking contingent upon running: To get a drink, the rats had to run. The result was that the time spent running increased. In other words, drinking reinforced running.

Premack's theory says that the *relative* value of activities determines their reinforcement value. This implies that the relationship between drinking and running could be reversed, that running could reinforce drinking if the relative value of running could be made greater than that of drinking. Premack tested this idea by providing rats with free access to water, but restricting their access to the exercise wheel. He then made running contingent upon drinking: To get to the exercise wheel, the rats had to drink. Under these circumstances, drinking increased. In other words, running reinforced drinking (see Figure 5-10).

In another experiment, Premack (1959) gave first-graders the opportunity to eat candy dispensed from a machine or to play a pinball machine. The children could stick with one activity or alternate between the two. Some children spent more time at the pinball machine;

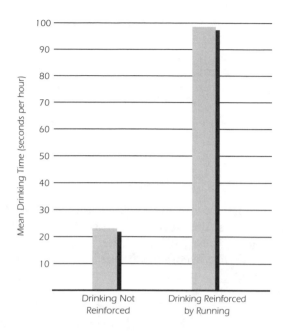

FIGURE 5-10   Relative value of reinforcement. In thirsty rats, water will reinforce running, but Premack showed that in rats deprived of exercise, running will reinforce drinking. SOURCE: Compiled from data in Premack, 1962.

others preferred to eat candy. After identifying these relative values, Premack made access to each child's more probable behavior contingent upon performance of that child's less probable behavior. For instance, a child who preferred to spend time playing pinball now had to eat candy to get access to the pinball machine. The result was that the less probable behavior increased.

The Premack Principle applies even to psychotic behavior. Some autistic children engage in what is called _echolalic speech_: They simply repeat, word for word, phrases they have just heard. If you say to them, "What's your name?" they answer, "What's your name?" If you say, "My name is Harriet," they reply, "My name is Harriet." Echolalic behavior occurs frequently in autistic children, while some normal behavior is relatively infrequent. Marjorie Charlop and her colleagues (1990) wondered if the high probability abnormal behavior could be used to reinforce low probability normal behavior. They provided the opportunity to echo speech if the youngsters performed normal activities. The result was an increase in normal activities.

Premack's theory of reinforcement has the advantage of being strictly empirical; no hypothetical concepts, such as drive, are required. An event is reinforcing simply because it provides the opportunity to engage in preferred behavior. The theory is not, however, without its problems. One problem concerns those troublesome secondary reinforcers. As Premack (1965) himself notes, this theory does not explain why the word _yes_ (for example) is often reinforcing. Another problem with the theory is the fact that *low* probability behavior will reinforce *high* probability behavior if the subject has been prevented from performing the low probability behavior for some time (Eisenberger et al., 1967; Timberlake, 1980). The latter problem has led some researchers to turn to response deprivation theory.

> Query: What does it mean to say that Premack's theory is "strictly empirical"?

■ Response Deprivation Theory

Because of the problems with Premack's relative value theory, William Timberlake and James Allison (1974; Timberlake, 1980) proposed the **response deprivation theory** of reinforcement. The central idea of this theory is that behavior becomes reinforcing when the organism is prevented from engaging in it.

Any behavior that occurs with some frequency has a baseline level. For instance, if a rat is given the opportunity to drink or run in an exercise wheel whenever it likes, it will, over a period of time, establish steady rates for each behavior. Response deprivation theory predicts that if we restrict access to drinking, so that the rate of drinking falls below the baseline level, the rat will engage in behavior that provides access to water. In other words, drinking will be reinforcing. If the rat is allowed to drink freely, but its access to the exercise wheel is restricted so that the rate of running falls below the baseline level, the rat will engage in behavior that provides access to the exercise wheel. In other words, running will be reinforcing.

This sounds similar to Premack's relative value theory, and indeed, response deprivation theory is an extension of Premack's work. The difference is that response deprivation theory says that the relative value of one reinforcer to another is not vital; what is vital is the extent to which each behavior occurs below its baseline rate. Put another way, a response is reinforcing to the extent that the organism has been deprived of that response.

Response deprivation theory predicts that the opportunity to engage in any behavior that has fallen below the baseline level will be reinforcing. For instance, suppose a child normally watches television for three or four hours each evening. This, then, is the child's baseline rate for this activity. Now suppose that something disrupts this pattern of behavior. With television viewing reduced to, say, one hour, the child is likely to engage in activities that provide access to a television. If carrying out the garbage or performing other household chores earns the child a chance to watch television, the frequency of such activities is likely to increase.

> Query: According to response deprivation theory, why are schoolchildren eager to go to recess?

Response deprivation theory works well enough for many reinforcers, but like Premack's theory, it has trouble explaining the reinforcing power of *yes.* Words such as *yes, right,* and *correct* can be powerfully reinforcing. Had someone looked over Thorndike's shoulder as he tried to draw a 4-inch line while blindfolded and said "good" each time his effort showed improvement, it is certain that he would have improved rapidly. How are we to fit such findings into response deprivation theory? Are we to believe that if Thorndike had had the opportunity to hear *good* many times, it would no longer reinforce his behavior? This hardly seems likely. Still, response deprivation theory provides an intriguing way of looking at the problem of reinforcement.

Psychologists have not entirely resolved the question of why some stimuli reinforce (or why others punish) the behavior they follow. They have, however, removed all doubt about the value of operant procedures in animal and human learning. Like Pavlov, Thorndike and Skinner profoundly altered our views of human nature. They showed that complex human behavior is not due to mysterious forces lurking in an unexplorable mind, but can be understood in terms of functional relations between behavior and environmental events.

Chapter Six shows how operant learning can aid our understanding of six topics: self-awareness, language, problem solving, creativity, superstition, and delusions and hallucinations. Once understood in terms of operant learning, these topics can never be viewed in quite the same way again.

SUMMARY

The scientific study of operant learning began with the puzzle box experiments of E. L. Thorndike and his formulation of the Law of Effect. B. F. Skinner built upon this foundation with his studies of response rate change in rats and pigeons using an experimental chamber known as the Skinner box.

The term *operant learning* takes its name from the fact that the organism operates on its surroundings. The behavior is usually instrumental in producing important effects, so this kind of learning is also called *instrumental learning.* Of the four basic procedures, two strengthen behavior and two weaken it. Those that increase the rate of behavior are called *reinforcement procedures.* Those that decrease the rate of behavior are called *punishment procedures.* There are two types of reinforcement and two types of punishment.

Operant and Pavlovian learning are sometimes confused, but there are important differences: Pavlovian conditioning involves pairing stimuli, while operant learning involves responses and consequences; Pavlovian conditioning usually involves reflexes, while operant learning involves voluntary behavior; and so on. Though different, Pavlovian and operant experiences often occur together.

Through shaping and chaining, new complex forms of behavior can be acquired. Shaping is the process of reinforcing successive approximations of a desired response. Chaining is the process of sequentially shaping a series of connected responses.

The apparently simple procedures of operant learning are actually quite complex, because their outcomes depend upon a number of variables. These include the degree of R-S contingency, R-S contiguity, response features, the distribution of practice sessions, and the level of deprivation.

Many theorists have wondered what makes reinforcers reinforcing. Hull proposed the drive-reduction theory, based on the idea that reinforcers reduce a drive caused by physiological deprivation. Premack discarded the drive concept and argued that reinforcers are effective because they provide access to preferred kinds of behavior. Timberlake and Allison suggest that reinforcement depends upon the discrepancy between the baseline rate of a response and recent opportunities to make the response.

The discovery and analysis of operant learning has provided an entirely different view of behavior, including human behavior. Interestingly, it was through operant learning that we arrived at this new view.

REVIEW QUESTIONS

1. Define the following terms in your own words:

   chaining   punishment
   operant learning   reinforcer
   Premack Principle   shaping

2. Apply Thorndike's reasoning about animal anecdotes to anecdotes about other remarkable phenomena, such as telepathy, astrology, and dreams about the future.

3. Why did Thorndike object to the term *trial-and-error learning*?   success → reinforcement

4. One of Skinner's chief contributions to psychology is said to be the use of response rate as a dependent variable. How does this approach differ from Thorndike's studies of chicks running mazes?

5. How did the Skinner box improve upon Thorndike's puzzle boxes?

6. Explain the difference between negative and positive reinforcement.

7. If Pavlovian conditioning is S-S learning, what is operant learning?

8. What is the single most important difference between Pavlovian and operant learning?

9. A worker used to slip away from the plant every afternoon to hunt rabbits. When his employer found out, he gave the man a raise as an incentive to work harder. What did the employer reinforce?

10. Does the children's game "Hot and Cold" make use of shaping?

11. How could a Spanish instructor use shaping to teach a student to roll r's?

12. Describe the procedure you would use to train a dog to retrieve the morning newspaper from your front porch. (*Hint:* A chain has many links.)

13. How is chaining a form of shaping?

14. What is a chain of chains? Give an example not mentioned in the text.

15. What is the R-S interval? What is its counterpart in Pavlovian conditioning?

16. Why is the Premack Principle sometimes called Grandmother's Rule?

17. Design an experiment to determine the optimum distribution of student study sessions. Plot a hypothetical graph of the data you would expect to obtain.

18. What problems does the drive-reduction theory present?

19. What is the chief difference between Premack's relative value theory and Timberlake and Allison's response deprivation theory?

20. How has your study of operant learning changed your views of human nature?

Suggested Readings

The two classics in operant learning are Thorndike's *Animal Intelligence* and Skinner's *The Behavior of Organisms*. These two works, like most classics, are talked about more often than they are read. This is unfortunate because both books are well worth reading. Thorndike's *Animal Intelligence* is a fast read, but *The Behavior of Organisms* is slower going.

Most of Skinner's other books were written for the general reader. *Science and Human Behavior* is particularly recommended for its discussion of the role that operant learning plays in human behavior. Skinner's controversial *Beyond Freedom and Dignity* has been misrepresented so often you might want to read it just to see what Skinner *really* said about freedom and dignity.

Skinner was arguably the most influential behavioral scientist who ever lived, and his life and work are well worth study. His auto-biographical volumes—*Particulars of My Life, The Shaping of a Behaviorist,* and *A Matter of Consequences*—make fascinating reading.

Answers to Queries

Page 108: Both positive and negative reinforcement procedures reinforce behavior. That is, they increase the strength of a response (for example, the likelihood that it will be repeated).

Page 111: Operant learning is called R-S learning because it involves responses (R) and their consequences (S).

Page 112: In shaping, each time behavior gets closer to the desired response, it is reinforced. Each of these improvements toward the final goal is a successive approximation.

Page 113: Turning in a clockwise circle means turning to the right 360 degrees. We might reinforce any turn to the right of 5 degrees or more, then gradually increase the number of degrees that must be turned to receive reinforcement.

Page 113: This is a trick question, like the one about the chicken and the egg. In operant learning, there is a reciprocal relationship between the teacher (or the teaching environment) and the "student." The student's behavior is modified by the consequences provided by the teacher; the teacher's behavior is modified by the consequences provided by the student.

Page 116: Answers will vary. A typical chain might include picking up a toothbrush, dampening the brush under the spigot, putting toothpaste on it, moving the brush against the teeth, rinsing the mouth, rinsing the brush, and returning the brush to its container. Obviously, the chain could be extended considerably. *The Odd Couple*'s Felix Ungar would specify the precise manner in which each tooth is to be brushed.

Page 118: Put food in the goal box (the end of the maze), put the rat just outside the goal box, and release it. On the next trial, put the rat further away from the goal box. Keep backing the rat up in this way until it is starting at the beginning.

Page 119: Weil wanted to separate the effects of *delay* of reinforcement and *number* of reinforcements. He found that reinforcement delay does affect learning.

Page 122: If you can't figure this one out, you might need to study more often for short periods instead of studying less often for long periods.

Page 125: Hull identified primary and secondary (or conditioned) reinforcers.

Page 126: The relation that interests Premack is between the response that is being reinforced and the response that is reinforcing it. Premack's terminology changes R-S learning (see the answer to the query from page 111) into R-R learning.

Page 128: Premack deals only in observable events, not hypothetical concepts such as drive.

Page 128: In school, children typically are required to sit at their desks for long periods. They are deprived of the opportunity to engage in their normal level of activity.

six

Operant Learning: Applications

From so simple a beginning endless forms most beautiful and most wonderful have been, and are being, evolved.
—CHARLES DARWIN

BACKGROUND

In operant learning, B. F. Skinner often suggested, the environment selects behavior in much the same way that the environment selects species characteristics. Behavior that is useful, that contributes to survival, endures; behavior that is harmful or useless dies out. In this way the environment shapes behavior. An organism behaves in a certain way, and the environment reinforces, punishes, or ignores that behavior.

In saying this, Skinner draws a clear parallel between operant learning and evolution. The parallel is apt, but it is important to remember that the organism is affecting its environment, as well as being affected by it.

Organisms interact with their environments. Both the organisms and the environment "behave," in the sense that each acts upon the other. This is what operant learning is all about: An organism acts on its surroundings, and the surroundings act upon the organism. Each shapes the other.

We have seen that this simple process, this business of acting on our environment and being acted upon by that environment, can change behavior. Simple responses, such as lever presses and disk pecks, will increase or decrease in frequency depending upon their consequences. More complex behavior can be shaped by the selective reinforcement of successive approximations of the behavior to be learned. And long sequences of behavior can be constructed through the reinforcement of response chains.

Clearly, humans and other animals can and do learn in this way, but can the threads that form the rich fabric of human experience be understood in terms of operant learning? Let us examine some of those threads and see.

SELF-AWARENESS

Self-awareness seems so basic, so fundamental to experience, that we rarely examine the concept closely. What is the self of which we are aware, and how do we become aware of it?

Let us consider first what it means to be aware of someone else. Suppose you are sitting at a table in a school cafeteria. A friend sits across from you and engages you in conversation. She has recently taken an important test that you will soon have to take, so you are intensely interested in what she has to report. During the conversation, another student sits next to you and listens silently to the conversation, but you are so absorbed in what your friend is saying that you are later surprised to find someone sitting next to you. We say that we are aware of someone, then, when we observe their behavior.

If the self is our behavior, then we are aware of the self when we observe our own behavior. "I was angry" means, "I observed myself behaving in ways commonly identified as anger." A more scrupulous self-observer might say, "I noticed that my voice trembled, my face and neck felt warm, I clenched my teeth, made fists with my hands, felt my heart beat fast, and cursed silently."

B. F. Skinner (1953) notes that we often observe subtle forms of behavior in ourselves and make inferences from them about our future behavior. We do this all the time when we speak of future plans. When we say, for example, "I think I'll quit school," we are really saying, "I have observed myself behaving in ways that suggest I will quit school." Saying, "I think I'll quit school" is not, in any fundamental way, different from saying, "I think Joe will quit school." The events that lead to either observation will be nearly identical: negative statements about school, failure to attend classes, poor grades, unsuccessful efforts to make friends or join social clubs or athletic teams, and so on. In other words, we make observations about our own behavior that are essentially the same as the observations we make about others.

To be aware of one's self means, then, to observe one's own behavior, just as we observe the behavior of others. How is it that we come to observe our behavior? Why do we become self-aware?

Query: What is the briefest definition of self-awareness you can produce?

It is easy to see why we observe the behavior of others: Doing so is reinforced. We may notice that Mary is in a good mood, and our efforts to engage her in conversation on such occasions are followed by pleasant exchanges. Or we may notice that Mary is in a foul mood, and this observation allows us to avoid the aversive consequences that are likely to follow certains kinds of behavior, such as attempting to engage her in conversation. We never actually observe the private events that are Mary's feelings, of course; rather, we observe subtle forms of behavior such as a smile or a frown. Such behavior serves as signals that certain kinds of behavior will be reinforced, and other kinds of behavior will be punished. The signals vary from person to person, which is why it takes a while to learn a person's moods. When we know someone well, however, we say that we "can read her (or him) like a book." And so we do.

We become expert at reading a person's behavior because it pays to do so, but why do we observe our own behavior? Again, the answer is that it pays to do so. If we are able to detect from our own behavior that we are in the early stages of flu, we might speed our recovery by getting additional rest before the symptoms hit with full force. Similarly, if we notice that we are in a bad mood, we might avoid an unpleasant argument by postponing a meeting to discuss wedding plans with our future in-laws. Or consider the case of a man who is not a careful observer of his own behavior. When such a person says at various times during a conversation that he is going to college, that he is going to join the Navy, and that he is going to work in his uncle's garage, we say that he doesn't know what he will do. But there are aversive consequences for being a person who "doesn't know his (or her) own mind": People may not take such a person's statements seriously (remember the little boy who cried "wolf"); a banker may be reluctant to loan money to a person who changes his or her mind so often; and people are apt to deny opportunities to someone who seems indecisive. When we observe our behavior carefully, however, we can more accurately predict what we will do, just as we can predict the behavior of a close friend. This sort of self-awareness (often called personal insight), is reinforced because it allows us to behave more effectively.

It was once thought that such self-knowledge was available only to humans. Two prominent psychologists not so long ago wrote in a psychology textbook that "one of man's unique distinctions, setting him off most sharply from other animals, may be just this extraordinary capacity to look at himself" (Krech & Crutchfield, 1961, p. 202). But recent research has shown that other animals appear to be quite capable of at least a primitive form of self-awareness.

Gordon Gallup (1970, 1979) was apparently the first to provide experimental evidence of self-awareness in animals. In his first study (Gallup, 1970), he exposed chimpanzees to a full-length mirror for several days. Initially, the animals responded to their reflections as if to another animal, but these social responses were gradually replaced by self-directed behavior. Increasingly, the animals used the mirrors to groom parts of their bodies they could not otherwise see, to pick food from between their teeth, to look at themselves as they made faces or blew bubbles, and so on. After this, each animal was anesthetized and dabbed with an odorless red dye on one eyebrow ridge and the upper part of one ear. Upon recovering from anesthesia, the animals were observed for 30 minutes with the mirror removed and then for 30 minutes with the mirror present. The chimps made almost no effort to touch the dyed parts of their bodies when there was no mirror, but made from 4 to 10 responses with the mirror present. Sometimes the animals would look in the mirror, touch the dye with their fingers, and then examine their fingers closely. When chimps that had not had experience with mirrors were anesthetized and dyed, they did not touch the dyed spots and showed no signs of using the mirror to inspect themselves. Gallup concluded that "insofar as self-recognition of one's mirror image implies a concept of self, these data would seem to qualify as the first experimental demonstration of self-concept in a subhuman form" (p. 87). Gallup repeated his experiment with monkeys but was unsuccessful. He concluded that "the capacity for self-recognition may not extend below man and the great apes" (p. 87). But other research has proved him wrong.

Robert Epstein and others (Epstein et al., 1981) found that even pigeons are capable of performing in the manner of Gallup's chimps. These researchers first trained pigeons to peck dots on their own bodies, then to peck a wall after seeing a dot flashed there, and then to peck the wall after seeing the flashing dot reflected in a mirror. After this, the researchers put a blue dot on each bird's breast beneath a bib. The bib prevented the bird from seeing the dot directly, but it could see the dot reflected in a mirror. Each bird was tested first with the mirror covered; none of the birds tried to peck the blue dot. Next, the birds were tested with the mirror uncovered, and each of them soon began pecking at a spot on the bib corresponding to the dot on its breast.

Whether chimpanzees and pigeons are self-aware in the same sense as humans is a matter for conjecture. These studies demonstrate that animals can become careful observers of their own bodies, at least the outer surface of their bodies. They do not, of course, demonstrate that animals observe their own moods and thoughts and other private behavior the way humans do. But the experiments do support the notion that self-awareness means observing one's own behavior and that such self-awareness "can be accounted for in terms of an environmental history" (Epstein et al., 1981, p. 696). In other words, self-awareness is learned.

Humans learn to observe themselves—to be self-aware—not so much from mirrors as from other people. "Strangely enough," writes Skinner (1953), "it is the community which teaches the individual to 'know thyself' " (p. 261; see also Cooley, 1902; Mead, 1934). Skinner adds that we teach a child to say "that itches," "that tickles," "that hurts," by suggesting such terms when we observe behavior or events that ordinarily accompany such experiences. For instance, scratching

The Shaping of Awareness

Most people think of coma as deep sleep, but in long-term cases, patients often behave as though they are about to wake. They may open their eyes, turn their heads, move a hand. Often, they seem trapped in a foglike state somewhere between sleep and wakefulness. Operant learning may help some coma victims break through the fog.

Mary Boyle (Boyle & Greer, 1983) worked with three people who had been comatose for at least six months. Each of the patients made some slight spontaneous movements, such as squinting or moving the head from side to side. Boyle tried to increase the frequency of these acts by reinforcing them with music. First, she asked the patient to make some movement that he or she had been seen to make spontaneously. Then she encouraged the desired act by, for example, moving the patient's hand from side to side. After this, she repeatedly asked the patient to make that movement. Each time the patient complied with the request, Boyle played a short selection of the patient's favorite music. Training continued for two sessions a day, seven days a week, for four months.

There was nothing new about the idea of playing music for coma victims; what was new was making music contingent upon the patient's behavior. But coma victims are, by definition, not responsive to the environment. Would the procedure modify their behavior?

Results varied. The patient who had been in coma for the shortest period of time produced the best results: a clear increase in the likelihood of making a response when asked to do so. Eventually, this patient came out of coma. Did the reinforcement procedure have anything to do with the patient's recovery? Boyle is cautious, but she thinks the answer is *yes*.

Boyle holds out the hope that reinforcement of spontaneous behavior will one day be part of the standard treatment for coma. Perhaps successively more wakeful behavior (for example, opening the eyes, keeping the eyes open for longer periods, tracking moving objects with the eyes, and so on) could be reinforced. In essence, therapy would consist of reinforcing successive approximations of wakefulness. Awareness would be shaped.

suggests itching, giggling when brushed with a feather suggests tickling, moans and tears suggest pain. By observing and commenting upon behavior that suggests certain experiences, we teach the child to observe those private events.

Skinner also notes that we teach children to make comments upon and predictions from self-observations. We do this, in part, by asking the child questions: What are you doing? What are you going to do? Why are you doing that? How do you feel? Are you in a good mood? Do you want to play? Are you sleepy? These and countless other questions direct the child to observe and comment upon private experiences— that is, thoughts and feelings. When the observations are accurate, they are likely to be reinforced. At noon, we ask a child if she is hungry, and if she says yes, we provide food. If the child has accurately reported her private state (if she is correct in saying she is hungry), food will reinforce her observation. If the child says she is hungry when she is not, the food may not be reinforcing and may even be aversive if she is made to eat it. By means of such experiences, the child learns to observe herself carefully.

VERBAL BEHAVIOR

The traditional view holds that language is a system of symbols for communicating ideas. Through language, we "get our ideas across." Ideas are said to be encoded (usually in the form of words) by one person and sent to another person in speech or writing. The receiver of the message decodes it and thereby achieves understanding.

This ancient approach to language is still the view held by most people. Another approach is, however, possible. It may have had its roots in the early work of Thorndike, but it received its fullest expression in a book by Skinner called *Verbal Behavior.* Skinner's analysis is very complex, and we can do no more here than make a brief survey of its key features. Even a brief survey, however, will reveal a stimulating and promising approach to language.

Skinner rejected the view that ideas are encoded into language by one person and decoded by another. Indeed, he rejected the view that the purpose of language was communication! Instead, he proposed that to understand speech, writing, and other uses of language, we must first of all recognize that they are forms of behavior. Moreover, he proposed that verbal bahavior is in no essential way different from any other behavior. And, like other behavior, verbal behavior is to be understood in terms of functional relationships between it and events in the environment, particularly its consequences. Like the pawing of a cat at a loop and the lever pressing of a rat, verbal behavior is a function of its consequences.

If we want to understand language, then, we must examine the effects of verbal behavior on the environment, particularly the social environment. For it is the social environment, the behavior of other people, said Skinner, that shapes and maintains verbal behavior.

Parents encourage their infant children to make certain kinds of sounds, and when these sounds approximate *Ma-ma* or *Da-da*, all sorts of wonderful things are apt to happen: Adults smile, tickle the child, provide food, remove uncomfortable diapers, and so on. Through shaping, parents teach their children the rudiments of language. After a time, *Da-da* and *Ma-ma* no longer result in reinforcement; the child must say *Daddy* and *Mommy*. In the same way, *cook* must give way to *cookie* or no treat is forthcoming. Later the child may be required to use complete, grammatically correct sentences, such as, "May I have a cookie, please?"

In the normal course of events, we learn to speak because speaking produces reinforcers more reliably than other forms of behavior. To say, "Please pass the sugar" is to behave in such a way as to increase the probability of receiving sugar. This consequence reinforces the tendency to make similar requests in similar situations. When the professor says, "Why weren't you in class Monday?" he behaves in a way that is apt to produce various kinds of reinforcers: a satisfactory explanation, perhaps, or an apology. The student may reply, "My aunt died. I had to go to her funeral." The student's behavior is apt to produce reinforcing consequences: expressions of sympathy, for example, or the opportunity to make up a missed exam. Of course, verbal behavior need not correspond perfectly with reality in order to produce reinforcement, so the relatives of college students are notoriously susceptible to fatal illnesses, especially around midterm exams.

Skinner's analysis of verbal behavior is fascinating, but it is entirely theoretical; *Verbal Behavior* does not include a single study. This is not to say that relevant research has not been done, however.

Perhaps the first studies of language as behavior were done by Thorndike (1931/1968). In one study, he showed adults 160 incomplete words (for example, aw_y, d_ _n, bet_ _ _) and asked them to fill in the missing letters. These efforts produced one of two consequences: "Right" or "Wrong." For example, when shown b_at, the "right" response was the letter *l*; all other responses were judged "wrong." At first, of course, the letter *o* was the most popular response (to form *boat*); other popular responses formed the words *brat* and *beat.* After many trials, however, these responses tended to decline and were replaced by *blat.*

In a more sophisticated experiment, Joel Greenspoon (1955) asked college students to say as many words as they could think of in a given period. The exact instructions were, "What I want you to do is to say all the words that you can think of. Say them individually. Do not use any sentences or phrases. Do not count. Please continue until I say stop. Go ahead" (p. 410). In one condition, the experimenter said, "Mmm-hmm" after each plural noun emitted by the student. In another condition, the experimenter said, "Huh-uh" after each plural noun. Control subjects heard nothing from the experimenter regardless of what they said. The results showed that the frequency of plural nouns varied with the consequences. Reinforcement ("Mmm-hmm") resulted in more plural nouns compared with the control group, while punishment ("Huh-uh") resulted in fewer plural nouns compared with the control group.

Query: Is verbal behavior governed by the Law of Effect?

The work of Thorndike, Greenspoon, and others clearly showed that verbal behavior is a function of its consequences. Unfortunately, it did not closely resemble the ordinary use of language. Research by William Verplanck (1955) came closer to the mark. In one experiment, Verplanck or a colleague engaged one person at a time in casual conversation under ordinary circumstances. For the first ten minutes, the researchers surreptitiously kept track of the number of times the subject started a sentence with the phrases "I think that," "I believe that," and the like. During the next ten minutes, the experimenter reinforced such expressions of opinion by paraphrasing them or expressing agreement. For the final ten-minute period, the experimenter no longer reinforced opinions. The object was to see if the frequency of opinion statements would vary with the availability of reinforcement. The result was that every one of the 23 subjects in the experiment showed a higher rate of opinion statements during the reinforcement period than during the periods when reinforcement was unavailable.

> Query: What sort of experimental design did Verplanck use in the opinion study?

In a second experiment, Verplanck engaged subjects in conversation for ten minutes and then introduced a new topic. For the next ten minutes, some of the subjects received reinforcement for any statement bearing on the suggested topic, while the other subjects did not. The results showed that those who did not receive reinforcement dropped the suggested topic within two or three minutes, while those who received reinforcement talked about almost nothing else for the next ten minutes. When the experimenter stopped reinforcing discussion of the topic, statements on the topic fell to zero.

Herbert Quay (1959) wondered whether the tendency of psychotherapy patients to talk about family experiences was due to the unique importance of these experiences, or if this tendency might be the result of subtle forms of reinforcement from the therapist. To find out, he engaged people in conversation. For some people, any recollection about a family experience resulted in reinforcement in the form of "a flat, noncommittal, 'uh-huh,' spoken in a low conversational tone" (p. 255). Other people received the same reinforcement, but for recollections that had nothing to do with family experiences. The result was an increase in family memories when those recollections were reinforced, and an increase in nonfamily memories when those recollections were reinforced.

Further evidence for the operant view of language comes from developmental research. It has been found that as infants acquire verbal skill, their tendency to cry declines (Bell & Ainsworth, 1972). Babies who can get parental help by requesting it need not cry. Similarly, toddlers become less aggressive when they learn to obtain reinforcement by talking (Brownlee & Bakeman, 1981). All of which suggests that verbal behavior is merely one of many ways of obtaining reinforcement.

If a child's verbal behavior does not produce satisfactory results, other forms of behavior will emerge. Edward Carr (1977, 1985, 1988) has suggested that the aggressive and self-injurious behavior of some psychotic children may be a substitute for speech. Having violent tantrums, biting oneself or others, and breaking objects may be, according to Carr, "functionally equivalent" to making requests and statements. (By *functionally equivalent*, he means that they may produce the same kinds of reinforcers.) If Carr is right, it follows that the abnormal behavior may disappear if we teach the child effective verbal skills. Carr and his colleagues have gotten excellent results by doing just that. In one study, Carr and Mark Durand (1985) taught four disturbed youngsters alternative ways of obtaining reinforcers they were accustomed to obtaining through disruptive acts. They learned, for example, to obtain attention by asking their teacher, "Am I doing good work?" instead of by throwing things about the room. Following the training, all four children showed greater than 90% reduction in unacceptable behavior within 10 to 20 minutes.

Of course, it is not merely the current reinforcement contingencies that determine verbal behavior. The speaker comes to his or her audience after a long and complicated history of reinforcement. This history, as well as the listener's reactions, mold his or her speech. Skinner (1953) notes that when people are asked to call out numbers at random, they inevitably produce a nonrandom series of numbers. He suggests that the reason has to do with the history of reinforcement. "Various sequences of numbers are reinforced as we learn to count by ones, twos, threes, or fives, to recite multiplication tables, to give telephone numbers, and so on" (p. 211f).

The importance of reinforcement history in determining verbal behavior can also be seen in word associations. Given the word *black*, far more people will say "white" than would be expected if their replies were simply random answers. It is likely that this has to do with the tendency for the words *black* and *white* to appear together. (For example, "They're as different as black and white"; "It's right there in the contract in black and white"; "I prefer black and white photos for portraits.") It is often suggested that such responses occur because the words are associated. But it is probably not so much their association that is responsible as the reinforcement for saying both. We receive reinforcement (in the form of smiles, nods, or other signs of understanding) when we say, "Here it is in black and white." We do not receive reinforcement if we say, "Here it is in black and green."

Much of the learning involving verbal behavior occurs without our awareness. It is interesting to note, for example, that in the studies by Greenspoon, Verplanck, and Quay, there was no evidence that the subjects knew there was a reinforcement contingency in force. Verplanck's subjects were not even aware that they were the subjects of an experiment. In fact, Verplanck reports that he described his research to someone in casual conversation and that, while they talked, the person listening to him began systematically reinforcing Verplanck's verbal behavior, with predictable results. And Verplanck was completely unaware that his companion was providing reinforcement!

Many other studies show verbal learning without awareness (Krasner, 1958). Whether verbal learning regularly occurs without awareness is not, however, particularly important. What is important is that verbal behavior, like other behavior, is a function of its consequences. The idea that what we say and write depends upon the effects of our behavior on others may seem, in hindsight, like nothing more than common sense. But it represents a radical departure from the traditional view of language.

INSIGHTFUL PROBLEM SOLVING

Problem solving is shrouded in mystery. It is often spoken of in conjunction with references to "the mysteries of mind" and is said to be one of those subjects that defy scientific analysis. However, researchers who have approached problem solving from the standpoint of operant learning have given the lie to that view.

A problem exists when reinforcement is available but the response necessary to produce reinforcement is not forthcoming. Often, the necessary response is not currently in the organism's repertoire. Consider Thorndike's cats: Food was available, but to reach it the cats had to make a response they had never performed, at least not in that situation. Thorndike noticed that the cats solved the problem by scratching and pawing at things in the box until they happened to trigger the mechanism that opened their cage door. When placed in the box repeatedly, they gradually learned to escape without delay. Thorndike said they learned to solve the problem through "trial and accidental success."

Query: What is a problem?

Problem solving would seem, then, to be a special case of operant learning: The organism responds to a new situation in a variety of ways; some of those responses have reinforcing consequences (for example, they result in escape and food), and others do not. A solution to a problem is, by definition, then, a response that produces reinforcement.

Reaching a solution usually involves several unsuccessful attempts. But there are instances of problem solving in which the solution does not appear to occur in this typically slow, rather haphazard way. Sometimes the solution appears suddenly, in full form, like Athena springing from the head of Zeus. In these instances, problems are said to be solved "by insight."

Insight is a vague term, but it is often said to be a form of learning that is at least partly independent of the consequences of one's behavior. Discussions of insight often imply that it is an inherently mysterious process, probably involving the "unconscious mind."

The best-known experiments on insightful problem solving are those described in The Mentality of Apes by the German psychologist

Wolfgang Kohler. In one of Kohler's most famous experiments, Kohler gave a chimpanzee named Sultan two hollow bamboo rods. The end of one bamboo rod could be inserted into the end of the other to make one long rod. Outside Sultan's cage lay a bit of fruit, just far enough from the bars so it could not be reached with either short stick alone. After an hour of unproductive work, Sultan sat down on a box and examined the sticks. His keeper wrote that "while doing this, it happens that [Sultan] finds himself holding one rod in either hand in such a way that they lie in a straight line; he pushes the thinner one a little way into the opening of the thicker, jumps up and is already on the run towards the railings . . . and begins to draw a banana towards him with the double stick" (1973, p. 127).

Sultan, Kohler said, solved the problem through insight: Sitting there on the box, looking at the two sticks, he had a sudden flash of understanding into the problem. Such insightful problem solving, it was said, could not be accounted for by operant learning, since the correct solution appeared suddenly, without benefit of reinforcement. Or did it?

Some years after Kohler's work, Louis Peckstein and Forrest Brown (1939) performed experiments similar to Kohler's and found no evidence of solutions emerging suddenly without benefit of reinforcement. In a replication of Kohler's two-stick problem, for example, they found that it took a chimpanzee 11 trials over a period of four days to learn to put two sticks together to retrieve food. Their chimpanzee first learned to retrieve food with a single stick, and then learned to combine two sticks while playing with them. It then *gradually* learned to use the combined sticks to retrieve food.

Other experiments have added doubts about the apparent suddenness of insight into problems. Harry Harlow (1949) provided monkeys with a problem in which a bit of food could be found under one of two lids that varied in some way, such as color, size, or shape. In one series of trials, the prize would always be under the larger lid; in another series, it would always be under the square lid; and so on. Success on the first trial of any series was necessarily a matter of chance; there was no way of telling which lid covered food on the first trial. Attempts on the second and subsequent trials could be successful if the monkeys selected the same kind of lid that hid food on the first trial. Unfortunately, Harlow's monkeys showed no inclination to behave in this way.

In any given series, Harlow's monkeys would slowly learn to pick the right lid. Gradually, over many series of learning trials, their learning rate improved (see Figure 6-1). Eventually, they would get the second problem in a new series right about 90% of the time. This insight emerged slowly, however, and was clearly the result of the animal's reinforcement history. Harlow repeated the same experiment with children between the ages of 2 and 7 and got the same result: no sudden emergence of solutions, but a gradual improvement in performance due, apparently, to the reinforcement of correct responses.

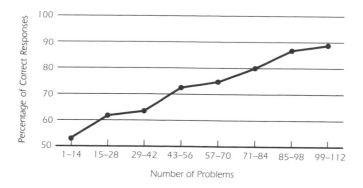

FIGURE 6-1 *The evolution of insight. The percentage of correct solutions on Trial 2 of a series increased gradually with training.* SOURCE: *After Harlow, 1949.*

Nevertheless, people and animals do sometimes solve problems suddenly. They may struggle unsuccessfully with a problem for some time, and then abruptly perform the necessary response. If, however, the sudden appearance of a solution can be shown to be dependent upon previous operant learning, the notion that insightful problem solving is a distinct form of learning is seriously challenged.

One of the most frequently cited demonstrations of insightful problem solving is Kohler's suspended fruit problem. In this experiment, Kohler suspended a banana or other piece of fruit from the ceiling of a cage in a corner and placed a large box in the center of the cage. The chimpanzees under study attempted to reach the fruit by jumping, but the fruit was too high to reach. Sultan "soon relinquished this attempt, paced restlessly up and down, suddenly stood still in front of the box, seized it, tipped it hastily straight towards the objective, but began to climb upon it at a [horizontal] distance of half a metre, and springing upwards with all his force, tore down the banana" (1927/ 1973, p. 40).

In such instances of problem solving, the solution's abrupt appearance is said to be an inexplicable "act of mind," not to be accounted for in terms of the reinforcement of previous behavior. The claim is that such insight is different from the gradual selection of correct responses seen, for example, in Thorndike's cats. But is insight really independent of prior reinforcement? Unfortunately, Kohler's records of the experiences of the animals prior to testing are spotty. In the case just cited, it is not clear what sort of experiences Sultan had had in the use of boxes or the retrieval of fruit from high places. However, if the same sort of insight could be demonstrated in animals with a particular reinforcement history, but not in animals that lacked that history, this would suggest that the insight was due to previous reinforcement.

In a brilliant experiment, Robert Epstein and his colleagues (1984) taught a pigeon (1) to push a small box toward a target and (2) to climb on a box that was already beneath a toy banana and peck the banana.

Once this was accomplished, the researchers hung the toy banana from the ceiling of one corner and put the box in another corner. Note that this represented a new situation for the bird, a situation quite similar to that confronted by Sultan. The bird's behavior was also remarkably like that of Sultan:

> It paced and looked perplexed, stretched toward the banana, glanced back and forth from box to banana and then energetically pushed the box toward it, looking up at it repeatedly as it did so, then stopped just short of it, climbed, and pecked. The solution appeared in about a minute for each of three birds. (Epstein, 1984b, p. 48f).

One could argue that the birds had solved the problem through some mysterious process (for example, the workings of the unconscious), but it is more parsimonious to attribute the solution to the animal's reinforcement history.

Note that in this experiment, the solution required new behavior, so the birds may be said to have shown insight. The point is that this insight depended upon previous reinforcement of the necessary behavior. Birds that had been trained to climb the box and peck the banana, but not to push the box, did not solve the problem. Insightful problem solving is dependent upon previous reinforcement of behavior related to a problem's solution.

Query: What is the point of Epstein's banana experiment?

We humans are, of course, far better at solving problems than other animals, but this does not mean that our reinforcement history is less important. Indeed, our greater success may be largely due to our being more adept at learning from the consequences of our behavior. As Thorndike observed in 1911, "Because he learns fast and learns much, in the animal way, man seems to learn by intuitions of his own (p. 281)." Efforts to account for insight in terms of operant learning have not solved all the mysteries of insightful problem solving, but they have cleared away some of the clouds in which this subject has for so long been shrouded.

CREATIVITY

If insightful problem solving has been shrouded in mystery, it is nothing compared to that surrounding creativity. This realm of behavior is often said to defy scientific or logical analysis. But is creativity really so unfathomable?

Let us begin with a definition. Creativity has been defined in many ways, but one feature that is always mentioned is novelty. For a drawing, sculpture, story, invention, dance, idea, or anything else to be judged creative, it must be novel; that is, it must be relatively unlike other drawings, sculptures, stories, inventions, dances, or ideas.

Novelty is seldom sufficient, in and of itself, for a product to be judged worthwhile. A child scribbling on the wall with a crayon might produce a composition unlike any the world has ever seen, but it is not likely to be called art. A biologist might theorize that plant life evolved out of animal life. If no one has made a similar suggestion, then the biologist has produced a creative idea, but that does not mean that other biologists will embrace the theory. However, nothing (regardless of its merits), is judged creative unless it is different from other products of its type. To be creative, then, is to behave in original ways.

Where does original behavior come from? In ancient Greece, people believed that the muses (spirits that specialized in art, music, or literature) visited a person. If one wanted to write poetry, one waited upon Erato, the muse of poetry. The poet was merely an instrument of Erato's work. This theory is still expressed occasionally by people in the arts today. A more modern version of the theory moves the muse into the person, usually lodging her in the unconscious mind. Today the poet waits for inspiration from the muse in his or her unconscious.

An analysis of creativity in terms of operant learning looks to the history of reinforcement. The idea that reinforcement may lead to creativity may seem a logical absurdity. A reinforcer is, by definition, something that strengthens the response it follows. How can you get novel behavior by reinforcing responses that have already occurred? The whole point of creativity is to get *new* forms of behavior, not old behavior. How is it possible to increase the frequency of novel behavior with reinforcement? A sea mammal called a porpoise provided an answer.

> **Query:** Why does the idea of increasing creativity by means of reinforcement seem illogical at first?

In the 1960s, Karen Pryor (1975/1991) was an animal trainer at the Ocean Science Theater in Hawaii. The theater was a kind of museum at which people could, among other things, watch porpoises and other sea animals perform tricks. One day Pryor and the other trainers realized that the show they put on for the public was getting stale. Both the trainers and the animals were getting "a little too good, a little too slick, a little too polished" (p. 234). To enliven things a bit, they decided to demonstrate how the animals were trained by waiting for Malia, one of their star performers, to do something and then reinforcing that response. The audience would actually see learning take place as the reinforced behavior increased rapidly in frequency. The plan worked extraordinarily well, and the trainers made it a regular part of the show.

In the next few days, Malia received reinforcement for all sorts of typical porpoise behavior: tail slapping, swimming upside down, rising out of the water, and so on. After only 14 shows, however, the trainers had a new problem: They were running out of behavior to reinforce.

Malia solved the problem for them. One day Malia "got up a good head of steam, rolled over on her back, stuck her tail in the air, and coasted about 15 feet with her tail out" (p. 236). It was a delightful sight, and everyone, including the trainers, roared with laughter. Malia received a fish and repeated the stunt a dozen times.

Pryor gradually realized that all a trainer had to do to get novel responses was to reinforce novel responses. Malia was soon producing novel responses on a regular basis; she had learned to be creative.

Pryor repeated the experiment in a more formal fashion with a new animal, a porpoise named Hou. The new pupil was not as fast a learner as Malia had been, but Hou eventually produced four novel responses in one training session. After this, Hou "came up with novelty after novelty, sinking head downwards, spitting water at the trainer, jumping upside down" (p. 242). By the 13th training session, Hou had produced a novel response in 6 out of 7 consecutive sessions. Pryor and her coworkers published these and other experiments in a scientific journal (Pryor et al., 1969), and those findings have not been successfully challenged.

Even some small-brained species can show remarkable creativity if originality is systematically reinforced. Pryor and her group (1969) used reinforcement to train novel behavior in pigeons. Some of the birds engaged in such unusual behavior as lying on their backs or hovering two inches above the cage floor.

A number of studies have shown that the same basic technique, reinforcing novel responses, can increase the creativity of children. In one study, John Glover and A. L. Gary (1976), asked fourth- and fifth-graders to think of uses for various objects (such as a can, brick, or pencil). The students worked in teams and earned points by coming up with uses for a particular object. At various times, different kinds of criteria had to be met to earn points. The results showed that reinforcement affected the kinds of responses produced. When unusual responses were reinforced, the number of unusual responses rose sharply. For instance, during the baseline period, students asked to come up with uses for a box might suggest variations on the idea that a box is used to store things in (for example, "hold books in," "hold leaves in," and so on). But when originality earned points, some very unusual uses appeared. Asked for uses of a brick, for example, one student suggested attaching a brick to each foot as a way to develop leg strength. Another, asked to come up with an original use for blackboard erasers, proposed that they could be stuffed into his shirt "to make my shoulders look bigger." Originality and other measures of creativity showed a strong increase as a result of reinforcement for creative ideas.

Kathy Chambers and her colleagues (1977) obtained similar results when they reinforced originality in blockbuilding. In this study, one of the experimenters asked first- and second-graders to build things with blocks. Each time a child in the experimental group produced a new form of construction, the experimenter praised him or her. The experimenter watched children in the control group work, but made no comment about their constructions. Reinforcement resulted in nearly twice as many different constructional forms being produced by children in the experimental group.

> Query: How could an auto manufacturer increase the creativity of its designers?

Other studies of the effects of reinforcement on creative behavior have produced similar results (Sloane et al., 1980; Winston & Baker, 1985). It seems to be no great trick to increase creativity in children; all one need do is reinforce creative acts whenever they occur.

Like insightful problem solving, creativity now seems less mysterious than it once did. Instead of attributing the creative act to a muse or some dark, hidden recess of the soul, we can see that creativity is a function of reinforcement. While this reduces the mystery of the creative process, it need not reduce our enjoyment of creative activities or our appreciation of creative products. We simply recognize the old ideas about creativity for what they are: superstitions.

SUPERSTITION

In the experiments cited so far, the behavior produces, or at least is reliably followed by, a reinforcer or punisher. This raises an interesting question: What is the effect of a reinforcer if its appearance following a response is merely coincidental?

Suppose that you put a pigeon into a Skinner box and modified the feeding mechanism so that grain became available at intervals of, say, 15 seconds, *regardless* of what the animal happened to be doing at that time. Would the delivery of food in this way affect the pigeon's behavior?

Skinner (1948a) performed an experiment very much like this. He found that out of eight pigeons, six acquired some clear-cut response: One bird turned in counterclockwise circles, another raised its head toward one of the corners of the cage, one pigeon bobbed its head up and down, two birds swung their heads to and fro, and the sixth pigeon made brushing movements toward the floor, as if trying to peck it. The birds appeared to have learned to perform strange rituals, in spite of the fact that the reinforcer came whether or not the birds engaged in the behavior. Skinner called these acts **superstitious behavior** since the birds behaved as though their rituals produced reinforcement, when in fact they did not.

Skinner's explanation of this phenomenon is quite simple. When the first reinforcer arrived, the animal had to be doing *something.* If the bird happened to be bobbing its head up and down (something that pigeons are inclined to do occasionally), then head bobbing was accidentally reinforced. This meant that head bobbing was likely to occur again, which meant it was still more likely to be reinforced, and so on.

Superstitious behavior is not restricted to pigeons. Gregory Wagner and Edward Morris (1987) conducted a carefully designed study of superstitious behavior in children. They began by introducing preschool children to a mechanical clown named Bobo that periodically dispensed marbles. Bobo released marbles at fixed intervals regardless of what the child did. The children learned that "sometimes Bobo will give marbles" and that they should take any marbles Bobo might provide and put them into a box. When they had put enough marbles into the box, they would be able to trade them for a toy. The researchers worked with one child at a time and, after explaining about the marbles and the toys, left the child alone with Bobo. They then videotaped the children so that they could do a detailed, minute-by-minute analysis of the child's behavior. What Wagner and Morris found was that new, superstitious behavior emerged in 7 of the 12 children studied. Some children sucked their thumbs; some swung their hips back and forth; some touched Bobo or kissed him on the nose.

In another study, Alfred Bruner and Samuel Revusky (1961) used adventitious (that is, accidental, coincidental) reinforcement to establish superstitious behavior in four high school students. Each student sat in front of four telegraph keys. If the student pressed the right key, a bell would sound, a red light would go on, and a counter would record the response. Each time this happened, the student would have earned five cents, which could be collected later on. The correct response consisted of depressing the third key from the student's left, but this response was reinforced only when it occurred after an interval of several seconds. The students began plunking the other keys during these periods of nonreinforcement. Eventually, the nonreinforcement period would end, the student would happen to hit key 3 again, and this act would be reinforced. However, the responses that immediately preceded hitting key 3 also were reinforced, even though they had nothing to do with producing the reinforcers. Eventually, each student worked out a pattern of key processes, such as 1, 2, 3, 4, 1, 2, 3. Interestingly, the experimenters report that none of the students suspected that any part of their behavior was superstitious. The students believed that they had discovered the one correct formula for producing reinforcement.

Richard Herrnstein (1966) has argued that superstitious behavior can occur as a by-product of training. He notes that in many instances, a particular feature of a response is essential for reinforcement, but other features are not. If the essential feature produces reinforcement, the other features are adventitiously reinforced. He cites handwriting as an example. In making the various letters of the alphabet, reinforcement is contingent upon producing certain features of the letters. However, there is a good deal of latitude in how the letters may be formed. For example, in making a cursive, lowercase *t*, it is necessary to produce a nearly vertical straight line and to cross that line with a horizontal line. But the vertical line may, in fact, be a loop (like the cursive letter *l*), and it can be short or long; likewise, the horizontal line can be short or long, perfectly horizontal or angled up or down, and it can appear near the top of the vertical line or near the bottom. If essential features are performed in such a way as to gain reinforcement, other nonessential features of handwriting are adventitiously reinforced. The implication is that the wide differences in handwriting, among other idiosyncrasies, are superstitious behavior. Some research supports Herrnstein's hypothesis (see, for example, Leander et al., 1968; Vyse & Heltzer, 1990).

Skinner (1948a) suggests that a good deal of everyday human activity may be superstitious behavior established through adventitious reinforcement. He cites as a likely candidate "the bowler who has released a ball down the alley but continues to behave as if he were controlling it by twisting and turning his arm and shoulder. . . . These behaviors have, of course, no real effect upon . . . a ball halfway down an alley" (p. 171). Other examples may include a baseball player who flaps one arm as he awaits the pitch, the stockbroker who never buys or sells on Tuesdays, the woman who never dates men named Bruce, and the student who always takes a seat in the next-to-last row.

Query: *What reinforces the superstitious gyrations of the bowler?*

Many human superstitions seem too complex and too widespread to be attributed to adventitious reinforcement. Lots of people sprinkle salt over their shoulders and carry good-luck charms. In some societies, people have engaged in rain dances and human sacrifice. Can such practices be attributed to adventitious reinforcement of individual behavior? Herrnstein (1966) argues that it is unlikely that such behavior is shaped by adventitious reinforcement, but that it may be maintained by such reinforcement.

Herrnstein argued that any behavior, if made likely to occur, might be maintained by adventitious reinforcement. To test this idea, he trained a pigeon to peck a disk by reinforcing each disk peck that occurred after an 11-second interval. (In other words, the bird received no reinforcement for disk pecks during the interval.) When disk pecking was well established, Herrnstein stopped reinforcing this behavior and began providing food every 11 seconds *regardless* of what the animal did; in other words, he switched to Skinner's superstition procedure. Note that though the reinforcement contingencies had changed, the bird was expected to show a relatively high frequency of disk pecking, at least initially. Thus, the now ineffectual behavior of disk pecking could easily be adventitiously reinforced. Under these conditions, the rate of disk pecking declined somewhat but did not die out. Apparently, the adventitious reinforcement was sufficient to maintain the behavior. (See also Neuringer, 1970, and Gleeson et al., 1989.)

The significance of Herrnstein's experiment is that it suggests that any behavior, however complex and improbable, can be maintained through adventitious reinforcement if the organism can be induced to perform it at least once. He notes further that the most common human superstitions arise in a social context. We hear about rabbits' feet, about the dangers of black cats, about Friday the 13th, about spilling salt. Further, we are encouraged to perform superstitious acts. Children, for example, may be required by a parent to throw a bit of salt over one shoulder after spilling salt on the dinner table. Or a child may be encouraged to carry a rabbit's foot "for luck." Once performed, there is the chance that such behavior will be adventitiously reinforced. If a child who carries a rabbit's foot is unhurt in a minor bicycle accident, then carrying a rabbit's foot has been reinforced.

Of course, it should be noted that the social context to which Herrnstein refers often provides ample reinforcement for the maintenance of superstitious behavior. Not only are we advised of the wisdom of carrying a rabbit's foot, but following this advice is reinforced by the approval of those who recommend it. This kind of reinforcement is not adventitious since it depends upon the performance of the superstitious behavior. Superstitious behavior in humans is therefore likely to be maintained both by adventitious and contingent reinforcement.

It is perhaps for this reason that superstitious behavior persists in spite of its apparent lack of adaptive value. Herrnstein (1966) notes that behavior may be expected to "drift" toward the minimal essential features; that is, we may expect that only the behavior required for reinforcement will persist. If no feature is essential for reinforcement (as is the case in superstitious behavior), then we may expect that it will disappear. However, if reinforcement occurs occasionally, superstitious behavior may be maintained indefinitely (see Schwartz & Reilly, 1985).

John Staddon and Virginia Simmelhag (1971) have questioned the significance of Skinner's superstition experiment. They suggest that the procedure merely increases the rate at which innately dominant responses occur. Pigeons will, from time to time, flap their wings, turn in clockwise circles, stand on one foot, move their head from side to side, and so on. Adventitious reinforcement, Staddon and Simmelhag argue, merely strengthens these natural tendencies. Skinner (1983b) replies that all organisms are innately inclined to behave in certain ways, so of course superstitious behavior is likely to "drift toward" these inclinations. This does not make the behavior any less superstitious. It merely explains why pigeon superstitions are likely to involve wing flapping, and human superstitions are not. (See Timberlake & Lucas, 1985, for a discussion of these issues.)

Although researchers continue to argue about the precise role of adventitious reinforcement in superstitious behavior, operant learning goes a long way toward helping us understand this once-mysterious behavior.

DELUSIONS AND HALLUCINATIONS

We have seen that ordinary thoughts and sensory experiences appear to fall within the realm of behavior and to be amenable to analysis in terms of operant learning. What about bizarre thoughts and sensory experiences?

People in mental hospitals often have delusions (false beliefs such as "everyone is out to get me" or "there are little green men inside my stomach") or hallucinations (they might hear voices that say "You're no good" or "you shouldn't have done what you did"). Can such delusions and hallucinations be understood in terms of an operant analysis, or must we attribute them to a disordered mind?

Delusions and hallucinations can and often do have an organic basis. Schizophrenia, senile paresis, Alzheimer's disease, brain damage, and some drugs can induce such behavior. But even when an organic disorder exists, the frequency of delusions, hallucinations, and other forms of bizarre behavior may be a function of reinforcement.

Joe Layng and Paul Andronis (1984) provide the example of a psychiatric patient who complained that her head was falling off. She seemed quite frightened, so a member of the staff sat with her to calm her down. The delusion got worse. She began to hear popping sounds that preceded the feeling that she was losing her head. A discussion with the patient led to the discovery that she found it very difficult to approach the staff members to engage them in conversation. Sometimes when she approached them, they responded with obvious annoyance. Her delusional behavior produced the desirable effect (interaction with the staff) without the risk of hostile reactions. In other words, the delusion was reinforced. Once the woman learned how to approach the staff without incurring hostile reactions, the delusion disappeared, and her head seemed securely attached.

Layng and Andronis (1984) also describe the case of a middle-aged man admitted to a locked hospital ward after he tried to pull a pair of clothesline poles out of the ground in his backyard. He shouted that the poles were blasphemous statues of the cross and that Jesus had

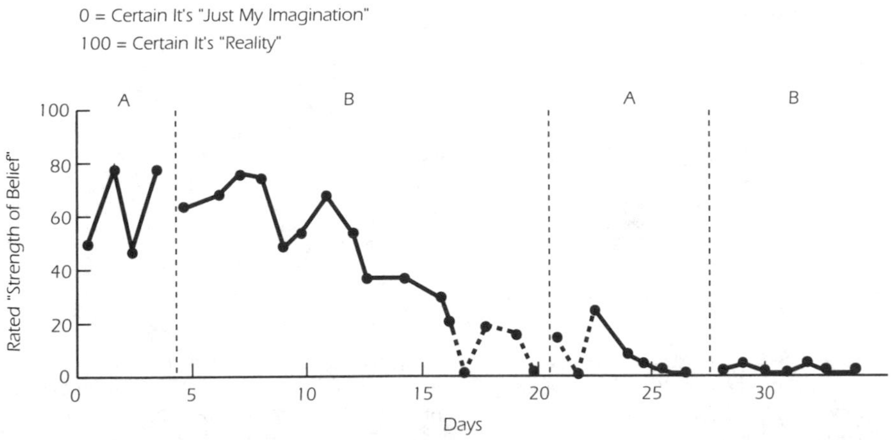

0 = Certain It's "Just My Imagination"
100 = Certain It's "Reality"

FIGURE 6-2   Strength of delusional belief. During treatment (B) phases, the patient's confidence in the reality of the "haggly old witch" declined. SOURCE: From "Behavioral Treatment of Schizophrenic Delusions: A Single-Case Experimental Analysis" by B. A. Alford. In *Behavior Therapy, 17*, pp. 637–644. Copyright © 1968 by The Association for Advancement of Behavior Therapy. Reprinted by permission of the publisher and author.

told him to tear them down. It turned out the man's efforts to involve his wife in his demanding business problems had been unsuccessful; she showed concern only when his behavior changed for the worse. In other words, she inadvertently shaped up increasingly pathological behavior, until he finally behaved so bizarrely that he was hospitalized. When she learned to show concern for her husband's business problems instead of his bizarre behavior, his symptoms began to subside.

> Query: Why might a person have delusions at home but not in a hospital?

Another example is provided by Brad Alford (1986). He worked with a young schizophrenic patient in a psychiatric hospital. The man was greatly helped by medication but continued to complain that a "haggly old witch" followed him about.

Alford asked the patient to keep a record of his feeling that he was being followed. The patient also indicated the strength of his belief, from zero (certainty that the belief was just his imagination) to 100 (certainty that there really was a witch). During the treatment phases, Alford reinforced expressions of doubt about the veridicality of the delusional belief. The result was that the patient's reported confidence in the delusion declined (see Figure 6-2).

It might be argued that the patient believed in the witch as much as ever and merely learned not to admit it. To test this idea, Alford looked at the medication the patient received before and during the study. He found that the man received one kind of medication, a

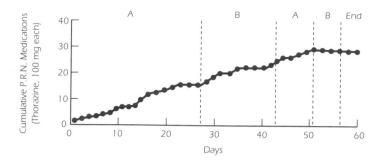

FIGURE 6-3 Tranquilizer consumption. During treatment (B) phases, the rate at which the patient received tranquilizer pills declined. SOURCE: From "Behavioral Treatment of Schizophrenic Delusions: A Single-Case Experimental Analysis" by B. A. Alford. In *Behavior Therapy, 17*, pp. 637–644. Copyright © 1968 by The Association for Advancement of Behavior Therapy. Reprinted by permission of the publisher and author.

traquilizer, only when he seemed agitated. If the patient remained convinced that the witch was real, then there should be no decline in the rate at which he consumed tranquilizers. In fact, however, his use of tranquilizers declined sharply with treatment (see Figure 6-3).

To the extent that schizophrenia means displaying a high rate of bizarre behavior, then, this study demonstrates that schizophrenics can be helped by the application of operant learning principles. This does not mean that psychotic behavior is entirely the product of learning. Diseases of the brain *do* produce bizarre behavior. However, even when psychotic behavior arises from a diseased brain, it may be modified by operant procedures.

One objection to the operant analysis of psychotic behavior is that such behavior often occurs even when it is not reinforced. Goldiamond (1975) describes a woman virtually paralyzed by her fear of cockroaches. She remained in bed, too afraid to move about. Her husband was sympathetic and gave her the attention she had previously been denied. This attention was apparently the reinforcer that maintained her phobic behavior. But this introduces a dilemma because the woman's husband was not always at home. Ordinarily, we would expect that the woman would become an invalid when reinforcement was available for invalidism (that is, when the husband was present), but would go about her business when reinforcement was not available (when the husband was absent). But this did not occur: The woman stayed in bed whether her husband was present or not. This is what might be called **Goldiamond's paradox**, which states that in order for bizarre behavior to be reinforced, it must sometimes occur on occasions when it cannot be reinforced (Goldiamond, 1975).

The reason is simple. If a person behaves bizarrely only when reinforcement for bizarre behavior is available, people catch on. The reinforcer controlling the behavior becomes apparent and is soon withheld. Reinforcement for bizarre behavior is therefore often contingent not only upon the occurrence of the behavior but upon the occurrence of the behavior *at times when reinforcement is unavailable.* "In other words," write Layng and Andronis (1984), "the apparent absence of maintaining consequences or the presence of aversive consequences on some occasions, may be requirements that must be met for reinforcement to be available on other occasions" (p. 142). The idea is familiar to every person who, as a child, got out of going to school by feigning illness: As soon as you leap for joy at being allowed to stay home, you get sent to school![1]

Layng and Andronis note that the traditional approach to delusions and hallucinations assumes that disordered thoughts reflect a disordered private world. The traditional clinician therefore attempts to understand more about this private world, often by inviting the patient to describe it in great depth. But a simpler, more scientific approach is possible. This approach assumes that delusions and hallucinations reflect a disordered environment. (That is, an environment that reinforces inappropriate behavior.) According to this view, the clinician's task is to understand and modify the patient's disordered environment.

It appears, then, that operant learning can help us understand psychotic behavior, just as it helps us understand self-awareness, language, insightful problem solving, creativity, and superstition. And these are merely examples of the role operant learning plays in everyday behavior.

Some lower organisms may get by with innate behavior and Pavlovian conditioning, but operant learning is clearly essential to the survival of higher life forms. Foraging, hunting, avoiding predators, gaining access to mates, and other forms of complex behavior all require that the animal learn from its successes and its failures—that is, from the consequences of its behavior.

The importance of operant learning to human adaptation is especially great. It is largely through operant learning that we are able not only to find edible fruits and berries, but to grow crops; not only to find safety and comfort in caves, but to build houses; not only to find warmth in the hides of animals, but to fashion clothes; not only to develop languages, but to write books. Indeed, most of what we think of as culture would not be possible were we unable to profit from the effects of our behavior.

The fact that humans live in homes with hot and cold running water, and chimpanzees do not, has little to do with our respective reflexes, fixed action patterns, or with differences in our ability to benefit from the pairing of stimuli. It has a great deal to do with differences in our ability to benefit from the consequences of our behavior.

---

[1] This may have something to do with the fact that many children who are at death's door at 7 A.M. are completely recovered by about 1 P.M., at which time, coincidentally, there is little point in taking the child to school.

SUMMARY

Many kinds of behavior have been analyzed in terms of operant procedures; we have considered just a few as illustrations.

Self-awareness is so basic a human experience that we hardly think of it at all, let alone think of it as dependent upon operant learning. To be self-aware means to observe our own behavior, including our thoughts and feelings. Studies with animals suggest that we learn to observe ourselves, perhaps mainly as a result of consequences provided by others.

The traditional view of language holds that ideas are coded by one person and decoded by another. An operant analysis suggests that language can be more usefully thought of as verbal behavior that varies as a function of its consequences. Experiments by Thorndike, Greenspoon, Verplanck, and others provided empirical support for this suggestion.

Operant research has also provided insight into insightful problem solving. Kohler's experiments with apes were said to demonstrate that solutions to problems appear suddenly, without "trial and error." It turns out, however, that the apparent suddenness of solutions is often a delusion, that many attempts are made before an effective response appears. Furthermore, recent research, especially the work of Epstein and his colleagues, shows that the appearance of a solution depends upon previous learning. This research shows that insightful problem solving depends upon an operant learning history that includes the acquisition of components required for solving new problems.

Another mysterious topic, creativity, has also succumbed to operant analysis. The work of Pryor and her colleagues showed that porpoises could learn to produce novel behavior, to be creative, if novel behavior were systematically reinforced. Other research has shown that creatures as different as pigeons and people can learn to be more creative if creative acts produce reinforcing consequences.

Superstition, once thought to be the oblique expression of unconscious fears and desires, is now understood in terms of learning history. Skinner showed that regular noncontingent reinforcement will reliably produce superstitious behavior. Other researchers showed that the same contingencies will produce superstitious behavior in humans. Herrnstein has suggested that human superstitions may be more often initiated by the community than by adventitious reinforcement, but adventitious reinforcement is important to their maintenance.

Delusions and hallucinations would seem at first to fall beyond the reach of an operant analysis. But work by Goldiamond, Layng, Andronis, and others suggests otherwise. These researchers show that delusional beliefs and hallucinatory experiences may be modified by their consequences. This has led to new, effective treatments for victims of psychosis.

The simple processes called operant learning have proven remarkably effective in helping us understand complex behavior, including behavior that had seemed for hundreds of years to be hopelessly beyond the reach of science. It is now clear that human nature cannot be understood without an appreciation of the role played by the consequences of behavior. This realization marks a major turning point in our effort to understand ourselves and our struggle for survival.

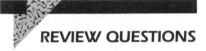

REVIEW QUESTIONS

1. Define the following terms in your own words:

    adventitious reinforcement   *self-awareness*
    Goldiamond's paradox   *superstition*
    insight   *verbal behavior*

2. In what sense is the relationship between an organism and its environment reciprocal?

3. How is self-awareness like the awareness we have of others? How is it different?

4. Janet hypothesizes that people who are good at observing others are good at observing themselves. Design a study to test her hypothesis.

5. Does the use of a mirror by Gallup's chimps imply a concept of self?

6. How is an operant analysis of verbal behavior different from the traditional approach to language?

7. Given the role of reinforcement in verbal behavior, how do you account for the fact that some people talk to themselves when alone?

8. In supporting the operant view of verbal behavior, which work described in this chapter is more important, that of Thorndike or that of Verplanck?

9. Occasionally the solution to a problem comes to a person in a dream. Can you account for this in terms of operant learning?

10. Why is insight not an adequate *explanation* of problem solving?

11. Studies show that students who have difficulty learning higher-level skills, such as algebra, often perform poorly at lower-level skills, such as arithmetic. Explain why.

12. You head the product development division of a major corporation. How can you get the people in your division to come up with more ideas for new products?

13. How can a writing instructor get his or her students to write more creative stories?

14. There is some evidence that very creative people are more inclined toward mental illness. Assuming this is true, how might you account for it in terms of operant learning?

15. Why are so many gamblers inclined to be superstitious?

16. Explain why people within the same family often share the same superstitious beliefs.

17. Could some delusions be a form of superstitious behavior?

18. Suppose a psychiatric patient claims he is Napoleon. How could you determine whether this delusion is under the control of reinforcing consequences?

19. Why have the topics covered in this chapter resisted scientific analysis for so long?

20. What mysteries of human nature not covered in this chapter might succumb to an operant analysis?

Suggested Readings

Although Skinner is often accused of being preoccupied with lever-pressing rats, in fact he seems to have been fascinated with the sort of complex human behavior described in this chapter. Indeed, the work summarized here owes a great deal to Skinner's thinking. Skinner discusses many of the topics dealt with here, and others, in *Science and Human Behavior* and *About Behaviorism*. His analysis of verbal behavior, said by some to be his most important contribution, is set forth in great detail in *Verbal Behavior*.

Other fascinating work on the role of operant learning in complex behavior can be found in the articles by Goldiamond, Layng and Andronis, and Epstein cited in this chapter. For more on the role of reinforcement in the etiology of "mental illness," see Benjamin Braginsky et al., *Methods of Madness: The Mental Hospital as a Last Resort*.

For a more traditional approach to some of the topics covered here, see *Human Information Processing: An Introduction to Psychology* by Peter Lindsay and Donald Norman, or *Human Cognition* by John Bransford.

Answers to Queries:

Page 136: How about: "observation of one's own behavior," or maybe "self-observation"?
Page 141: Yes. This is what Greenspoon's work clearly demonstrates.
Page 142: Verplanck used an ABA reversal design.

Page 144: A problem is a situation in which reinforcement for a response is available, but the response is not. The subject is often capable of performing the response (recall Thorndike's cats) but does not perform it.

Page 147: Epstein's experiment demonstrates that insightful problem solving is largely the product of the organism's learning history.

Page 148: It might seem at first that reinforcing a response would reduce creativity, since it means that the same response is more likely to occur. But when the object is to increase creativity, the response that is reinforced is novel behavior.

Page 150: The company might try providing bonuses, promotions, or awards to people when they produce creative designs. These actions should reinforce creative responses.

Page 152: This would be a good subject for an experiment. Very likely an experiment would show that strikes and spares reinforce superstitious behavior in the bowler.

Page 155: Answers may vary. One possibility is that someone in the home environment reinforces delusional behavior.

seven

Observational Learning

Well, he raised up two or three times, and looked away off and around on the water. That started me at it, too. A body is always doing what he sees somebody else doing, though there mayn't be no sense in it.
—MARK TWAIN

BACKGROUND

Sometimes the history of science is the story of a steady progression, rather like the climb up a winding staircase. Progress requires effort, and occasionally the scientist is found panting on a landing, but movement is always forward and usually upward. The study of classical conditioning, for example, began with the brilliant experiments of Pavlov and his coworkers and progressed more or less steadily until today our understanding of this phenomenon is fairly sophisticated. The study of operant learning followed a similar course. But sometimes the history of science is more like a roller coaster ride than the climb up a staircase: One moment we're plummeting toward ruin, the next we seem to be headed for the stars. Observational (or vicarious) learning is a case in point.

The problem posed by observational learning seems simple enough: Can one organism learn by observing the behavior of another? The search for an answer to this question began with Thorndike. In Thorndike's day, it was widely believed that animals often learned by observing others. Everyone knew that the house cat watched people opening cabinet doors and then imitated their behavior. Could cats and other animals really learn this way? According to anecdotal evidence, the answer was yes.

Thorndike was not so sure, so he dealt with this belief the same way he had dealt with beliefs about animal intelligence: He submitted it to experimental test. His subjects were, once again, chicks, cats, and dogs. In a typical experiment, Thorndike (1898) put one cat in a puzzle box and another cat in a nearby cage. The first cat had already learned how to escape the box, and the second had only to observe its neighbor to learn the trick. But when Thorndike put this cat into the puzzle box, he found that it did not imitate its more learned fellow. Instead, it went through the same sort of operant learning any other cat went through in learning to solve the problem. No matter how often one cat watched another escape, it seemed to learn nothing.

> Query: What is the basic question posed by observational learning?

Thorndike found that there was not the slightest difference between the behavior of cats that had observed a successful model and those that had not. He got similar results with chicks and dogs and concluded that "we should give up imitation as an a priori explanation of any novel intelligent performance" (p. 62). In other words, until someone demonstrates that animals learn by observing others, we ought not to assume that they do.

These experiments on observational learning, perhaps the first ever done, were published in 1898 as part of Thorndike's classic treatise on animal intelligence. Shortly thereafter, Thorndike (1901) conducted similar experiments with monkeys, but despite the popular belief that "monkey see, monkey do," Thorndike concluded that "nothing in my experience with these animals . . . favors the hypothesis that they have any general ability to learn to do things from seeing others do them" (p. 42). A few years after this, John B. Watson (1908) performed a similar series of experiments on monkeys with nearly identical results.

These negative findings seem to have had a devastating effect on research on observational learning. There was, in fact, almost no experimental investigation of this problem for a generation. Then, in the 1930s, Carl Warden and his colleagues conducted a number of carefully controlled experiments and clearly demonstrated that monkeys can learn by observing others.

> Query: How might the lack of research on observational learning have been due to observational learning?

Warden began by constructing a special duplicate cage (see Figure 7-1) with identical problems to be solved in each chamber. Warden put an observer monkey in one chamber and restrained it so that it could not get to the problem apparatus. Then he put another monkey, the model, in the other chamber. The model had already learned to perform whatever act was necessary to obtain reinforcement.

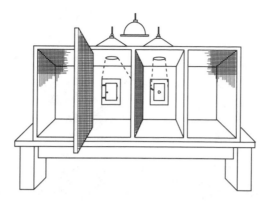

FIGURE 7-1 The duplicate cage developed by Warden and used by him and his colleagues to study observational learning. SOURCE: From Carl Warden and T. A. Jackson, "Imitative Behavior in the Rhesus Monkey," *Journal of Genetic Psychology*, 1935, 46, p. 106, figure 1. Copyright 1935 by the Journal Press. Reprinted by permission.

In one study (Warden & Jackson, 1935), the simplest problem involved pulling a chain that opened a door and revealed a raisin the model could retrieve and eat. After watching the model perform this act five times, the observer got a chance to tackle the same problem in its own chamber. If the observer did not solve the problem within 60 seconds, the experimenters pulled the monkey away from the apparatus and restrained it for about half a minute before letting it have a second trial. The researchers repeated this procedure on the next two days for a total of six trials before going on to the next problem. According to the early work of Thorndike and Watson, this procedure should not have resulted in much learning; the observing monkeys should have spent their time exactly as if they had never seen the model.

They did not. In fact, the observers made it quite clear that they had benefitted substantially from watching the model, often responding correctly on the very first trial. Furthermore, when an animal succeeded, it often did so in far less time than would have been expected had they not watched a model. Forty-seven percent of all the solutions occurred within 10 seconds (almost as fast as the model's performance), and about 75% of the solutions occurred within 30 seconds.

Warden and his coworkers performed other, similar experiments with equally encouraging results. For instance, in one study (Warden et al., 1940), observer monkeys made the correct responses on 76% of 144 trials, and about half of the solutions occurred within 10 seconds.

In addition to noting the number of correct responses, Warden and his colleagues also kept tabs on the nature of their monkeys' failures. In many instances the monkey made the correct response, but with too little force to operate the mechanisms; in other instances the monkeys approached the right part of the apparatus, but manipulated it in the

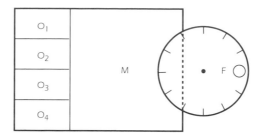

FIGURE 7-2 View from above the Herbert and Harsh cage, showing the turn table problem installed. Observers sat in chambers at O_1, O_2, O_3, and O_4 and watched as a model, at M, worked on the problem of getting the food at F. SOURCE: After Herbert & Harsh, 1944.

wrong way. Thus, even when a monkey failed to solve a problem, the topography of its behavior suggested some learning had occurred.

Following Warden's lead, Marvin Herbert and Charles Harsh (1944) demonstrated observational learning in cats. They designed a structure that would allow as many as four cats at a time to watch a model as it worked at one of five problems (see Figure 7-2). In the turntable problem, a circular platform rotated on a bicycle axle (see Figure 7-3). By grasping the black cleats on the turntable, a cat could spin the platform so that a food dish came into its cage. On any given problem, the cat that served as model would have 30 trials while observer cats looked on. Some observers watched all 30 of a model's trials before tackling a problem; others watched only the last 15 trials. By comparing the performances of the observers with those of the models, the experimenters could determine how much observational learning had taken place.

The results showed that the observer cats outperformed the models. Moreover, the more trials a cat observed, the more it learned. On the turntable problem, for instance, the models took an average of 62 seconds to solve the problem on the first trial, cats that had observed 15 trials took an average of 57 seconds, and those that had observed 30 trials took an average of only 16 seconds.

These and other successful studies should have prompted an upswing in research on observational learning, but it continued to receive little attention. Then, in the 1960s, research on observational learning began to take off. Much of the impetus for this change was the work of Albert Bandura and his colleagues. In one study, Bandura and Fred McDonald (1963) had children listen to stories and judge which of two characters was naughtier. In a typical story, John breaks 15 cups while answering his mother's call to dinner; in another story, Henry breaks one cup while in the act of stealing cookies. In pretesting, the experimenters found that some children tended to make their moral judgments on the basis of the intent of the protagonist; on this *subjective* basis, Henry is naughtier than John because he was stealing. Other children based their decision on the amount of damage done; on

FIGURE 7-3 Miss White working at the turntable problem. SOURCE: After Herbert & Harsh, 1944.

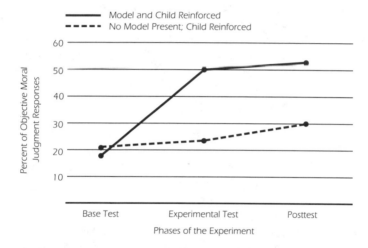

FIGURE 7-4 Average percentage of objective moral judgments as a function of reinforcement. SOURCE: Adapted from Albert Bandura and Frederick McDonald, "The Influence of Social Reinforcement and the Behavior of Models in Shaping Children's Moral Judgments," *Journal of Abnormal and Social Psychology*, 1963, *67*, p. 278, figure 2. Copyright by the American Psychological Association. Reprinted by permission.

this *objective* basis, John is naughtier because he broke more cups. The experiment consisted, in part, of attempting to teach subjective children to use the objective approach. The children were assigned to one of three conditions, two of which are of special interest. In one condition, the child and an adult female model took turns in evaluating stories. The model always used the objective approach to make her judgment, and an experimenter approved these judgments. The experimenter also approved the child's judgments when they reflected the objective approach. In the second condition there was no model, but the experimenter approved the child's choice whenever it was based on the objective method. After this training, the researchers tested the children again on their own to see how the training had influenced their moral judgments. The results showed that the reinforcement of a model's behavior added substantially to the effects of direct reinforcement (see Figure 7-4).

Studies of this sort showed the importance of observational learning in child development and spurred interest in the subject. Many psychologists now believe that observational learning deserves the same sort of attention that classical and operant procedures have received (Kymissis & Poulson, 1990; Robert, 1990).

BASIC PROCEDURES

Learning is a change in behavior brought about by experience. In **observational** or **vicarious learning**, the experience consists of observing the performance of a model and the consequences of the model's behavior. For instance, a monkey (the observer, O) might look on as one of its peers (the model) lifts a cup, under which it finds a raisin:

$$0 \left[\begin{array}{c} R \rightarrow S^R \\ \text{lift cup} \rightarrow \text{find raisin} \end{array} \right]$$

If, as a result of this experience, the observer lifts the cup and retrieves the raisin when given the opportunity, or if it learns to do so more quickly than it would have had it not observed the model, then observational learning has taken place.

Similarly, an observer may look on as a model's behavior is punished. For instance, a monkey might watch as a model reaches for a raisin in a bowl and receives a rap on its knuckles (and no raisin) each time it does so.

$$0 \left[\begin{array}{c} R \rightarrow S^P \\ \text{reach for raisin} \rightarrow \text{receive rap} \end{array} \right]$$

The model will soon give up reaching into the bowl. If the observer behaves in a similar manner when in this situation, then observational learning has occurred.

Query: Is observational learning limited to those who can see? Explain.

Most studies of observational learning involve live or filmed models. However, it should be noted that, with humans at least, behavior and its consequences may be "modeled" with words. Bandura (1962) refers to this as **symbolic modeling**. A study by Michael Spiegler and Adrea Weiland (1976) provides an example.

Spiegler and Weiland had college students read a short story about the conflicts between the principal and students at a hypothetical high school. The story explained that a new principal made a number of changes the students did not like. He eliminated extracurricular activities, outlawed talking in the hallways, and "generally ruled with an iron hand." The story went on to describe the actions taken by Janet Halloran, the president of the senior class, and the consequences of her behavior. The researchers used three different versions of the story. In one version the student's efforts had positive consequences, in another her acts were punished, and in a third variation the consequences were neutral. For instance, one step that Janet took was to write a letter to a neighborhood newspaper complaining about the principal's actions. That step won her either praise, criticism, or an ambiguous reaction. After reading one of the three versions of the story, the subjects were asked what they would do if they found themselves in a similar situation. Their answers depended upon the consequences of the fictitious Janet's behavior. If writing to the neighborhood paper got good results for Janet, people were likely to say they would write to the local paper; if that behavior was punished in the story, the subjects were likely to avoid that tactic and try something else.

As Bandura points out, it is clear that similar symbolic modeling is important in everyday human affairs:

> People are aided in assembling and operating complicated mechanical equipment, in acquiring social, vocational, and recreational skills, and in learning appropriate behavior for almost any situation by consulting the written descriptions in instructional manuals. Verbal forms of modeling are used extensively because one can transmit through words an almost infinite variety of behavioral patterns that would be exceedingly difficult and time consuming to portray behaviorally. (Bandura, 1971a, p. 41)

Although verbal modeling is important, it is a subject that falls beyond the scope of this text. We will confine ourselves to studies in which observers view the actions of live or filmed models. Even this relatively simple form of observational learning is complicated by the influence of a number of variables.

VARIABLES AFFECTING OBSERVATIONAL LEARNING

The same variables that are important in operant learning apparently affect observational learning in a similar manner. For example, the course of operant learning varies with the degree of contingency between a response and a consequence. The same seems to hold true for observational learning. When a model's behavior is consistently reinforced, the observer tends to imitate it; when it is consistently punished, the observer tends to avoid making it; and when the model's

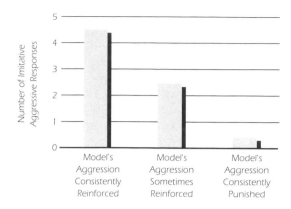

FIGURE 7-5 *Average number of imitative aggressive responses by observers who saw aggressive acts consistently reinforced; sometimes reinforced and sometimes punished; or consistently punished.* SOURCE: *Compiled from data in Rosekrans & Hartup, 1967.*

behavior is sometimes reinforced and sometimes punished, the observer's tendency to imitate the model falls between the other two conditions (for example, Rosekrans & Hartup, 1967; see Figure 7-5). However, the variables that have received the most systematic attention are the characteristics of the model and of the observer.

■ Characteristics of the Model

Numerous studies have demonstrated that human observers tend to learn more from models who are competent, attractive, likable, and prestigious than from models who lack these characteristics. A study by Seymour Berger (1971), in which college students participated in what was ostensibly an investigation of extrasensory perception (ESP), will serve as an example. The model was introduced to the observer either as a fellow subject or as an assistant to the experimenter. Later, observers who thought they had watched a fellow student showed less evidence of learning than those who thought they had observed the experimenter's assistant. Since the model was actually the same person in each case and behaved in the same way, the difference in the observer's behavior must have been due to the model's status. Studies of this sort raise an interesting question: Why should model characteristics, such as status, attractiveness, competence, and so on, affect what an observer learns?

Research by Judith Fisher and Mary Harris (1976) provides a plausible answer. Fisher and Harris approached people in a shopping center or on a college campus and asked them to guess the prices of certain items. An experimenter would appear to approach two subjects simultaneously, but one of the people was actually a confederate of the researchers. In one experiment, the model sometimes wore an eye

Observational Learning and Human Nature

Viki probably had no memory of her natural parents. After all, she was only a few days old when Keith and Catherine Hayes (1952) adopted her and took her home. The Hayeses reared their adopted daughter with great care and affection. Their devotion paid off, for Viki proved to be extraordinarily precocious. For example, when she was less than a year-and-a-half old, she began to learn, simply by observing her parents, how to dust the furniture and wash dishes. Before she was 2 years old, she would look in the mirror and put on lipstick as she had seen her mother do.

When Viki was between 2 and 3, her parents, who were psychologists, decided to test her to see just how well she could learn vicariously. They gave her, and some other youngsters of about the same age, a series of problems. For instance, in the stick and string problem, the Hayeses put an object in a wooden box. The object could be retrieved from the box only by hitting a string with a stick. The Hayeses demonstrated the correct solution to the problem and then gave Viki a shot at it.

Overall, Viki did quite well. She solved the stick and string problem, for instance, after only one demonstration. Some children who worked on that problem required four demonstrations before they could solve it. Viki's performance did more than demonstrate observational learning, however. It raised all sorts of questions about human nature. Viki, you see, wasn't like the children with whom she competed on those problems.

Viki was a chimpanzee.

patch. The model would guess at the price of an item, and then the observer would make a guess. Later, when the observers tried to remember the answers the model had given, it turned out that people usually recalled responses more accurately when the model wore an eye patch.

In a second experiment, the researchers manipulated the mood of the model. In one condition, the model smiled and nodded her head as the experimenter asked her questions. In another condition, the model frowned and shook her head. In a third condition, the model behaved in a neutral manner. In other respects, this experiment was similar to the first. The results showed that observers who had witnessed one of the more expressive models recalled her behavior more accurately than observers who saw an impassive model. It made no difference whether the model's mood was positive or negative, so long as it was not neutral.

According to Fisher and Harris, these model characteristics (eye patch and moodiness) affected the observer's learning because they attracted the observer's attention. Status, likability, age, sex, competence, and other model characteristics affect observational learning because they influence how carefully the observer studies the model.

And the more attentive an observer is to a model, the more likely he or she is to learn from the model's behavior.

■ Characteristics of the Observer

The success of observational procedures varies greatly with the learner. Whereas Pavlovian and operant learning occur readily in hundreds of species, observational learning seems to be restricted to a handful. Humans and other primates often learn vicariously with little trouble (Aronfreed, 1969; Hall, 1968), but dogs and cats appear to learn little from models, and many lower species seem to be incapable of learning vicariously. (On the other hand, at least one invertebrate, the octopus, is capable of vicarious learning; Fiorito & Scotto, 1992).

There is also tremendous variability within a given species in the ability to profit from the experience of others. This variability seems to be due to a number of characteristics, one of which is the age of the learner. In general, adults learn better than children from observation, and older children learn better than younger ones (Coates & Hartup, 1969; Yando et al., 1978). Those advanced in years, however, often are slower to benefit from the experiences of others than are the young (Kawamura, 1963).

Another important characteristic is the learning history of the observer. John Wolfe (1936) taught chimpanzees how to use a poker chip or brass slug to get fruit from a kind of vending machine. Wolfe would pick up a token, show it to the animal, and then put the token into a slot, thereby tripping a mechanism in the machine and causing a grape to fall into a food tray. Wolfe found that the animals could learn to use tokens in this way, but that some chimps learned the task much more readily than others. A chimp named Moos learned the trick after only 1 demonstration, while others required as many as 237 demonstrations. Apparently, one factor that contributed to this wide range of learning abilities was the learning histories of the various animals. Moos, for example, had participated in other experiments and may have learned that it is sometimes a good idea to pay attention to what humans do.

The emotional state of the learner while observing the model is also important. Warden and Jackson (1935) found, for instance, that some of their monkeys became sexually excited by the model and that this arousal severely interfered with learning (see Figure 7–6).

THEORIES OF OBSERVATIONAL LEARNING

The two main theories of observational learning are the cognitive mediation theory of Albert Bandura and the operant learning theory of Neal Miller and John Dollard.

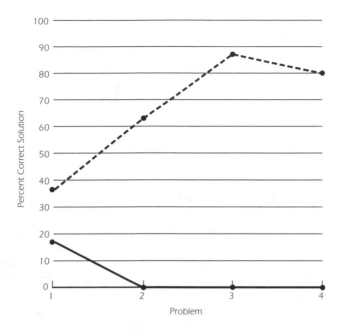

FIGURE 7-6 Percent of subjects solving each problem on first trial. Broken line shows performance of observers who attended to the problem; solid line shows performance of observers who were sexually aroused and attended to other matters. SOURCE: Compiled from data in Warden & Jackson, 1935.

■ Bandura's Theory

Albert Bandura (1965, 1971a, 1971b, 1971c, 1977) argues that observational learning is explained by acts performed while observing the model. Often these acts are performed covertly; that is, they involve thinking. Two types of covert behavior are especially important to observational learning: **attentional processes** and **retentional processes**.

Attentional processes have to do with the organism observing the relevant aspects of the model's behavior and its consequences. Various studies have demonstrated that if the observer does not attend to the model, or attends to irrelevant aspects of the model's behavior, little learning will take place (for example, Warden & Jackson, 1935). As we saw earlier, a number of variables affect the extent to which an observer attends to the appropriate aspects of a model's behavior.

Once an organism is attending to the relevant aspects of the model's behavior, Bandura reasons, retentional processes come into play. These are acts the observer performs to aid recall of the model's behavior. One important retentional process consists of representing the model's behavior in some way, often in words. With the acquisition of language, it is often possible to reduce complex behavior to a few words. A cooking student observing a tutor might say to himself, "He *folds* the batter; he doesn't whip it."

Another important retentional activity consists of repeatedly performing the model's behavior, or a verbal representation of that behavior, in some covert way. After seeing a tennis pro demonstrate the perfect backhand, for example, you might covertly imitate that behavior without making any perceptible movement of your arm. Or you might silently repeat some verbal representation of the model's behavior, such as "Keep the wrist straight."

> **Query:** What sort of process would Bandura say this query
> involves?

Attentional and retentional activities can be easily illustrated. Suppose that your aunt points to a wall safe and says, "I'm going to open that safe and then lock it again. I will then give you one chance to open it; if you succeed, you can keep whatever you find inside." Your aunt then proceeds to open the safe. She turns the dial clockwise to 20, counterclockwise to 40, clockwise to 20. She pulls down the handle and swings open the door, then immediately closes it.

Now, as you watch your aunt work, you carefully note which way she turns the safe dial and the numbers at which she stops. You may also represent her behavior by picturing a little potbellied Santa Claus whose measurements are 20-40-20. More likely, however, you repeat to yourself (or perhaps aloud), "Right 20; left 40; right 20." The point is that you do not merely observe your aunt's behavior; you are busy behaving (albeit covertly) while you watch her.

Bandura's theory includes other factors that affect the performance of modeled behavior, but it is the attentional and retentional processes that, according to Bandura, account for observational learning. In fact, Bandura insists that observational learning cannot be explained without reference to the observer's attentional and retentional activities.

Bandura's theory has tremendous intuitive appeal. It seems to capture the experience of observational learning as humans know it. Probably because of this, it is very popular. The theory is not, however, without its problems.

We might question, for example, the explanatory value of attentional processes. Whether you attend to the relative features of your aunt's behavior depends largely upon your previous learning experiences. If you know that your aunt is rich, that rich people often keep valuable things in safes, and that safes are often opened by turning a dial this way and that, then you are apt to observe the relevant features of your aunt's behavior. If you had not previously learned these things, you might observe irrelevant aspects of the environment. But if prior learning accounts for what is observed, what does the notion of attention add?

We might also question the explanatory value of retentional processes for a different reason. Bats, pigeons, rats, and other lower organisms can learn vicariously. Is it realistic to assume that such animals learn through the sort of retentional processes Bandura describes? And if these creatures can learn without sophisticated retentional processes, why must we assume they are essential to observational learning in humans?

Bandura might respond to the first criticism by suggesting that while the learning history determines what is observed, the act of observing, of attending, is still essential to learning and must be addressed. He might add that the fact that lower organisms are less likely to learn from models implies that retentional activities are important. Not everyone is satisfied by these defenses, however, so many researchers prefer the Miller-Dollard theory.

■ The Miller-Dollard Theory

It is possible to treat observational learning as merely a variation of operant learning. According to this view, set forth by Neal Miller and John Dollard (1941; see Skinner, 1969, for a similar analysis), the changes in an observer's behavior are due to the consequences of the *observer's* behavior, not those of the model.

Suppose, Miller and Dollard suggest, that a boy hears his father returning from work and runs to greet him. Suppose also that the boy's younger brother follows him to the door. If the father greets both boys cheerfully and gives them pieces of candy, what behavior has he reinforced? In the case of the elder boy, the reinforced behavior is the act of running to the door when his father comes home. In the case of the younger boy, the reinforced behavior is the act of imitating his elder brother in going to the door. Put another way, the younger boy learns that going to the door when big brother does pays off.

Miller and Dollard performed a number of experiments that supported their theory. They found, for example, that rats would learn to follow another rat through a maze if such imitative acts were reinforced. They also showed that imitation in children was a function of reinforcement. In one study, children could get candy from a machine if they manipulated the handle the right way. A model used the machine just before the subject. In one condition, if the child imitated the model's behavior, the machine provided candy. In another condition, the machine provided candy only if the child did *not* imitate the model. The children learned to imitate the model when imitating paid off, and they learned *not* to imitate the model when not imitating the model paid off (see also Baer & Sherman, 1967).

Some psychologists have asked why, if an observer receives reinforcement for imitating a model's behavior, imitative acts occur even when the model is no longer present. A boy may see his elder brother run to the door, for example, but be prevented from imitating this act. Several minutes later, when the boy is free, he may run for the door even though his elder brother is no longer modeling this behavior. This phenomenon seems troublesome at first, but it poses no special problem for Miller and Dollard. We often continue to be influenced by a stimulus that is no longer present. You may, for example, see an ad for a movie on one day and go to the theater the next. The ad is no longer present, yet it still affects your behavior. Stimuli usually have their most powerful effects immediately, but they may continue to affect behavior long after they have disappeared.

A more serious problem with the theory is that imitation often occurs in the absence of reinforcement of the observer's behavior. For instance, the children who learned to imitate a model to get candy from a machine later imitated other models in other situations though they received no reinforcement for imitating these models. If imitative behavior is the product of reinforcement, why did the children imitate these models?

Such behavior can be explained in terms of generalization, a subject to be covered in the next chapter. Any learned response tends to occur not only in the situation in which it was learned, but in new situations as well. Thus, if we use operant procedures to train a pigeon to peck a *red* disk, it is then likely to peck an *orange* disk as well, though the bird has never received food for pecking an orange disk. In the same way, a child who has learned to imitate one adult doing one thing is then likely to imitate other adults doing other things. The implication is that observers learn, through reinforcement of their behavior, to observe and imitate the behavior of successful models and to avoid imitating the behavior of unsuccessful models.

> Query: According to Miller and Dollard, why do people imitate successful models but not unsuccessful ones?

The Miller-Dollard and Bandura theories are in active contention as explanations of observational learning and will probably remain so for some time. Perhaps the real difference between them has to do with different ideas about the nature of scientific explanation. Bandura's theory looks for explanation inside the individual, appealing to thoughts to account for learning. The Miller-Dollard theory looks for explanation in the relation between behavior and environmental events. To choose between these two theories is to choose between two different views of science.

Attempts have been made to examine the role of observational learning in the modification of many kinds of behavior. For illustrative purposes, we will consider two areas in which observational learning seems to be important: foraging in animals and social aggression in children.

FORAGING

Surviving means finding food, and a number of field studies suggest that observational learning plays a role in that quest.

One fascinating report involves British songbirds. J. Fisher and R. A. Hinde (1949; Hinde & Fisher, 1972) reported that songbirds made a regular practice of opening and drinking from milk bottles left on porches. It appeared that a few birds learned the trick on their own and were imitated by other birds.

Less ambiguous evidence of the role of observational learning in foraging is provided by a study by Syumzo Kawamura (1963). In order to make naturalistic observations of macaque monkeys. Kawamura placed sweet potatoes (a monkey treat) near a lake, thus attracting the animals to the lakeshore so that they tended to congregate and could be easily observed interacting. Since the potatoes were placed on the beach, they tended to get sand on them. One of the monkeys learned that the sand could be removed by dipping the potatoes into the water. Soon, other macaques followed this monkey's lead, and eventually, all but the oldest animals regularly washed their potatoes before eating them. Here, it seems, was a very clear instance of observational learning (see also Eaton, 1976).

Although field studies of this sort are fascinating, they are of limited scientific value in understanding observational learning. The significance of Fisher and Hinde's milk-drinking birds, for example, is a subject of some debate. David Sherry and B. G. Galef (1984) point out that the fact that many birds are drinking from bottles does not necessarily mean that birds have learned to open the bottles by observing others. They note that the presence of a bottle opened by one bird would provide the opportunity for many birds to feed without their having learned anything.

Such issues can be resolved only through experimental research. In this case, Sherry and Galef captured black-capped chickadees on the campus of the University of Toronto and presented each with a foil-covered plastic cream tub of the sort restaurants serve with coffee. Four of the birds spontaneously pecked through the foil top and fed upon the cream. These four birds then served as models for four birds that had not opened the tubs. Each model demonstrated the technique for an observer on five trials. Another four birds received five trials with a sealed tub, but no training. After this, the researchers presented each of the birds with a sealed tub to see what it had learned. They found that birds in the observational learning group opened the tubs, while the untrained group did not. The researchers concluded that some birds probably learn to open milk bottles by observing others do so.

In another experiment, Connie Gaudet and M. Brock Fenton (1984) studied observational learning in three species of bats. They began by training one member of each species to find a bit of mealworm from a target fastened to a wall. The bats would fly to the target, remove the food, return to their starting point about 2 yards away, and eat the meal. A bat of the same species was allowed to observe the model up to 20 times a day for 5 days. (Contrary to popular belief, most bats are *not* blind.) There were two control groups. In one group, the bats were simply put into the experimental chamber alone; in the other, the bats were individually trained, through an operant procedure, to find the food. The result was that the bats that were allowed to observe a model learned faster than those that were trained. Bats that were placed in the chamber without benefit of a model or operant training did not find the food.

Some forms of food gathering that may seem innate turn out to be at least partly the result of observational learning. Zing Yang Kuo (1930) reared kittens under different conditions. Some kittens were reared with their mothers and had the opportunity to watch her kill rats. Other kittens were separated from their mothers and never saw rats killed. When the kittens had matured, Kuo gave them the opportunity to kill rats. He found that 86% of those that had seen their mothers kill rats did so, but only 45% of those that had not seen rats killed did so. Observational learning clearly plays a role in the cat's diet.

> Query: How do you use observational learning in your own foraging efforts?

SOCIAL AGGRESSION

Social aggression plays a major role not only in individual survival but in the survival of the species. Numerous studies have shown how observational learning influences the aggressive tendencies of people toward one another.

The best-known studies of vicariously acquired aggression are those of Albert Bandura and his colleagues. In one famous study (Bandura et al., 1963), nursery school children watched a five-minute videotape of two men, Rocky and Johnny, interacting in a playroom. In the video, Johnny plays with toy cars, plastic farm animals, and various other appealing toys. Rocky asks Johnny to share the toys, but Johnny refuses. Rocky then hits Johnny several times with a rubber ball, overpowers him when he tries to defend his property, hits him with a baton, and generally gives poor Johnny a rough time. Rocky's aggressive behavior is reinforced, since he ends up having all the fun. The researchers write:

> The final scene shows Johnny seated dejectedly in the corner while Rocky is playing with the toys, serving himself generous helpings of 7-Up and cookies, and riding a large bouncing hobby horse with gusto. As the scene closes, Rocky packs the playthings in a sack and sings a merry tune, "Hi, ho, hi, ho, it's off to play I go," as he departs with the hobby horse under his arm and the bulging sack of loot over his shoulder. A commentator's voice announces that Rocky is the victor. (p. 602)

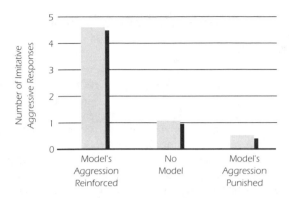

FIGURE 7-7 *Average number of imitative aggressive responses by observers who saw the aggressive acts reinforced or punished or who saw no model.* SOURCE: *Compiled from data in Rosekrans & Hartup, 1967.*

After watching the videotape, each child went to a playroom that contained a number of toys, including those shown in the film and several others. Each child spent 20 minutes in the room while judges watched through a one-way mirror and noted how often the child hit a Bobo doll (a large, inflated doll) or performed other aggressive acts. The data indicated that children were far more likely to commit aggressive acts if they had seen the same behavior reinforced in a model. The similarity of the children's behavior to that of the model was sometimes striking. At the end of one session, a little girl who had imitated a good deal of Rocky's behavior looked at the experimenter and asked, "Do you have a sack here?" (p. 605).

> **Query:** *A child watches as a sibling is spanked for stealing. What two things is the child likely to learn from observing this?*

A study by Mary Rosekrans and Willard Hartup (1967) shows the differential effects of observing aggressive behavior reinforced and punished. The researchers had nursery school children watch an adult model as she played with some toys, at times beating a Bobo doll on the head with a mallet and poking a clay figure with a fork. As she played, the model made such comments as, "Wham, bam, I'll knock your head off," and "Punch him, punch him, punch his legs full of holes." In one condition, these aggressive acts were reinforced by an adult who made remarks such as, "Good for you! I guess you really fixed him that time." In another condition, the model's behavior was repeatedly punished by an adult who said things such as, "Now look what you've done, you've ruined it." After watching the model play and seeing her behavior either reinforced or punished, the observer then got a chance to play with the same toys. The results showed that children who saw aggressive behavior reinforced tended to play aggressively, while those who saw aggressive behavior punished tended to play more peacefully (see Figure 7-7).

Pie in the Sky

On Wednesday, December 1, 1971, a passenger on Northwest Airlines flight 305 handed a stewardess a note demanding that the airline give him $200,000. Then he opened his briefcase and revealed what looked very much like a bomb.

The passenger, registered under the name D. B. Cooper, had thought things out carefully: The airline would have the cash, and four parachutes, ready when the plane touched down at Seattle-Tacoma International Airport in Washington, or the airline would lose one Boeing 727, 36 passengers, and a crew. The airline came up with the money and the parachutes. Cooper let everyone deplane in Tacoma except the cockpit crew and one flight attendant; then he ordered the pilot to head for Mexico. Once aloft, however, Cooper made his escape 10,000 feet above the forested countryside of southwestern Washington. He was never captured.

Naturally, Cooper's very clever crime got a lot of coverage in the news media, so much so that anyone who cared to follow his lead had access to all the pertinent details. And follow his lead they did. Bandura (1973) later wrote that "within the next few months . . . a number of hijackers, emboldened by the successful example, copied the specific tactics, including threats of bombing unless passengers were exchanged for ransom money and parachutes" (p. 107).

This incident demonstrates very nicely the role observational learning plays in crime. When you think about it, it becomes clear that it would be very difficult for the novice criminal to learn his trade strictly through operant learning. It is only through observational learning that people can efficiently acquire the sophisticated skills necessary for pulling off a successful burglary, extortion scheme, bank robbery, or bookie operation. This raises two intriguing questions: If people were not so adept at learning from models, would crime cease to be an important social problem? And if so, would we gain more than we would lose?

Questions like these are not easily answered. Except, perhaps, by D. B. Cooper.

One particularly undesirable form of aggressive behavior is crime. Bandura (1973) has analyzed this problem and provides a great deal of evidence that criminal behavior is powerfully influenced by observation. He notes that, thanks to television, both children and adults have unlimited opportunities to learn "the whole gamut of felonious behavior within the comfort of their homes" (p. 101). As Bandura points out, people often put such learning to use: "Children have been apprehended for writing bad checks to obtain money for candy, for sniping at strangers with BB guns, for sending threatening letters to teachers and for injurious switchblade fights after witnessing similar performances on television" (p. 101f).

The studies reported in this chapter suggest that people are unlikely to imitate criminal acts unless the model's behavior is reinforced. But often television crime is reinforced. Otto Larsen and his coworkers (1968) found that in television programs intended for children, TV characters achieved their goals by violent or illegal acts 56%

of the time. It is little wonder, then, that a link has been found between violence viewed on television and criminal behavior. Leonard Eron (reported in DeAngelis, 1992) reports that a longitudinal study found that the more time children spent watching television at age 8, the more likely they were at age 30 to have been convicted of a serious crime, to be aggressive when under the influence of alcohol, and to use harsh punishment with their children.

Many animals get along quite well without observational learning. The story is quite different when it comes to people. It is impossible to say what proportion of human learning is due to direct experience and what proportion is due to observation. It is clear, however, that if people suddenly lost their ability to learn vicariously, the effect would be noticeable immediately. Imagine, for example, the difficulties one would encounter in teaching preschoolers to tie their shoes, first-graders to write, or employees to operate machines. Not only would shaping such behavior through reinforcement be much slower, but in many cases, reliance on operant procedures would be dangerous. As Bandura (1971a) has pointed out, it would be extremely unwise to ignore vicarious procedures in teaching children to swim, adolescents to drive automobiles, or medical students to perform operations.

This is not to say that Pavlovian and operant procedures are un-important in the lives of human beings. Both have a good deal to do with our daily activities. But we humans also rely heavily upon observational learning in our efforts to cope with the changing world around us.

SUMMARY

Observational learning has received less attention over the years than Pavlovian and operant procedures, partly because of the early failures of Thorndike and Watson. Even Warden's successes in the 1930s did not entirely overcome the doubts spawned by the earlier studies, and it was another 30 years before observational learning received serious attention from a number of researchers.

In vicarious procedures, an observer looks on as a model performs a response. Model responses that are reinforced tend to be imitated by the observer, while model responses that are punished tend not to be imitated.

As with Pavlovian and operant learning, the effectiveness of observational procedures depends upon many variables. Variables that have received the greatest attention involve characteristics of the model and observer. Observers learn more from models who are competent, attractive, likable, and prestigious than from models who lack these features. Although observational learning has been demonstrated in species at least as low as the octopus, it proceeds much more quickly in higher species. The age of the observer is another important characteristic, as are the individual's emotional state and previous learning experiences.

There are two prominent theories of observational learning. Bandura's theory argues that what the observer does (in the way of attentional and retentional processes) while observing a model is crucial. The Miller-Dollard theory assumes that observational learning is really a form of operant learning; it depends upon a history of reinforcement for imitative behavior.

The role of observational learning in adaptation can be seen in studies of aggression and foraging, among other areas. It is especially important in human adaptation.

REVIEW QUESTIONS

1. Define the following terms in your own words:

   Miller-Dollard theory   *retentional processes*
   observational learning   *symbolic modeling*

2. Why has observational learning received less attention than other forms of learning?

3. If observational learning can lead to the widespread use of certain practices, how can one determine whether those practices are innate or learned?

4. Given what you know about observational learning, what advice would you give a friend whose children watch four to five hours of television daily?

5. How could you use vicarious procedures to create a fad on a college campus?

6. How might the value of Bandura's retentional processes be demonstrated experimentally? (*Hint:* Look to chimps for a sign.)

7. If you wanted to ensure that a human observer would learn from a model, what sort of model would you choose?

8. How would you determine whether snakes can learn through observation?

9. How could you teach a child to tie his or her shoes *without* using modeling?

10. Studies of observational learning of aggression usually involve children. Why?

11. After Marilyn Monroe died, apparently by suicide, many other people took their own lives. Explain these copycat suicides.

12. Why do so many fads get started by rock groups and movie stars?

13. Design an experiment to determine the role of delayed reinforcement of a model's behavior in observational learning.

14. How might superstitious behavior be acquired through vicarious experiences?

15. What is the chief difference between the Miller-Dollard theory and Bandura's theory of observational learning?

16. According to the Miller-Dollard theory, observational learning is merely a form of operant learning. Describe their reasoning.

17. Design a study to determine whether Kawamura's monkeys really learned vicariously.

18. Suppose you proved that observational learning ability improves markedly as children develop speech. How would Bandura account for this finding? How would Miller and Dollard account for it?

19. How might our view of human nature differ if psychologists had never succeeded in demonstrating observational learning in animals?

20. If you could learn in only one way (through Pavlovian, operant, or observational procedures), which would you choose?

Suggested Readings

Thorndike's experiments on observational learning are reported in *Animal Intelligence: Experimental Studies* and in a monograph, "The Mental Life of the Monkeys." Watson's work appears in "Imitation in Monkeys," an article published in 1908. Despite their age (or perhaps because of it), all three make fascinating reading, even though the reported studies are failures.

Social Learning and Personality Development, by Albert Bandura and Richard Walters, is a fascinating study of how children are influenced by adult models. Neal Miller and John Dollard's *Social Learning and Imitation* and Bandura's *Social Learning Theory* offer their respective theories of observational learning.

Answers to Queries

Page 164: The question posed is, Can one organism learn by observing the behavior of another?

Page 164: Early efforts to demonstrate observational learning failed. Other researchers observed this behavior and its consequences and learned that such research does not pay off.

Page 168: No. We can observe with our ears and other senses in much the same way that we observe with our eyes.

Page 184: Bandura might say the query involves an attentional process, since it draws attention to certain parts of the text. Or, he might say it involves a retentional process, since it elicits behavior that may improve recall.

Page 176: We imitate successful models because such acts are likely to be reinforced; imitating unsuccessful models is unlikely to be reinforced, so we tend not to do it.

Page 178: Answers will vary. They might include stopping at restaurants with nearly full parking lots—if the restaurant did not serve good food, it would not be busy; imitating the actions of an older shopper in the produce section of a grocery store; and, while camping, avoiding wild berries eaten by another camper who has just tried them and fallen over dead.

Page 179: (1) Do not steal. (Or, if you do steal, do not get caught.) (2) When you do not like the way people behave, hit them.

eight

Generalization and Discrimination

When you've seen one redwood tree, you've seen them all.
—RONALD REAGAN

Like—but oh! how different!
—WILLIAM WORDSWORTH

BACKGROUND

We have discussed three kinds of learning, three kinds of experiences that change behavior. To say that learning is the product of certain kinds of experiences is to say that it arises in certain kinds of situations. Pair a white rat with a frightening noise, and a child will become fearful whenever confronted with that rat; put a cat in a box from which it can escape by pressing a treadle, and it will press the treadle when placed in that box; let a child get candy from a machine by imitating the actions of an adult, and the child will imitate that adult in getting candy from that machine.

However, learning would be of little value as an adaptive mechanism if it helped us adapt only to precisely the same environment in which learning occurred. We rarely, if ever, find ourselves in precisely the same situation twice, so it is important that what we learn in one situation carry over to new situations. And it does: The child who has learned to fear one white rat fears other white rats and may fear things that resemble white rats; the cat that has learned to escape a box by stepping on a treadle is likely to step on treadles when placed in other boxes; the child who learns to imitate one adult in operating one machine imitates other adults operating other machines. This tendency for learned behavior to spread to situations not involved in training is called *generalization.*

You can see that generalization is of great value. On the other hand, learning would be a handicap if what was learned carried over to situations where the behavior was inappropriate. The child who has learned to fear a white rat is not better off if he or she fears a black dog as well; the cat that has learned to escape a box by stepping on a treadle is not better off stepping on things in a box with a hook-and-eye latch; the child who imitates an adult's method of operating a candy machine does not do well to apply the same technique to the operation of a telephone. It is often best if behavior learned in one situation does not carry over to very different situations. This tendency to behave differently in different situations is called *discrimination*.

These two phenomena, generalization and discrimination, are the subjects of this chapter. Although treated as two separate phenomena, they are really two sides of the same coin. It is a coin without which we could not survive.

GENERALIZATION

Generalization is the tendency for learned behavior to occur in the presence of stimuli that were *not* present during training.[1] For instance, in Pavlovian conditioning, a dog may learn to salivate to the sound of a tuning fork vibrating at 1,000 cycles per second (cps). After this training, the dog may then be found to salivate to the sound of a tuning fork vibrating at, say, 950 cps to 1,100 cps, even though it was never exposed to these stimuli. The conditional response spreads, or generalizes, to stimuli somewhat different from the CS.

The famous Watson and Rayner study (see Chapter Four) provides another example of the generalization of a conditional response. You will recall that Little Albert learned to fear a white rat. After establishing this fear, Watson and Rayner tested Albert to see whether other, previously neutral stimuli would also elicit the fear reaction. They presented Albert with a rabbit, cotton wool, and a Santa Claus mask. None of these stimuli had been present when the rat was paired with the loud noise, yet Albert was afraid of them. Albert's fear had spread, or generalized, from the white rat to other white, furry objects.

Perhaps the first report of generalization following operant learning came from Thorndike (1898) when he observed that "a cat that has learned to escape from [box] A by clawing has, when put into C or G, a greater tendency to claw at things than it instinctively had at the start" (p. 14). In other words, clawing generalized from box A to boxes C and G.

---

[1] This is also called *stimulus generalization*, to distinguish it from *response generalization*. The latter has to do with variations in the response to a given stimulus. In this text, the term *generalization* refers only to stimulus generalization.

Generalized Therapy

The patient was a 37-year-old woman who stood 5 feet 4 inches and weighed 47 pounds. She looked like a survivor of a Nazi concentration camp, but the emaciation that threatened to kill her was due to self-starvation. She had a mysterious aversion to eating called anorexia.

Arthur Bachrach and his colleagues (1965) took on the task of ending this woman's self-destructive refusal to eat. They used shaping and reinforcement principles to get her to eat more. The strategy worked, and she gained enough weight to be released from the hospital. But what would happen when she went home? Would she go back to starving herself again, or would the effects of the therapy generalize to the new situation?

The problem of generalization is critical for therapists: There is little value in changing a person's behavior in the hospital or clinic if those changes do not carry over to the person's home and workplace. One way to attack the problem of generalization is to try to alter the natural environment so that appropriate behavior continues to be reinforced at a high rate. Bachrach and his coworkers used this approach. They asked the patient's family to cooperate in various ways. Among other things, they asked the family to avoid reinforcing invalidism; to reinforce maintenance of weight by, for example, complimenting the patient's appearance; and to encourage her to eat with other people under pleasant circumstances.

With reinforcement of appropriate behavior in the home, the behavior might then generalize to other settings. The reinforcement that naturally occurs in these settings would, it was hoped, maintain the desired behavior. The hope seems to have been fulfilled. For instance, the patient attended a social function at which refreshments were served. It had always been the woman's custom to refuse food on such occasions, but she surprised everyone by asking for a doughnut. All eyes were on her as she devoured the snack, and she later admitted that she got considerable pleasure from all the attention.

Generalization is not always established this easily (Holland, 1978; Miller & Sloane, 1976; Wolf et al, 1987). The juvenile delinquent who acquires cooperative social skills in a special rehabilitation center and then returns to a home and community where aggressive, antisocial acts are reinforced and cooperative behavior is punished is apt to revert to old habits. The chain smoker who quits while on a vacation with nonsmokers must return to a world of smoke-filled rooms. The rehabilitated and repentant child abuser returns to a neighborhood filled with naive and easily seduced children. The problem of getting therapeutic gains to generalize to the natural environment is one of the most difficult the therapist faces, but understanding the principles of generalization helps.

Those who followed Thorndike studied operant generalization in a more rigorous manner. In a typical experiment, a pigeon might receive food when it pecks a yellow disk. After this training, the bird is given the opportunity to peck the disk, but sometimes the disk is yellow, sometimes a yellowish orange, sometimes dark orange, sometimes red. Regardless of the color, pecking is not reinforced. The experimenter records the number of times the bird pecks each colored disk. The inevitable outcome is that the bird pecks the disk most often when it is the color used during training, but it also pecks the disk when it is other colors. The same thing may be observed in people. When punching a Bobo doll is reinforced, children later tend to be more aggressive when interacting with their peers (Walters & Brown, 1963). Behavior learned in one situation generalizes to other, similar situations.

> Query: Teachers want students to apply what they learn. Is this generalization? Explain.

■ Generalization Gradients

The fact that a response generalizes to stimuli not present during training does not mean that all new stimuli are equally effective in eliciting the response. Nor is generalization an arbitrary and unpredictable phenomenon that occurs in some situations and not others. Indeed, generalization is a reliable and orderly phenomenon that has "a pattern and sense" (Guttman, 1963, p. 144).

When stimuli can be arranged in an orderly way along some dimension (such as pitch or hue), from most like the training stimulus to least like it, a clear association between stimulus similarity and generalization can be seen. This can be demonstrated by training an animal to respond in the presence of a stimulus in a particular way and then presenting the animal with several new stimuli of varying degrees of similarity to the training stimulus. The typical finding is that the more similar a novel stimulus is to the training stimulus, the more likely the organism is to respond as though it *were* the training stimulus. When these results are plotted, they yield a figure called the **generalization gradient**. The slope of the gradient indicates the amount of generalization: The flatter the line, the more generalization; the steeper the line, the less generalization.

> Query: What does a generalization gradient show?

Carl Hovland (1937a) produced a generalization gradient following Pavlovian conditioning. He began by training college students to respond to a tone. The US was a mild electric shock, and the UR was the galvanic skin response, or GSR (a measure of emotional arousal). The CS was a tone of a particular pitch. After 16 pairings of the CS and US, Hovland then presented four different tones, including the CS. The results showed that the CR diminished as the stimuli grew less like the CS. Hovland plotted the data to produce the generalization gradient shown in Figure 8-1.

Another sort of generalization gradient is illustrated in Figure 8-2. This gradient is the product of a classic study by Norman Guttman and Harry Kalish (1956). In their experiment, birds learned to peck a disk of a particular color and later had the opportunity to peck disks of

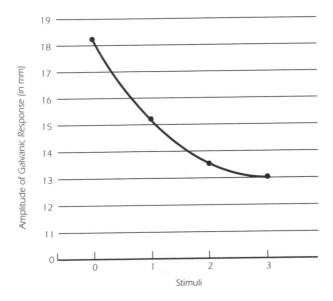

FIGURE 8-1 Generalization gradient. Average strength of conditional response (GSR) to the CS (0), and to other tones of increasing dissimilarity to the CS (1, 2, 3). SOURCE: Carl Hovland, "The Generalization of Conditioned Responses: I. The Sensory Generalization of Conditioned Responses with Varying Frequencies of Tone," *Journal of General Psychology*, 1937, *17*, p. 136, figure 2. Copyright 1937 by the Journal Press. Reprinted by permission of the Helen Dwight Reid Educational Foundation. Published by Heldref Publications.

various colors, including the color used in training, for 30 seconds each. Pigeons pecked the disk most frequently when it was the color used during training, but they also pecked the disk when it was other colors. As the generalization gradient reveals, the more closely the disk resembled the training disk, the more often the birds pecked it. When a disk was almost the same color as the training disk, the birds pecked at it almost as much as if it were the training disk; when the color of the disk was very different, the pigeons seldom touched it.

> Query: Fire drills are meant to teach appropriate behavior during
> a fire, yet people don't always behave during fires as they
> do during drills. Why?

The generalization gradients depicted here are typical of those found in learning texts, but it would be a mistake to assume that all generalization gradients are more or less alike. The form of the gradient depends upon many variables, including the amount of training, the method of testing for generalization, and the kind of stimuli involved (Honig & Urcuioli, 1981). Nevertheless, there is a systematic relationship between an organism's response to a stimulus and the similarity of that stimulus to stimuli present during training. That systematic relationship is usually based upon some physical aspect of the stimuli in question. However, generalization can be based on more abstract features, as studies of semantic generalization make clear.

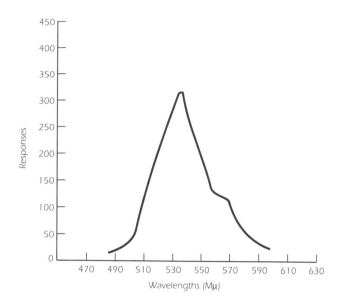

FIGURE 8-2 Generalization gradient. When pecking a disk of a particular color (in this case, 550 Mμ) had been reinforced, pigeons were likely to peck that disk at a high rate. However, they would also peck disks that were similar to the original disk. Source: After Guttman & Kalish, 1956.

■ Semantic Generalization

Most studies of generalization, like those just described, are based on the physical properties of the stimuli involved—color, size, shape, pitch, loudness, and so on. But learned behavior sometimes generalizes on the basis of the meaning of the stimulus. This phenomenon is known as **semantic generalization**.

Gregory Razran (1939) conducted what may have been the first study of semantic generalization. Razran had three adults chew gum, lick lollipops, or eat sandwiches to make them salivate. As they ate, they watched the words *style, urn, freeze,* and *surf* flash on a screen. Then Razran presented the words alone and collected saliva in cotton balls that rested under each individual's tongue. Razran weighed the cotton after each testing period to determine the effectiveness of the procedure: the heavier the cotton, the stronger the CR. After the people had learned to salivate at the sight of the words, Razran showed them words that were either homophones (words with similar sounds but different meanings, such as *stile, earn, frieze, serf*) or synonyms (*fashion, vase, chill, wave*) of the words used in training. The idea was to determine whether the CR would generalize more to words that had similar sounds or to words that had similar meanings. The results showed that, on average, the subjects salivated about one-third as much to the homophones as they had to the conditional stimuli.

Mental Rotation and Generalization

Roger Shepard is a cognitive psychologist who has studied what he calls *mental rotation*. In a typical experiment (Cooper & Shepard, 1973), people saw letters rotated by varying degrees from their normal, upright position and said whether the letters were backward (that is, mirror images of the original) or not. The result was that the greater the rotation, the longer it took people to answer. Shepard concludes from such data that people mentally rotate an image of the errant letter until it is in its normal, upright position, and then decide whether it is backward. But is mental rotation the best explanation of this phenomenon?

It is interesting to note that when the data are plotted graphically, the resulting curve looks remarkably like a generalization gradient. Subjects respond most quickly to the training stimulus (the letter they were trained in school to recognize), and less quickly the less the stimulus resembles the training stimulus.

We humans tend to look for explanations of behavior in terms of higher mental processes, such as mental rotation. But such explanations often do little more than name the behavior that needs to be explained. Scientific explanation of mental rotation requires an explication of the kinds of experiences that produce it.

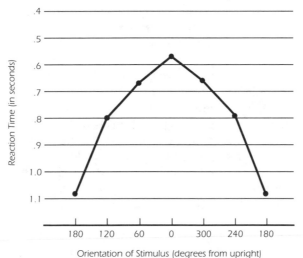

Mean reaction time to a familiar stimulus as a function of the orientation of the stimulus. The shortest reaction times occurred when the stimulus was in its normal position (0 degrees from upright). The less the stimulus resembled the normal position, the longer the reaction time. SOURCE: Compiled from data in Cooper and Shepard, 1973.

However, the subjects salivated more than half as much to the synonyms as they had to the conditional stimuli. Thus, while there was some generalization based on the sounds of the words, there was even more generalization based on word meanings.

Semantic generalization has been demonstrated in a number of other studies. John Lacey and his colleagues (1955) paired farm words such as *corn* with electric shocks, so that they became conditional stimuli that would elicit an increase in heart rate. Then the researchers presented words that were semantically related (other farms words, such as *cow, plow, tractor*) but that had never been paired with shock. They found that these related words also caused hearts to beat faster. Words that were not related to farming did not have this effect.

Studies of semantic generalization demonstrate that, at least among humans, stimulus generalization can be based on abstract concepts as well as on physical properties. It is easy to see how this phenomenon might be an important influence on human behavior. For example, in the United States during World War II, the word *Japanese* was often paired with unpleasant words such as *dirty, sneaky, cruel,* and *enemy.* The work of Carolyn and Arthur Staats (see Chapter Four) showed that such pairings are likely to result in the word *Japanese* eliciting negative emotional reactions. The work on semantic generalization suggests that such emotional responses may generalize to other, semantically related words, such as *Oriental* and *Asian.*

It is reasonable to suppose that there might be generalization from words to the people the words represent. During World War II, American citizens of Japanese descent were treated with suspicion and hostility; they were even imprisoned merely because of their ancestry. Recently, hostility toward Japan has reappeared, a phenomenon related to what some have termed an "economic war" (Thurow, 1992). This hostility has included discrimination, racial slurs, and beatings. It has also generalized to other people of Asian descent, including people from Korea, China, and Vietnam.

> Query: How is semantic generalization involved in racial
> prejudice?

Positive emotions generalize in the same way. When an American president takes an action that is favorable to another country, Americans visiting that country are welcomed and treated kindly, even though they had nothing whatever to do with the president's action. Positive emotions toward the president generalize to other Americans. Thus, semantic generalization appears to play an important role in prejudice and other kinds of emotional behavior.

You can see that part of the great power of learning comes from the tendency of learned behavior to generalize. There are times, however, when generalizing is inappropriate. In fact, sometimes survival depends upon the tendency to discriminate.

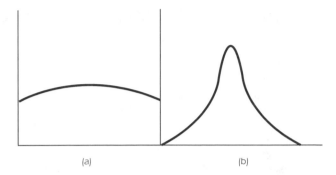

FIGURE 8-3 Discrimination and the generalization gradient. A relatively flat gradient (a) indicates little discrimination; a steep gradient (b) indicates considerable discrimination. (Hypothetical data.)

DISCRIMINATION

Discrimination is the tendency for learned behavior to occur in one situation, such as the presence of a red light, but not in other situations, such as the presence of a blue or green light. The organism differentiates, or discriminates, among the situations.

Discrimination and generalization are inversely related: The more discrimination, the less generalization. Generalization gradients therefore also reflect the degree of discrimination. A relatively flat gradient (see Figure 8-3a) indicates little or no discrimination; a steep gradient (see Figure 8-3b) indicates considerable discrimination.

We saw earlier that the more a stimulus resembles the training stimulus, the greater the degree of generalization. It is therefore clear that the less similar a stimulus to the training stimulus, the greater the degree of discrimination. It is often possible, however, to establish a discrimination between very similar stimuli through training.

■ Discrimination Training

The procedure for establishing a discrimination is called **discrimination training**. In Pavlovian discrimination training, one stimulus (designated CS+) indicates that a US is forthcoming, while another stimulus (designated CS−) indicates that the US is *not* coming. For example, we might put food into a dog's mouth each time a buzzer sounds, and give the dog nothing when a bell rings. As a result, the dog will salivate at the sound of the buzzer (the CS+) but not at the sound of the bell (the CS−).

Pavlov (1927) conducted many experiments on discrimination training. In one, a dog saw a rotating object. Whenever the object rotated in a clockwise direction, the dog received food; whenever the

Worlds Apart: Punks and Skinheads

To many people, birds are birds. Sparrows, starlings, finches—they all look alike. The same thing is often said of certain groups of people. Yet members of these groups have no trouble at all distinguishing members of their group from members of other groups. This is nicely illustrated in an article by Bill Bartlett (1992), who is himself a member of the variety of humans known as punks.

Punks and skinheads are people who adorn their persons in highly unconventional ways. To many people, they are all one sort of bird, indistinguishable. But punks and skins have no trouble telling each other apart. Bartlett explains the difference for those of us who have not learned to discriminate between them.

Punks, he says, usually wear spike-studded leather jackets or denims. They also wear T-shirts with the names of punk bands or anti-government slogans, spiked belts, tight-fitting jeans, and combat boots or Doc Martens. Sometimes they have anti-government slogans tattooed on their arms, and most have pierced noses, lips, or eyebrows.

Skins, on the other hand, wear army flight jackets, Fred Perry or polo shirts, and suspenders. They also wear jeans or khaki slacks that fit around the ankles, and Doc Marten shoes. They wear tattoos of the American flag, swastikas, or the letters *SWP* (for "supreme white power").

Skins and punks have very different political views (punks lean toward anarchy; skins, toward fascism), so they are not, as a rule, inclined to picnic in the park together. Because of this mutual hostility, it is important that they be able to discriminate between members of the two groups. The rest of us are usually not too comfortable around either skins or punks, so we have less need to discriminate between them. To most of us, they are "birds of a feather."

---

object rotated in the opposite direction, the dog did not get food. The dog soon learned to salivate to the CS+ (clockwise rotation) and not to the CS− (counterclockwise rotation).

Other experiments yielded similar results. Pavlov's dogs learned to discriminate between different volumes of a particular sound, different pitches of a tone, different geometric forms, different temperatures, and so on. Sometimes the level of discrimination achieved was remarkable. One dog even learned to discriminate between a metronome that ticked at the rate of 100 beats a minute and one that ticked at a rate of 96 times a minute.

In Pavlovian discrimination training, a stimulus indicates whether the US is coming or is not coming. In operant discrimination training, a stimulus (often called a **discriminative stimulus**) indicates whether a particular response, if made, will be reinforced. An S^D (pronounced ess-dee) indicates that responding will be reinforced, while an S^Δ (pronounced ess-delta) indicates that responding will either not be reinforced or will be punished.

In one kind of operant discrimination procedure, a pigeon that has learned to peck a disk for food may receive food after pecking a red disk, but not after pecking a green one. Under such conditions, the bird soon learns to ignore the green disk and pecks steadily at the red one.

In another kind of discrimination procedure, Karl Lashley (1930) trained rats to jump from a stand to a platform on which they would find food. To reach the platform, they had to jump through a door. The rats had a choice of two doors, one with vertical lines, the other with horizontal lines; only one door would open. If the animals jumped toward the correct door, the door flew open and the rat passed through to the food; if they chose the wrong door, the door did not open and they fell to a net below and got no food. In this procedure, responding was either reinforced or punished, depending upon the stimulus to which the rat responded. The rats soon learned to jump toward the proper door.

Query: How does operant discrimination training differ from ordinary operant learning?

■ Errorless Discrimination Training

In the procedures just described, the organism undergoing training inevitably makes a number of mistakes; that is, it responds to the S^Δ. When discriminative stimuli are very similar, the subject at first responds at about the same rate to both S^D and S^Δ, but since responses in the presence of S^Δ are not reinforced (and in some instances are punished), they tend to die out. It typically takes some time for a discrimination to develop, and subjects can make dozens of errors in the process.

Herbert Terrace (1963, 1964, 1972) found that many of the errors that occur in discrimination training could be avoided through a procedure he called **errorless discrimination training**. He presented the S^D in the usual manner and reinforced appropriate responses. But instead of presenting the S^Δ in the usual manner, he introduced it in a form so weak that the subject did not respond to it. Gradually, Terrace increased the strength of the S^Δ while reinforcing responses made to the S^D. Finally, Terrace was able to present the S^Δ in full strength without the subject responding to it. With this procedure, a discrimination can be developed with the subject making few errors. This is important, since errors tend to arouse undesirable emotional reactions in the subjects.

After discrimination training—with or without errors—the organism discriminates: It responds to certain stimuli, but not to other, similar stimuli. At this point, we can say that the discriminative stimuli exert a certain amount of control over the organism's behavior.

Query: How would you use errorless discrimination training to train a pigeon to peck a red disk but not an orange one?

■ Stimulus Control

Consider a rat that has learned to press a lever when a light is on, but not when the light is off. The environment has gained a measure of control over the rat's behavior: When the light goes on, the rat presses the lever at a rapid rate; when the light goes off, lever pressing falls off. When discrimination training brings behavior under the control of discriminative stimuli, the phenomenon is known as **stimulus control** (for a review, see Thomas, 1991).

Rats are not the only creatures that come under stimulus control. While driving, if you approach an intersection and the traffic light turns red, you move your foot to the brake pedal; when the light turns green, you press the gas pedal again. It is not a coincidence that you press the brake pedal on red and the gas pedal on green; as the result of discrimination training, your behavior has come under the control of these stimuli. Similarly, you tend to enter stores that display signs that read "Open," and you walk past stores that are marked "Closed." People who live on a tight budget are especially likely to respond to signs that say, "Sale," "Reduced Prices," "Clearance," "Going Out of Business," and the like. Retailers know the control such signs exert, of course, and use them to attract shoppers.

Sometimes the control exerted by stimuli in our environment is very subtle (Hickis and Thomas, 1991). A student may sit at her desk to study and find herself getting sleepy, even in the morning. The reason may be that the desk faces the student's bed, a discriminative stimulus for sleep. Another student may attempt to study while his roommates watch television. If television viewing is usually more reinforcing than studying, then he will find his eyes drifting from the text to the tube.

Stimulus control in everyday experience is apt to go unrecognized partly because the stimuli involved are not always as salient as those used in the lab. In the simplified world of the Skinner box, the relation between behavior and a light that goes on and off is quite noticeable. The connection between the location of a student's bed and her sleepiness is harder to see.

Sometimes discriminative control is exerted not by a single stimulus, but by a complex array of stimuli that, collectively, elicit behavior. We behave differently at a formal ball than we do at a square dance, and behavior that would be acceptable at a beach party is unacceptable at a dinner party. The differential control exerted by such situations probably has to do with a number of stimuli including attire, furniture, food, and the behavior of other people present.

Stimulus control can work against us. We may find ourselves eating food we don't need, or particularly want, merely because it is available. The food exerts a kind of control over us; so does the sign on a restaurant that says "Eat," or the photograph of a delicious dessert on a menu. Similarly, studies have shown that the mere presence of a weapon increases the likelihood of a violent act (Berkowitz, 1964;

Berkowitz & LePage, 1967). Leonard Berkowitz (1968) warns that while the finger pulls the trigger of a gun, the trigger also pulls the finger. He is talking about stimulus control.

But being under the control of discriminative stimuli also conveys power over the environment. Consider the rat that learns to press a lever when a light is on, but not when it is off. The light is said to control the rat's behavior, but the rat has also gained control over its environment: It no longer wastes time and energy pressing a lever when doing so is useless. Similarly, the behavior of motorists comes under the control of traffic lights and signs. But it is this stimulus control that permits us to travel more or less safely and efficiently. Without stimulus control, traffic jams would be routine, and our highways would be dangerous gauntlets.

An understanding of the control exerted by stimuli can also give us the power to change our environment appropriately. Dieters who learn that the mere presence of certain foods can affect how much they eat can avoid situations in which those foods are present. People who want to smoke less and who know that they are more likely to smoke when they see other people smoking can reduce their impulse to light up by avoiding areas where smokers congregate. Similarly, once the student understands that her drowsiness is the result of control exerted by the sight of her bed, she can rearrange the furniture and remain alert.

Researchers have explored other ways stimulus control can be turned to advantage. G. Alan Marlatt and his colleagues (Marlatt & Gordon, 1985; see also Hickis & Thomas, 1991) have postulated that one reason drug abusers so often relapse after treatment is that they return to an environment that elicits drug use. Treatment takes place in hospitals and clinics far away from the environment in which drug abuse occurred. After treatment, however, former addicts typically return to the same situation in which the drug abuse arose. They see the drug peddlers who once sold them drugs, they see friends and neighbors "shooting up," they walk the same streets where they walked when high on drugs. In such an environment, it is difficult indeed to continue a life of drug abstinence. The implication is that therapy must include learning to avoid or cope with the control exerted by the addict's home environment.

Our environment exerts control over our behavior. Paradoxically, that control increases the control we have, in turn, over our environment.

■ Discrimination Training and Secondary Reinforcement

In operant discrimination training, an S^D signals that a response will be reinforced. A rat may receive food for pressing a lever, for example, but only if a red light is on. This pairing of the red light and food results in the red light acquiring reinforcing properties. In other words, one result of operant discrimination training is that the S^D

becomes a secondary or conditional reinforcer (Bugelski, 1938; also see Chapter Five).

You may recall that Skinner once trained a dog to jump (1983a; see Chapter Four). Skinner accomplished the task by reinforcing successive approximations of jumping: first a slightly raised nose would result in reinforcement, then the dog had to raise its front legs to earn a reinforcer, then stand on its hind legs, and so on. The requirement for reinforcement continued to increase until the dog jumped to the desired height.

Skinner might have tossed the dog a bit of food each time he wanted to reinforce a response. However, tossing food to the dog would have meant a slight delay in reinforcement, and such delays usually reduce a reinforcer's effectiveness. To get around this problem, Skinner used a camera flash. A camera flash is not, under ordinary circumstances, reinforcing. How could the flash of a camera function as a reinforcer? The answer was to use the flash as an S^D for approaching an area where food was available. After several pairings of the flash and food, the light flash became an S^D for approaching and receiving food. After this, the dog's behavior could be reinforced by the camera flash, and it was used to shape jumping.

> Query: What is the process by which an S^D becomes a
> conditioned reinforcer?

Kent Burgess (1968) used a similar technique to train Shamu, a killer whale. Like Skinner, Burgess could have trained his subject by tossing it a bit of food. But the whale was swimming in a large pool, and it might have taken some time before the whale found a fish tossed to it. When the whale found the food, it might be doing something other than performing the response Burgess wanted to reinforce. Hence, all sorts of behavior might be accidentally shaped, and this would interefere with training. To avoid this problem, Burgess blew a whistle and then provided food when the animal approached. Thus, the whistle became an S^D for approaching the trainer. After this, Burgess could reinforce selected responses by blowing the whistle. If, for example, the whale spouted water, Burgess would blow the whistle and the animal would immediately swim to the trainer and receive a bit of food:

$$R \quad \rightarrow \quad S^D \quad \rightarrow \quad R \quad \rightarrow \quad S^R$$

spout	whistle	approach	receive
water	sounds	trainer	food

Note that the whistle is both a discriminative stimulus and a reinforcer.

Response chains typically involve several discriminative stimuli; these stimuli reinforce the behavior throughout the chain. Climbing a ramp is reinforced by reaching a bridge, the S^D for crossing it; crossing the bridge is reinforced by reaching a ladder, the S^D for climbing, and so on. Each S^D reinforces the previous response and provides the signal for the next response.

The reinforcing properties of a discriminative stimulus can be demonstrated by using it as a reinforcer in a new situation. J. T. Cowles (1937) taught chimpanzees to use poker chips to get food from a vending machine. A poker chip thus became a discriminative stimulus for approaching the machine and inserting the chip. At this point, Cowles found that he could use the poker chips as reinforcers to train other responses. Of course, the poker chips would eventually lose their reinforcing value if they could not eventually be exchanged for food.

Research on generalization and discrimination has provided insights into several topics. We will consider how they have changed our views of two phenomena, neurosis and concept formation.

NEUROSIS

Errors during discrimination training arouse negative emotions in the subject. During a difficult discrimination, these emotional reactions are sometimes quite pronounced. N. R. Shenger-Krestovnikova (in Pavlov, 1927), working in Pavlov's laboratory, trained a dog to salivate at the sight of a circle flashed upon a screen, but not to salivate at the sight of an oval (see Figure 8-4a). Next, the researcher modified the oval so that it more closely resembled the circle, and then resumed training (see Figure 8-4b). When the animal discriminated between the two figures, Shenger-Krestovnikova modified the oval again, making it still more like the circle, and resumed training. He repeated this procedure again and again. Finally, when the two forms were nearly identical, progress stopped. Not only did the animal fail to discriminate between the two forms, but, as Pavlov (1927) wrote:

> The whole behavior of the animal underwent an abrupt change. The hitherto quiet dog began to squeal in its stand, kept wriggling about, tore off with its teeth the apparatus for mechanical stimulation of the skin, and bit through the tubes connecting the animal's room with the observer, a behavior which never happened before. (p. 291)

Pavlov called the dog's bizarre behavior an **experimental neurosis** since it seemed to him that the behavior resembled that sometimes seen in people who had had "nervous breakdowns." Analogous findings have been obtained during operant discrimination training (Brown, 1942).

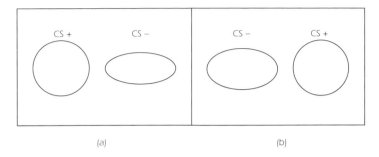

FIGURE 8-4 *Discrimination and experimental neurosis. A dog learned to salivate at the sight of a circle, but not of an oval (a). As training proceeded, the discrimination became progressively more difficult, with the oval becoming more and more like the circle (b). Eventually, the dog could not discriminate and became "emotionally disturbed."*

We must be careful in using experimental neurosis as an analog for human neurosis. Yet people do sometimes find themselves in situations that require extremely subtle discriminations, and such situations do seem to be stressful. Teenagers, for example, sometimes are praised by their parents for "accepting responsibility," but on other occasions they are criticized for not "knowing their place." The discriminations the adults require of their children are often nearly as subtle as those Shenger-Krestovnikova required of his dog. And often the results are similar. Whether the "nervous breakdowns" that sometimes result in hospitalization are ever the result of this sort of discrimination training is uncertain, but the possibility cannot be ignored.

Query: What can parents learn from the Shenger-Krestovnikova experiment?

CONCEPT FORMATION

The word **concept** usually refers to any class whose members share one or more defining features. The defining feature allows us to discriminate the members of one class from the members of another class. For example, all spiders have eight legs; this distinguishes them from other animals, including insects, which have fewer than or more than eight legs. All ice creams have in common that they are sweet, cold, and soft, and it is these features that allow us to distinguish ice cream from, say, popsicles, which are sweet and cold but hard.

Understanding a concept means responding appropriately to any stimulus in the concept class, not merely the training stimuli. We do not say that a child understands the concept "car" just because she calls the family car by that name. Understanding a concept also implies discriminating between members of the concept class and other items. A child understands the concept, "car," only if she calls certain kinds of vehicles by that name but not others (for example, trucks and vans). Obviously, then, understanding a concept means generalizing within a class and discriminating between classes. There is considerable evidence that concepts are acquired through discrimination training.

> Query: How does understanding a concept involve
>   generalization?

Every parent can provide anecdotal evidence of the role of discrimination training in concept learning. The baby's babbling is eventually shaped through reinforcement to forms words, such as *Da-da*. But the child does not, at first, use the terms altogether correctly. A baby may say "Da-Da! " when his father approaches, but he may also greet any other man in the same way, which can be a source of some embarrassment to his parents. Through discrimination training, the child learns to reserve *Da-da* for one particular man. In the same way, a child may point at everything on wheels, from a tricycle to a farm tractor, and proudly pronounce it a car. At first, parents and other adults accept this broad definition of the term, but eventually they provide reinforcement only when the term is used correctly.

Experimental evidence also supports the notion that concepts are learned through discrimination training. Richard Herrnstein and his colleagues performed a series of brilliant experiments in which they used discrimination training to teach various concepts to pigeons. In one study, Herrnstein (1979) projected photographic slides on one wall of a pigeon's chamber. Some of the slides included one or more trees or parts of trees; the others did not. The birds received food if they pecked a disk, but only if the picture currently on their wall included a tree. Herrnstein was amazed at how rapidly the birds learned to discriminate between photographs with trees and those without them. Moreover, when Herrnstein tested the birds with slides they had never seen before, they responded correctly. Thus, the birds appear to have learned the concept, "tree."

In another study (Herrnstein et al., 1976), the researchers taught pigeons the concept, "human being." The researchers again projected slides on the wall of the pigeon's chamber. This time some of the slides contained images of people, while others did not. The birds received food for pecking a disk, but only when the current slide included people. This was no easy task: Sometimes the people depicted appeared alone, sometimes in groups; they were of different sizes, shapes, ages, and sexes; they wore different kinds of clothing, and sometimes no clothing; they were sometimes in full view, other times partially hidden by objects. Nevertheless, the pigeons learned to peck only when human beings were depicted. And when the birds saw new slides, they pecked or did not peck, depending upon whether the slide included a person. The results are particularly impressive when you consider that the researchers themselves were unable to pinpoint any single defining feature upon which the birds might have discriminated.

Some concepts differ from the examples given in that they express relationships between two or more items: taller, cheapest, biggest, and so on. We say that one desk is bigger than another, or that it is the biggest of three desks. We say that one job is easier than another or that it is the easiest job in a plant. These relational concepts appear, however, to be learned through the same discrimination process.

In one study, Kenneth Spence (1937) trained chimpanzees to find food under one of two white, metal covers that differed only in size. One chimp got a choice between covers that were 160 and 100 square centimeters. Whenever it chose the larger cover, it found food; whenever it chose the smaller cover, it found nothing. After the chimp had learned to choose the larger cover reliably, Spence presented it with new covers, identical to the first set except that the choice was now between covers that were 320 and 200 centimeters. We might expect that the chimp would select the 200 cm cover, since that one more closely resembled the cover that previously hid food. Instead, the chimp chose the larger cover. It apparently had learned the relational concept, "larger than."

In a similar experiment, Wolfgang Kohler (1939) trained chickens and chimpanzees to select the lighter of two gray squares. After training, he tested them with the light gray square that had always led to food, and with a still lighter gray square they had never seen before. Again, we might expect the subjects to select the original gray stimulus, since that had previously led to food. In fact, the apes chose the new, lighter square. Kohler called the phenomenon **transposition**, since it seemed analogous to musical transposition, in which a composition is played in a key different from the original. But the behavior of the subjects also fits our criterion for concept learning.

Query: What sort of concept is involved in transposition?

Richard and Maria Malott (1970) used discrimination to teach pigeons the concept of sameness. In this study, two halves of a key were illuminated independently and could therefore have different colors. When both halves were the same color (either all red or all violet), pecking the key produced food; when the two halves were different colors (one half red, the other violet), pecking did not produce food. After the birds learned this discrimination, they were tested on four new patterns: blue-blue, yellow-yellow, blue-yellow, and yellow-blue. Three out of the four pigeons pecked more often when the key halves were the same color than when they were different colors.

K. Fujita has used a similar procedure to study the acquisition of the sameness concept in monkeys. In one experiment (Fujita, 1983, reported in Pisacreta et al., 1984), monkeys learned to press a lever when two disks were the same color (either red or purple), and not to press the lever when the disks did not match (red and purple). When the animals mastered this discrimination, Fujita found that the response generalized to novel stimuli. When presented with two yellow or two green disks, for example, the monkeys pressed the lever; when presented with one yellow and one green disk, they did not press the lever.

Children learn relational concepts quite readily. Elizabeth Alberts and David Ehrenfreund (1951) trained children ages 3 to 5 to find a gumdrop by opening the correct door on a box. The doors differed only in size, and the smaller door always provided the gumdrop. After the children reached a criterion of nine out of ten correct responses, they tried their hands at a number of new boxes. The doors on these new boxes differed in size from those on the training box, but the smaller door always produced the gumdrop. Overall, the results showed that the children continued to choose the smaller doors. That is, they responded on the basis of the relative sizes of the doors, rather than their similarity to the training doors.

Researchers have demonstrated that pigeons and monkeys, to say nothing of humans, can master the concepts *fish*, *cats*, *flowers*, *ships*, *oak leaves*, *cars*, *letters*, and *chairs*, among others. Teaching more abstract concepts (such as *up* and *down*, *right* and *left*, *horizontal* and *vertical*, *attractive* and *unattractive*) may be more difficult. Yet it is surprising what can be accomplished, even with animals. Discrimination training does seem to provide an explanation of concept learning in the natural environment. Explaining discrimination and generalization is, however, another matter, one to which we must now turn our attention.

THEORIES OF GENERALIZATION AND DISCRIMINATION

Three theories of generalization and discrimination have dominated the field: those of Pavlov, Spence, and Lashley and Wade.

■ Pavlov's Theory

Pavlov's theory is physiological. He speculated that discrimination training produces physiological changes in the brain's cerebral cortex. Specifically, it establishes an area of excitation associated with the CS+, and an area of inhibition associated with the CS−. If a novel stimulus is similar to the CS+, it will excite an area of the cortex near the CS+ area. The excitation will irradiate to the CS+ area and elicit the CR (see Figure 8-5). Similarly, if a novel stimulus resembles the CS−, it will excite an area of the cortex near the CS− area. The excitation of this area will irradiate to the CS− area and inhibit the CR.

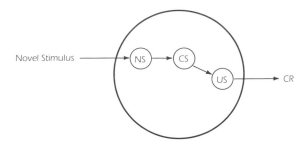

FIGURE 8-5 *Pavlov's theory of generalization and discrimination.*

A similar explanation could be applied to generalization and discrimination following operant learning.

Pavlov's theory provides an intuitively appealing explanation and, wrapped as it is in physiology, it has the smell of science. Unfortunately, the physiological events are merely inferred from observed behavior. Pavlov never saw or measured cortical activity association with conditioning. He assumed that cortical irradiation occurred only because generalization occurred, but there is no independent validation of its occurrence. The theory therefore suffers from circularity and is for this reason not popular with psychologists. Pavlov's ideas have been modified by other theorists, however, most notably by Kenneth Spence.

> **Query**: How is Pavlov's explanation of generalization and discrimination circular?

■ Spence's Theory

Pavlov's theory deals with hypothetical physiological events. What Pavlov actually observed, however, was not what went on in the brain, but how an animal responded to different stimuli. Kenneth Spence (1936, 1937, 1960) put Pavlov's physiology aside but accepted the notion that discrimination training does produce generalization to CS− as well as CS+.

Pairing a CS+ with a US results in an increased tendency to respond to the CS+ and to stimuli resembling the CS+. Similarly, reinforcement for responding in the presence of an S^D results in an increased tendency to respond not only to the S^D but to similar stimuli. The generalization gradient that results is called an **excitatory gradient**. In the same way, presenting a CS− without the US results in a *decreased* tendency to respond to the CS− and to stimuli resembling the CS−. Likewise, withholding reinforcement when responses occur in the presence of an S^Δ results in a decreased tendency to respond to the S^Δ and to similar stimuli. The generalization gradient that results is often called an **inhibitory gradient**.

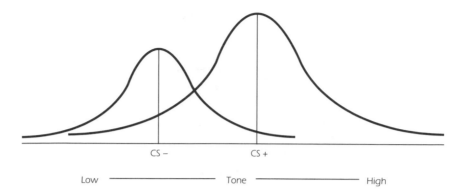

FIGURE 8-6 Spence's theory of generalization and discrimination. CS+ training produces a gradient of excitation; CS− training produces a gradient of inhibition. The tendency to respond to a stimulus near the CS+ is reduced to the extent that it resembles the CS−. The tendency *not* to respond to a simulus near the CS− is reduced to the extent that it resembles the CS+.

Spence proposed that the tendency to respond to any given stimulus was the result of the interaction of the increased and decreased tendencies to respond, as reflected in gradients of excitation and inhibition. Consider a dog that is trained to salivate to the sound of a high-pitched tone, and another that is trained *not* to salivate to the sound of a low-pitched tone. The first dog will show generalization of excitation around CS+; the second will show generalization of inhibition around CS−. We can plot the excitatory and inhibitory gradients that result and place them next to one another, as depicted in Figure 8-6. Notice that the two curves overlap.

Discrimination training produces much the same effect within an organism. That is, the increased tendency to respond to stimuli resembling the CS+ (or S^D) overlaps with the decreased tendency to respond to stimuli resembling the CS− (or S^{Δ}). What Spence proposed was that the tendency to respond to a novel stimulus following discrimination training would be equal to the net difference between the excitatory and inhibitory tendencies. In other words, the tendency *to* respond to a novel stimulus will be reduced by the tendency *not* to respond to that stimulus.

Consider a hypothetical experiment in which a pigeon is trained to peck an orange disk, but not a red one. After training, we give the bird the opportunity to peck the disk when it is a variety of colors, from pale yellow to deep red. What color disk will it peck most often? We know that if the bird had merely received food for pecking the orange disk, it would peck that same color most often. But discrimination training, according to Spence, should result in inhibition of the tendency to peck stimuli resembling the S^{Δ}. Spence's theory therefore predicts that the peak of responding will not occur at the S^D, but at a stimulus further away from the S^{Δ}. In other words, the peak of responding will

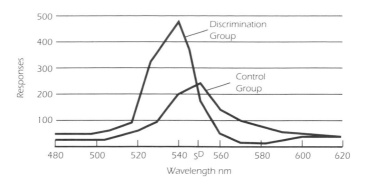

FIGURE 8-7 Peak shift. Pigeons trained to discriminate between an S^D (550 nm) and an S^Δ (560 nm) responded more often to a 540 nm stimulus than to the S^D. Birds that had been trained only on the S^D (control group) did not show this peak shift. SOURCE: After Hanson, 1959.

not be on the orange disk, but on one that is less reddish (less like the S^Δ).

This prediction, made in the 1930s, was actually confirmed in the 1950s in an experiment much like that just described. H. M. Hanson (1959) trained pigeons to peck a yellow-green disk (550 nm, or nanometers, a measure of wavelength) and not to peck a slightly more yellowish (560 nm) disk. A control group of birds did not undergo discrimination training but did receive food for pecking the yellow-green disk. After training, Hanson let the birds peck disks of various colors, from yellow to green. The control group showed a peak of responding to the discriminative stimulus. Birds that had received discrimination training, however, showed a shift away from the S^D; their peak of responding was to a stimulus of about 540 nm (see Figure 8-7). The **peak shift** has proved to be a robust phenomenon (see, for example, Thomas et al., 1991).

> Query: Suppose Hanson had used a disk of 540 nm as the S^Δ. Where do you think the peak of responding would have occurred? (Consider Figure 8-7.)

The ability of Spence's theory to predict the peak shift phenomenon is impressive. But the Lashley-Wade theory also has much to recommend it.

■ The Lashley-Wade Theory

Karl Lashley and M. Wade (1946) proposed an explanation of generalization and discrimination that differs sharply from those of Pavlov and Spence. These researchers argued that generalization gradients depend upon prior experience with stimuli similar to those used in testing. Discrimination training increases the steepness of the generalization gradient because it teaches the animal to tell the difference between the S^D and other stimuli. But the generalization gradient is not usually flat even in the absence of training. Why is this so if the gradient depends on training? Lashley and Wade's answer is that the animal has, in fact, undergone a kind of discrimination training in its everyday life. A pigeon, for example, learns to discriminate colors long before a researcher trains it to peck colored disks. The more experience a pigeon has had with colors, especially those resembling the S^D, the steeper its generalization gradient will be; the less experience the bird has had, the flatter the gradient will be.

The theory implies that if an animal is prevented from having any experience with a certain kind of stimulus, such as color, its behavior following training will be affected. If such a color-naive animal is trained to respond in the presence of a red disk, for example, it will later respond just as frequently to a green disk as to a red one. In other words, its gradient of generalization will be flat.

Several researchers have attempted to test this hypothesis. In the typical experiment, animals are reared from birth in the dark in order to deprive them of experiences with color. Then they are trained to respond to a stimulus such as a green disk. After this, the animals are tested for generalization by presenting them with disks of other colors and noting the extent to which they discriminate. The results can be compared with those obtained from animals that had been reared normally. If the gradients of the color-deprived animals are flatter, the Lashley-Wade theory is supported; if rearing in the dark makes no difference in the shape of the gradient, the theory is unsupported.

Unfortunately, the results of such experiments have been ambiguous, with one study tending to support the theory and another study tending to undermine it. Moreover, interpretation of the results is subject to argument. When there is no difference in the gradients of deprived and normally reared animals, proponents of the Lashley-Wade theory argue that the rearing procedure does not entirely preclude experience with the relevant stimuli; when deprivation produces a flat gradient, opponents of the theory argue that the deprivation procedure has damaged the eyes of the animals so that their physical capacity for discriminating colors has been limited. A stronger test of the Lashley-Wade theory is needed than deprivation studies can provide.

If the theory is valid, it can be argued that it should not be necessary to deprive an animal of all experience with a stimulus, but merely to restrict its experience with the stimulus during training. To test this idea, Herbert Jenkins and Robert Harrison (1960) trained pigeons to peck a disk. Some pigeons could hear a tone periodically; pecking was reinforced in the presence of the tone, but not during periods of quiet. Other pigeons heard the same tone without interruption. In both cases, then, disk pecking was reinforced in the presence of a tone, but in one case, there were periods of silence during which pecking was not reinforced. Next, the experimenters tested all the pigeons for generalization to other tones and to periods of silence. They found that pigeons that had been exposed to a periodic tone were much less likely to peck the disk during periods of silence than when the tone sounded. The other pigeons, however, pecked the disk just as much when the tone was on as when it was off. This much is to be expected, since the birds that heard the tone constantly had no opportunity to discriminate, while those that heard the tone periodically were taught to discriminate. But what would happen when the pigeons were exposed to different tones, sounds that neither group had heard before? The pigeons that had learned to discriminate between periods of tone and periods of silence also discriminated between the original tone and other tones. Pigeons that had been reinforced during constant sound did not discriminate between tones. These results are just what the Lashley-Wade theory would predict.

Not all tests of the Lashley-Wade theory have yielded positive results, but it is now generally acknowledged that the steepness of a generalization gradient depends to some extent upon the experience the subject has had with the stimuli under study before training.

GENERALIZATION, DISCRIMINATION, AND ADAPTATION

The tendency to generalize is a blessing bestowed upon us by evolution because it has survival value. Conditioned taste aversion offers a powerful illustration of this fact: Animals and people made sick by a particular kind of food then refuse to eat not only that food but other foods that resemble it. When a blue jay eats a monarch butterfly and gets sick (see Chapter Four), it not only stops eating that particular butterfly, it thereafter eschews all monarch butterflies.

We can see the same sort of benefit from the generalization of food gathering skills. In hunter-gatherer societies, young boys practice the skills of the hunt by shooting arrows at leaves. The survival of the group depends not upon the boy's ability to shoot a leaf, however, but upon his ability to shoot a bird. The mastery of archery skills in the training situation must, and fortunately does, generalize to other situations.

Academic education also would be of little value if what we learned did not generalize. Schoolchildren do not write essays about their summer vacations because they will one day be required to write about those experiences; they write so that they will be able to write about other experiences. Similarly, they do not solve the problems in an algebra textbook so that they will be able to solve those same problems later on; they solve them so that they will be able to solve other problems.

Like generalization, discrimination plays an important role in survival. The blue jay that learns not to eat monarch butterflies is not helped if it avoids eating all kinds of butterflies. In fact, the blue jay that has been made sick by a monarch tends also to avoid viceroys, a kind of butterfly that closely resembles the monarch. The bird's failure to discriminate handicaps it in its search for food.

In hunter-gatherer societies, girls learn to collect fruits and vegetables for food. They must be able to tell the difference between edible plants and poisonous ones. They also learn to collect medicinal plants, and, again, discriminating is important: While some plants heal, others kill.

Discrimination is also important in industrialized societies. The motorist who does not reliably respond differentially to red and green traffic signals is unlikely to survive for long on our highways. Similarly, the patient whose doctor cannot discriminate between the symptoms of appendicitis and those of indigestion is in serious trouble.

Organisms also sometimes benefit from the inability of other organisms to discriminate. The angler fish waves a fleshy protuberance about in its gaping mouth, and its victims swim after what looks like a tasty morsel. The fish profits from the inability of its prey to discriminate between the fish's lure and the real thing. Some biologists theorize that the rattlesnake's rattle might also provide a kind of lure, citing as evidence the fact that frogs fail to discriminate between insects and the rattler's tail (Schuett et al., 1984). As the frog lunges for what it takes to be a meal, it instead falls victim to the snake. Human hunters also use decoys to attract prey within reach of their weapons.

Camouflage can be viewed as an adaptive technique based upon the principle of generalization. The chameleon escapes its enemies by changing its color to resemble that of its background. The more it resembles the surface on which it stands, the less likely it is to be eaten. The walking stick, a kind of insect, goes unmolested because it resembles a twig. Human hunters wear uniforms that blend in with their surroundings to escape detection by their prey. Such animal and human disguises are effective because other organisms fail to discriminate between the organisms and their surroundings.

We see, then, that for both humans and animals, generalization and discrimination play major roles in adaptation. These phenomena greatly complicate the role of learning in survival.

SUMMARY

As earlier chapters show, learning is an adaptive mechanism that plays an essential role in survival. This chapter shows that learning itself would be of limited value were it not for the phenomena of generalization and discrimination.

Generalization is the tendency to respond in situations that are somewhat different from the situation in which the behavior was learned. Without generalization, all learning would be specific to a particular situation. Generalization is measured by putting the subject in situations that are different from the training situation. When the subject's response frequencies are plotted on a graph, the result is a generalization gradient. The flatter the resulting line, the more generalization.

Most studies of generalization involve the physical properties of stimuli—sound, color, shape, and so on. But responses sometimes generalize on the basis of the meaning of a stimulus, a phenomenon called semantic generalization.

Discrimination is also important for adaptation. Behavior that is appropriate in one situation may be highly inappropriate in another. When an organism responds in the presence of a particular stimulus, but not in the presence of another stimulus, we say the organism discriminates. The procedure for establishing a discrimination is called discrimination training. Errorless discrimination training establishes a discrimination with a minimum of errors. When a discrimination is established, the generalization gradient shows a much steeper slope than is found prior to such training. One by-product of operant discrimination training is that the S^D becomes a secondary reinforcer. When a discrimination has been established, the behavior is said to be under stimulus control.

The study of generalization and discrimination has led to an improved understanding of other phenomena. An example is the learning of concepts. Research has also shown that discrimination procedures can produce experimental neuroses, which may provide a model for some naturally occurring human neuroses.

Various theories have been proposed to account for generalization and discrimination. Pavlov explained the phenomena in terms of the irradiation of excitation. When generalization occurs, for instance, it is because a stimulus has excited an area of the brain near the part of the brain affected by the CS+. Spence believed that the net difference between gradients of excitation and inhibition predicts the response to novel stimuli. His theory accurately predicted the peak shift phenomenon. The Lashley-Wade theory maintains that generalization occurs because the organism has had too little experience with the stimuli involved to be able to discriminate among them.

Generalization and discrimination are vital to adaptation. Behavior that does not generalize where appropriate is of limited value, and behavior that generalizes to situations in which it is not appropriate can be dangerous. The use of lures to capture prey and of camouflage to avoid detection are examples of adaptive behavior that depend upon the principles of generalization and discrimination. Predators put evolutionary pressure upon their prey to develop more sophisticated defensive techniques. By developing those techniques, prey animals put evolutionary pressure upon predators to develop more sophisticated predatory techniques. In this way, predator and prey contribute to each other's evolution.

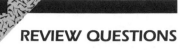

REVIEW QUESTIONS

1. Define the following terms:

concept	generalization
discrimination	peak shift
discrimination training	semantic generalization

2. Describe the relationship between generalization and discrimination.

3. How is semantic generalization different from other examples of generalization?

4. A student learns to draw human figures. How could you determine if this learning had improved the student's ability to draw animal figures? What phenomenon would you be studying?

5. "He who has been bitten by a snake fears a rope." What phenomenon does this proverb implicitly recognize?

6. Mark Twain once said that a cat that gets burned on a hot stove thereafter avoids cold stoves as well as hot ones. How could you train such a cat to discriminate between hot and cold stoves?

7. B. F. Skinner (1951) once taught pigeons to "read." They would peck a disk when a sign read "Peck," and would not peck when a sign read "Don't peck." Describe how Skinner might have accomplished this.

8. Thorndike (1911) wrote that "by taking a certain well-defined position in front of [a monkey's] cage and feeding him whenever he did scratch himself I got him to always scratch himself within a few seconds after I took that position" (p. 236). Explain what sort of training is going on here. Be sure to identify the S^D, the S^Δ, the response being learned, and the reinforcer.

9. Diane says that in the experiment described in question 8, it is not the monkey that is undergoing discrimination training, but Thorndike. Why might she say this?

10. Why is generalization important to the teacher?

11. How would you test the hypothesis, Experimental neurosis can be avoided through errorless discrimination training?

12. How might you use discrimination training to make someone capable of recognizing, from facial expressions and other "body language," when people were lying?

13. What might be the role of discrimination training in racial prejudice?

14. Many feminists object to the practice of using the pronoun *he* to refer to people in traditionally male roles (for example, scientists) while using *she* to refer to people in traditionally female roles (for example, chambermaids). Are they right to object?

15. How does Spence's theory differ from Pavlov's?

16. A music teacher has trained students to recognize middle C on the piano. She then tests for generalization by playing other keys. Draw a hypothetical generalization gradient of the results.

17. How could you teach a fellow student the concept of generalization?

18. What are the implications of research on errorless discrimination training for the construction of educational software?

19. Explain why a stimulus that becomes an S^D also becomes a secondary reinforcer.

20. Explain why a person who is red-green color blind (that is, a person to whom red and green objects look gray) is at a disadvantage compared to his or her peers.

Suggested Readings

Most of the important works on generalization and discrimination are technical papers published in professional journals. They are difficult reading and tend to focus on narrow aspects of these phenomena. However, there are some publications that you might find both readable and intriguing.

Two are books already recommended: Pavlov's *Conditioned Reflexes* and Thorndike's *Animal Intelligence.*

B. F. Skinner's article, "How to Teach Animals," published in *Scientific American* in 1951, illustrates the practical application of discrimination training and secondary reinforcers. The principles Skinner describes are not limited to animals. One of Skinner's most important books, *Science and Human Behavior,* deals in part with topics covered here. See especially Chapter Seven, "Operant Discrimination," and Chapter Eight, "The Controlling Environment."

Answers to Queries

Page 188: Yes. Students apply skills they have learned when they use those skills in situations different from those used in instruction. You did not write essays about your summer vacation in order to prepare you for a job in which you would write essays about that summer vacation.

Page 188: A generalization gradient shows the tendency to respond in a given way to stimuli that differ systematically from the training stimulus.

Page 191: The building in which we conduct fire drills presents a very different situation when it is on fire.

*Page 192:*If we hear negative things about a person of a given race, the feelings aroused will tend to generalize to other people of the same race and probably to similar races. This might explain why many people dislike races with which they have had no firsthand experience.

Page 195: In ordinary operant learning (see Chapter Five), reinforcement is contingent upon a given response. In operant discrimination training, reinforcement is contingent upon a given response and the presence of a given stimulus. It is the difference between reinforcing a lever press and reinforcing a lever press only if a green light is on.

*Page 195:*You might reinforce disk pecking only when the disk is red and then illuminate the disk with a very, very faint orange lamp. You would then very gradually increase the brightness of the orange disk. Pecking the red disk would always be reinforced; pecking the orange disk never would be reinforced.

Page 198: Pavlovian conditioning.

Page 200: Parents might have less neurotic children if they made the conditions under which certain behavior was and was not acceptable very clear.

Page 201: Training in a concept seldom involves exposure to all possible stimuli in the concept class. To understand a concept means to generalize from the training stimuli to other stimuli in that class.

Page 202: Transposition involves a relational concept.

Page 204: Pavlov infers the physiological events from observations about generalization and discrimination and then explains generalization and discrimination by pointing to the supposed physiological events. This is like saying, "Evil spirits cause disease," and then citing illness as proof that evil spirits exist.

Page 206: It would have shifted in the other direction, probably to around 560 nm.

nine

Schedules
of Reinforcement

The tendencies to respond eventually correspond to
the probabilities of reinforcement.
—B. F. SKINNER

The communist production system? We pretend to
work, and they pretend to pay us.
—JOKE TOLD BY FACTORY WORKERS IN THE FORMER
  SOVIET UNION

BACKGROUND

Most people use the term *learning* to refer to the
acquisition of new behavior. A pigeon that never turned in counterclockwise circles now does so reliably and efficiently. A child who could
not ride a bicycle at all now rides with skill and ease. A college student
for whom the equation $F = ma$ previously meant nothing now uses the
formula to solve physics problems.

But we have seen that learning also includes changes in which no
new behavior appears. One such change is an increase in the rate of
behavior. A pigeon that turns in counterclockwise circles at the rate of
3 or 4 turns a minute may learn to make 10 or 15 turns a minute. A
child who previously took ten minutes to ride a bicycle through an
obstacle course now navigates the course in three minutes. A physics
student who used to solve textbook problems involving force and mass
at the rate of one every ten minutes now solves the same kinds of
problems in five minutes.

Learning can also mean a reduction in response rate. A bird that
turns counterclockwise ten times a minute can learn to make one turn
a minute. The child who races around on a bicycle can learn to ride

more slowly. The student who whips through physics problems can learn to take the time to check her work.

Learning can mean a change in the pattern of responses as well as the rate. If a pan of cookies must bake for ten minutes, it is pointless to check the cookies during the first five minutes or so, but it is essential to check on them after an interval of about eight or nine minutes. The cook learns to avoid opening the oven in the first few minutes, but to check on the cookies more and more often during the last few minutes of baking time.

We can see the same phenomenon in the workplace. Consider a factory worker who is employed at two factories. In one plant he is paid an hourly wage for spray-painting lawn chairs; in the other, he is paid so much per chair for the same work. Very likely the employee will eventually behave differently in the two factories. Not only will he turn out more lawn chairs per hour when on piece work, but he will probably work more steadily and take fewer breaks.

Just as acquisition of new behavior is partly the product of reinforcement contingencies, so response rate and pattern are partly due to reinforcement contingencies. The changes in the cook's behavior reflect the fact that reinforcement (seeing cookies that are done or nearly done) is available near the end of baking time but not earlier. Similarly, the factory worker on piece work paints more chairs because his earnings reflect the number of chairs painted. For him, each chair painted is a secondary reinforcer. This is not the case when he works on an hourly wage.

The pattern of response consequences is called a **schedule of reinforcement.** We shall see that a particular kind of reinforcement schedule tends to produce a particular pattern and rate of responding, and these **schedule effects** are remarkably reliable. When a given schedule is in force for some time, the organism responds in a predictable way. If the organism is removed from the schedule environment for a time and then returned to it, it typically resumes its previous behavior. Moreover, if different schedules are in force for different kinds of behavior, the rates of response will reflect the different schedules. And if an organism is responding at a steady rate and the reinforcement schedule changes, the behavior will change in predictable ways.

> Query: What does the term *schedule* mean in the phrase *schedule of reinforcement?*

Such schedule effects are often attributed to character traits, such as laziness and ambition. But the factory worker does not work at different rates in two plants because he is lazy in one factory and ambitious in the other. The difference in behavior merely reflects the different reinforcement schedules in force.

There are schedules of punishment as well as reinforcement, and behavior can be followed by both reinforcing and punishing events simultaneously. However, in this chapter we will concentrate on reinforcement schedules and their effects on operant behavior, beginning with simple schedules of reinforcement.

SIMPLE SCHEDULES

■ Continuous Reinforcement

The simplest of simple schedules is called **continuous reinforcement, or CRF.** In continuous reinforcement, each response of a designated nature is reinforced. If, for example, a rat receives food each and every time it presses a lever, then lever pressing is on a continuous reinforcement schedule, as is the disk pecking of a pigeon if it receives a bit of grain each time it pecks a disk. Likewise, a child's behavior is on CRF if she is praised every time she hangs up her coat, and your behavior is on CRF when you operate a vending machine if, each time you insert the requisite amount of money, you receive the item selected.[1]

Each reinforcement strengthens behavior, so continuous reinforcement leads to very rapid increases in response rates. It is especially useful, then, when the task is to shape up some new behavior or chain of responses. You can see that it would be much easier to teach a pigeon to make counterclockwise turns by reinforcing each successive approximation of the desired response than it would be if one were to reinforce successive approximations only occasionally.

Although continuous reinforcement typically leads to the most rapid learning of new behavior, it is not the most common schedule in the natural environment. Most behavior is reinforced on some occasions, but not on others. A parent is not able to praise a child every time she hangs up her coat, and vending machines sometimes take our money and give us nothing in return. When reinforcement occurs on some occasions but not others, it is said to be **intermittent.** There are many kinds of intermittent schedules (see Ferster & Skinner, 1957), but the most important fall into four groups. Let us begin with those called fixed ratio schedules.

INTERMITTENT:

■ Fixed Ratio Schedules

In a **fixed ratio, or FR, schedule,** reinforcement occurs after a fixed number of responses. For instance, a rat may be trained to press a lever for food. After the response is established, the experimenter may switch to a schedule in which every third lever press is reinforced. In

---

[1] Note that it is the response that is on a reinforcement schedule, not the organism. It is common for people to say that a rat is on a particular reinforcement schedule, but it is the rat's behavior, and not the rat itself, that is reinforced.

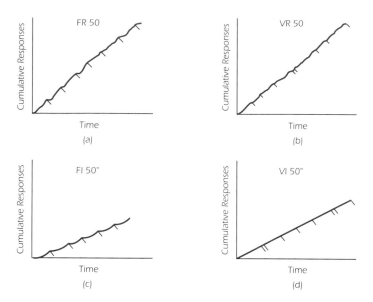

FIGURE 9-1   Intermittent schedules of reinforcement. In an FR 50 schedule (a), every 50th response is reinforced; in a VR 50 schedule (b), an average of 50 responses is required for each reinforcement; in an FI 50" schedule (c), a response is reinforced when it occurs after a 50-second interval; in a VI 50" schedule (d), a response is reinforced after an average interval of 50 seconds. Short diagonal lines indicate delivery of a reinforcer. (Hypothetical data.)

other words, the rat must press the lever three times before it receives a bit of food. There is a ratio of three responses to each reinforcement. The schedule is usually indicated by the letters *FR*, followed by the number of responses required for reinforcement. The lever pressing of our hypothetical rat, for example, is on an FR 3 schedule. (Continuous reinforcement is a fixed ratio schedule, then, and may be designated FR 1.)

> **Query:** Which schedule reinforces more often, FR 10 or FR 5?

Animals on fixed ratio schedules respond at a high rate, often punctuated by short pauses after each reinforcement. A rat that lever presses on an FR 5 schedule will press the lever quickly five times, eat the food that appears in the food tray, pause for a moment, and then return to work at the lever. A rat on an FR 50 schedule will show much the same pattern, except that the **postreinforcement pauses,** as they are called, will be longer. The greater the number of responses required for reinforcement, the longer the postreinforcement pause. Thus, reducing the ratio of responses to reinforcers from, say, 50:1 to 10:1 (that is, from FR 50 to FR 10) does not substantially increase the rate at which the animal responds once it has set to work; what it does do is shorten the breaks it takes after each reinforcer (see Figure 9-1a).

The reason for postreinforcement pauses is not clear. It is tempting to assume that they are due to fatigue. The animal makes a number of responses and then pauses as if to catch its breath before starting the next long run. But animals on other types of schedules often work even harder without pauses, so fatigue does not seem to be the answer.

Fixed ratio schedules are common outside the laboratory. Many games make use of fixed ratio schedules. In board games, for example, players often get one point for each correct answer. Perhaps the best examples of FR schedules involve work. Many employees are paid on a fixed ratio schedule, though it is usually called piece work. Often they are paid a certain amount for each piece (or for every 5, 10, or 100 pieces) they produce, as in the case of the garment worker who is paid so much for each shirt sewn, or the farm worker who is paid so much per basket of apples picked. Actually, in these two examples, as in most work examples, payment is not usually made upon completion of a set number of responses, but rather at the end of some period, such as the workweek (in the case of the garment worker) or the workday (in the case of the farm worker). Nevertheless, it is fair to call these FR schedules, because some record is kept of the number of responses, and this record serves as a secondary reinforcer. The farm worker may, for example, receive a token for each basket of apples picked. This token is a secondary reinforcer since it can be exchanged for payment at the end of the day.

■ Variable Ratio Schedules

Instead of reinforcing after a fixed number of responses, it is possible to vary the number of responses required around some average. For example, instead of reinforcing every fifth lever press, we might reinforce after the second response, then after the eighth response, then the sixth, the fourth, and so on. On such **variable ratio schedules,** usually abbreviated **VR,** the number of responses required for reinforcement varies around some average. In a VR 5 schedule, an average of five responses is required for each reinforcement.

Variable ratio schedules produce slightly higher response rates than fixed ratio schedules. Thus, an animal on a VR 50 schedule will produce more responses in an hour than an animal on an FR 50 schedule. This is so even though the actual payoff is the same for both animals. That is, the animal on an FR 50 schedule earns as much food for its 50 responses as the animal on a VR 50 schedule does (on average) for its 50 responses. Yet the animal on VR 50 responds at a higher rate (see Figure 9-1b). The difference in response rate is largely due to the postreinforcement pauses in the FR schedule, since such pauses are not a regular feature of VR schedules.

Variable ratio schedules are quite common in natural environments. As fast as the cheetah is, it does not bring down a victim every time it gives chase, nor can it depend on being successful on the second, third, or fourth try. There is no predicting which particular effort will be successful. It may be successful on two succeeding at-

The Unlucky Gambler

Most people look for an explanation of gambling, especially excessive gambling, in the gamblers themselves: They are morally weak; they are stupid; they have masochistic impulses. One way or another, the theory goes, there is something about them, some flaw, that makes them behave as they do.

Skinner (1953) suggests that the source of the problem might not be in the gambler, but in the gambler's experience. He notes that games of chance have variable ratio schedules of reinforcement and that behavior on such schedules can be extraordinarily persistent. But many people gamble without getting hooked. Why do some become compulsive gamblers while others do not? Psychiatrist Robert Custer (1984) suggested that the answer might be a winning streak and a big win early on.

Alan Christopher (1988) put the Skinner-Custer theory to the test. First, he trained two pigeons to obtain their daily food by pecking at an illuminated disk. Pecking at the disk paid off at a steady rate: 50 pecks earned three seconds at a food tray. This schedule allowed the birds to maintain normal body weight by working only about half an hour a day.

Next Christopher gave the birds a choice between working and gambling. He illuminated a disk that, like the lottery, paid off in an unpredictable way. But Christopher arranged things so that novice gamblers got "lucky": During the first three days, the pigeons could earn far more food by gambling than they could by working. And Christopher made sure that now and then the birds had a big win—up to 15 seconds at the food tray. After the third day, however, the birds were better off working than gambling. The question was, would they go back to work, or were they hooked on gambling?

They were hooked. The birds pounded relentlessly at the less rewarding gambling disk, so much so that they began to lose weight. Christopher prevented them from gambling for fear that they would starve themselves. Unable to gamble, the birds went back to work and began gaining weight. Christopher provided the gambling disk again to see if the birds had learned their lesson.

They had not. Once again they banged away at the gambler's disk and began losing weight. Christopher ended the experiment.

Whether the same sort of reinforcement history turns people into compulsive gamblers is uncertain. It is interesting to note, however, that pool hustlers and card sharks regularly let their "pigeons" win several games early on. It may be that a little good luck at the wrong time can turn anyone into a pigeon.

tempts, and then it may fail on the next ten tries. All that can be said is that, on average, one in every so many attempts will be reinforced.

Probably most predatory behavior is reinforced on VR schedules, though the exact schedule varies depending upon many factors. For instance, if the elk in a particular area are heavily infested by parasites, they will be easier for wolves to bring down. The reinforcement schedule for hunting elk will be relatively rich. As the wolves remove the sicker animals from the herd, however, the remaining elk will be harder to catch and kill, and the reinforcement ratio will thin out.

Variable ratio schedules are important in human society as well. A teacher may praise a student for good attendance, but the praise is not likely to come after every 30 days of uninterrupted attendance; the teacher may praise the student after 10 days, then after 40 days, then after 20. (This is not to say that the teacher works out this schedule in advance. Nevertheless, a schedule of reinforcement is in force.) The studying of college students is on a VR schedule when their instructor bases their grades on unannounced quizzes given an average of once a week but varying between zero and three times a week. Since the opportunities for reinforcement are unpredictable, students on such schedules who find good grades desirable (reinforcing) will tend to study frequently. And any student who regularly tries to find a parking space close to campus, even when success is unlikely, should be able to identify with the rat that presses a lever on a VR schedule. Gambling provides a more pernicious example of VR schedules in human life (see "The Unlucky Gambler").

> Query: Why do gambling casinos provide free chips to their newly arrived patrons? (See "The Unlucky Gambler.")

■ Fixed Interval Schedules

Reinforcement need not be based solely on the number of responses. In interval schedules, reinforcement is dispensed following a response, but only when the response occurs after a given period of time. In **fixed interval,** or **FI, schedules,** the response under study is reinforced the first time it occurs after a specified interval. Note that the reinforcer is not delivered merely because a given period of time has elapsed; a response is still required. For example, a pigeon that has learned to peck a disk may be put on an FI 5″ (read FI 5 second) reinforcement schedule. The first time the bird pecks the disk, food is delivered into its food tray, but for the next five seconds, disk pecking produces no reinforcement. Then, at the end of the five-second interval, the very next disk peck is reinforced.

Like fixed ratio schedules, fixed interval schedules produce postreinforcement pauses. Typically, the animal on an FI schedule makes few or no responses for some time after reinforcement, but gradually increases the rate of responding so that by the time the interval has elapsed, the response rate is quite high. Thus, FI schedules typically produce a scalloped-shaped response curve (see Figure 9-1c).

Why should FI schedules produce a scalloped-shaped curve while FR schedules produce a steady response rate between pauses? Possibly it is because the FR schedule reinforces steady responding, while the FI schedule does not. Consider first the case of a rat pressing a lever on an FR 50 schedule. The animal has a lot of work to do before it receives its next reinforcer, and any pause delays its arrival. Now consider the rat on an FI 50″ schedule. No responses will be reinforced until 50 seconds have passed, so responding during this period brings the animal no closer to reinforcement. The animal therefore makes relatively few responses until well into the interval—after, say, 20 seconds. Then it begins responding slowly, and rapidly increases its response rate until reinforcement.

We might expect that after some experience with this schedule, the rat would become more efficient. There is no advantage to responding after 20 seconds, so the rat might delay until, say, 40 seconds had elapsed. Surprisingly, this does not happen. No matter how long an organism is on an FI schedule, it persists in responding long before responding pays off, producing the familiar scalloped-shape cumulative response curve.

Good examples of FI schedules in the animal world are hard to come by. In many animal species, the females become sexually receptive at fairly regular intervals, and attempts by males to mate with them at other times are seldom reinforced. This therefore looks like an FI schedule. But estrus (sexual receptivity) is indicated by specific odors and other discriminative stimuli, and male sexual behavior is more likely to be under the control of these stimuli than of the passage of time.

Examples of fixed interval schedules in humans are easier to think of, perhaps because we more often live by the clock. Your behavior is on an FI schedule when you bake bread in an oven since checking the bread will be reinforced only when it occurs after a specified period. The first time you bake bread, you may open the oven door repeatedly to check on its progress. But with experience you learn to wait until the required baking time has nearly elapsed before peeking inside the oven.

Studying may provide another example. Many students show little inclination to study during the early days of the semester, but spend increasing amounts of time studying as midterm exams approach. After midterms, their study time falls off sharply until shortly before finals. Plotted on a curve, studying would then show the familiar scalloped curve of FI schedules. It has been said that studying is not an example of an FI schedule, since the behavior that is reinforced is not studying but rather writing answers to test questions (Malone, 1990). However, being able to write good test answers may be a reinforcer for studying. The closer students get to the availability of reinforcement for studying, the more they study. Student procrastination, it would seem, is partly the result of FI reinforcement schedules.

Query: Assuming that a response takes one second to perform, on which schedule are more reinforcements available, FR 10 or FI 10"?

■ Variable Interval Schedules

Instead of reinforcing a response after a fixed interval, it is possible to vary the interval during which responses are not reinforced around some average. For example, instead of reinforcing disk pecking after a fixed interval of five seconds, we might reinforce a response after two seconds, then after eight seconds, six seconds, four seconds, and so forth. On such **variable interval,** or **VI, schedules,** the length of the interval during which responses are not reinforced varies around some average. In a VI 5″ schedule, the average interval between reinforced responses is five seconds.

Variable interval schedules produce higher response rates than FI schedules, though not so high as FR and VR schedules. As with VR schedules, variable interval schedules are free of postreinforcement pauses. The animal responds at a steady rate, pausing only long enough to consume the reinforcers delivered to it (see Figure 9-1d).

We can find VI schedules in natural environments as well as in the lab. Leopards often lie in wait for their prey rather than stalk it. Sometimes the wait is short, sometimes long, but remaining alert and waiting quietly are eventually reinforced by the appearance of prey. The same sort of behavior may be seen in many other predators, including spiders and snakes.

Human hunters also lie in wait for game. Deer hunters typically take a position in a tree or another high point and wait for a deer to appear within range. Sometimes they wait for hours; sometimes a deer appears almost immediately. Similarly, the nature photographer is on a VI schedule since he or she must wait varying lengths of time before having the opportunity to get a good picture. Air traffic controllers who watch a radar screen are also on a VI schedule, since the signals for which they watch occur at irregular intervals. We also find ourselves on VI schedules when we must wait in line at the bank or the theater.

■ Other Simple Schedules

The reinforcement schedules just described are the bedrock of schedules work: Quite possibly more research has been done involving these schedules than all other schedules combined. Yet there are other simple schedules that have received considerable attention.

In a **fixed time,** or **FT, schedule,** a reinforcer is delivered after a given period of time without regard to behavior. You will recall from Chapter Six that Skinner established superstitious behavior in pigeons by providing reinforcement every 15 seconds regardless of what the birds did. The birds were on an FT 15″ schedule. The birds were not required to do anything at the end of the 15 seconds to obtain reinforcement; reinforcement was time contingent, but not response contingent.

Fixed time schedules resemble fixed interval schedules except that in the latter the performance of a particular response is required. In an FI 10″ schedule, for instance, a rat may receive food after a ten-second interval, but only if it presses a lever. In an FT 10″ schedule, the rat would receive food every ten seconds whether it pressed the lever or not. Research on superstitious behavior suggests that animals and people on FT schedules have a tendency to respond as if reinforcement were response contingent (see Chapter Six).

Fixed time schedules are not common outside of the laboratory. Unemployment compensation and welfare payments do not precisely meet the definition of fixed time schedules, but they come close. Although certain responses are nominally required (for example, those receiving unemployment compensation are required to look for work), in fact money is provided more or less independently of what the person does. The only true response requirement is standing in line for the check. Social critics who would replace welfare with "workfare" are suggesting that money should be response contingent rather than time contingent.

In **variable time,** or **VT, schedules,** reinforcement is delivered periodically at irregular intervals. As in FT schedules, reinforcement does not depend upon the performance of a response, but in VT schedules the reinforcer is delivered at intervals that vary about some average. VT schedules resemble situations in which superstitious behavior is common. Some people would argue, for example, that sports fishing is largely a matter of luck, rather than skill, which means success is not particularly response contingent. Periodically the angler gets lucky, and the use of a particular lure or kind of bait is adventitiously reinforced. This may explain why people who fish a lot are apt to be enthusiastic about many different kinds of lures and baits. (Dedicated anglers will insist, of course, that there is nothing superstitious about their behavior.)

In another schedule, reinforcement is response contingent, but a response is reinforced only if it occurs after a specified interval of time since the last response. A rat might receive food for pressing a lever, for instance, but only if there has been a pause of, say, five seconds since the last lever press. This schedule, called **differential reinforcement of low rate,** or **DRL,** can result in very low response rates.

DRL schedules are easy to confuse with FI schedules, but there is one important difference. In an FI schedule, the interval begins after reinforcement; in a DRL schedule, the interval begins after the last response. In an FI 5″ schedule, a pigeon that pecks a disk receives reinforcement for pecking so long as five seconds have elapsed since the last reinforcement. It need only respond once after five seconds, but there is no penalty for responding before the five seconds have elapsed. In a DRL 5″ schedule, a pigeon that pecks a disk receives reinforcement only if five seconds have elapsed since the last disk peck. Each response resets the clock, as it were, so that responding before the interval is up delays reinforcement.

The longer the interval required between responses, the slower the rate of responding. A DRL 5″ schedule would permit a maximum of 12 responses per minute. Responding before the prescribed interval is up further reduces the number of reinforcements received per minute, as does responding after a longer interval than is required.

You can see that DRL schedules can produce extremely low response rates.

We may see something close to a DRL schedule in situations where it is necessary to work with great care. Small children are likely to have accidents when pouring milk, so they are often admonished to take their time and are praised for doing so. Adults who work in art restoration may be under a similar reinforcement schedule. If they work quickly, they may do irreparable damage; success depends upon performing at a low rate.

> Query: In a DRL 10″ schedule, what would be the effect of responding eight seconds after reinforcement?

The logical opposite of the DRL schedule is the **DRH** schedule, short for **differential reinforcement of high rate.** DRH schedules require that a minimum number of responses occur in a given period. A pigeon might be required, for example, to peck a disk five times in a ten-second period. If it produces fewer than five responses during the interval, it receives nothing. DRH schedules can produce extremely high rates of responding, higher than any other kind of schedule.

DRL and DRH schedules are not often encountered outside of the laboratory. They may, however, be put to good use in applied settings. DRL schedules might be used, for example, to help a person reduce the rate of a particular response, such as smoking. Similarly, DRH schedules might find use where the problem is a low rate of responding, as in the case of the student who seldom participates in class discussions.

Another schedule that has been particularly useful in applied settings is called **differential reinforcement of other behavior,** or **DRO.** DRO is used as an alternative to punishment as a way of reducing the frequency of unwanted behavior. Some nursing home residents spend almost all of their time watching television. This contributes to their physical deterioration and possibly to their intellectual deterioration as well. The staff could restrict access to the television, but this is apt to cause resentment. A better approach is to reinforce other kinds of behavior. This can be done by providing reinforcement (in the form of additional attention, treats, compliments, and the like) whenever a resident reads, visits with other people, walks about, or does anything except watch TV.

A similar schedule, **differential reinforcement of incompatible behavior,** or **DRI,** serves much the same purpose. In DRI, a response that is incompatible with an undesired response is reinforced. Moving is incompatible with remaining still, standing is incompatible with sitting, smiling is incompatible with frowning. Reinforcing a response that is incompatible with the unwanted behavior rapidly reduces the frequency of the unwanted behavior. The child who earns admiration from others by getting into fights will change his behavior quickly if praise can be earned only through cooperative behavior. The person who speaks far too loudly will lower his or her voice if people look at him only when he or she speaks more softly.

■ Stretching the Ratio

Rats will press levers and pigeons will peck disks hundreds of times for a single reinforcer, even if that reinforcer is a small amount of food. People have also been known to respond steadily on a very thin schedule of reinforcement. How is this possible?

The answer is shaping. An experimenter does not train a rat to press a lever and then put the animal on, say, an FR 1,000 schedule. The experimenter gradually shapes persistent responding. The experimenter might start with a CRF schedule and, when the animal is responding at a steady rate, increase the ratio to FR 3; when this schedule has been in force awhile, the experimenter may go to FR 5, then FR 8, FR 12, FR 20, FR 30, and so on. This procedure is known as **stretching the ratio** (Skinner, 1968), but you can see that it is the same shaping process used to shape any new behavior.

Card sharks and pool hustlers let their competitors win frequently during the early stages and then gradually win more and more of the games. They stretch the ratio gradually because they do not want to "lose their pigeon." Stretching the ratio can be put to more benevolent purposes. Parents, for example, may reinforce the behavior called studying each time it occurs. Gradually, however, they may reinforce the behavior less often. This thinning of the reinforcement schedule is very useful, up to a point, since it makes it more likely that the behavior will persist when the parents are not around to provide reinforcement.

> Query: How could stretching the ratio be used to establish the personality trait called perseverance?

Stretching the ratio must be done with some care since, if we stretch too rapidly, responding will be disrupted, a phenomenon called **ratio strain.** Even if great care is used, there is a limit to how thin the schedule can get. The more we stretch the schedule, the closer we get to an extinction schedule.

■ Extinction

One way reinforcement schedules differ is in the density of reinforcement. At one extreme we find continuous reinforcement, in which every single occurrence of a response is reinforced. At the other ex-

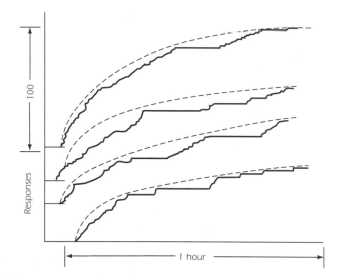

FIGURE 9-2 Extinction curves. Lever pressing was reinforced on a CRF schedule, then put on extinction. The curves show typical decreases in response rate in four rats. SOURCE: B. F. Skinner, *The Behavior of Organisms: An Experimental Analysis.* Copyright 1938, renewed 1966, p. 75. Reprinted by permission of B. F. Skinner.

treme we find **extinction,** a schedule in which a response is never reinforced. Although extinction is a schedule of nonreinforcement, it can be thought of as a fixed ratio schedule in which an infinite number of responses are required for reinforcement.

In an early study of extinction, Skinner (1938) trained rats to press a lever and then, after about 100 responses had been reinforced, disconnected the feeding magazine. Everything was as it had been during training, except that now lever pressing no longer produced food. The result, as you might expect, was a gradual decline in the rate of lever pressing (see Figure 9-2).

Extinction was later used outside the laboratory to get rid of unwanted behavior. A well-known study by Carl Williams (1959) provides an example. A 21-month-old boy insisted that someone stay with him when he took his afternoon nap. If the adult left the room before the child was asleep, the boy would go into a rage and cry until the adult returned. Of course, when the adult returned, this reinforced crying. What were the parents to do? Williams advised them to put the tantrums on extinction: The child was to be put to bed and left alone. No matter how loudly the child protested, the parents were not to return to the room until the child's nap time was over. As you can see from Figure 9-3, the result was a steady decline in the time spent throwing tantrums, the same sort of decline in response rate Skinner found in his rats.

extinction = no reinforcement

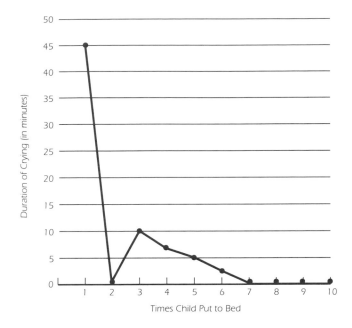

FIGURE 9-3 Extinction of crying. (After Williams, 1959.)

The principal effect of extinction, as the foregoing examples illustrate, is the steady decline in the rate of a previously reinforced response. A second effect is an increase in the variability of behavior. A rat that has learned to press a lever for food may, during extinction, press the lever harder, or use its nose instead of its forepaw, or use two forepaws instead of one. Other behavior, not previously much in evidence, may become more common. The rat may sniff about the lever, stand on its hind legs, move about the cage, and look into the empty food tray. We see the same increase in the variability of human behavior during extinction. A person who repeatedly puts coins into a vending machine only to have them fall into the return tray is apt to insert the coins in a different order, shove them into the slot more forcefully or more gently, and so on. If these efforts are not reinforced, other behavior will appear: The customer is apt to look around, press the coin return several times, reach into the food tray, and talk aloud to the machine.

A third effect of extinction is the appearance of emotional behavior, particularly aggression. Rats that have received food for pressing a lever have been known to bite the lever when pressing it no longer produced reinforcement. The aggression will be directed at another animal if one is handy, even though the other animal was in no way responsible for the failure of the reinforcer to arrive (Azrin et al., 1966; Rilling & Caplan, 1973). Research also provides evidence that extinction can produce an increase in aggressive behavior in humans (for example, Todd et al., 1989). Such behavior will be familiar to anyone

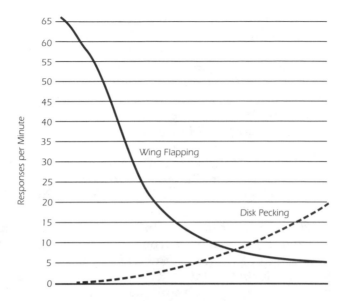

FIGURE 9-4 Resurgence. When a response (wing flapping) is put on extinction, a previously reinforced response (disk pecking) reappears. (Hypothetical data.)

who has ever kicked a stuck door, slammed down a telephone receiver when a call did not go through, or pounded on a defective vending machine.

Extinction sometimes has a fourth effect upon behavior: the appearance of previously effective behavior. Suppose a pigeon is trained to peck a disk on a VI schedule, and then this response is put on extinction. Now suppose some new response, such as wing flapping, is reinforced. When the bird is flapping steadily, we again withhold reinforcement. During this second extinction, the frequency of wing flapping declines as expected, but something else also occurs: The bird begins to peck the disk again. As the rate of wing flapping declines, the rate of disk pecking increases (see Figure 9-4). Robert Epstein (1983, 1985) has named this phenomenon **resurgence,** since the earlier behavior resurges.

Resurgence has only recently been submitted to experimental analysis, but it has been observed by many researchers over the past 50 years (Epstein, 1983, 1985). Karen Pryor and her colleagues (1969) describe an instance of resurgence in a porpoise. An animal named Hou often received reinforcement for performing a response learned in the previous training session. If this response was not reinforced, Hou would then run through its repertoire of previously learned responses: breaching, swimming upside down, and so on.

The notion of resurgence may help us understand what clinicians call regression, the tendency to return to more primitive, infantile modes of behavior (Epstein, 1983, 1985). The husband who is unable to get his wife to behave as he would like by asking her nicely may resort to having a tantrum, a form of behavior that got good results with his mother when he was a boy. The behavior "asking nicely" is on extinction, and the man reverts to a form of behavior that had been reinforced in similar situations in the past. However, Epstein notes that there is no need to assume, as Sigmund Freud did, that the response that resurges will be more primitive than the behavior it replaces. It need only be a response that had once been effective; it may be more primitive than the behavior now on extinction, but it need not be.

One extinction session is often not enough to extinguish behavior. This is often so even when the extinction session lasts for several hours and involves hundreds or even thousands of unreinforced responses. What usually happens is this: The response rate declines and finally stabilizes at or near its pretraining level. Extinction appears to be complete, and the animal is returned to its home cage. If, however, the animal is later put back into the training situation, it again responds as it had during training. This reappearance of a previously extinguished response is called **spontaneous recovery.** The longer the interval between the two sessions, the greater the recovery.

We may witness spontaneous recovery in everyday situations. A person who has made a number of unsuccessful attempts to get food from a defective vending machine may give up, but may try once again when passing by the machine later in the day. This reappearance of the behavior is spontaneous recovery. Likewise, the teacher who finds that he or she has been reinforcing silly comments by smiling when they are made may put the behavior on extinction by not smiling. The frequency of silly remarks will fall off, only to reappear unexpectedly. This reappearance is spontaneous recovery.

Spontaneous recovery is not much of a problem in the laboratory, but it can undermine gains in applied settings. The trouble is that when an extinguished response reappears, it is likely to be reinforced. In the Williams experiment, crying recovered spontaneously and was inadvertently reinforced when an adult looked in on the child. The tantrums reappeared and had to be extinguished again. The second extinction proceeded rapidly, and the problem behavior was soon gone for good.

If a response is kept continuously on an extinction schedule, it will continue to decline in frequency. When the response no longer occurs, or occurs no more often than it did before training, it is said to have been extinguished. The rate at which extinction occurs depends upon a number of factors, including the number of reinforced responses (Williams, 1938; see Figure 9-5) and the effort required in responding (Capehart et al., 1958; see Figure 9-6). The most important variable, however, is the reinforcement schedule before extinction.

Extinction proceeds rapidly following continuous reinforcement but much more slowly following intermittent reinforcement, a phenomenon known as the **partial reinforcement effect** or PRE

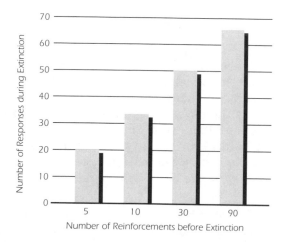

FIGURE 9-5   Extinction as a function of reinforcement. The average number of responses made during extinction increased with the number of reinforced responses prior to extinction. (After Williams, 1938.)

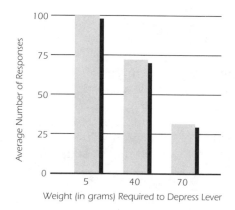

FIGURE 9-6   Effort and extinction. The more force required to depress a lever, the fewer responses made during extinction. SOURCE: Compiled from data in Capehart et al., 1958.

(Humphreys, 1939). It is a very robust phenomenon and has been demonstrated in both animals and humans many times. Thin reinforcement schedules can result in remarkable resistance to extinction. Harlan Lane and Paul Shinkman (1963), for example, put a college student on extinction after reinforcing responses on a VI 100" schedule. The student then worked for 11 hours without reinforcement, and made over 8,000 unreinforced responses!

The fact that intermittent reinforcement produces extinction-resistant behavior can cause considerable difficulty. You may recall the story about the people who shaped persistent barking in their dog by requiring longer and longer periods of barking (see Chapter Five). They had shaped persistent barking by reinforcing on an intermittent schedule and gradually stretching the ratio. Very likely the dog's owners had no idea that they created the problem by occasionally reinforcing barking. Similarly, the parents whose child has terrible, hour-long tantrums may reject the psychologist's suggestion that the tantrums are the product of parental reinforcement. "That can't be it," they may say, "After all, we hardly ever give in to her demands." The key words are, of course, *hardly ever.* By occasionally reinforcing tantrumming, the parents have taught the child that persistence pays off.

> Query: Explain why occasional reinforcement of misbehavior can
> be worse than frequent reinforcement.

Nevertheless, even behavior maintained on an intermittent schedule will eventually succumb to an extinction schedule. It is not possible to say, however, that extinction has entirely undone the effects of training. Even after many hours of extinction and thousands of unreinforced responses, the behavior may occur with a frequency that exceeds its baseline level. There is considerable doubt, in fact, as to whether a well-established response can ever be truly extinguished, in the sense that the organism's tendency to make the response is no greater than it was before training (see, for example, Razran, 1956). To paraphrase Shakespeare: What's done can ne'er be (entirely) undone.

Extinction and the other simple schedules discussed thus far are the elements of schedules research. These simple elements can be combined to form a variety of complex schedules.

COMPLEX SCHEDULES

Complex schedules consist of various combinations of simple schedules. We will consider only a few complex schedules here.

In a **multiple schedule,** a response is under the control of two or more simple schedules, each associated with a particular stimulus. A pigeon that has learned to peck a disk for grain may be put on a multiple schedule in which pecking is reinforced on an FI 10″ schedule when a red light is on, but on a VR 10 schedule when a yellow light is on. The two reinforcement schedules alternate, with the changes indicated by changes in the light. The experimenter refers to this as a MULT FI 10″ VR 10 schedule. The bird's cumulative record shows the familiar scalloped curve of FI schedules when the red light is on, followed by the rapid, steady responding associated with VR schedules when the yellow light is on (see Figure 9-7).

In a **chain schedule,** reinforcement is delivered only upon comple-

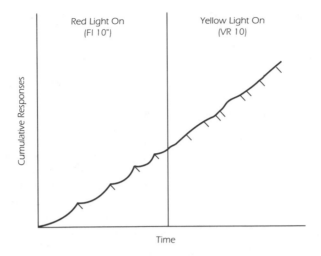

FIGURE 9-7 *Multiple schedule. A pigeon's rate and pattern of responding changes when a stimulus indicates a change in the reinforcement schedule in force. (Hypothetical data.)*

tion of the last in a series of schedules. Consider a pigeon on a CHAIN FR 10 FI 15″ VR 20 schedule: The bird pecks a red disk; after the tenth response, the disk changes from red to yellow. The yellow disk signals that an FI 15″ schedule is in effect; after 15 seconds, pecking the disk changes it from yellow to green. Pecking the green disk results, after an average of 20 responses, in food. The disk also becomes red again, indicating that the FR 10 schedule is once again in force. Note that, unlike the multiple schedule, the bird receives food only after completing the response requirement of the last schedule. Despite this, the bird typically responds just as though food were provided on each of the separate schedules. When it is on the FI 15 schedule, for example, it shows the typical scalloped response curve.

Chain schedules give rise to an interesting question: What reinforces responding? Apparently, discriminative stimuli, such as the disk colors, indicate not only that a new schedule is in force but that the organism is one step closer to reinforcement. These discriminative stimuli act as secondary reinforcers.

In the schedules discussed thus far, only one schedule is available at any given moment. In **concurrent schedules,** two or more schedules are available at once. A pigeon may have the option of pecking a red disk on a VR 50 schedule or pecking a yellow disk on a VR 20 schedule. In other words, the concurrent schedule involves a choice. In the example just given, the bird would soon choose the yellow disk and the VR 20 schedule.

Since a great deal of behavior can be thought of as involving choices, we will consider this problem in greater detail.

Scheduled Neurosis

There are many ways to become neurotic. We saw in Chapter Eight that an animal will behave bizarrely if required to make increasingly subtle discriminations for reinforcement. Other research shows that animals behave peculiarly under certain reinforcement schedules. Schedules that include both reinforcement and punishment seem especially likely to produce neurotic behavior.

For instance, Jules Masserman (1943) taught a cat to lift a cover to find food. When this response was well established, Masserman changed the consequences: Now when the cat lifted a cover, it would find food, but sometimes it would receive a blast of air or a brief electric shock as well. The result was that the cat quickly learned not to make the response, but in addition, it displayed rather unusual behavior. "For instance," writes Masserman, "Cat 53 was a moderately quiet animal in which two air-blasts abolished further feeding responses but produced a fidgety, incessant pacing and shifting from side to side," among other symptoms. Other cats became extremely passive. One animal would lie so still "he appeared to be asleep; moreover, he could be placed in various cataleptic postures for periods of from ten to twenty minutes" (p. 67).

All of us have had experiences similar to those of Masserman's cats, though usually the consequences involved are secondary reinforcers and punishers. The woman who feels she is due for a raise may become irritable and fidgety before knocking at the boss's door if past requests for raises have been acceded to only after unpleasant scenes. The man who has trouble getting dates may agree to go out with a woman who treats him with contempt but will probably be ambivalent about doing so and may become depressed.

It is not certain whether such mixed consequences play an important role in human neurosis, but it seems certain that they complicate our lives. If the environment always answered us in a clear and consistent manner, there might be fewer troubled people; unfortunately, our environment often has us on a more complex schedule. Sometimes it seems to be a schedule designed for neurosis.

CHOICE AND THE MATCHING LAW

A concurrent schedule represents a choice. The pigeon on such a schedule may make one response (peck the red disk) or another (peck the yellow disk). It cannot do both simultaneously, so a choice exists. In recent years, psychologists have become increasingly interested in the study of behavior in such situations.

Making a choice may involve a great deal of thought. Human beings faced with a choice often verbalize silently, and sometimes aloud, about the relative merits of the various response alternatives. It is possible that animals engage in analogous behavior when faced with a choice. However, our interest in choice is not in these cogitations, but in the effect that the reinforcement schedules have upon the choices made. The task is to be able to predict, from the reinforcement schedules in force, how the person or animal will respond in a choice situation.

Sometimes this is easy to do. Imagine a rat in a T-maze arranged so that if the rat enters the arm on the right, it will receive food, but if it enters the arm on the left, it will receive a shock. We have no difficulty in predicting that after a few trials, the rat will regularly choose to turn right rather than left. A choice situation in which response A is always reinforced and response B is always punished quickly results in the reliable performance of response A. We can also predict with confidence the outcome of a choice between a CRF schedule and an extinction schedule.

Prediction becomes more difficult, however, when both alternatives are reinforced, and the only difference is in the relative frequency of reinforcement. Consider the case of a pigeon given a choice between pecking either of two disks, one red, the other yellow. Pecking the red disk is reinforced on an FR 50 schedule, and pecking the yellow disk is reinforced on an FR 75 schedule. What will the pigeon do? Perhaps it will go back and forth repeatedly between the two disks. Or perhaps it will work steadily at one disk, but the disk will be selected at random, so that one pigeon will peck at yellow, another at red.

What happens is that the pigeon initially spends some time at each disk, moving back and forth between them, but it eventually settles on the disk associated with the richer reinforcement schedule. In fact, some animals have an uncanny knack for selecting the more rewarding work. Humans have the same ability to discriminate between similar reinforcement schedules (Pierce & Epling, 1983).

Richard Herrnstein (1961, 1970; Herrnstein & Mazur, 1987) has led the way in the study of choice and has shown that the tendency to choose the better of two reinforcement schedules can be expressed by the formula

$$\frac{R_1}{R_2} = \frac{r_1}{r_2}$$

What this formula means is that, given two responses, R_1 and R_2, each on its own reinforcement schedule, r_1 and r_2, respectively, the relative frequency of each response equals the relative frequency of reinforcement available. This statement is called the **Matching Law** since the response frequency matches the reinforcement frequency (Herrnstein, 1961, 1970; see Davison & McCarthy, 1988, for a review).

A choice situation involving different schedules of reinforcement can be viewed as a kind of discrimination task (see Chapter Eight). In the case of two ratio schedules, such as FR 30 and FR 40, the subject samples each and then settles on the denser schedule. In concurrent ratio schedules, it makes sense to identify the higher-paying schedule as quickly as possible and to remain loyal to it. Switching back and forth between two ratio schedules is pointless. In the same way, if you can pick beans for Farmer Able for $5 a bushel, or for Farmer Baker for $4 a bushel, it makes little sense to switch back and forth. Other things being equal, your behavior will follow the Matching Law: You will pick steadily for Farmer Able.

Query: State the Matching Law in your own words.

Switching makes more sense when concurrent interval schedules are involved. Consider the case of an animal on a concurrent FI 10″ FI 30″ schedule. Clearly, the payoff is better on the FI 10″ schedule, so it makes sense for the animal to spend most of its time working on that schedule. But even on that schedule, there are periods during which responding is useless. Some of this time could be spent responding on the FI 30″ schedule. And the longer the animal works on the FI 10″ schedule, the more likely it is that a response on the FI 30″ schedule will be reinforced. It therefore makes sense for the animal to devote most of its effort to the FI 10″ schedule but to make a few responses on the FI 30″ schedule. In fact, this is what happens.

What about concurrent VI schedules? Suppose a rat has a choice between VI 10″ and VI 30″ schedules. Once again it makes sense for the rat to devote most of its time to the VI 10″ schedule, but occasional responses on the VI 30″ schedule are also likely to be reinforced. This is so even though delivery of reinforcement is variable and therefore unpredictable. Once again, animals behave in the most sensible manner: They focus on the VI 10″ schedule, but periodically abandon this schedule to respond on the VI 30″ schedule. In this way, they receive more reinforcements than they would if they focused solely on the better-paying VI 10″ schedule. Even when the differences in schedules are fairly subtle, animals usually respond in a manner that is in their best interests.

We have seen that, given a choice between two interval schedules, an animal will alternate between them. Is it possible to predict, on the basis of the schedules in force, how often an animal will respond on each schedule? Herrnstein (1961, 1970) has found that it is indeed possible. He reports that in a two-choice situation, response choice can be predicted according to the mathematical expression

$$\frac{R_A}{R_A + R_B} = \frac{r_A}{r_A + r_B}$$

where R_A and R_B represent two responses, A and B, and r_A and r_B represent the reinforcement rates for responses A and B, respectively. This equation is merely a reformulation of the Matching Law. The idea is that the proportion of responses matches the proportion of reinforcement available.

Take the case of a rat trained to press a lever for food. Presses on lever A are reinforced on a VI 10″ schedule; presses on lever B are reinforced on a VI 30″ schedule. If the rat were to respond solely on the VI 10″ schedule, it would receive a maximum of six reinforcers per minute. If it occasionally responded to the VI 30″ schedule, it could obtain a maximum of two more reinforcers. Thus, of the total reinforcers obtainable, 75% (six out of eight) are available on the VI 10″ schedule, and 25% are available on the VI 30″ schedule. The value of r_A is therefore .75; that of r_B is .25. This means that the rat will devote approximately three-fourths of its responses (.75 = 75%) to schedule A (the VI 10″ schedule) and one-fourth of its responses to schedule B (VI 30″). Experimental tests show that such predictions are surprisingly accurate.

Herrnstein has extended the Matching Law beyond the two-choice situation, suggesting that every situation represents a kind of choice. Consider the pigeon that receives food when it pecks a disk. There are many responses the pigeon can make besides pecking the disk. The bird might, for instance, groom itself, wander around the cage, peck at objects on the floor or on the walls, or sleep. In pecking the disk, it is making a choice between that response and several alternative responses. Indeed, even when the pigeon pecks the disk at a high rate, it continues to engage in other kinds of behavior, such as bobbing its head and turning to the left and right. Theoretically, it is possible to identify all of these responses and the reinforcers that maintain them and to predict the relative frequency of any one of them. This idea can be expressed by the formula

$$\frac{R_A}{R_A + R_O} = \frac{r_A}{r_A + r_O}$$

where R_A represents the particular response we are studying, R_O represents all other responses, r_A represents the reinforcers available for R_A, and r_O represents the reinforcers available for all other responses (Herrnstein, 1970). This formula has less predictive value than the formula for the two-choice situation, since it is not usually possible to specify all the responses that may occur, nor all the reinforcers those responses may produce. Some responses may, for example, be reinforced by events not readily subject to observation, as in the case of the reinforcement a rat receives when it scratches an itch. Still, the formula reminds us that behavior is a function of the reinforcers available for any behavior that might occur, not merely the reinforcers available for the behavior that interests us at the moment.

It is not clear how animals and people discriminate between subtle differences in reinforcement schedules. However, it is clear that the ability to do so is highly adaptive. The value of matching response choice to reinforcement schedules is easy to see in the case of foraging for food. If food is more plentiful in one area than another, the animal that chooses to forage where food is more abundant has a better chance of surviving. Similarly, predators often have a choice of prey animals. The lion probably works on the best schedule when it pursues

Experimental Economics

Some psychologists and economists have drawn a parallel between research on reinforcement schedules and economics and have made them the foundation of a new field called **experimental economics.**

Certain economic principles have been found to hold in animal experiments. For instance, economists know that when the price of a luxury item rises, the consumption of that item declines. But when the price of an essential item, such as food, rises, there is little change in consumption. The same phenomenon has been demonstrated in rats. Rats will work for psychoactive drugs (a luxury), but increases in the price of a drug (the number of lever presses required for a dose) usually result in decreased consumption; yet large increases in the price of food (an essential) do not lower consumption substantially (Hursh, 1980, 1984).

Other studies have examined economic principles experimentally in human groups. In one study, Ray Battalio and John Kagel (reported in Alexander, 1980) studied the behavior of female patients on the psychiatric ward of a state hospital. The patients could earn tokens for performing various tasks and exchange them for cigarettes, candy, and other items. This can be construed as a choice between activities (making one's bed, doing laundry) for which tokens are available, and activities (watching television, sleeping) for which other reinforcers are available. The situation resembles the society outside the hospital, where people usually have a choice between working for pay or participating in various leisure activities.

One thing the researchers were interested in was how the reinforcers would be distributed among the patients. That is, would each person accumulate about the same number of tokens or would some people end up with far more than others, as is the case for the United States population as a whole? The results revealed that those in the top 20% of patients held a total of 41% of all tokens, while those in the bottom 20% held only 7%. This distribution of wealth closely approximated that of the general population at the time.

It appears from such research that economics might be well on its way to becoming a true experimental science.

---

animals that are old, sick, or injured, and this is what it usually does. It fares even better if it chooses to take a prize away from a weaker predator, such as the cheetah, and it will do this when the opportunity arises.

Humans likewise benefit from the ability to match responses to reinforcement. No doubt for most of human existence, people have made good use of the ability to apportion responses appropriately among the hunting and foraging areas available. Today, a farmer might do this by devoting most available farmland to a crop that produces a nice profit under typical weather conditions and planting a smaller area in a less lucrative crop that does well under adverse weather conditions. The rest of us do the same thing when we spend more time at a high-paying job than at a low-paying one. College students obey the Matching Law when they devote more time to a five-credit course than to a one-credit course, since a high grade in the former pays better (contributes more to grade point average) than a high grade in the latter. We follow the same principle when we spend more time with someone whose company we enjoy than with someone we find tiresome.

The Matching Law has been found to be a robust phenomenon. It holds for a wide variety of species, responses, reinforcers, and reinforcement schedules (see deVilliers, 1977, for a review). It holds, for example, whether we are considering different rates of reinforcement (Herrnstein, 1970), different amounts of reinforcement (Todorov et al., 1984), or different reinforcement delays (Catania, 1966). And it holds for punishment schedules as well as reinforcement schedules (Baum, 1975). The Matching Law does not always work, and it is the subject of considerable debate, some of it quite rancorous (Binmore, 1991; Herrnstein, 1990, 1991; Staddon, 1991). It has, however, proved its worth as a stimulus to research.

There are, of course, choice situations in which humans and beasts do not respond intelligently. The peculiar nature of the contingencies in these situations trick us into behaving foolishly. Let us now consider these contingency traps.

CONTINGENCY TRAPS

The typical mousetrap is a simple affair: A bit of bait, when taken, releases a metal bar that is under tension. There is an economic exchange: The mouse gets to eat a bit of cheese, and it pays for that treat at the risk of its life. When looked at closely, many situations in both animal and human life bear a striking resemblance to the mousetrap.

John Platt (1973; cf. Hardin, 1968), a physicist turned behavioral scientist, identified the contingencies implicit in traps. The trap provides some consequences that are reinforcing and other consequences that are punishing. The reinforcing consequences are immediate and nearly certain, while the punishing consequences are delayed and uncertain. The immediate, high-probability events outweigh the remote, low-probability events.

Platt proposed that many kinds of apparently senseless behavior are the products of situations with these same kinds of contingencies. He called these situations *social traps,* but since their essence is not their social nature but their contingencies, a better term would be **contingency traps.** A great deal of research has been done on contingency traps (see Cross & Guyer, 1980, for a review); this research shows that they account for a good deal of otherwise puzzling behavior.

The most frequently cited example of a contingency trap is cigarette smoking. The positive consequences of smoking include peer approval (especially for children and adolescents) and escape from withdrawal symptoms. The negative consequences include emphysema, heart disease, stroke, cancer, and other diseases. By any objective measure, the negative consequences of smoking far outweigh the positive consequences. Why then do people smoke?

The answer appears to be that the positive consequences are immediate and certain, while the negative consequences are remote and uncertain. Smoking might kill a person or turn him or her into an invalid, but it takes years to do it. Moreover, these adverse consequences are not sure to occur. Even some heavy smokers outlive their nonsmoking peers. Such contingencies are the essence of a contingency trap, and this is what catches the smoker.

Contingency traps also help explain why people perform many other unsafe acts, such as driving a car at excessive speeds (Fuller, 1991). The reinforcing consequences of driving fast (the excitement, the admiration of one's peers, reaching a destination on time) are immediate and almost certain, while the aversive consequences (having an accident) are unlikely to occur during any given ride.

Credit card debt offers a different kind of example of a contingency trap. Americans who had credit cards owed, on average, over $1,400 on their cards in 1986 (Sivy, 1987). More than 20 million Americans are financially overextended (Sivy, 1987; Rudoph, 1986), and this is no doubt partly due to the misuse of credit cards.

Why do people misuse credit cards? Again, the answer seems to be that a contingency trap is involved. Buying an item with plastic is immediately reinforced. If you are hungry, you can go into a restaurant and eat. If you see a pair of shoes that are exactly what you need to go with that brown suit you just bought, then you can take those shoes immediately and start wearing the suit. The negative consequences of buying on credit are less certain and far more remote. The bill does not arrive until the end of the month, and you need only make a partial payment, so even then it's not very painful. Of course, if you continue to run up bills, you may eventually have to sell your car, move to a smaller apartment, quit school, and go to work full time—but that might never happen. And, here, today, is this beautiful yellow sweater—and it's on sale!

The use of drugs during pregnancy may provide another example of a contingency trap. Using alcohol, cocaine, and other psychoactive drugs while pregnant can result in hyperactivity, learning disabilities, lower IQs, and physical deformities in offspring (Hawkins, 1983; Overholser, 1990). Although heavy doses of such drugs are most likely to damage the fetus, even small doses may be harmful (Bolton, 1983). These facts have been widely publicized in magazines and newspapers, yet the behavior persists. Apparently this is because the reinforcing consequences are certain and immediate, while the aversive consequences are uncertain and distant.

> **Query:** Teen pregnancy is a serious problem in the United States. How might this problem be the result of a contingency trap?

A different kind of contingency trap may induce us to avoid doing something we ought to do. A common example is putting off a visit to the dentist. Everyone recognizes that this is foolish, yet many people do it. Probably this is because putting off the visit means avoiding discomfort and expense, and these consequences are immediate and certain. The negative consequences of putting off the visit (serious and costly dental work) are distant and uncertain. When a dental problem becomes very painful, one benefit of delaying a visit no longer exists. This may explain why dentists commonly see people in agony who could have saved themselves some suffering had they come in sooner. The same contingencies probably account for the failure of many women to have routine mammograms and of men to have prostate exams.

Groups as well as individuals are affected by contingency traps. Consider the company that produces thousands of tons of toxins each year. If released into the air, these toxins contribute to lung cancer and emphysema and to the acid rain that destroys our forests and eats away the granite sculptures in our cities. Disposing of the toxins in this way seems insane, but consider the contingencies in force: By releasing the toxins into the air, the company saves millions of dollars on pollution control measures, and this consequence is immediate and certain. The negative consequences of polluting (bad publicity, fines, a boycott) are remote and by no means certain.

In the same way, equatorial countries with millions of acres of rain forest cut trees much faster than the forest can replace them. This pushes countless species into extinction and contributes to the greenhouse effect. It is all very well to say that this is foolish, even suicidal behavior, but the fact is that the immediate and certain consequences of clearing the forest are positive: It generates desperately needed income from the lumber and opens up land for agricultural use. The negative consequences (the loss of future medicines from plants and animals forced into extinction, famine from prolonged droughts, and the like) may be devastating, but they might not occur. Even if the worst happens, it will occur at some unspecified point in the future, possibly after all of the present policy makers are dead.

Of course, each of these situations represents a choice. The problem is to avail ourselves of the wiser options. There is reason to believe that we can learn to make intelligent choices and avoid the perils of contingency traps. For instance, given a choice between a small prize immediately and a bigger prize later, young children typically opt for the immediate prize (Neidert & Linder, 1990). But children can learn to delay gratification (Bandura & Mischel, 1965; Bandura & Walters, 1963). Perhaps, with proper instruction adults can learn to avoid more sophisticated traps.

The ideal way to cope with contingency traps, however, is to change the reinforcement contingencies. Corporations will use anti-pollution devices willingly when the positive consequences for doing so are immediate and certain, and the negative consequences are remote and uncertain. This might be arranged by legislation that provides tax incentives and low-interest loans for corporations that take anti-pollution measures. Many other societal problems might be solved partly or wholly by changing the consequences of behavior.

> Query: How could the incidence of teen pregnancy be reduced by altering the consequences of behavior?

Similarly, equatorial countries will preserve the rain forests if the positive consequences for doing so are immediate and certain, and the negative consequences are remote and uncertain. Other countries might arrange these contingencies by agreeing to share the cost of maintaining the forests and by agreeing to support tourism to the rain forests, a practice that has helped save wildlife habitat in some African nations.

There are, then, ways of coping with contingency traps. But they all begin with the realization that it is contingencies of reinforcement that are responsible for behavior, not greed, stupidity, a poor attitude, destructiveness, a death wish, or other mental states.

In light of the apparent relevance of reinforcement schedules to everyday human behavior, there would seem to be no doubt about the value of research in this area. However, the importance of reinforcement schedules has been questioned.

THE IMPORTANCE OF REINFORCEMENT SCHEDULES

A great deal of research has been done on schedules of reinforcement and their differential effects. But some psychologists have raised doubts about the significance of this research (see, for example, Schwartz et al., 1978). Some argue that the schedules of reinforcement studied in the laboratory are artificial constructions not found in the real world. Others complain that research on schedule effects has generated reams of data on hundreds of schedules, but that these data contribute little of real importance to an understanding of behavior.

It is true that schedules found outside the laboratory are seldom as simple as those created by researchers. But this is true of all laboratory science; researchers take a problem into the laboratory precisely because the laboratory allows them to simplify it. Thus, a psychologist studies a rat's behavior on a concurrent VR 10 VR 15 schedule not because this schedule is particularly representative of the rat's natural environment, but because it is a convenient way of determining the animal's ability to discriminate between similar schedules. The goal is to discover rules that describe the way the environment affects behavior. It is difficult if not impossible to discover such rules unless the experimenter simplifies the environment.

The second charge is that studies of schedules usually produce trivial findings. But it is not trivial to note that personality (the characteristic behavior of a given individual) is a function of the individual's history of reinforcement. Traditional explanations attribute personality differences to qualities of mind: John is said to smoke because he "lacks will power"; Mary is a compulsive gambler because of "masochistic urges"; Bill is persistent in his efforts to break the school track record because he "has 'stick-to-itiveness' "; Harry gives up easily because he "lacks 'stick-to-itiveness"; Phyllis comes up with novel ideas because she "has a lot of imagination." The trouble with all such explanations is that they merely name the behavior to be explained. Harry's tendency to give up is called a lack of stick-to-itiveness; Phyllis's high rate of original ideas is called imagination.

The study of reinforcement schedules gives us a more scientific way of accounting for differences in response frequency. If Harry gives up at the first sign of failure, perhaps it is because his reinforcement history has not included reinforcement for persisting in the face of failure. Harry need not have had considerable failure: A steady diet of easy success (otherwise known as continuous reinforcement) makes one especially likely to quit trying when success is not forthcoming (otherwise known as extinction). Phyllis's high rate of creative ideas might be due to a history of reinforcement for creative ideas. We cannot say with certainty that regular differences in behavior are due to differences in reinforcement schedules, but at least this hypothesis can be put to empirical test. There is no way of determining whether someone has lots of perseverance or imagination as a factor independent of their perseverant or imaginative behavior.

> Query: What is wrong with using a personality trait, such as
> stick-to-itiveness, to explain behavior?

Some critics charge that reinforcement schedules reveal considerably more about rats and pigeons than they do about people. Studies with human subjects do sometimes reveal patterns of responding that differ from those obtained with animals on the same schedules. A rat placed on an FI 15″ schedule soon produces the familiar scalloped-shaped response curve; a person on the same schedule might respond at a steady rate. Typically, such differences are due to the fact that human subjects often receive instructions about what they are to do. Instead of shaping the behavior through continuous reinforcement and then moving to an FI schedule (the usual procedure with animal subjects), human subjects are often given instructions. "Just press this bar like so," they may be told, "and every once in a while a coin will

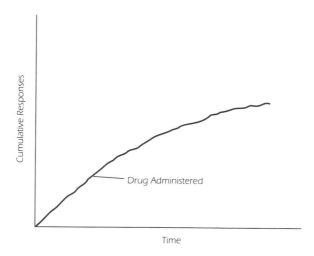

FIGURE 9-8 Use of schedules in pharmaceutical research. Behavioral effects of a drug can be studied by administering it to an animal responding steadily on a given schedule. (Hypothetical data.)

drop into this tray." Such instructions often have a more powerful effect on human behavior than the reinforcement contingencies. People who have been instructed to press a bar or push a button will often do so at a steady rate even though the reinforcement schedule does not support this behavior. (People, unlike other creatures, usually have long histories of reinforcement for doing as they are told, even when doing so seems pointless.) However, human schedule behavior shows remarkable similarity to animal behavior when both are shaped by reinforcement contingencies (Matthews et al., 1977; Weiner, 1983). Indeed, as one psychologist puts it, "those who feel that an unfathomable gulf exists between human and beast are well advised to watch a pigeon pecking for food delivered according to a VR schedule and then go to a video arcade" (Malone, 1990, p. 245).

Schedules research has also led to useful insights into education and rehabilitation. We know that it is not enough to shape behavior with reinforcement. If we want the behavior to persist, we must shift from continuous to intermittent reinforcement. We also know that we must take care not to stretch the ratio too quickly or too far. And we know that we can often eliminate dangerous or otherwise troublesome behavior by changing the reinforcement schedule. It is probably safe to say that we have only just begun to appreciate the practical utility of schedule research.

But even if schedule research had no immediate relevance to human behavior, it would be worthwhile as a research tool. For instance, one can study the effects of a new drug by giving it to an animal that is responding steadily on, say, a VR 15 reinforcement schedule. The response rate on such a schedule is so steady that if the rate of response increases or decreases, or if the pattern of responding changes, we can safely attribute the changes to the drug (see Figure 9-8). In this way, we can detect drug effects that would go unnoticed if we merely observed the animals in their cages. In a similar manner, schedules can be used to study the effects of toxins, diet, sleep deprivation, exercise, brain stimulation, and other independent variables.

Reinforcement schedules have been called the "sleeping giant" of behavioral research (Zeiler, 1984). Whether important new insights and useful techniques remain to be discovered from schedules research is unclear, but there can be no doubt that past research in this area has been of great value.

SUMMARY

Learning is a change in behavior, and that includes changes in the rate and pattern of a response over time. Response rates and patterns are functions of the pattern, or schedule, of reinforcement in effect.

There are several kinds of reinforcement schedules, each of which has distinctive effects on behavior. In continuous reinforcement, each time an organism makes the response under study, it receives food or another reinforcer. Continuous reinforcement results in rapid increases in the rate of response and is therefore very effective in shaping new behavior. Continuous reinforcement differs from intermittent schedules in that, in the latter, responses are not always reinforced.

One kind of intermittent schedule is the fixed ratio schedule. In this kind of schedule, every nth response is reinforced. Thus, a lever-pressing response on an FR 10 schedule is reinforced after a lever is pressed ten times. FR schedules produce bursts of rapid and continuous responding punctuated by pauses after each reinforcement. The length of these postreinforcement pauses varies with the schedule: the higher the ratio of responses to reinforcers, the longer the pauses. Piece work is a common example of a fixed ratio schedule.

In variable ratio, or VR, schedules, the number of responses required for reinforcement varies around an average. An animal on a VR 50 schedule makes an average of 50 responses for each reinforcer. Like fixed ratio schedules, variable ratio schedules produce high rates of responding. However, VR schedules do not produce postreinforcement pauses; instead, the organism responds at a steady, uninterrupted pace. A good example of behavior on variable ratio schedules in human society is gambling.

Ratio schedules are based on the number of responses. Interval schedules reinforce a response only when it occurs after a specified interval. In fixed interval, or FI, schedules, a response is reinforced the first time it occurs after an interval. An animal on an FI 50″ schedule receives food or another reinforcer when it performs a specified response after a specified period of 50 seconds. Once a response is reinforced, responding has no effect until the 50 seconds have elapsed. Organisms on FI schedules make few responses during the early part of the interval, but respond more frequently as the end of the period approaches. This results in a scalloped-shaped cumulative record. College students often find themselves studying very little during the early part of the semester and then burning the midnight oil near midsemester when reinforcers for studying become available.

In variable interval, or VI, schedules, a response is reinforced only after a period of time, but the interval varies around some average. An animal on a VI 50″ schedule receives reinforcement for responding after intervals of varying lengths that average 50 seconds. Variable interval schedules produce higher response rates than fixed interval schedules, but not as high as ratio schedules. Like VR schedules, VI schedules produce steady response rates without postreinforcement pauses. Predatory animals lying in wait for prey and air traffic controllers watching a radar screen provide examples of VI schedules.

Other simple schedules include fixed time (used in superstition studies), variable time, and various differential reinforcement schedules, including DRL, DRH, DRO, and DRI.

Animals and humans have been known to perform hundreds of responses for a single reinforcer, but it is necessary to begin with a relatively rich schedule and gradually stretch the ratio. That is, the number of responses required for reinforcement is gradually increased. An analogous procedure is applied to interval schedules.

In an extinction schedule, a response is never reinforced. The chief effect of an extinction schedule is a gradual return of the response rate to or near its baseline level. Other effects of extinction include an increase in the variability of behavior; an increase in emotional behavior; and the appearance of previously effective behavior, a phenomenon called resurgence. Extinguished responses are apt to reappear after extinction, a phenomenon called spontaneous recovery. Several variables affect the rate at which a response extinguishes, the most important being the schedule of reinforcement in force before extinction begins. The Partial Reinforcement Effect refers to the fact that extinction occurs more slowly after intermittent reinforcement than after continuous reinforcement.

Two or more simple schedules can be combined to form various kinds of complex schedules. When the schedules alternate and each is identified by a particular stimulus, a multiple schedule is said to be in force. In a chain schedule, reinforcement occurs only upon completion of the last in a series of reinforcement schedules, with each schedule change signaled by a change in stimulus.

Humans and animals have a remarkable ability to obtain the maximum amount of reinforcement available under concurrent schedules. The tendency to apportion responses in proportion to the reinforcement available is so reliable it is called the Matching Law. In the case of a choice among ratio schedules, the Matching Law correctly predicts responding on the schedule with the highest reinforcement frequency.

In the case of a choice among interval schedules, the Matching Law predicts responding to each schedule in proportion to the amount of reinforcers available on each.

Sometimes a choice exists between responses that have different immediate and long-term consequences. When the consequences are likely to result in inappropriate behavior, the situation is called a contingency trap. A common form of contingency trap involves positive consequences that are immediate and certain and negative consequences that are delayed and uncertain. Smoking provides a familiar example. Another form of contingency trap involves negative consequences that are immediate and certain and positive consequences that are delayed and less certain. An example is visiting the dentist. Many social problems, such as pollution, can be understood as contingency traps.

The significance of research on schedules has been challenged in recent years. Some argue that laboratory studies of schedules are artificial because the schedules studied are seldom found in nature. But the artificiality of laboratory studies allows the researcher to arrive at reliable generalizations which, when tested in natural environments, often hold true. The analysis of reinforcement schedules has provided new insights into behavior previously attributed to "character" and other vague constructs. Human schedule performance, unlike that of animals, is affected by the nature of the instructions given. If behavior is shaped solely by the reinforcement schedules, schedule effects tend to be much the same for humans and animals. Schedule research has led to applications in education, rehabilitation, and other areas. Finally, the study of schedules of reinforcement has proved useful as a research tool for studying the effects of drugs and other variables on behavior.

REVIEW QUESTIONS

1. Define the following terms:

   complex schedule   Matching Law
   FR 20   postreinforcement pause
   intermittent schedule   VI 20"

2. Give an example (not provided by the text) of a decrease in responding that indicates learning has occurred.

3. John wants to teach Cindy, age 5, the alphabet. He plans to reinforce correct responses with praise and small pieces of candy. What sort of schedule should he use?

4. Mary complains that her dog jumps up on her when she gets home from school. You explain that she reinforces

this behavior by petting and talking to the dog when it jumps up, but Mary replies that you must be wrong, since she hardly ever does this. How would you respond to Mary's comment?

5. Five-year-old David gives up easily in the face of frustration. How could you develop his persistence?

6. Joyce is annoyed because some of her employees fail to take the periodic rest breaks required by the union and the state's safety regulations. Why do you suppose this happens, and what can Joyce do to correct the problem?

7. Every Saturday at noon, the local fire department tests the fire signal. Is this a reinforcement schedule, and if so, what sort of schedule is it?

8. Many people regularly check the coin return after using a public telephone even though their call went through. Explain this behavior.

9. Mr. Smith and Ms. Jones both give their students new spelling words on Friday. Mr. Smith always tests his students on the following Friday. Ms. Jones also tests her students once a week, but the day varies, and she does not announce the test day in advance. Whose students are more likely to study on Tuesday nights? Explain why.

10. How might casino operators increase their income by stretching the ratio?

11. Concurrent schedules are said to represent a choice. Why is a multiple schedule not said to represent a choice?

12. Describe the similarities and differences between multiple and chain schedules.

13. Rat X's lever pressing is put on a concurrent FR 10 FR 20 schedule. Rat Y's behavior is put on a concurrent VR 10 VR 20 schedule. Which rat will select the more reinforcing schedule first?

14. How might you use what you know about reinforcement schedules to study the effects of the presence of observers on human performance?

15. Someone says to you, "George is a nasty fellow. He was born that way." How else could you account for George's personality?

16. A student tells you that studying reinforcement schedules is a waste of time. Give arguments for the opposing view.

17. A teacher reinforces longer and longer periods of quiet behavior in her students. How can she avoid creating ratio strain?

18. This chapter describes schedules of reinforcement. How would schedules of punishment work? Use, as an example, a VR 10 punishment schedule.

19. Pretend you are a behavioral economist who wants to understand the effect of inflation on purchasing. Describe an experiment that will shed light on the problem.

20. How might an understanding of schedules of reinforcement help account for the poor economic performance of communist countries?

Suggested Readings

The classic work on reinforcement schedules is *Schedules of Reinforcement* by C. B. Ferster and B. F. Skinner. It describes the basic kinds of reinforcement schedules and provides many charts illustrating the response rates and patterns associated with each.

The Matching Law was formulated in an article by Richard Herrnstein, "On the Law of Effect," published in the *Journal of the Experimental Analysis of Behavior* in 1970. Howard Rachlin deals with this subject in an intriguing little book called *Judgment, Decision and Choice*.

A nontechnical survey of research on the application of reinforcement schedules to problems in economics is provided by Tom Alexander in a 1980 *Fortune* magazine article, "Economics According to the Rat."

For a discussion of the relevance of reinforcement schedules to the analysis of human behavior and to concepts such as personality, see Skinner's *Science and Human Behavior*.

Answers to Queries

Page 216: A schedule is a timetable or program of events. In this case, the programmed events are reinforcers.

Page 218: FR 5. The number indicates the number of times a response must be performed before reinforcement. Thus, FR 5 pays off twice as often as FR 10.

Page 221: The free chips make it likely that people will gamble long enough for the behavior to be reinforced by an occasional win, after which they may then gamble their own money. Any money lost by the casino during this early stage is apt to be gained back several times over.

Page 222: If a response takes one second, 60 responses can be performed in a minute, so reinforcement is available a maximum of six times a minute on an FR 10 schedule. On an FI 10" schedule, reinforcement is available once every ten seconds, or six times a minute. There is no difference in the availability of reinforcement. However, the two schedules produce very different patterns of response.

Page 225: Reinforcement would be delayed. On a DRL 10″ schedule, any response that occurs less than ten seconds after the last response resets the clock.

Page 226: You might first reinforce short periods at a task and gradually require longer periods for reinforcement. To make persistence a tendency in a wide range of situations (that is, to make it a personality trait), you would have to stretch the ratio in a number of different tasks.

Page 232: Intermittent reinforcement can produce high rates of responding and increase resistance to extinction. This means the misbehavior is likely to occur more often and will endure through long periods without reinforcement.

Page 236: Your answer should be something like this: The rate of responding matches (or is proportional to) the rate of reinforcement.

Page 241: Getting pregnant and bearing a child often produce immediate reinforcers (for example, increased status among peers, welfare payments). The aversive consequences (for example, nighttime feedings, remaining in poverty) are remote.

Page 242: We might provide reinforcing consequences (for example, money) to girls aged 12 to 17 contingent upon *not* bearing children. (Incidentally, this might save taxpayers money.)

Page 243: Personality traits merely name behavior. To say that a person "has stick-to-itiveness" merely means that he or she persists at a task. Thus, the behavior is said to be explained by the behavior. To really explain the behavior, we must identify the learning history that produced it.

ten

Aversive Control

Fear preserves you by a dread of punishment that
never fails.
—MACHIAVELLI

Those who are feared, are hated.
—BENJAMIN FRANKLIN

BACKGROUND

The story is told of a young king who wanted to
know what lessons could be learned from the study of history. He called
for the finest historians in his land and commanded them to write the
history of humanity so that he might study their work, and learn what
history had to teach. The historians set to work, and after 20 years of
labor, presented the king with a 30-volume history of human progress.
The king protested that he was far too busy with matters of state to
read so many books, and commanded them to reduce it to a single
volume. After several years, the historians offered a large book. Again
the king said, "It is too much yet. Distill it into one slim volume." Two
years later, the historians presented the king with a short book. "I am
old and ill, and even this work is more than I can manage. Reduce it
further." The historians returned after some months with a short
monograph, but found the king on his deathbed. "I am dying," said the
king, "but still I would know the lessons to be learned from the history
of our species. Pray, tell me in a few words." The historians looked at
one another in puzzlement. Finally, the oldest and wisest of their
members approached the king, and whispered into the dying monarch's ear: "Majesty, the great lesson of history is this: We are born, we
suffer, and we die."

The old historian may have been a terrible cynic, but there can be
no doubt that suffering is part of life. Babies are greeted at birth with a
slap, and go on to suffer from hunger, ear infections, tooth eruptions,

and numerous maladies. When they get older, they learn to walk, and in the process they inevitably fall, with uncomfortable results. They eat things they ought not to eat and get sick. They play with things they ought not to play with and get injured. As they get older, the nature of their suffering changes, but the suffering continues. Disease and injury are the benchmarks of our lives.

Many of the slings and arrows outrageous fortune throws our way come at the hands of other people. Children are disciplined in the home by being made to suffer. Even babies are sometimes shouted at, insulted, confined in closets, shaken, slapped, whipped—and much, much worse.

One might expect that school would provide a safe haven from such mistreatment, but this is not always so. Students who do not learn are held up for ridicule. Those who misbehave may receive harsher treatment. More than a million American schoolchildren experience some sort of corporal punishment at the hands of teachers or administrators every year (Wolk, 1992). And society sanctions these tactics: Surveys show that half of us approve the use of corporal punishment in school (Gallup & Elam, 1988).

Children who are made to suffer grow up to be adults who make others suffer (Bandura & Walters, 1959; Sears et al., 1957). As we become spouse, friend, coworker, and employee, we deal with the troublesome behavior of others by inflicting injury upon them. We threaten a roommate with dire harm for using our property; say hurtful things to friends and lovers; shirk our duties on the job (thus injuring our employer and coworkers); and deny hardworking subordinates the pay raises they deserve. Few can justly claim to have been only the victim of suffering and never its cause. The old historian might well have said, "We live, we cause suffering, and we die."

Of course, not all human interactions involve one person hurting another. Many parents would not dream of beating a child and rear their children successfully by relying largely on smiles, praise, and other forms of positive reinforcement. Many teachers totally reject both sarcasm and the paddle, and instead praise good efforts. Many employers provide recognition, awards, bonuses, raises, and promotions for a job well done. And most of us do not make a habit of murdering, assaulting, raping, or stealing.

Many people, including behavior scientists, deplore the widespread use of aversives to control behavior. Deploring it, however, is not enough. We must try to understand such **aversive control**: its nature, its appeal, and its drawbacks. And we must learn what alternatives are available. Let us begin our study with an examination of noncontingent aversives.

NONCONTINGENT AVERSIVES

Most of the aversive events we experience are, to some extent at least, contingent upon our behavior. We get an electric shock from a faulty toaster, but only if we touch the toaster. We hit our thumb with a hammer, but only if we swing the hammer incorrectly. We catch cold, but only if we consort with those who are sick. The ill treatment we receive at the hands of others is likewise usually dependent upon our behavior: Neighbors shout at us if we play the trombone too loudly; teachers threaten students with dire harm if they misbehave; employers reprimand workers if they arrive late.

But sometimes aversive events happen without regard to our behavior. People are sometimes struck by lightning even though they stay indoors, where it is apparently safe; they sometimes get cancer despite a healthy lifestyle; they sometimes are arrested by the police though they have done nothing wrong. Bad things do sometimes happen to us without our having earned them.

Noncontinent aversives (those that occur independently of behavior) can be studied in the laboratory. Suppose, for example, that a rat has learned to press a lever for food and is doing so at a steady rate. Now suppose we run an electrical charge through the grid floor of the rat's cage, so that it periodically receives a shock. Notice that lever pressing does not cause the shock, nor does *not* pressing the lever terminate the shock. The rat receives a shock whether it presses the lever or not. The aversive stimulation is noncontingent.

> Query: What does it mean to say that an aversive is
>   noncontingent?

A regular effect of noncontingent aversive stimulation is a decrease in the rate of ongoing behavior. A study by Erling Boe and Russel Church (1967) will illustrate. Boe and Church trained rats to press a lever for food and then put lever pressing on extinction. During extinction, some rats received shocks every 30 seconds, regardless of what they were doing; others did not. After the first extinction period, there were nine more extinction sessions during which neither group of rats received shocks. A comparison of the cumulative response rates of rats in the two conditions showed that the shocked rats pressed the lever less often than those that were not shocked. The shocks had depressed the rate of lever pressing even though they had not been contingent upon lever pressing.

You will recall from your reading of Pavlovian conditioning that any stimulus that is regularly paired with an aversive stimulus will itself become aversive. This means that any stimulus that is paired with an aversive stimulus should also suppress responding. The first researchers to demonstrate this clearly were William Estes and B. F. Skinner (1941). They trained a rat to press a lever and, when the animal was responding at a steady rate, periodically sounded a tone; when the tone stopped, the rat received a shock. At first, the tone had no noticeable effect—the rat continued to press the lever at the same rate. But after the tone and shock had been paired several times, the rat decreased its rate of lever pressing when it heard the tone and did not resume its

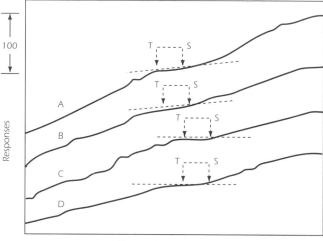

Responses

100

A

B

C

D

T - - - - - S

T - - - - - S

T - - - - - S

T - - - - - S

Time (each record one hour)

FIGURE 10-1 Conditioned suppression. When a tone (T) was paired with a shock (S), the tone suppressed the rate of an ongoing behavior. The curves show the average response rates for six rats on four consecutive days. SOURCE: from Estes & Skinner, 1941.

previous rate of activity until after it had received the shock (see Figure 10-1).

Note that the rat's activity had absolutely no effect on the appearance of the tone or the delivery of the shock. Yet the tone clearly altered the rat's behavior. Since the disruption of ongoing behavior occurs after pairing with an aversive US, this phenomenon is called **conditioned suppression.**

A history of continuous noncontingent aversives can suppress behavior in new situations. Some years ago, Martin Seligman and his colleagues (Overmier & Seligman, 1967; Seligman & Maier, 1967) strapped a dog into a harness and exposed it to shock. Since the dog was restrained by a harness, it could not escape the shock. Next, the experimenters put the dog into one side of a shuttle box. (This is a box divided by a barrier placed so the animal can "shuttle" from compartment to compartment by jumping the barrier.) Shortly afterwards the researchers delivered a shock through the floor of the dog's compartment. Now the dog was no longer restrained by a harness and could easily escape the shock by jumping the barrier to the other compartment. Normally, dogs learn this escape task very quickly, but the experimenters found that dogs that had been exposed to inescapable shocks behaved very differently. Seligman (1975) writes:

> The dog's first reactions to shock in the shuttle box were much the same as those of a naive dog: it ran around frantically for about thirty seconds. But then it stopped moving; to our surprise, it lay down and quietly whined. After one minute of this we turned the shock off. . . . On the next trial the dog did it again; at first it struggled a bit and then, after a few seconds, it seemed to give up and to accept the shock passively. (p. 22)

Seligman called this phenomenon **learned helplessness** because the inescapable shock seemed to teach the dog to do nothing, to be helpless. Researchers have demonstrated this phenomenon in other species, including humans (Hiroto, 1974).

Seligman used learned helplessness as a model for depression in people. Depression is characterized not only by sadness but by general inactivity. Depressed people often stop going to school or work and spend a great deal of time lounging about or sleeping. Faced with a problem, they may do nothing about it. Most of us soon recover from depression, but some do not. Seligman suggested that those who do not bounce back from life's cruelties may have a history of inescapable aversives, the noncontingent "shocks" of life. Some parents, for example, seldom interact with their children without providing some sort of aversive stimulation (criticism, beatings, work assignments). To the extent that these aversives are not contingent upon the child's behavior and are inescapable, the parent is providing the kind of experience that made Seligman's dogs helpless.

> **Query**: What is the opposite of learned helplessness? How could you produce it?

Aversives that are not response contingent have important effects upon behavior; they may suppress responding and can even cause helplessness. The most important forms of aversive control, however, are those that are in some way contingent upon behavior. In one of these, the reduction or removal of aversive stimulation depends upon behavior. It is to this form of aversive control that we now turn.

NEGATIVE REINFORCEMENT

Reinforcement occurs when a response is followed by a stimulus that makes the response more likely to occur in the future. In previous chapters we have mainly considered positive reinforcement, in which a response is followed by a stimulus, such as food or kind words, that the organism usually seeks out. In negative reinforcement, a response is strengthened when it is followed by the *removal* of a stimulus, such as shock or criticism, that the organism usually tries to escape or avoid.

> **Query**: What do positive and negative reinforcement have in common?

Richard Solomon did pioneer research on negative reinforcement involving shuttle boxes. In one study Solomon and Lyman Wynne (1953) put a dog in one compartment of a shuttle box. After a time the light in the compartment went off, and ten seconds later the dog received a shock through the floor. Typically the dog whimpered and moved about in an agitated manner for awhile and then jumped over the hurdle to the second compartment. The light in this compartment was on, and there was no shock. Some time later the light in this compartment went out and, ten seconds later, the floor would again provide a shock. The dog again escaped the shock by jumping to the other compartment. With each trial the dog endured the shock for a shorter period before jumping. Soon it jumped the instant the shock began. Eventually the dog began jumping *before* the shock started, and thereby avoided shock entirely. After this first avoidance response, most dogs received few additional shocks. As this study illustrates, negative reinforcement often starts out with an escape response and ends up with an avoidance response. For this reason, negative reinforcement is often referred to as **escape-avoidance learning**.

Laboratory studies of negative reinforcement have proved their worth by providing insights into many kinds of behavior. Lying, for instance. Paul Ekman (Ekman & Patterson, 1992), a social psychologist famous for his work on nonverbal communication, reports that 91% of Americans lie routinely. He adds that 86% lie regularly to parents, 75% to friends, and 69% to spouses. Why is lying so popular?

No doubt people sometimes lie because lying has been positively reinforced in the past. Suppose, for example, that a classmate asks, "What did you think of my speech?" It was really mediocre, but you lie and say, "I thought it was great!" We may lie in such situations because there are sometimes positive consequences for doing so: The speech maker smiles pleasantly and may offer to do us some kindness. ("Well, I'm glad you liked it. How are you coming in calculus? Need any help?")

Most lying, however, probably has less to do with positive reinforcement than with escaping or avoiding aversive stimulation. By lying about the speech, we avoid rejection, criticism, and other unpleasantness. People realize this, of course, and so are apt to implore us to be honest and tell them what we *really* think. "Don't hold back," they tell us, "I can take it." Only sometimes they cannot. After begging us to critique a speech honestly, they then rebuke us for having done so. We may then try to escape the unpleasant situation our honesty has created by temporizing our earlier opinion (that is, by lying).

A good deal of behavior is controlled by negative reinforcement without being recognized as such. Teens and young adults are said to become sexually active, use drugs, drive while intoxicated, and ignore their studies because of peer pressure. What is this peer pressure we hear so much about? What do peers actually do to exert pressure? The answer seems to be that they create an unpleasant situation from which others can escape by participating in the behavior demanded. When a child is afraid to jump from a diving board, other children might tease him or her. The child can escape the teasing quickly by jumping, and doing so is negatively reinforced. In the same way, the teen or young adult who feels no great urgency to have sex might do so anyway to escape social rejection.

Having escaped an aversive stimulus once in a certain way (by lying or doing what our peers demand, for example) we are thereafter more likely to escape similar aversive stimuli by similar means. Each time we make use of the escape route more quickly. Finally, we avoid unpleasantness altogether by acting before it starts.

We do many things, both noble and shameful, in order to escape or avoid aversive stimulation. We learn to escape pain by taking analgesics; insomnia by drinking milk; noise by covering our ears; horrible sights by looking away; a dull movie by leaving the theater; academic failure by quitting school; stress by using drugs; a bad marriage by obtaining a divorce; unpleasant work conditions by resigning; and so on.

Studies of negative reinforcement have also led to insights into abnormal behavior. Psychotic and retarded children often behave in ways that make teaching them extremely difficult. They may bite and scratch the teacher, have screaming tantrums, or injure themselves in various ways. Such behavior was once thought to be merely the result of the children's psychoses or retardation. Then evidence began to suggest the behavior was due, at least in part, to negative reinforcement.

Montrose Wolf and his colleagues (1967) discovered, for instance, that self-injurious behavior in disturbed children seemed to be precipitated by teacher requests. When a teacher stopped asking a child to perform tasks, the self-injurious behavior would subside. Sometime after this, Edward Carr began to speculate that inappropriate behavior might be negatively reinforced by escape from an aversive situation. In a study of the self-injurious behavior of an 8-year-old boy (Carr et al., 1976), Carr tallied the number of self-injurious acts that occurred during lessions and compared it with the number that occurred during free play. He found a marked difference: Almost all of the self-injurious behavior occurred during the lessons (see Figure 10-2).

Carr and his coworkers found that self-injury, tantrums, aggression, and other forms of bizarre behavior were often negatively reinforced (Carr & Newsom, 1985; Carr, Taylor, & Robinson, 1991; Carr et al., 1980). What happens is that children find themselves in aversive situations from which they can escape by behaving in a bizarre or disruptive fashion.

The discovery that abnormal behavior is often due to negative reinforcement ultimately led to new, more effective treatment approaches (for example, Carr & Durand, 1985; Bird et al., 1988). It is unlikely, however, that these new approaches would have been discovered had it not been for laboratory research on negative reinforcement. The same sort of laboratory research has also helped resolve some theoretical issues.

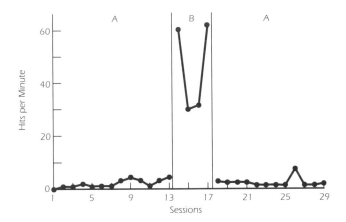

FIGURE 10-2 Negative reinforcement and self-injury. Number of times 8-year-old Tim hit himself each minute during free time (A) and during lessons (B). The data suggest that escape from lessons might have reinforced the behavior. SOURCE: From "Stimulus Control of Self-Destructive Behavior in a Psychotic Child" by E. G. Carr, D. D. Newsom, and J. A. Binkoff. In *Journal of Abnormal Child Psychology*, 1976, 4, pp. 139–153.

■ Theories of Negative Reinforcement

Negative reinforcement raises interesting theoretical questions. There are two principle ways of answering these questions: two-factor theory and one-factor theory.

Two-factor theory. **Two-factor theory** says that two kinds of learning experiences are involved in escape-avoidance learning: Pavlovian and operant learning (Mowrer, 1947). Consider the dog that learns to jump a hurdle to escape shock. A light goes off, and shortly afterwards the dog is shocked. Soon the dog jumps over the hurdle to a shock-free compartment. The termination of an aversive stimulus is negatively reinforcing, so jumping the hurdle becomes more likely each time shock begins. Thus, the escape response is the result of an operant procedure.

But wait: The dog eventually learns not only to escape shock, but to avoid it. How can jumping a hurdle be reinforced by the termination of shock if the response avoids shock? As Murray Sidman (1989b) noted, "Successful avoidance meant that something—the shock—did not happen, but how could something that did not happen be a reinforcer?" (p. 191). After all, Sidman adds, things are not happening all the time.

It seems illogical to say that things that do not happen can explain things that do happen. This is where Pavlovian conditioning comes in. Recall that before the shock begins, a light goes out. Shock is a US for fear. Any stimulus that reliably precedes a US for fear becomes a CS for fear. So, through Pavlovian conditioning, the extinguished light becomes a CS for fear. The dog can escape the fearful stimulus (the dark) by jumping the hurdle to the compartment where the light is on, and this is what it does. Thus, jumping before receiving a shock is reinforced by termination of an aversive stimulus, the dark compartment.

According to two-factor theory, then, Pavlovian and operant procedures are both required to explain escape-avoidance learning. Escape is reinforced by termination of the shock (or other aversive stimulus); avoidance is reinforced by termination of an extinguished light (or other CS for fear).

Query: *What are the two factors in two-factor theory?*

Two-factor theory fits all the essential facts. In addition, the theory leads to logical predictions that can be tested. A number of these tests have led to evidence supporting two-factor theory.

In one experiment, Neal Miller (1948) tested the idea that escape from an aversive CS reinforced avoidance behavior. He put rats into a white compartment (the CS) and shocked them. Then he permitted the rats to escape from the compartment by running in an exercise wheel. No further shocks were given, so the rats were not escaping from shocks. Yet the rats quickly learned to use the exercise wheel to get out of the white compartment. This experiment demonstrated that escape from an aversive CS could reinforce avoidance behavior.

Unfortunately, not all tests of two-factor theory have produced supportive evidence. The idea that the avoidance response is reinforced by escape from an aversive CS leads to the prediction that if the CS were to lose its aversiveness, the avoidance response would break down. There is evidence that the signal for shock does lose its aversiveness, yet the avoidance response persists.

Solomon and Wynne (1953; see above) noticed that the dogs in their study showed considerable evidence of fear of the CS in the early stages of learning, but once they had learned to avoid shock, the CS no longer seemed to trouble them. Leon Kamin and his colleagues (1963) conducted an experiment to see if Solomon and Wynne were right. In their experiment, they first trained rats to press a lever for food on a VI schedule. Then they trained the animals to avoid shock in a shuttle box, with the shock preceded by a sound. Finally, after from 1 to 27 trials in the shuttle box, the researchers returned the rats to the original training cage where they could press a lever for food.

Recall that an aversive CS will reduce the rate of ongoing behavior. Kamin and his colleagues used this phenomenon as a measure of the aversiveness of the CS (the sound that signaled shock). While the rats were in the cage with the lever, the researchers sounded the tone to see if it would depress the rate of responding. Two-factor theory predicts that the more avoidance trials a rat has had, the greater the suppression of lever pressing. This is because more avoidance trials mean more pairing of CS (sound) and US (shock). In fact, however, the greatest suppression occurred with rats that had had the fewest avoid-ance trials. Once the avoidance response was well established, present-ing the CS produced little conditioned suppression. In other words, the CS loses its aversiveness as avoidance learning proceeds. But if the CS loses its aversiveness, then escape from the CS cannot account for persistence of the avoidance response.

A second major problem for two-factor theory concerns the failure of the avoidance response to extinguish. Consider the rat that learns to avoid a shock by jumping a hurdle when a tone sounds. As learning proceeds, the rat receives fewer and fewer shocks until finally it re-ceives no shocks at all. This means that the CS (the sound) should lose its value as a negative reinforcer for the avoidance response. Two-factor theory therefore leads to the prediction that the avoidance re-sponse, once learned, will begin to extinguish. The dog will delay longer and longer before jumping the hurdle. Finally, it will not jump until it is shocked.

The predicted scenario is not, however, what happens. Instead, the animal continues responding. Indeed, avoidance responses are re-markable for their persistence. Even if the shock apparatus is dis-connected so the animal cannot receive shocks, it nevertheless con-tinues to jump the hurdle.

Two-factor theory lost still more ground with Murray Sidman's research on what is now known as the **Sidman avoidance procedure** (Sidman, 1953, 1966). In this procedure, the shock or other aversive stimulus is not signaled. A rat in a Skinner box might receive shocks at regular intervals through the grid floor. The rat might avoid the shocks for 15 seconds by pressing a lever. If it pressed the lever again before the end of this delay period, it would earn another 15-second delay. Thus, by pressing the lever regularly, the rat could completely avoid shock. The key aspect of the Sidman procedure, however, is that there is no signal (no light going off, no tone sounding) indicating impending shock.

Sidman found that not much happened at first: The rat would receive shocks periodically and, between shocks, it would explore the cage. But after half an hour or so, the rat would begin to press the lever and delay some shocks. This would mean that it would receive fewer shocks each minute. Thus, avoidance learning occurred, apparently in the absence of a signal. This was bad news for two-factor theory since, if there was no signal for shock, then termination of a signal could not reinforce the avoidance response.

Douglas Anger (1963) proposed that there is a signal in the Sidman procedure: time. The shocks, said Anger, occur at regular intervals. The passage of time therefore signals the approach of shock. The animal does not escape the CS in the same way as it might by jumping a hurdle, but it does allow the animal to get "further away" from the shocks—further away in terms of time, not distance.

Query: Why is a signal an essential part of two-factor theory?

Anger's proposal raised a new dilemma: How could one rule out the possibility that time became a CS in escape-avoidance situations? Richard Herrnstein and Phillip Hineline (1966) provided an elegant solution to this problem. Whereas Sidman had used a fixed time schedule, Herrnstein and Hineline used a variable time schedule. In their experiment, rats had a choice of two shock schedules: If they pressed a lever at a steady rate, they would receive shocks an average of once every 20 seconds; if they did not press the lever, they would receive shocks an average of about once every 7 seconds. Note that these shock intervals are merely averages: A rat might press the lever and get an immediate shock, or it might not press the lever and receive no shock for several seconds. Still, the rat is better off, in the long run, if it presses the lever. What Herrnstein and Hineline had done was to render time useless as a possible signal for shock. According to two-factor theory, no signal means no avoidance learning. Yet 17 out of 18 of Herrnstein and Hineline's rats learned to press the lever and avoid a great many shocks.

The problems with two-factor theory have cost it the allegiance of most learning researchers, although it still has its supporters (Malott, 1992). With the depreciation of two-factor theory, one-factor theory has gained adherents.

One-factor theory. One-factor theory proposes that escape-avoidance involves only one factor, operant learning (Sidman, 1962; Herrnstein, 1969). We learn to make escape and avoidance responses because those responses are reinforced by a reduction in aversive stimulation. Consider, once again, the rat in a shuttle box. A light goes off, and a few seconds later it receives a shock. Jumping a hurdle is reinforced by the termination of shock. So far, so good. But what is the reinforcer for avoiding shock? Two-factor theorists had gotten caught up on this question, because they assumed that the absence of shock could not be said to reinforce behavior. How can something that does not happen be a reinforcer? But one-factor theory assumes that something *does* happen: There is a reduction in the number of shocks, and this is reinforcing.

Perhaps it will be helpful to think for a moment about positive reinforcement. We know that hungry rats will press a lever if doing so produces food. More than that, we know that if a rat has a choice of two levers, both of which produce food, it will work at the lever that pays off better. If one lever produces food on an FR 3 schedule, and the other lever produces food on an FR 5 schedule, the rat will work steadily on the FR 3 lever. Now suppose that we put light bulbs above each lever and arrange things so that the lever with an illuminated bulb will be the one with the higher reinforcement schedule (in this example, FR 3). The rat would soon learn to go immediately to the lever with the illuminated bulb. And if, while the rat was working at this lever, we turned the light off and turned on the light above the second lever, the rat would move to that lever. We would say that the illuminated bulb had become a discriminative stimulus for lever pressing.

Now, one-factor theory says that the avoidance response is reinforced by a lower density of shocks in the same way as the lever pressing in our example is reinforced by a higher density of food. Learning proceeds when the reinforcer is *fewer* shocks in the same way that learning proceeds when the reinforcer is *more* food.

The Herrnstein and Hineline (1966) study just described supports one-factor theory, and so do other experiments. But what about the extreme resistance of avoidance responses to extinction? Can one-factor theory explain this? Again it may be helpful to consider positive reinforcement. Suppose you have trained a rat to press a lever for food and have stretched the ratio from VR 1 to VR 500. The animal now must press the lever an average of 500 times to receive food, but sometimes it might press the lever 600 or 700 times without reinforcement. At such high ratio schedules, the difference between a reinforcement schedule and an extinction schedule is slight and hard to discriminate. Extinction therefore takes a long time. It can be argued that the same process is involved in avoidance learning. The rat continues to press the lever or jump the hurdle because it is not possible to tell that responding no longer prevents shocks. In fact, one quick way to extinguish an avoidance response is to prevent the response in the absence of aversive stimulation.

One-factor theory currently holds sway among psychologists. It fits the data well, and it has an elegant simplicity. In all, it provides a good explanation of negative reinforcement. Negative reinforcement is not, however, the only form of contingent aversive control to be explained. Another widespread form of aversive control is punishment.

PUNISHMENT

"The commonest technique of control in modern life," wrote B. F. Skinner in 1953, "is punishment" (p. 182). Skinner deplored the human preoccupation with punishment and continued to protest against its use until his death in 1990. Yet there has been no discernable abatement in the popularity of punishment. It is still the most common method of influencing behavior, widely used by parents, teachers, employers, and governments. Parents spank their children, teachers send students to the principal, police ticket motorists, states imprison criminals, nations bomb neighbors.

The term *punishment* is often used as a synonym for *abuse* (Sherman, 1991; Starin, 1991). To most people, to punish is to hurt. A sportscaster might say of a boxer's right cross, "That was a punishing blow." The owner of an automobile might brag, "This car will stand up to a lot of punishment." To the person on the street, punishment means pain and suffering; it is defined by the nature of the stimulus involved: Any event that causes damage, pain, or discomfort is punishing.

To the behavioral scientist, however, punishment (like reinforcement) is defined by its effects on behavior. It has less to do with the nature of the stimulus than with the relationship between the stimulus and the behavior. The term *punishment* refers to procedures that reduce the probability of a response. As we saw in Chapter Five, there are two kinds of punishment. In Type 1, an aversive stimulus is contingent upon a response: A rat presses a lever and is shocked; a child refuses to eat his vegetables and is sent to his room; a prisoner steals and is put to hard labor. In Type 2 punishment, removal of a positive reinforcer is contingent upon a response: A rat presses a lever and a light indicating the availability of food goes out; a child refuses to eat her vegetables and has her dinner taken away; a prisoner steals and is denied visitors. Since something is taken away in Type 2 punishment, the procedure is often called *response cost.*

All of these examples sound like punishment procedures, and usually they are. It is important to remember, however, that punishment is defined by its effect on behavior. If the contingency between a response and a consequence does not reduce the probability of the response, then the procedure is not punishment. This is particularly important since, if the procedure does not reduce the response rate, what is done in the name of punishment may be merely abuse.

Punishment and negative reinforcement are closely related and often confused. This is partly because the same aversive stimuli (shocks, spankings, pinches, criticism, denial of privileges, and the like) may be used in either procedure. But there is an important difference: Punishment weakens a response, while negative reinforcement strengthens it.

Query: What is the essential difference between negative reinforcement and punishment?

The first formal experiments on punishment were probably done by E. L. Thorndike around the turn of the century. Thorndike (1898) noted that while behavior followed by a "satisfying state of affairs" became stronger, behavior followed by an "annoying state of affairs" became weaker.

Other early research supported Thorndike's view (Yerkes, 1912; Warden & Aylesworth, 1927). Yet there were doubts, serious doubts. Thorndike, who originally believed that punishment affected behavior in a manner parallel to reinforcement, later questioned this view. In one study, Thorndike (1932) presented college students with Spanish words or uncommon English words and asked them to choose a synonym from a selection of five alternatives. If they guessed correctly, the experimenter said, "Right"; if incorrectly, the experimenter said,

"Wrong." Thorndike then looked at the likelihood that a correct or incorrect answer would be repeated on subsequent trials. He found that saying "right" after a response strengthened it, as expected, but saying "wrong" did not particularly weaken it. "Indeed," he wrote, "the announcement of 'Wrong'. . . . in our experiments does not weaken the connection at all, so far as we can see" (1968, p. 45).

B. F. Skinner (1938) shared Thorndike's doubts about punishment. After training rats to press a lever, he put the response on extinction. In addition, some of the rats received a slap from the lever whenever they pressed it during the first ten minutes of extinction. Skinner then compared the cumulative records of these rats with those that were not slapped. His reasoning was that if punishment suppresses responding, then it should result in fewer total responses during extinction. What Skinner found was that responding markedly slowed during punishment but increased sharply after punishment stopped. The end result was that punished rats pressed the lever about as often as those that were not punished (see Chapter Five, Figure 5-7). There was, in other words, no net effect from punishment. Skinner concluded from this study that the effects of punishment are short-lived (1938; see also Skinner, 1953, 1971).

A series of experiments by W. K. Estes (1944) bolstered Skinner's position. Estes trained rats to press a lever for food and then punished lever pressing with shocks for various lengths of time. In most experiments, rats no longer received food once the shocks started. The principal finding was that the rate of lever pressing dropped sharply when lever pressing produced shocks but recovered when the shocks stopped. Given enough time on extinction, the shocked rats eventually pressed the lever as often as rats that had never received shocks. This was so even when the rats never again received food for lever pressing. Like Skinner, Estes concluded that punishment reliably suppresses responding but that the effects are only temporary.

This view of punishment held sway for a number of years, but many studies found that punishment did produce a net reduction of responses. One reason for the discrepancy was that Thorndike and Skinner used very mild forms of punishment, and research showed that the effects of punishment vary greatly with the intensity of the stimulus used. In one experiment, Boe and Church (1967) trained rats to press a lever for food and then put them on an extinction schedule for nine sessions. During the first of these extinction sessions, some rats occasionally received shocks when they pressed the lever. The intensity of these shocks varied from very mild to quite severe. The results showed that responding varied with the intensity of shock (see Figure 10-3). The mildest shock had almost no effect on lever pressing, while each increase in intensity did a better job of suppressing responses. The strongest shock resulted in almost total suppression of responding. Today, the consensus is that the effects of punishment can be quite long-lasting.

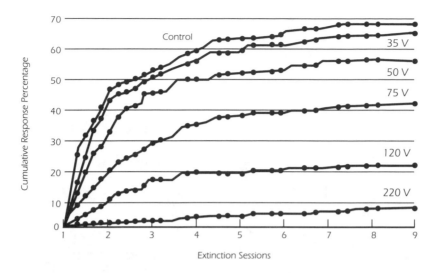

FIGURE 10-3 *Stimulus intensity and punishment. Cumulative record of the median number of responses (as a percentage of responses before punishment) during extinction varied with the intensity of shock. A mild shock had very little effect; a severe shock resulted in nearly complete suppression of the response.* Source: From "Permanent Effects of Punishment during Extinction," by E. E. Boe and R. M. Church, *Journal of Comparative and Physiological Psychology,* 1967, *63,* p. 491. Copyright 1967 by the American Psychological Association. Reprinted by permission.

Punishment has been put to practical use. Paradoxically, this source of so much suffering has alleviated suffering when used properly by experts. Ivar Lovaas pioneered in the use of punishment to suppress self-injurious behavior in psychotic children. In one study, Lovaas and J. Q. Simmons (1969) worked with a boy who hit himself up to 300 times in a ten-minute period if not restrained. (That is one blow every two seconds.) This behavior ended abruptly when the experimenters shocked the boy on the leg after he hit himself. Incredibly, a single shock practically ended the self-injurious behavior. The boy hit himself a few times on subsequent days, and these responses were also punished. After a total of four contingent shocks, the self-injurious behavior did not recur. An extremely high rate of self-injurious behavior had been stopped with just a few contingent shocks.

Edward Carr and Jack McDowell (1980) treated a case of self-injurious scratching in an otherwise healthy 10-year-old boy. Jim began scratching following exposure to poison oak. The dermatitis cleared up after a few weeks, but Jim continued to scratch for *three years.* When Carr and McDowell finally saw Jim for treatment, his skin was covered with scars and sores and he was the object of ridicule among his peers. The experimenters found that nearly all the scratching occurred at home and seemed to be maintained by attention from

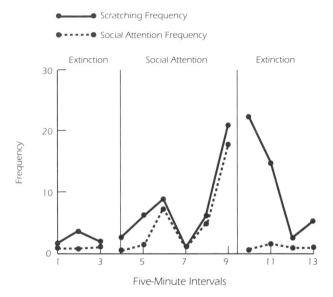

FIGURE 10-4 Attention and scratching. Scratching declined when ignored (extinction) and increased when reinforced (social attention). Note the high degree of correspondence between scratching and reinforcement (telling the child to stop scratching). SOURCE: From "Social Control of Self-Injurious Behavior of Organic Etiology" by E. G. Carr and J. J. McDowell. In *Behavior Therapy,* 1980, *11,* pp. 402–409. Copyright © 1980 by the Association for the Advancement of Behavior Therapy.

his parents. When Jim's parents saw him scratching, they would often make comments about it ("Jim, stop scratching") or attempt to stop it by restraining his hands. To verify that this attention was acting as a reinforcer, the experimenters had the parents systematically withhold or provide attention for scratching. The results clearly showed that scratching depended upon attention (see Figure 10-4).

Jim's scratching might have been treated by having the parents simply ignore scratching entirely—that is, by putting the behavior on extinction. Unfortunately, the scratching so annoyed the boy's parents that they were unable to ignore it for long. Carr and McDowell therefore asked the parents to use punishment in the form of "time out": Each time they saw Jim scratch, they were to send him to a small, rather uninteresting room for 20 minutes. (The researchers also recommended reinforcement for *not* scratching: Jim earned weekly rewards, such as a trip to a museum or a skating rink, by reducing the number of sores on his body. Thus, the researchers combined punishment with positive reinforcement.) This treatment resulted in a sharp reduction in the number of sores (see Figure 10-5).

Query: What reason might Carr and McDowell (1980) have had for using sores rather than scratching as their dependent measure?

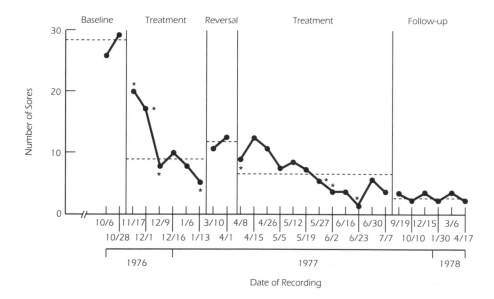

FIGURE 10-5   Reducing scratching. Number of body sores recorded over a one-and-a-half-year period. Treatment consisted of time out contingent upon scratching and positive reinforcement (indicated by asterisks) for reduction in sores. Source: From "Social Control of Self-Injurious Behavior of Organic Etiology" by E. G. Carr and J. J. McDowell. In *Behavior Therapy*, 1980, *11*, pp. 402–409. Copyright © 1980 by the Association for the Advancement of Behavior Therapy.

Punishment has also been used successfully to reduce criminal behavior. A clear example of the potential of punishment in crime reduction is provided by the work of Leonard Jason and his colleagues on the sale of cigarettes to minors (Jason, 1991; Jason et al., 1991). Jason and his coworkers (1991) found that 80% of stores in the Chicago area were selling cigarettes to minors in violation of state law. Officer Talbot, a member of the Woodbridge, Illinois, police department, contacted Jason about his work, and the two decided to see what could be done about cigarette sales in Woodbridge, a suburb of Chicago. First they sent minors into stores to buy cigarettes to see if the stores were violating state law. They found that 70% of the stores were selling cigarettes to minors. Next, Talbott and Jason persuaded the town council to pass an ordinance providing for punishment of store owners who sold cigarettes to minors. The first offense would produce a warning; the second offense would result in a $400 fine and a one-day suspension of the right to sell cigarettes. The researchers monitored compliance with the law by periodically sending minors into the stores to buy cigarettes.

The results showed a sharp drop in cigarette sales to minors with the passage of the new legislation, but about one-third of merchants continued to sell to minors. These merchants received warnings, but

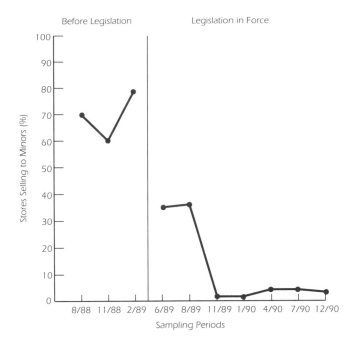

FIGURE 10-6 Cigarette sales to minors. The percentage of stores selling cigarettes to minors fell sharply when punitive legislation went into force. Note that sampling periods are not evenly spaced. SOURCE: Compiled from data in Jason et al., 1991.

many of the warned merchants continued to violate the law. The merchants were subsequently fined and had their cigarette licenses suspended for a day. After this, the rate of violations fell to zero and remained at a very low level for the remainder of the study (see Figure 10-6).

Such studies demonstrate that punishment can be extremely beneficial if properly used. Punishment has reduced the frequency of hallucinations (Bucher & Fabricatore, 1970; Samaan, 1975); obsessional thinking (Anthony & Edelstein, 1975); compulsions (Minnes, 1980; O'Brien & Raynes, 1973); stereotypic behavior (Foxx & Azrin, 1973); nonstop sneezing (Kushner, 1968); persistent vomiting (Lang & Melamed, 1969); and many other forms of troublesome behavior. Explaining why punishment works is, however, another matter.

■ Theories of Punishment

Early theories of punishment (Estes, 1944; E. R. Guthrie, 1960; Skinner, 1953) proposed that response suppression was due to the disruptive effects of aversive stimuli. They pointed out that when a rat is shocked, for example, it may jump, then freeze or run hurriedly about. This behavior is clearly incompatible with, say, pressing a lever, so the rate of lever pressing is bound to decline. Skinner (1953) gives the

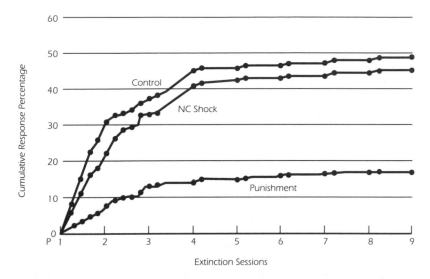

FIGURE 10-7 Contingent versus noncontingent shocks. Cumulative record of the median number of responses (as a percentage of responses before punishment) following no shocks (control), noncontingent shocks, and response-contingent shocks (punishment). SOURCE: From "Permanent Effects of Punishment During Extinction," by E. E. Boe and R. M. Church. *Journal of Comparative and Physiological Psychology*, 1967, *63*, pp. 486–492. Copyright 1967 by the American Psychological Association. Reprinted by permission.

example of a child who giggles in church. If the parent pinches the child, this arouses emotional behavior that is incompatible with giggling, so the giggling stops or declines. The punished behavior, said Skinner, "is merely temporarily suppressed, more or less effectively, by an emotional reaction" (p. 188).

Research on punishment undermined this explanation by producing two key findings: First, as we have seen, the effects of punishment are not as transient as Skinner thought if sufficiently strong aversives are used. Second, punishment has a greater suppressive effect on behavior than noncontingent aversive stimulation. This last point takes a bit of explaining.

If punishment reduces response rates merely because it arouses incompatible behavior, then it should make no difference whether the aversive stimuli used are response contingent or not. But in fact it makes a great deal of difference. Recall the study by Boe and Church (1967), described earlier, in which some rats received noncontingent shocks. The experimenters also studied a group of rats that received occasional shocks, but in this group the shocks were contingent upon lever pressing. Thus, some rats received shocks contingent upon lever pressing, others received the same number of shocks independent of their behavior, and a control group received no shocks at all. As noted earlier, the noncontingent shocks did suppress lever pressing. But this effect was nothing compared with that of contingent shocks (see Figure 10-7).

The early theories of punishment could not explain this discrepancy between contingent and noncontingent aversives, and it is this discrepancy that current theories must explain. The two leading theories are the two-factor and one-factor theories we encountered in considering negative reinforcement.

Two-factor theory.   Two-factor theory can be applied to punishment much as it is applied to negative reinforcement (Mowrer, 1947; Dinsmoor, 1954, 1955). If a rat presses a lever and receives a shock, the lever is paired with the shock. Through Pavlovian conditioning, the lever then becomes a CS for the same behavior aroused by the shock, including fear. Put another way, if shock is aversive, then the lever becomes aversive. The rat might escape the lever by moving away from it. Moving away from the lever is reinforced by a reduction of fear. And, of course, moving away from the lever necessarily reduces the rate of lever pressing.

A human example may clarify the theory: Suppose that you sat on a balcony railing, slipped, and fell 10 feet to the pavement below. You experienced considerable pain, but no permanent injury. After such an experience, you might find that sitting on a railing frightened you, and even being on a balcony might make you uneasy. You could escape this discomfort by leaving the balcony, so walking away from the balcony would be reinforced. So would milling about, talking with friends, and anything else that keeps you away from the railing. Thus, punishment reduces responding because it creates a CS the avoidance of which is reinforcing.

Critics of two-factor theory charge that the theory has all the flaws when applied to punishment that it has when explaining negative reinforcement. In addition, some studies meant to test the theory have not been very supportive. For instance, the theory predicts that punishment will reduce responding in proportion to its proximity to the punished response. A rat that has been shocked when it pressed a lever should be less inclined to press the lever than to touch it, less inclined to touch it than to stand near it, less inclined to stand near it than to approach it, and so on. But this may not be the case.

In one study, R. Mansfield and Howard Rachlin (1970) trained pigeons to peck two disks for food. The birds received food only if they pecked both disks in the proper sequence, first the right disk, then the left. Next the experimenters began shocking the birds each time they pecked the disks in the proper, right-left, sequence. They began with mild shocks and each day increased their intensity. They reasoned that if two-factor theory were correct, at some point the birds would peck the right disk, but not the left. The right disk, being further removed from punishment, would be less aversive than the left and therefore would be more likely to be pecked. It is as though a student were punished for calling out answers instead of waiting to be called upon by the teacher. After being punished, the student might *start* to call out an answer, and catch himself (or herself). Similarly, the birds might start the key peck sequence, but catch themselves and stop. It turned out, however, that response rates on the two keys declined together. If the birds pecked the right disk, they nearly always went on to peck the left.

Because of such failures, two-factor theory has lost ground to the more elegant one-factor theory of punishment.

One-factor theory.   The one-factor theory of punishment is similar to the one-factor theory of negative reinforcement: It says that only one process, operant learning, is involved. Punishment, these theories argue, weakens behavior just as reinforcement strengthens it.

The idea goes back to Thorndike (1911), who originally thought that punishment was the mirror image of reinforcement. He later abandoned the idea (Thorndike, 1932), but other researchers resurrected it (Azrin & Holz, 1966; Premack, 1971; Rachlin & Herrnstein, 1969). The theory wins points partly because it is not subject to the criticisms made against the two-factor theory. There is also, however, research evidence in its favor.

Recall that the Premack Principle states that high-probability behavior reinforces low-probability behavior. If one-factor theory is correct, then the opposite of Premack's reinforcement rule should apply to punishment: Low-probability behavior should punish high-probability behavior (Premack, 1971). This is, in fact, what happens (Mazur, 1975). If, for example, a hungry rat is made to run following eating, it will eat less. The low-probability behavior (running), suppresses the high-probability behavior (eating). One-factor theorists conclude that Thorndike was right in the first place: Punishment and reinforcement have symmetrical (though opposite) effects on behavior.

But while reinforcement and punishment might show a certain symmetry, this does not mean they are equally desirable ways of changing behavior. Indeed, punishment and negative reinforcement both leave much to be desired as agents of change. They work, but they work for a high price.

THE PRICE OF AVERSIVES

One reason that negative reinforcement and punishment are so widely used is that they are effective, at least in the short run. In other words, we use aversives because we are reinforced for doing so. Sometimes the reinforcement is positive, as when a teacher is praised by a principal for "running a tight ship." Sometimes the reinforcement is negative, as when we escape criticism by rebuking our critics, or when we take away a child's radio to escape loud music.

Unfortunately, aversive control, especially punishment, has three very undesirable side effects: escape, aggression, and apathy (Skinner, 1953; Sidman, 1989b). Escape is a reasonable and predictable response to aversive control. The dog that has been punished after answering its master's call runs away when called; the failing student ditches school; the employee who has botched an assignment "hides out" until the boss has cooled down.

Sometimes it is possible to escape without actually fleeing. Nathan Azrin once put a rat in a cage where it would receive both food and shock when it pressed a lever. The rat eventually learned to lie on its back while pressing the lever. Presumably the rat's fur insulated it somewhat and reduced the intensity of the shocks. Murray Sidman (1989b) notes that we humans often escape aversives by "tuning out." We "close our ears," for example, to a spouse, parent, or employer who nags incessantly.

We can also escape aversives by cheating and lying. The student who did not do his homework escapes criticism by copying someone else's work or by saying, "The dog ate it." Making excuses, fawning, crying, and professing remorse are other means of escape. If such tactics are reinforced by escape from aversives, they will be repeated. As a result, people often become quite expert at avoiding aversive control.

The ultimate escape, as Sidman (1989b) notes, is suicide. Those who suffer the ravages of advanced age or the intractable pain of incurable disease are, not surprisingly, among those most likely to kill themselves. But otherwise healthy people will sometimes commit suicide to escape aversive control. People who live in abusive relationships or who are victims of harassment by government sometimes escape these intolerable situations by removing themselves irrevocably from them.

An alternative to escaping aversive conditions is to attack those who create them. We criticize our critics, disparage those who disparage us, and answer each blow in kind. Aggression is particularly likely when escape is impossible: It is the cornered rat that is dangerous. Like escape, aggression is often an effective way of exerting control over those who use aversives.

Aggression is a more troublesome side effect of aversives than escape for two reasons. First, the aggression is not necessarily directed at the source of injury. If two animals are put into the same cage and one of them is shocked, the shocked animal will attack its neighbor (Ulrich & Azrin, 1962; Ulrich et al., 1965). This is so even though the other animal had nothing to do with the attacker's pain. "The aggression is neither ritualistic nor momentary," writes Sidman (1989b); "if we do not separate the two, the attack will end with a kill" (p. 186). Shocked animals will even attack much larger neighbors: A mouse will attack a rat, a rat will attack a cat.

If no other animal is available, shocked animals will attack inanimate objects. Again, the inanimate object need not be in any way responsible for the shocks. If no suitable object is available, a rat will learn to pull a chain that provides an object to bite (Azrin et al., 1965).

We can see much the same phenomenon in people. Steven Oliver and his colleagues (1974) found, for instance, that both boys and men would inflict pain on others following aversive stimulation, even though their victims were not responsible for their suffering. A familiar example suggests the way aggression sometimes "progresses" through a family: A husband strikes his wife, the wife strikes a child, the child strikes a younger sibling, the sibling strikes the family dog. Humans, like animals, will also attack inanimate objects if no living creature is handy. Most of us have slammed a door after being insulted.

People, unlike other animals, often try to make their aggression against innocent parties seem rational. The British philosopher and mathematician Bertrand Russell reports that while a lad in school he saw one of his classmates beating a younger boy. When he reproached the elder boy, the latter replied, "The Bigs beat on me, so I beat the babies. That's fair." Of course, there is nothing fair about it. The boy has at least recognized, however, that the beating he gives is in some way connected to the beating he receives from others.

Sometimes physical aggression is not an option. Employees cannot assault the boss who insults or badgers them, but they can attack in other ways. Employees who are mistreated often steal materials, sabotage products, or slow production rates. Students who are miserable in school and cannot escape may vandalize school property or set the school on fire.

A third side effect of aversives is a generalized suppression of behavior. If aversives are a common consequence of many kinds of behavior, they will suppress not only the punished behavior, but behavior in general. A kind of malaise, or apathy, is a by-product of situations in which aversives are commonplace. If responding produces only punishment or negative reinforcement, then we are apt to behave as little as possible except when responding is required to escape or avoid aversives. Unless strong positive reinforcers balance the use of aversives, the best thing to do is to do nothing.

When Carl Warden and Mercy Aylesworth (1927) punished rats for entering one of two passageways, they found that the rats tended to avoid entering either. Instead, they stayed in the release chamber. We may see a similar phenomenon in the classroom when a teacher ridicules children for asking "stupid" questions. Those children not only become less likely to ask questions; they may be reluctant to answer questions or participate in other classroom activities.

Query: What are the three main side effects of aversive control?

Aside from the side effects of aversive control, there are practical limitations in its use (Stachnik, 1972). These limitations often prevent us from using aversives effectively. The fact that aversive control often leads to efforts to escape or counterattack means that it is sometimes difficult to apply aversives. A teacher can use aversives to control students, but if this leads to high absenteeism, the students might not learn much. And if a student reacts to aversives by vandalizing school property, the student and the school might be worse off.

Another difficulty with the use of aversives is that they tend to get out of control. The use of corporal punishment in schools has resulted in broken bones, ruptured blood vessels, hematomas, muscle and nerve damage, whiplash, spinal injuries, and even death (Gursky, 1992). Child abuse is often punishment that got out of hand. A parent slaps a child harder than intended and breaks a jaw, boxes the child's ears and breaks an eardrum, shakes a crying baby and puts it into a coma. Sometimes parents ignore a child's annoying behavior until they become enraged. Then, instead of striking the child once on the buttocks with the open hand, the parent may hit the child about the head and face with a belt.

A common mistake in the use of punishment is to begin with an aversive stimulus that is too weak to suppress the unwanted behavior and gradually go to stronger stimuli. The end result may be the use of more severe forms of punishment than are necessary. Neal Miller (1960) demonstrated this in a study of rats. He first exposed rats to very weak electric shock when they entered an alley where they found food. Gradually he increased the level of shock the rats received when they entered the alley. The result was that rats eventually endured levels of shock that would have suppressed their behavior had they received them at the outset. Parents sometimes make the same mistake: They begin with a very mild aversive stimulus and gradually use stronger and stronger forms of aversives. Eventually they may find themselves using aversives that risk bodily injury. Our courts regularly do the same thing when they dismiss charges or give a light sentence for a first or second offense.

Finally, the use of aversive control raises ethical questions. Is it right, for example, to punish children to get them to behave properly? Questions of this sort are not, of course, scientific questions. The science of behavior can demonstrate that aversives can be used effectively. It can even demonstrate that they can alleviate suffering, as when self-injury is eliminated by the use of punishment. But science cannot tell us whether what *can* be done *should* be done. The use of aversives inevitably proves to be controversial.

Of course, not all means of aversive control are equally troublesome. There is a great deal of difference between striking a child with a paddle and denying the child access to a television. Even mild forms of aversive control can, however, cause problems. Because of these problems, it is wise to consider alternatives whenever possible. Let us take a brief look at some of those alternatives.

ALTERNATIVES TO AVERSIVE CONTROL

Because of the unfortunate side effects of aversive control, psychologists have sought alternative ways of modifying troublesome behavior (LaVigna & Donnellan, 1986). The simplest of these is response prevention.

■ Response Prevention

One tempting alternative to aversive control of unwanted behavior is to prevent the behavior from occurring. Often this can be achieved by altering the environment in some way. A child who plays with the family's precious china can be prevented from doing so if the china is put out of reach. A telephone lock might curb a child's tendency to make expensive telephone calls to people on the other side of the globe. Poisons and firearms can be put under lock and key. A 6-year-old child who wets the bed can be prevented from drinking within the hour before retiring. A child who bites his hands can be made to wear boxing gloves.

Response prevention is often the simplest and fastest means of reducing unwanted behavior, especially in young children. Unfortunately, it has its limitations. The child who is prevented from drinking before bedtime has not gained bladder control and will wet the bed if allowed to drink. The child who bites his hands may be made to wear boxing gloves, but this effectively gives the child a severe disability. (It is impossible to feed oneself or use the bathroom while wearing boxing gloves.) Response prevention techniques that work well with young children do not always work well with teens or adults; they may pick the telephone lock or remove the hinges on the cabinet where drugs or firearms are kept. Moreover, some forms of behavior cannot be effectively prevented by modifying the environment. It is not clear, for example, how we could change a girl's environment to preclude her from holding her breath, or what we could do to prevent a boy from stealing from his classmates. Because of these limitations of response prevention, other tactics are sometimes necessary. One safe procedure that often works is extinction.

■ Extinction

We saw in Chapter Nine that withholding all reinforcement for a response reduces the frequency of that response. Carl Williams (1959) showed, for instance, that a child's tantrums could be eliminated simply by no longer providing the attention that reinforced them (see Figure 9-3).

Using extinction to get rid of unwanted behavior requires first of all identifying the reinforcer that maintains the behavior. In the case of

Williams's tantrum-prone child, the reinforcer was the parents' attention. Adult attention is frequently the reinforcer for misbehavior in children. Some parents make a big fuss over the child who wets the bed and express concern over the child's health. Similarly, teachers tell wandering students to return to their seats, perhaps lecturing them or explaining why roaming about is wrong. Studies have shown that such attention, though intended to punish behavior, often reinforces it. Research by K. Daniel O'Leary and his colleagues (O'Leary & Becker, 1968–1969; O'Leary et al., 1970) showed, for example, that when schoolchildren were reprimanded loudly for misbehaving, their behavior got worse, not better. In other words, loud reprimands, though intended as punishment, reinforced the unwanted behavior. By identifying and withholding reinforcers, the frequency of unwanted behavior can be reduced.

Adult attention is not the only source of reinforcement. The principle, however, is the same: If the reinforcer maintaining unwanted behavior can be identified and removed, the rate of that behavior will decline. Thus, extinction is sometimes an attractive alternative to aversives. It is not, unfortunately, an ideal alternative in all situations.

Query: *How does extinction differ from response prevention?*

As Chapter Nine indicates, extinction often provokes emotional behavior, especially aggression and angry displays. This is often annoying in itself, but in addition it can lead people to abandon the extinction procedure, at least temporarily. Alternating extinction with reinforcement amounts to intermittent reinforcement, which increases the rate of behavior and makes it more resistant to extinction. In theory, these problems can be avoided by maintaining the extinction procedure; in practice, people often give in to escape the obnoxious behavior, thereby reinforcing it on an intermittent schedule.

Another problem with extinction is that the unwanted behavior declines slowly. This is annoying when the behavior involved is throwing tantrums or running around a room; it is dangerous when the behavior can cause serious injury. Sometimes responses occur thousands of times during extinction before they reach acceptable levels, and by that time serious damage might have been done. If a child is hitting himself or herself in the eyes or stabbing others with pencils, a great deal of harm might be done before extinction is effective.

Extinction is also limited by the fact that the reinforcers maintaining troublesome behavior might not be under our control. Children sometimes steal to get adult attention, but they also steal to enjoy the toys, food, and other items they obtain through pilferage. Young students may roam about the room less because it earns them the attention of the teacher than because it gains them the company of another student. A student might make silly remarks not for the fun of annoying the teacher, but because of the laughter of peers. Extinction cannot be used if the relevant reinforcers cannot be withheld.

Where appropriate, extinction is safe and effective, and for these reasons it is a highly desirable alternative to aversives. Unfortunately, there are many situations in which it is inappropriate. In these situations, we may turn to differential reinforcement.

■ Differential Reinforcement

We saw in Chapter Nine that it is possible to change the rate of a response by modifying the reinforcement schedule in force. Certain of these schedules are particularly useful for getting rid of unwanted behavior.

One particularly effective schedule is DRI (differential reinforcement of incompatible responses). In DRI, we reinforce a response that is incompatible with the unwanted behavior. Moving rapidly is incompatible with moving slowly; smiling is usually incompatible with frowning; standing is incompatible with sitting down. By increasing the rate of a desirable response, we automatically reduce the rate of an incompatible undesirable response. Take the case of the teacher who has children moving about the room when they should be working at their desks. Sitting at a desk is incompatible with walking about the room; it is impossible to do one if you are doing the other. If a teacher systematically praises or talks to students who are seated at their desks, the time students spend at their desks will increase, and the time they spend wandering about will necessarily fall off.

Hughes Tarpley and Stephen Schroeder (1979) showed that DRI can reduce self-injurious behavior. In one case, they periodically provided food to an 8-year-old boy if, instead of hitting himself in the face, he played steadily with a ball. Within 40 minutes, the rate of face punching had fallen by more than 90%.

We need not, however, focus on incompatible responses. In DRO (differential reinforcement of other behavior), any behavior except the unwanted response can be reinforced. A child who constantly sucks his thumb, for example, might receive reinforcement periodically provided he is doing anything *except* sucking his thumb.

It is also possible to slow the rate of unwanted behavior by systematically reinforcing a lower rate of responding. This schedule, called differential reinforcement of low rate (DRL), involves providing reinforcement after an interval in which the unwanted response has not occurred. A child who bites her hands an average of once every two seconds, for instance, may be given a bit of candy each time she goes five seconds without biting. What is reinforced is not hand biting, but an interval of *not* biting. When hand biting occurs less than once every five seconds, we would begin requiring longer intervals for reinforcement, gradually shaping up prolonged periods of not biting.

James Luiselli and his colleagues (1985) used DRL to reduce aggressive behavior. They worked with a 15-year-old girl who was deaf, blind, and retarded and was inclined to hit and scratch other people. At first, she received food and attention contingent upon spending five minutes without hurting anyone. As her behavior improved, longer periods without aggression were required for reinforcement. Over a period of a few days, the procedure produced a reduction in aggressive acts of more than 90%.

Query: Name three kinds of differential reinforcement.

Differential reinforcement works best in conjunction with extinction. Thus, while reinforcing desirable behavior, every effort is made to avoid reinforcing undesirable behavior. This typically results in a reduction in unwanted behavior that is substantially more rapid than that obtained with extinction alone. Differential reinforcement is not always effective, however, perhaps because it ignores the function the misbehavior serves. This possibility brings us to functional communication training.

■ Functional Communication Training

We have seen that undesirable behavior, including aggressive and self-injurious behavior, is often maintained by the same sort of reinforcers, including attention and assistance, that usually strengthens more acceptable behavior. According to Carr (1985; 1988), having tantrums, biting oneself or others, breaking objects, and so on, may be equivalent to making requests, asking questions, pointing to desired objects, and the like. It follows, says Carr, that we may be able to reduce unwanted behavior by teaching the person more acceptable means of achieving the same ends. In a sense, the idea is to teach better ways of communicating, so the procedure is called **functional communication training**.

This new approach to reducing troublesome behavior has proved to be very effective. You might recall from Chapter Six that Carr and Mark Durand (1985) treated four children who engaged in various kinds of disruptive behavior. They taught the youngsters alternative ways of obtaining reinforcers they were accustomed to obtaining through unacceptable acts. Following the brief training period, all four children showed greater than 90% reduction in unacceptable behavior.

Other studies of functional communication training have yielded similar results (Carr & Carlson, in press; Carr & Kemp, 1989; Carr et al., 1990a, 1990b), making this arguably the most promising alternative to aversive control. Carr and his colleagues (1990a) have argued, in fact, that the debate concerning aversive treatments is the wrong issue. It focuses our attention on suppressing undesirable behavior. We should, they argue, be concerned less with tearing down behavior than with building up behavior. And we should ask whether a particular treatment will provide the individual with more effective forms of behavior. It is doubtful whether aversive techniques can always pass that test.

SUMMARY

Aversive stimulation, in one form or another, is a part of life. It is therefore important to understand the effects of aversives on behavior.

Sometimes aversive stimulation is not dependent upon a particular response. Such noncontingent aversives have the effect of suppressing responding, even though responding does not cause the aversives and not responding does not prevent the aversives. When noncontingent aversives are inescapable, the organism becomes less likely to escape aversives in new situations; they learn to be helpless. Learned helplessness has proved useful as a model for human depression.

Contingent aversives take one of two forms, negative reinforcement or punishment. In negative reinforcement, behavior is strengthened by the removal of an aversive stimulus. Negative reinforcement involves learning to escape or avoid aversive stimuli. Usually escape precedes avoidance, so psychologists speak of escape-avoidance learning. Lying provides a good example of behavior shaped by escape and avoidance of aversive stimulation, such as criticism. Recent research shows that the abnormal behavior of psychotic and retarded people is often shaped by negative reinforcement; it is often a way of escaping and avoiding unpleasant activities.

There are two major theories of negative reinforcement. The two-factor theory proposes that Pavlovian and operant learning are involved. Escape learning is the result of an operant procedure, with the termination of the aversive stimulus acting as a reinforcer. Avoidance learning is the result of Pavlovian conditioning, with the signal of an approaching aversive becoming a signal for fear. Some research supports the theory, but studies showing that avoidance learning occurs in the absence of a signal undermines it.

One-factor theory proposes that escape and avoidance are both due to operant learning. Just as escape from an aversive is reinforcing, so is the avoidance of an aversive.

Punishment is a procedure in which an aversive is contingent upon the performance of a response. The principle effect of punishment is a reduction in the rate of the punished behavior. This reduction in responding is usually more pronounced than that achieved with noncontingent aversives. The two-factor and one-factor theories of negative reinforcement have been applied to punishment; again, one-factor theory currently seems to hold sway.

In the hands of experts, punishment has proved to be an effective treatment for self-injurious behavior and certain other problems. Unfortunately, it also is likely to have unwanted effects, particularly when used by people who are not trained experts. The major side effects are escape, aggression, and apathy.

Fortunately, there are effective alternatives to aversive control.

These include response prevention, extinction, various forms of differential reinforcement, and functional communication training. While there may be instances in which aversives must be used, it is safe to say that the world would be a better place if all of us relied less upon aversives and more upon positive methods of influencing behavior.

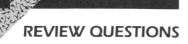

REVIEW QUESTIONS

1. Define the following terms:

   aversive control   *punishment*
   escape-avoidance learning   *response prevention*
   functional communication training   *Sidman avoidance*

2. Why do people rely so much upon aversive control?

3. Benjamin Franklin said that we hate those whom we fear. Do you think he was right? Explain.

4. What is the key difference between noncontingent aversives and punishment?

5. Suppose that you were the leader of a group in charge of new product development for your company. How would you avoid producing learned helplessness in the committee members? (*Hint:* First think of what you would do to produce learned helplessness.)

6. How might learned helplessness help us understand depression following the death of a loved one?

7. Paul argues that learned helplessness is the result of *contingent* aversives. How could you test his hypothesis?

8. What is the key difference between negative reinforcement and punishment?

9. People often say they seek "open, honest relationships." Why are such relationships so rare?

10. What is the key difference between two-factor theory and one-factor theory?

11. Why is the work of Sidman so troublesome to two-factor theory?

12. Why do you suppose it took researchers so long to appreciate the power of punishment?

13. Some psychologists have suggested that people could reduce unwanted behavior, such as nail biting, by wearing a rubber band around their wrist and snapping it against their skin whenever they perform the unwanted response. What do you think of this technique?

14. How could the work of Jason in Woodbridge, Illinois, be applied to campus crimes committed by students?

15. How would Premack define an aversive stimulus?

16. Give examples of the side effects you might expect if you used aversives to control the behavior of a spouse or friend.

17. If you were a practicing physician, how would you alter the behavior of an elderly person who frequently comes in complaining of vague, inconsequential symptoms?

18. Suppose you are a pediatric dentist, and many of your patients constantly suck their thumbs, a practice that may cause dental problems. What would you do?

19. How could a principal use differential reinforcement to reduce the use of punishment by teachers?

20. You are preparing guidelines for the use of corporal punishment in a reform school. What one point will you emphasize most?

Suggested Readings

The work of Nathan Azrin, Richard Foxx, Ivar Lovaas, and others provides ample evidence that aversives can be put to good use in therapeutic situations. However, great strides have been made in recent years in developing alternatives to aversive techniques. Edward Carr's work is particularly worth studying.

Probably the best critique of aversive control is *Coercion and Its Fallout* by Murray Sidman, a prominent researcher in the field. For examples of the horrific use of aversives throughout human history, see John Carey's *Eyewitness to History*.

Answers to Queries

Page 253: A noncontingent aversive is one that does not depend upon a particular response. For example, noncontingent shock is delivered regardless of what the organism does.

Page 255: The opposite of learned helplessness might be called learned resilience, or something of the sort. Perhaps the best way to produce learned resilience would be to reinforce responding after failure and gradually increase the amount of failure that must be endured before a response is reinforced.

Page 255: Both positive and negative reinforcement *increase* the strength (frequency, probability) of a response.

Page 259: The two factors are Pavlovian and operant learning.

Page 260: Pavlovian conditioning requires a CS. Therefore, some sort of stimulus must signal the aversive stimulus.

Page 263: Negative reinforcement makes a response more likely to occur, while punishment makes a response less likely to occur.

Page 266: Scratching can be suppressed in the presence of parents yet occur at a high rate in their absence. The goal was not merely to suppress scratching when the parents were around, but to suppress it all the time. Sores do not go away when a parent walks into the room.

Page 273: The organism tends to (1) escape from the source of aversive stimulation; (2) attack the source of aversive stimuli or other convenient targets; (3) reduce the rate of responding in general.

Page 276: In response prevention, we prevent the response from occurring; in extinction, we allow the response to occur but prevent its reinforcement.

Page 278: DRI (differential reinforcement of incompatible behavior), DRO (differential reinforcement of other behavior), and DRL (differential reinforcement of low rate). Other forms of differential reinforcement are used (for example, DRH; see Chapter Nine), but these three are particularly useful in reducing the frequency of unwanted behavior.

eleven

Forgetting

Memory is often spoken of as if it involved the actual persistence of the past. . . . This is mere mythology.
—BERTRAND RUSSELL

We do not remember experiences; we are changed by them.
—B. F. SKINNER

BACKGROUND

The history of memory is a story of metaphors. In ancient times, experiences were impressed upon the mind like marks on a wax tablet; to remember an experience, one had only to look upon one's mental tablet. In the Renaissance, experience wrote on a blank slate, which could be read so long as the message was not wiped off. In the Industrial Age, the blank slate gave way to memos and snapshots stored in mental filing cabinets. Experiences were filed away and retrieved by searching through the appropriate file when the need arose. In the 20th century, memories were once again recorded in wax, but this time the wax was Alexander Graham Bell's recording cylinder. Experiences could be replayed so long as one could set the needle at the right place on the cylinder. As magnetic tapes replaced records, memories became magnetic and lasted a long time if not erased or recorded over. The development of high-speed computers provided the current metaphor for memory. Today, by a curious coincidence, experiences are measured in bytes and stored in memory banks.

But while the metaphors have changed, the concept of memory has not. It is still viewed as an "internal record or representation" (as one of many texts puts it) of past experience. Plato would have no trouble recognizing that view of memory; it was his own.

Of course, few psychologists today believe that memories are verid-ical replicas of experience. Even in ages past memories were referred to as *"faint copies"* of experience, not exact duplicates. Our tendency to get things wrong (to remember a blue hat as green, to recall the date 1863 as 1836, and the like) argues compellingly against memories as exact copies of the past. But many psychologists, like most other people, believe that experiences are represented in some form with-in us.

One of B. F. Skinner's most important (and least understood) contributions may have been to offer an entirely different view. To Skinner, experiences are not stored away and retrieved for use later; rather, experiences change the organism's tendency to behave in cer-tain ways.[1] A dog that had little or no tendency to jump through hoops has, as a result of certain experiences, a greater tendency to do so. If this tendency persists the next day, it is wonderful and mysterious, but it is no more wonderful and mysterious than the fact that the behavior was learned in the first place.

This functional approach focuses on the behaving organism and its relation to events in its past and current environments. With this approach, there is no need to compare the organism to a wax tablet, a computer, or some other device. Memory requires a metaphor; living organisms do not.

We will not look for the internal record of the dog's trick, then. We will ask, rather, why it is that the dog, having learned to jump through hoops, is one day unable to do so, or does so less well. We will ask why behavior, once learned, is sometimes forgotten. Since our focus is to be on forgetting, we had better start with a definition.

DEFINING FORGETTING

Learning is a marvelous invention of genetic evolution, but it is far from perfect. The changes in behavior that we call learning are often lost, at least partially, with the passage of time. It is this loss to which we refer when we speak of forgetting. Thus, **forgetting** can be defined as deterioration in learned behavior over time.

Imagine that you return to your childhood home after an absence of several years. You have been assured that the town has changed little, yet you are astonished at how many landmarks seem unfamiliar. You visit the local library and discover that the floor plan is not as you remember it. Didn't the reference section used to be over there? Weren't these tables under the window? But you find that there has been no reorganization; things are where they have always been. While

---

[1] Changes in behavior are no doubt mediated by some sort of physiological change in tissue, but this change is not better understood by analogy with slates, filing cabinets, or computer chips.

in the library you pick up a book you read years ago, but its characters and plot are as unfamiliar to you as those of a book you have never seen. While leaving the library, you run into a friend and neighbor from years past. You were once "best friends," yet now you are unable to say her name.

This imaginary return home might seem like a story from *The Twilight Zone,* but it is quite plausible. The mysterious lapses in your behavior are merely everyday examples of forgetting.

In considering forgetting, it is important to realize that we are concerned with deterioration of behavior, not the deterioration of a mental or neurological record of experience. When we ask whether an individual has forgotten something, we are asking whether the individual can perform an act learned in the past. "Have you forgotten how to ride a bicycle?" is another way of saying, "Can you ride a bicycle?" "Do you remember algebra?" is a way of asking, "Can you still solve algebra problems?" "Did your dental appointment slip your mind?" means, "Did you go to the dentist?"

These examples imply that forgetting means a decline in the probability of some behavior, but this is not always the case. For example, a rat that has learned to press a lever for food might, as a result of discrimination training, learn *not* to press the lever when a red light is on. If we remove the rat from the cage and return it a month later, we may find that it presses the lever whether the light is on or not. If so, the rat has forgotten the discrimination learned earlier. In this instance, forgetting means the appearance of a response.

Of course, forgetting is often incomplete. An organism may fail to respond in exactly the same way it did at the conclusion of training, yet some evidence of learning may linger. You may not be able to solve as many algebra problems as you could at the conclusion of your algebra course, but you may still solve some problems. You may not be able to ride a bike as well as when you were 12, but you can still get around on two wheels. Thus, forgetting is not an all-or-none phenomenon; there are degrees of forgetting. The degree of forgetting can be measured in several ways.

Query: What is forgetting?

MEASURING FORGETTING

Forgetting, like learning, occurs in time. In measuring forgetting, we observe behavior after a period during which the learned behavior is not performed. After this period, usually called a **retention interval,** we test in various ways for evidence that the learned behavior is still intact.

In **free recall,** we simply give the organism the opportunity to perform the previously learned behavior. Consider the case of a pigeon that has learned to peck a disk for food. After training, the bird is removed from the experimental chamber and returned to its home cage. A month passes, during which time the bird has no opportunity to obtain food by pecking on a disk. (Note that it has not been punished for pecking the disk, nor has it been allowed to peck the disk without receiving food. It is simply deprived of the opportunity to peck the disk.) After the retention interval, we return the bird to the training cage. If it behaves as it did in the last training session, no forgetting has occurred. The less the bird's behavior resembles its former behavior, the greater the amount of forgetting.[2]

The free recall technique has been used in studies of human forgetting. A subject might be required to learn to recite a poem, such as "Jabberwocky," and then be asked to recite it again after a period of time. Or we might have someone learn a finger maze, a small maze that is run with a finger or stylus, and then have them run the maze after an interval.

Although free recall is what most of us think of when we think of measuring forgetting, it is sometimes a rather crude yardstick. The student who cannot recall a French word he studied earlier has not necessarily forgotten everything about the missing word. He may be able to say that the word has three syllables, that the emphasis is on the middle syllable, that the word starts with the letter *f*, and that it means "window." Clearly the effects of the learning experience have not been entirely lost, but the free recall method does not recognize this fact.

A variation of the free recall technique is sometimes used to get at these more subtle remnants of learning. Known as **prompted recall,** it consists of presenting hints, or prompts, to increase the likelihood that the behavior will be produced. A subject who has studied a list of French words, for example, might be given a list of anagrams of the words; the subject's task would then be to unscramble the letters. Failure to do so indicates forgetting. We may also provide a series of prompts and measure the degree of forgetting by the number of prompts required to produce the response. We might, for instance, give a subject the first letter of a French word learned earlier. If the subject does not respond correctly, we provide the second letter. If that does not prompt the correct response, we provide the third letter, and so on until the word is recalled.

Animal forgetting can also be studied with prompted recall. A chimp will learn to get fruit from a vending machine by inserting tokens into a slot (Cowles, 1937). If it fails to do so after a retention interval, we can prompt the behavior by offering the chimp a token. If

---

[2] Note that in this use of the term *forgetting* we are not speculating about the status of a memory for disk pecking. We are merely noting a difference in the bird's tendency to peck a disk.

the animal uses it correctly, we know that something of the previous learning experience remains.

Query: What is the difference between free recall and prompted recall?

Another way of measuring forgetting is called **recognition.** In this case, the subject has only to identify the material previously learned. Typically the subject is presented with the original learning materials as well as some new material. A person might be shown a list of French words and be asked to say which ones were on a list learned earlier. This test of forgetting is, of course, much easier to pass than one involving free or prompted recall.

Another kind of recognition procedure is often used to study forgetting in animals, particularly pigeons. The procedure is called **delayed matching to sample** (Blough, 1959). In a typical experiment, a pigeon is presented with a row of three disks. The middle disk is illuminated for a brief period by either a yellow or a blue light. After this, the two disks on either side are illuminated, one with a yellow light, the other with a blue one. If the bird pecks the disk that matches the sample, it receives food. Once the bird has learned to match the sample, the experimenter introduces a delay between the offset of the sample disk and the illumination of the two alternative disks. The bird is asked to recognize the training stimulus; failure to do so indicates forgetting.

Forgetting can also be measured by reinstating the original training procedure. This **relearning method** assumes that the less training required to reach the previous level of performance, the less forgetting has occurred. There is usually a savings compared with the original training program, so this technique is also called the **savings method.** Hermann Ebbinghaus (1885/1913), the German psychologist who conducted the world's first documented experiments on forgetting, used the relearning method to study forgetting. He memorized lists of nonsense syllables, such as *zak, kyl,* and *bof,* until he could produce the list twice without error. Then, after a retention interval, he relearned the list. If it took fewer trials to learn the list the second time, this savings provided a measure of forgetting. The greater the savings, the less the forgetting.

Relearning can also be used to study forgetting in animals. If a rat takes 30 trials to learn to run a maze without errors, and if it takes the rat 20 trials to reach that same criterion after a retention interval, then there has been a savings of 10 trials. If another rat has a savings of 15 trials, this second rat has forgotten less.

There are other ways of measuring forgetting, mainly variations on the methods just described. Together these methods have allowed researchers to tackle the problem of forgetting. Their research has provided considerable insight into why we forget.

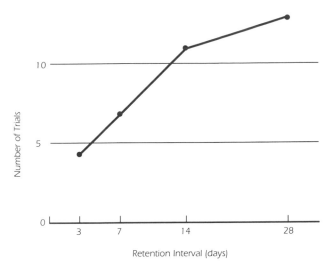

FIGURE 11-1 Retention interval and forgetting. Average number of trials required to relearn a response increased with the length of the retention interval. (After Gagne, 1941.)

WHY WE FORGET

Frédéric Chopin once said that if he went without practicing the piano for one day, only he knew it; if he skipped two days, only he and his tutor knew it; if he skipped three days, everyone knew it. Chopin was talking about forgetting. He recognized that even after mastering a skill at a very high level, that mastery deteriorates if the skill is neglected. Why?

Very likely Chopin believed that the passage of time since his last "training session" accounted for forgetting. This was the prevailing view of forgetting in his day, and it remains the dominant explanation outside the psychological laboratory. This view assumes that learning means storing up records of experience, and remembering means activating those records. With the passage of time, the record decays and we forget.

There is a strong relationship between the length of the retention interval and forgetting. Ebbinghaus found, for instance, that it took him longer to relearn lists of nonsense syllables after a long retention interval than after a short one. More carefully designed research with animals has shown much the same thing. R. M. Gagne (1941) trained rats to run down an alley to find food. After the training, Gagne tested the rats for forgetting using the relearning method. Some rats relearned after an interval of 3 days, others after 7 days, 14 days, and 28 days. The results showed clearly that the longer the interval between training and relearning, the greater the deterioration in performance (see Figure 11-1).

In another study, Henry Gleitman and J. W. Bernheim (1963) trained rats to press a lever on an FI schedule and then removed the animals from the training cage for either 24 hours or 24 days. The cumulative records from these sessions showed that there was less of the scalloping associated with FI schedules after the longer interval. After a period of 24 hours, rats were likely to pause following reinforcement; after a period of 24 days, they kept on responding. This failure to pause after reinforcement indicated greater forgetting with the longer retention interval.

Such studies clearly show that forgetting increases with the passage of time. The question is whether the passage of time *accounts for* the forgetting that occurs. John McGeoch (1932) argued that it did not. Time cannot explain forgetting, McGeoch said, because time itself is not an event. Time is not something that occurs, but rather an invention for talking about the occurrence of events. An hour, for example, is $\frac{1}{24}$ of the time it takes for the earth to rotate on its axis; a week is seven complete rotations of the earth; a year is one complete revolution of the earth around the sun, and so on. Time itself is not an event and can therefore not be said to cause other events.

Thus, the image on a film fades with time, but it is the action of sunlight, not time, that causes the fading. People develop illnesses over time, but it is bacteria and viruses and toxins that cause disease, not time. Learning occurs in time, but it is certain kinds of experiences, and not time, that produce learning. Likewise, forgetting occurs in time, but it is not time that causes forgetting. "Time, in and of itself," wrote McGeoch (1932), "does nothing" (p. 359).

To explain forgetting, then, we must identify the events that account for its occurrence. Some of those events have been identified, and we now turn our attention to them.

■ Degree of Learning

The better something is learned, the less likely it is to be forgotten. Ebbinghaus (1885) demonstrated this long ago. He found a systematic correlation between the number of learning trials and the amount of forgetting when tested the next day. When he practiced a list 8 times, for example, the next day he could recall very little; when he practiced a list 64 times, the next day his recall was nearly perfect.

Ebbinghaus demonstrated that learning apparently continues even after we seem to have achieved mastery. William Krueger (1929) performed a famous study that showed just how powerful such **overlearning** can be. He asked adults to learn three lists of words, with each list containing 12 one-syllable nouns. He presented the words one at a time at the rate of one word every two seconds. After going through the list the first time, the subject's task was to say each word before it was presented.

Training differed for each of the three lists. The subjects worked at one list until they produced all 12 words correctly and then stopped. On another list, they continued working beyond this level; this time they went through the list half again as many times as it took to reach one errorless trial. On the third list, the subjects went through twice as many trials as it took to learn the list. Suppose, for example, that a subject took 14 trials to get all 12 words correct on each of the three lists. On one of the lists, the subject would be allowed to quit (zero overlearning); on another he or she would be asked to do 7 more trials (50% overlearning); and on the third he or she would be asked to do another 14 trials (100% overlearning). After this initial training, Krueger had his subjects relearn the lists. Some subjects relearned after an interval of only one day; others relearned after 2, 4, 7, 14, or 28 days.

The results clearly showed that the subjects recalled more words from the lists they had overlearned. Moreover, the greater the amount of overlearning, the less they forgot. One hundred percent overlearning paid higher dividends than 50% overlearning, but the difference was not as great as that between no overlearning and 50% overlearning. This suggests that there is a point of diminishing returns in overlearning.

The benefits of overlearning may endure well beyond the final exam. Harry Bahrick (1984) found that a good indication of how well a person remembered the Spanish he or she studied 20, 30, or even 50 years earlier was how thoroughly the language had been learned. People who had studied Spanish for only a year and earned a grade of C remembered little of what they once knew. Those who had studied Spanish for three years and earned A's did very well when tested, even 50 years later. The difference was not due to differences in the opportunity to practice the language, but to how well the language was learned originally. Findings of this sort have obvious implications for students who want to retain what they learn after the graduation ceremony.

■ Prior Learning

Forgetting occurs rapidly when we learn unrelated words, random digits, and nonsense syllables. More meaningful material is, however, easier to retain.

K. Anders Ericsson and John Karat (1981; reported in Ericsson & Chase, 1982) demonstrated this with sentences from stories by John Steinbeck. They read the words in these sentences, one word per second, as though they were reading digits or nonsense syllables. Sometimes the words were in their correct order; sometimes the words were presented randomly. Not surprisingly, the original sentences were recalled far more successfully than the same words in scrambled order. Most people could recall only about six words correctly when the words were in scrambled order. But people could recall complete sentences of 12 or 14 words when presented in their Steinbeckian splendor. Two of the 20 subjects could even recall this 28-word sentence: "She brushed a cloud of hair out of her eyes with the back of her glove and left a smudge of earth on her cheek in doing it."

To say that the rate of forgetting varies with the meaningfulness of the material learned raises a question: What determines whether something is meaningful? We might get an idea by asking ourselves what would happen if we repeated the Ericsson and Karat study with subjects who did not speak a word of English. It is likely that in this case there would be little difference in recall between the original sentences and a random arrangement of words. Thus, when people speak of the meaningfulness of what is learned, they are really talking about the importance of prior learning.

We can see the benefit of previous learning in studies of forgetting and expertise. In one study, A. de Groot (1966) arranged pieces on a chessboard as though a game were in progress. He allowed chess players to study the boards for five seconds and then asked them to reproduce the arrangement of pieces on a cleared board. Some of de Groot's subjects were chess masters, while others were members of a chess club. When he compared the two kinds of players, he found that the chess masters were right 90% of the time, while club players were right only 40% of the time.

De Groot's data argue for the influence of previous learning on forgetting. But there is another possibility: Perhaps chess masters simply forget less than other people. To test this hypothesis, William Chase and Herbert Simon (1973) arranged chess pieces on the board in a random fashion and then showed it to chess masters and ordinary players. If the chess masters had fantastic ability to recall, the arrangement of pieces would make no difference; the experts would still come out on top. But Chase and Simon found that the chess masters' superb recall disappeared. In fact, under these conditions, they could recall no better than ordinary players. Their spectacular memories, it turns out, apply only when the chess pieces are placed on the board in "patterns that have become familiar with years of practice" (Ericsson & Chase, 1982, p. 608). Other studies show that past learning plays an important role in recall for contract bridge (Charness, 1979), circuit diagrams (Egan & Schwartz, 1979), and architectural drawings (Akin, 1983).

It is clear, then, that previous learning can reduce forgetting. Under some circumstances, however, old learning can interfere with recall, a phenomenon called **proactive interference.**

Proactive interference is often studied in people by means of **paired associate learning.** Typically, the object is to learn a list of word pairs, such as *hungry-beautiful,* so that when given the first word *(hungry),* the subject produces the second *(beautiful).* Usually, the list is taught by repeatedly presenting the subject with the first word in each pair,

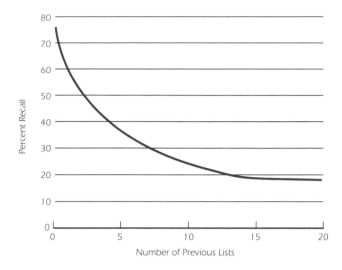

FIGURE 11-2 Interference and forgetting. Underwood plotted data from a number of studies and found that forgetting increased with the number of previously learned lists. (After Underwood, 1957.)

asking for the word that goes with it, and then presenting the correct word.

> Query: What sort of learning procedure (Pavlovian, operant, observational) is paired associate learning?

Typically in these studies all subjects learn an A-C list (for example, *hungry-beautiful*), but some subjects first learn an A-B list (for example, *hungry-fortunate*). Then, after a retention interval, all subjects try to recall the A-C list. Any difference between the two groups in recall can be attributed to learning the A-B list. These studies reliably show that learning the A-B list interferes with recall of items later learned on the A-C list. Moreover, the more lists one learns before the test (A-C) list, the more interference (Underwood, 1957; see Figure 11-2).

Interference from previous learning also accounts for forgetting in more complicated situations. Consider, for example, the findings of a classic study by the famous British psychologist, Sir Frederick Bartlett. Bartlett had people read a Native American folktale called *The War of the Ghosts*. Although the story runs well under 400 words, it is, by contemporary Western standards, disjointed and confusing. Bartlett had people read the story through twice and then, 15 minutes later, reproduce the story as accurately as they could. Bartlett also had the subjects recall the story on other occasions over the coming weeks and months "as opportunity offered." When Bartlett examined the successive recollections, he found that the story became simpler, more coherent, and more modern. This finding can be understood partly in

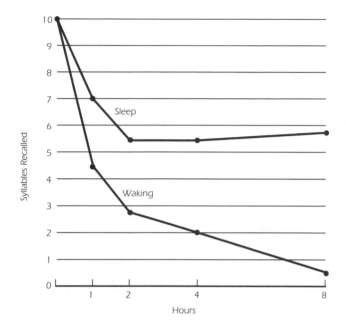

FIGURE 11-3 Forgetting and sleep. Average number of syllables recalled by one subject after intervals of sleep and waking. (After Jenkins & Dallenbach, 1924.)

terms of proactive interference: Previous learning about stories (about how they are constructed) interfered with recalling a different sort of story.

Social psychologists Jerome Levine and Gardner Murphy (1943) studied the effects of proactive interference in a different way. They had college students read a passage and then, 15 minutes later, reproduce it as accurately as possible. The students then read a second passage and, 15 minutes later, tried to reproduce it. The students read and attempted to reproduce the two passages each week for four weeks. Both passages were on what was then a very controversial subject, communism. One of the passages expressed anticommunist sentiments; the other was favorable to communism. Some of the students were strongly disposed toward communism, while others were strongly opposed to it. The researchers were interested in whether these personal inclinations would affect recollection.

They did. The results clearly showed that students who were pro-communist forgot more of the anticommunist passage, while students who were anticommunist forgot more of the procommunist passage.

Such findings are usually interpreted in terms of the effects of attitude or belief on forgetting. But since no one is born with particular attitudes or beliefs concerning communism (or capitalism, fascism, democracy, homosexuality, or other topics), we have to assume that such views are learned. Thus, studies that show that attitudes affect recall are really studies of proactive interference.

Prior learning can have a profound effect upon recall; so, we shall now see, can subsequent learning.

◼ Subsequent Learning

In a classic study by John Jenkins and Karl Dallenbach (1924), two college students learned lists of ten nonsense syllables in the morning and before retiring in the evening. They were then tested for forgetting after one, two, four, or eight hours. The results showed that they forgot less after a period of sleep than after a similar interval of activity. Indeed, after two hours of sleep, additional time had no effect on recall (see Figure 11-3).

Other studies showed that periods of inactivity produce less forgetting than comparable periods of activity. In one study, immobilized cockroaches forgot less than those allowed to move about (Minami & Dallenbach, 1946).

McGeoch (1932) hypothesized that part of the solution to the problem of forgetting was subsequent learning. Forgetting, he suggested, is "a result of an active interference from interpolated events" (p. 364). Or, as another psychologist phrases it, "We forget because we keep on learning" (Gleitman, 1971, p. 20).

When what we learn interferes with our ability to recall earlier learning, the phenomenon is called **retroactive interference.** New learning reaches into the past, as it were, to interfere with earlier learning.

Like proactive interference, retroactive interference is often studied by having people learn two or more lists of paired associates. First the A-B list is learned to a given criterion or for a given number of trials. Then the A-C list is learned. Finally, the subject's ability to recall the A-B list is measured. Evidence of forgetting the A-B list can be attributed to interference from learning the A-C list. If, for example, a person forgets the A-B pair, *hungry-fortunate*, this may be because of having later learned the A-C pair, *hungry-beautiful*.

Benton Underwood and his colleagues did a number of experiments with paired associates to study the interference effects of learning. In one experiment, he and Leland Thune (Thune & Underwood, 1943) had college students learn lists of ten paired associates made up of adjectives. Each subject learned an A-B list, then relearned the list after a 20-minute delay. During the delay period, some students just rested, while others had from 2 to 20 trials on an A-C list. Notice that the time lapse was the same for all subjects; the difference was in the learning that took place during the retention interval. The results showed that learning the A-C list interfered with recall of the A-B list. Moreover, the more thoroughly the A-C list had been learned, the more it interfered with recall of the A-B list.

Query: What measure of forgetting did Thune and Underwood use?

You experience much the same thing in your everyday life when, for example, you find that after learning your new license plate number, you can no longer recall the old one. Similarly, teachers often find it difficult to remember the names of previous students after learning the names of new students. And when an accountant learns new tax regulations, the old regulations may slip away. New learning often pushes out old learning.

Interference is an important factor in forgetting. Another important factor is the context in which learning and recall occur.

■ Context

McGeoch (1932) suggested that another important factor in forgetting was the context in which learning occurred. The idea is that learning inevitably occurs within a particular context, that is, in the presence of a given pattern of stimuli. These stimuli then act as cues that serve to elicit behavior. If, later on, these cues are absent, performance suffers.

Consider the case of a subject who learns a list of words in the morning and then is tested on those words in the afternoon. Both sessions occur in a research cubicle with a chair, two tables, and a window; the walls are painted a uniform off-white and there are no decorations. The two environments seem identical, but wait: In the morning the window looks out on a foggy landscape, but by afternoon the sun is shining; the researcher is rather abrupt and sour in the morning, but by afternoon he is all smiles; in the morning, the heating system blows warm air on the subject from a heat vent, by afternoon it is warm enough that the heat is off. Can such insignificant differences in the two situations affect forgetting?

A number of experiments suggest that they can. In one study, Charles Perkins and Robert Weyant (1958) trained rats to run a maze. Some rats learned to run a black maze; others learned to run a white maze. The mazes were in all other respects identical. After a retention interval of only one minute, the experimenters put the rats back into the mazes. This time, however, there was a difference. Some of the rats that had learned in a white maze were tested in a black one, and some of those that had learned in a black maze were tested in a white one. There was little evidence of forgetting when the animals ran the same maze they had been trained in, but performance suffered when the maze was a different color from the maze used during training.

The same sort of effects have been demonstrated with people. J. Greenspoon and R. Ranyard (1957) had students learn lists of words under two different conditions, standing up or sitting down. After this, the students recalled the lists as best they could. Some tried remembering while standing up, others while sitting down. The results showed that students performed best when tested under conditions similar to those under which they had learned. Those who had

The State of Learning

The findings on context raise an interesting possibility: The learner is part of the context in which learning occurs; can changes in the *learner* affect forgetting? There is evidence that they can.

Donald Overton (1964) gave rats a tranquilizing drug and then taught them to run a simple T-maze. Later, when the effects of the drug had worn off, Overton tested the rats and found that they appeared to have forgotten their earlier learning. There is nothing startling about this; we might easily believe that the drug interfered in some way with the brain's functioning. But Overton took one more step. He tranquilized the rats again and put them back into the maze. This time they performed well! The earlier forgetting was due to a change in the animal's internal state. Thus, behavior that is learned during a particular state is lost when that state passes, a phenomenon now called **state-dependent learning** (see also Girden & Culler, 1937; see Ho et al., 1978, for a review).

Anecdotes abound of people who show state-dependent learning as the result of alcoholic intoxication. A person hides his or her car keys while sober and then cannot find them after drinking; when the person sobers up, he or she knows right where to look. Another person stashes several bottles of whisky in various hiding places while drunk. Then when the person is sober and wants a drink, he or she cannot recall where the bottles are hidden. If the person manages to get drunk, he or she suddenly remembers where the bottles are.

There is some evidence that changes in emotional state may produce state-dependent learning. Gordon Bower and his colleagues (1978) had people learn one list of words while happy and another list while sad. When the subjects were tested later on, their recall varied with their mood. If their mood during testing matched their mood during training, their recall was very good; if not, their performance was poor.

It appears, then, that the context for learning includes the state of the learner as well as the state of the learner's surroundings. Students who drink beer while studying (which, by the way, may slow the rate of learning) would be well advised to consider the effects of their internal context on later forgetting.

---

learned the lists standing up remembered them best when standing up; those who had learned the lists while sitting down remembered them best while sitting down.

Duncan Godden and Alan Baddeley (1975) performed another imaginative study on the effects of context. In this study, adults learned a list of words. Some of them learned the list on dry land, while others learned the list while underwater! After training, the subjects tried to recall the list. The experimenters tested some subjects under the same conditions under which they learned, but they tested others under the opposite conditions. For example, some students who learned words on dry land tried to recall those words underwater. The results showed that recall suffered when the testing situation was different from the training situation.

The influence of context on recall can be illustrated from everyday experience. For instance, you may know the name of the person who sits next to you in history class, yet find you are unable to think of it when you run into him in a shopping mall. You may learn a speech to perfection at home, only to stumble over it when in front of an audience. And most of us have had the experience of studying until we have the material "down cold," and then "blanking out" in the classroom. Such anecdotes are consistent with studies showing that changes in context contribute to forgetting. Even subtle differences in the environment can have important effects on recall.

Query: What is meant by *context*?

Context, degree of learning, and the interfering effects of other learning experiences are some of the factors that contribute to forgetting. Other factors, such as the amount of material to be learned (Ebbinghaus, 1885), the nature of the recall test (Loftus & Palmer, 1974; Postman & Rau, 1957), and instructions (Epstein, 1972) also affect forgetting. Understanding forgetting and why it occurs has interested learning researchers because it is a phenomenon that can literally mean the difference between life and death.

FORGETTING AND SURVIVAL

We have seen again and again that learning has tremendous survival value. Like camouflage, flying, and razor-sharp fangs, learning ability evolved because it helped individuals survive and reproduce. Since all organisms must eat to survive, let us examine the role of forgetting in the search for food.

The Hawaiian honey creeper is a bird that feeds on the nectar of a particular kind of flower in its home territory. Once the bird has harvested the nectar from a plant, there is no point in its returning to that plant, for it takes some time for more nectar to be produced. The most efficient policy for the bird is to visit the flowers of each plant once and then avoid that plant for some time. Alan Kamil (1978) found that this is what the bird does. But does it actually remember which flowers it has harvested?

It is conceivable that the honey creeper discriminates between plants it has and has not visited on the basis of some physical feature. Perhaps it can smell the presence of nectar in unharvested plants, or perhaps harvesting the nectar alters the appearance of the plant in some way. But this seems not to be the case. Alan Kamil noticed that when other honey creepers invaded a bird's territory and fed on its flowers, the resident bird visited the flowers already harvested by the intruder. Apparently the birds remember what plants they have harvested and which ones they have not harvested. This greatly improves the efficiency of harvesting for the honey creeper, since a random search of flowers would mean much time wasted on barren flowers.

In the wild, the availability of food is variable. In particular, food crops tend to be abundant at certain times and scarce at others. One way around the problem is for an organism to eat as much as possible when food is plentiful, and then hibernate or sleep a great deal when food is in short supply. Another approach is for the organism to migrate when food supplies dwindle to areas where food is more plentiful. A third tactic that works well for some species, though it lacks appeal for the individual, is to have a short life cycle. Many insects are born in the spring, when food becomes available, and die in the fall, when the weather turns cold and food supplies dry up. Many animals, including humans, have taken a fourth course. They reduce the disparity in food supply by storing up excess food when it is plentiful and drawing on these caches when food runs short.

The Clark's nutcracker, a year-long resident of the U.S. Rocky Mountains, is a case in point (Kamil & Balda, 1985, 1990a, 1990b). It feeds, not on nuts, but on pine seeds. Each bird needs about 10,000 seeds to see it through the winter, so it must set aside seeds and retrieve them later. The birds can store more than 30,000 seeds in over 6,000 caches. But how do they find the 2,000 caches they must locate to make it through the winter?

With so many hiding places, the birds might just probe the ground with their beaks and find their own or some other bird's caches by chance. Kamil and Russell Balda (1990a) estimate that if nutcrackers relied upon luck, their success rate (the proportion of successful probes to all probes) would be only about 10%. In fact, their success rate is several times that level. Nor do the birds find the seeds by detecting their odor (Balda, 1980, reported in Kamil & Balda, 1990a). How, then, do they find the caches? By not forgetting where they are.

Kamil and Balda (1990b) conducted an experiment in which nutcrackers stored seeds and were then allowed to recover them one week, three months, and six months later. There was some decline in the ability to find caches after prolonged periods, but even after six months the birds found seeds with a level of success that could not be attributed to chance.

Further evidence supports the notion that learning accounts for the nutcracker's ability to find caches. In one study, Stephen Vander Wall (1982) allowed two Clark's nutcrackers to store seeds in an aviary and later retrieve them. Each bird found many of its own caches, but seldom found the other bird's caches. This suggests that the birds did not find seeds simply by searching likely cache sites or by "sniffing out" the seeds. Rather, they found seeds because they remembered where they had hidden them.

Other studies show similar evidence of the ability of animals to retrieve caches after prolonged periods, including chipmunks (Vander Wall, 1991), gray squirrels (Jacobs & Liman, 1991), and kangaroo rats

The Man Who Couldn't Forget

One day, around 1920, a young man named S. V. Shereshevski walked into the office of the now-famous Russian neuropsychologist, Aleksandr Luria. He had come to have his memory tested.

Testing a person's memory is ordinarily one of the easier tasks a neuropsychologist performs. But in the case of S, as Luria called Shereshevski, it was quite difficult. Luria read off long strings of words or numbers only to have S recite them with ease, as though reading over Luria's shoulder. Even lists of 70 items caused no problem, and S would repeat them without error as presented or, if Luria wished, in reverse order. And S could still repeat what he had learned a day later, a week later, a month later, a year later, even, it turned out, 15 or more years later—the man never seemed to forget.

Luria tried to discover how S accomplished his amazing feats. He found that S used a combination of mnemonic techniques, including the method of loci. But he also experienced synesthesia, a synthesis of different senses. A sound, for example, might produce an experience of light, color, taste, odor, and touch. For S, a rainbow was not merely an array of colors, it was a shower of sensations. These sensations evidently helped make every experience memorable.

Students who hear of S's talent are sure to envy him. For him, there was no need to spend hours struggling to learn formulas, historical dates and events, passages of poetry, the periodic table, or the principles of learning. All such material could be learned with ease and recalled years later as if read from an invisible book.

Yet the story of S is a rather sad one. It is sad, not in spite of his extraordinary talent, but in large measure because of it. You see, S's talent so preoccupied him that it interfered with his ability to do ordinary things. Sometimes he would get so engrossed in the sensory qualities of a person's voice that he could not follow what the person was saying. Sometimes S would interrupt a story Luria was telling. "This is too much," he would say. "Each word calls up images; they collide with one another, and the result is chaos. I can't make anything out of this" (p. 65).

The least little thing could trigger a whole series of experiences, along with all sorts of sensations. Most people struggle to remember, but S never stopped remembering. For him, the problem was not how to remember, but how to forget.

(Jacobs, 1992). Learning has survival value, and so does the persistence of what is learned. Forgetting has its positive side (see "The Man Who Couldn't Forget"), but most of us would like to reduce our tendency to forget. Let us consider that problem now.

LEARNING TO REMEMBER

History is replete with examples of people performing extraordinary feats of memory—which is to say, extraordinary feats of learning.

Tradition has it that Homer was blind and earned his living by reciting *The Iliad* and *The Odyssey*, which he had learned by heart. Cicero and other great poets of ancient times learned many long poems and recited them at banquets and other public functions. And it is said that Dame Judith Anderson, the actress, once performed *Hamlet—all* of *Hamlet,* not just one role.

How do they do it? There are, no doubt, genetic differences that affect recall. But is is clear that the ability to remember is to some extent a learned skill.

Animals have helped to prove this point. In one study, Michael D'Amato (1973) trained monkeys in a delayed matching to sample task. At first, the animals were successful only after very short delays, but they improved with practice. A monkey named Roscoe could remember the sample for only about nine seconds at first, but after several years of practice he was able to answer correctly about 70% of the time after a delay of nine *minutes*—a 6,000% improvement!

Ericsson and Chase (1982) demonstrated that ordinary humans can show similar improvement in recall. Their first subject was an average college student they called SF. SF showed no special skill at remembering but was eager to participate in the study. He worked with the researchers an hour at a time, three to five days a week, for almost two years, putting in a total of 230 hours. Training consisted of presenting SF with series of digits, one per second, which he then tried to reproduce. The experimenters gave no instruction or suggestions as to how SF was to learn the lists, and at first there was no improvement. He could reliably recall seven digits, but that was all. But after a time his "memory span" seemed to stretch. He could recall 9 digits, 12 digits, 15 digits. The previous record was 18 digits, a feat performed by a German mathematician named Ruckle. SF broke through that barrier and went on to set a new record of 82 digits![3]

Can we improve our ability to remember more useful kinds of things, such as mathematical formulas, French verbs, historical names and dates, lines of poetry, and where we parked our car? The answer is yes, but not without effort. There is, unfortunately, no way to exercise the "memory muscle" in the brain (wherever that might be) so that, ever after, we can easily recall anything we experience. But there are things we can do to reduce forgetting. Most of these memory strategies are really ways of improving learning. Let us consider a few of the more important of them.

■ Overlearn

We saw earlier that there is a strong, inverse relationship between the degree of learning and the rate of forgetting. The implication is clear: To forget less, study more.

---

[3] Ericsson and Chase replicated these results with another college student, called DD, who had reached a level of 75 digits as of the publication of their article.

Say All Fast Minute Each Day Shuffle

Almost everyone considers flash cards a bit old-fashioned today, but Ogden Lindsley believes that, old-fashioned or not, flash cards work—if they are used properly. The problem is that many students do not use them properly. How should they be used? Lindsley answers with an acronym to help you remember: SAFMEDS.

Say the answer before you turn a flash card over. Go through *All* of the cards, or as many as you can, as *Fast* as you can, in one *Minute.* Do this *Each Day.* After you go through the cards, *Shuffle* them.

This use of flash cards is very different from the way most students use them, and the differences are important. In particular, Lindsley puts great emphasis on the rate at which the student goes through the cards. Often students stare at a prompt for several seconds or even minutes, trying to recall the correct response. The one-minute time limit puts pressure on the student to work quickly. It also provides a convenient measure of learning. Each time you make an error, you can toss that card aside. At the end of a minute, you can count the number of cards you got right. At first, you may get only 20 or 30 correct answers in a minute. But with practice you may get 50, 60, 100, or even more correct answers in a minute. This means you can easily assess your degree of learning and the likelihood that you will forget.

Students are inclined to use massed practice and, as we have seen, this leads to rapid forgetting. Lindsley advises students to distribute their practice by using the cards once each day.

Finally, the sequence of cards can provide clues about the answers. The student may go through the cards without error but find he or she does not know the answers in a different context, such as a test. For this reason, it is important to shuffle the cards after each use.

Flash cards are out of favor with educational experts these days and have been for many years. Fortunately, this does not keep them from working.

Do not merely go through those German flash cards until you get all the words correct once; keep at it until you can do, say, 60 cards a minute without error. To give a good speech, continue practicing even after you are satisfied with your performance. To play a sonata brilliantly at the concert, continue practicing after you get through it without errors. To do a good job in the play, go to all the rehearsals and spend extra time practicing your lines.

It should be noted that there is a point of diminishing returns from overlearning, with each additional trial resulting in a smaller improvement in recall later. Kreuger (1929; see above) shows that there is a bigger difference between no overlearning and 50% overlearning than there is between 50% overlearning and 100% overlearning.

■ Use Mnemonics

A **mnemonic** (pronounced nee-mon-ic) is any device for aiding recall. Typically, mnemonics involve learning cues that will later prompt the behavior to be performed.

One common mnemonic is rhyme. Perhaps the best known example is the little ditty we all memorize to help us remember the spelling of certain words: "Use *i* before *e*, except after *c*, and in sounding like *a*, as in *neighbor* and *weigh*." Another is the rhyme that reminds us how many days are in each month: "Thirty days hath September, April, June, and November. . . ." In the film *My Fair Lady*, Professor Higgins has Eliza Doolittle learn pronunciation and enunciation by repeating the line, "The rain in Spain falls mainly in the plain." If the plains of Spain *do* get most of the country's rain, this bit of rhyme would help us remember that fact.

Sometimes a mnemonic combines rhyme with a code in which, for example, the first letter of each word to be learned is the first letter of a word in the rhyme. Medical students learn the names of the 12 cranial nerves by memorizing the following doggerel:

On Old Olympus's towering top,
a Finn and German
vault and hop

The first letter of each word provides the first letter of each cranial nerve (optic, otolaryngeal, and so on), and this hint helps prompt the appropriate response.

Sometimes we can get by with a sentence that does not rhyme. To recall the names of the planets in our solar system in their relation to the sun (Mercury, Venus, Earth, Mars, Jupiter, Saturn, Uranus, Neptune, Pluto), we have only to remember that "Many very early maps just show us nine planets."

A similar mnemonic is the acronym, a set of letters, often forming a pronounceable set, each of which stands for the first letter of a word. The North Atlantic Treaty Organization, for example, is NATO. The colors of the prism in their right order are remembered as Roy G. Biv, for red, orange, yellow, green, blue, indigo, and violet. And it is relatively easy to recall the names of the Great Lakes (Huron, Ontario, Michigan, Erie, and Superior) if you can just remember that they spell HOMES.

■ Try a Mnemonic System

Books that offer to improve memory typically devote considerable space to mnemonics, and to what are called mnemonic systems. Professional entertainers who do seemingly impossible memory feats, such as learning and recalling the names of 30 or 40 people in an audience, typically use a mnemonic system.

One popular system is the **method of loci.** This system dates back to the time of the ancient Greeks. Legend has it that a roof collapsed during a party, killing everyone inside and disfiguring many of the revelers so badly that they could not be recognized. A poet named Simonides, who had left the building just before the roof fell in, was able to identify the bodies by recalling where each person had been sitting. Thus, the method of loci fixes each fact to be recalled to a particular location. Later, when it is necessary to recall that fact, we simply "go to" the location and "see" what is there.

Typically, the locations used are familiar places. You might, for example, use the house in which you grew up, or a park where you regularly jog. Any place will do as long as it is sufficiently large to hold a large number of items, and so long as you can "see" it fairly clearly when you close your eyes.

Here is how the method of loci works: Suppose you must remember to buy several items at the grocery store: bread, milk, eggs, radishes, lettuce, paper towels, and toothpaste. And suppose the locus that you use is a park you frequently visit. You begin an imaginary walk through the park. Along the path there are various landmarks, and at each landmark you place one of the things to be remembered. You come to a park bench and put the loaf of bread on the bench, perhaps enlarging the loaf so that it takes up the entire bench. You continue your walk and come to the second landmark, a huge oak tree with a cavity where a branch has long since fallen off. You put a carton of milk in the cavity so that you will see it later on when you pass by. Just as you move on, you see that the carton is leaking, and milk is spilling down the side of the tree and onto the path. Next, you come to a small pond, where a family of ducks is often to be seen. You see a duck in harness pulling a barge laden with a carton of eggs. The rest of the items are distributed along the path in the same way.

When you arrive at the grocery store, you can recall the items on the list by walking through the park. As you approach the park bench, you see someone is taking a nap. When you get closer, you see that it is not a person at all, but a huge loaf of bread. You walk on, and come to the huge oak. The walk is covered with some sort of white liquid. You look up and see a leaky milk carton in the tree's cavity. Further along the trail you come to the pond, . . . and so on.

Another popular mnemonic system is called the **peg word system.** In this approach, one memorizes a list of pegs on which items can later be hung, much as you hang a hat on a peg. The pegs are numbered and made easy to remember by making them resemble items whose names rhyme with their numbers. For instance, the peg word for number one is usually the word *bun;* two is *shoe;* three is *tree;* four is *door;* five is *hive;* and so on.

Just about anything can be used as a peg, so long as it is a concrete object that can easily be imagined. (Abstract concepts such as beauty and truth do not work well as pegs because we cannot "see" them.) Now, if you want to learn a grocery list, you fasten each item to a peg. One is a bun. Let us imagine that it is a hot dog bun. You put the loaf of bread into the bun as you would a hot dog. Two is a shoe. It is an old-fashioned shoe, the type that Mother Hubbard wore. You put a carton of milk in the shoe. Three is a tree. You hang eggs from the tree like Christmas ornaments. And so on. To recall the list, you run through the numbers and look at the pegs.

Do such mnemonic systems really work? Yes, they do—if they are used regularly. The trouble is, people tend not to use them, at least not for long. Even memory researchers do not use them (Parks et al., 1986). The systems are not difficult to learn, but they probably have limited utility for most people. Memorizing a list of items to buy at the store is relatively easy, but it takes something of an expert to use the method of loci or the peg word system to recall the anatomical parts of a bird. It is even more difficult to use such a system to memorize abstract ideas, such as the tenets of Arthur Schopenhauer's philosophy.

■ Use Context Cues

We saw earlier that we remember better when cues present during learning are present during recall. It follows that we can improve recall by identifying cues that will be present during recall and then learning in the presence of those cues.

Students typically do exactly the opposite: They study in their rooms, often while lying on their beds and eating some sort of snack. Or, if the weather is pleasant, they sit under a large tree or on a park bench. Often friends stop by and chat, and studying gets mixed up with socializing. When they take a test on what they have studied, they are typically in a classroom, seated in a rather uncomfortable chair, usually in the presence of a number of other students with whom they cannot converse. The two situations, learning and testing, are very different, and these differences in context probably account for some forgetting. Students find themselves unable to recall facts that they "knew cold" before they walked into the classroom.

The clear implication is that students should study under conditions that closely resemble the conditions under which testing will take place. A student studying for a paper-and-pencil exam might even do well to spend some time studying in the classroom where the test will take place.

A less obvious implication of the work on context is that if we want to remember what we learn long after the final exam, we should study in a variety of situations. Why? Because what we learn is apt to be needed in a wide variety of situations. If you are to be an engineer, the mathematics you study today might be needed at a construction site, on a factory floor, or in an executive's office. If you are to be a historian, the history you study today might be needed not only in classrooms, but at historical sites, in libraries, and at meetings of historical societies. Or, to take an example of more immediate relevance, if you are trying to learn principles of learning that will reduce forgetting, then you should keep in mind that you will need to recall those principles not only where you usually study, but anywhere that you are likely to learn. Since what we learn is apt to be needed in many different situations, the best practice may be to study in many different situations: at home, on the bus, in classrooms and coffee shops, while walking across campus or relaxing on the beach—any place and every place is a good place to learn.

■ Distribute Practice

You may recall from Chapter Five that the rate of learning is apt to be faster if the learning trials are spread out over a period of time rather than crammed together. In addition to speeding up learning, such distributed practice also slows forgetting.

Bahrick (1983), in a study of the learning and forgetting of street names, found that the faster students learned street names, the more quickly they forgot them. That is, slower acquisition curves (fewer names learned each week) meant slower forgetting curves (fewer names forgotten each week). This does not mean, of course, that less intelligent people remember better. It simply means that if you cram a lot of learning into a short period, you will later cram a lot of forgetting into a short period. In another study, Bahrick and Elizabeth Phelps (1987) found that studying Spanish words *less* often (say, every 30 days) resulted in less forgetting over an eight-year period than studying at shorter intervals.

■ Use Prompts

A prompt is a discriminative stimulus, an S^D, that can be used to elicit behavior. One sort of prompt is the memorandum. To remember what groceries to buy, we make a list. To ensure that we do not forget an important meeting, we make a note on the calendar. Memoranda are obviously very useful memory aids. Even pigeons have been known to use a kind of memorandum (Epstein & Skinner, 1981). Some people would argue that memoranda do not aid recall, but rather remove the need for recall. But a memorandum usually provides no more than a hint, a reminder, of the behavior to be produced. A note to "Call Jim about Mary" would be meaningless to anyone except the person who wrote it.

Parents used to tie a piece of string around a child's finger to remind the child to ask the teacher when the costumes are needed for the school play, to buy bread on the way home, or to turn the oven off at four o'clock. The child sees or feels the string during the course of the day and this prompts the child to make the appropriate response. (Or someone else may see the string and ask what it is for, which has the same effect.) One problem with string is that it does not necessarily prompt the desired behavior at the right time. The string has given way to the electronic watch. Beep! It is time to take your medicine. Beep! It is time to call Margaret. Beep! It is time to turn off the oven.

But even an electronic watch can prompt a response only if we program it to do so in advance, and that is not always possible. Suppose that the weather report forecasts rain. The report prompts the response, "I should take my umbrella." But it is not time to leave, and walking around the house with an umbrella is a nuisance. On the other hand, when you are ready to leave, you may forget the umbrella. What we need to do in situations like this, says Skinner (1983c), is to arrange that a prompt will occur when it is needed. You cannot be sure just when you will leave, so an alarm watch is not helpful. But you can put the umbrella where you will see it when you are about to depart. So, Skinner suggests, when you hear rain is predicted, put the umbrella on the door handle. So long as you leave by that door, you will see the umbrella, and it will provide the necessary prompt.

In the same way, we can use prompts to induce ourselves to produce weak responses. Skinner (1953) suggests the problem of trying to recall someone's name. At one time you knew the person's name but find you are now unable to say it. You may be able to prod yourself into making the lost response by using various kinds of prompts (though, in this situation, Skinner prefers the term *self-probe*; see Skinner, 1953). You may, for example, be able to recall things about the person other than his or her name, such as the circumstances under which you met, the nature of conversations you have had with the person, his or her occupation, and where he or she works. You may also recall things about the name itself that will prove helpful: that it is Anglo-Saxon, two syllables, with hard consonants. Recalling such things may, in turn, elicit the person's name.

You might also go through the alphabet, trying to recognize the first letter or sound of the name. If this is successful, you might use the beginning of the name as a prompt for the rest of the name by trying out various names that start with that sound: "I think it starts with 'Ba.' Ba, Barns, Barnaby, Baker, Bantry, Battry, *Batman!*"

Skinner suggests that we can also try to prompt a forgotten name by practicing an introduction covertly (that is, to ourselves): "This is Mr ———," "I'd like you to meet ———." In doing so we create an unpleasant situation from which we can escape only by producing the person's name. We may be able to do the same sort of thing to recall the name of the sea captain who defeated the Spanish armada. We simply imagine introducing him to Queen Elizabeth I: "Your Majesty, it is a great honor to introduce to you the hero of the Atlantic, conqueror of the Spanish invaders,—Francis Drake."

As you know, any stimulus that is present during learning can later be used as a prompt for the behavior so learned. If, during a paper and pencil test on computer keyboard commands, you are unable to recall the command to begin an electronic search of a document, try putting your hands on the keyboard and typing the command. The keys may prompt the appropriate response. If a keyboard is not available, it may suffice to pretend that you are at the keyboard. Arrange your hands as you would if the keyboard were present, and try typing the wanted command.

Query: Name four techniques for improving recall.

A FINAL WORD ON FORGETTING

All of the techniques reviewed in this chapter—mnemonics, overlearning, and the rest—are established ways of reducing forgetting. Yet, even when we use these techniques, we forget. We may remember the rhyme about people vaulting and hopping on Olympus's towering top, yet be unable to remember any of the cranial nerves the rhyme is supposed to call up.

Sometimes the alacrity with which we forget is demoralizing. A comic (whose name I cannot recall!) suggests that what the typical college student remembers from a year of coursework in American history is, "North wore blue; South wore gray." This is an exaggeration, but it is an exaggeration that reveals a basic truth. We *do* forget a great deal of what we learn. So why bother learning? In particular, why spend years in school learning if much of that learning is bound to slip away from us?

Skinner's view of memory proposes an answer: We do not *remember* experiences, Skinner argues, we are *changed* by them. He means that the effect of an experience is to change us so that we behave differently. We are, in a very real sense, different people each time we learn something. The white, middle class student who reads *The Autobiography of Malcolm X* may recall little about the book, or about Malcolm X, years later. But despite all that the student has forgotten, he or she may behave differently toward African Americans. And if you one day forget most of what you now know about learning, you might still view behavior differently than you would have had you not taken the course. Learning means a change in behavior due to experience; it does not necessarily mean that we recall the experience that changed the behavior.

We are bound to forget. But even the experiences we have forgotten leave their mark upon us.

SUMMARY

Most people assume that experience leaves some sort of mental or physiological record, and this record, or memory, is then activated when we perform a skill or recall an experience. An alternative approach suggests that there is no such thing as memory; rather, experience changes us so that we behave differently. This approach leads us to ask why forgetting occurs.

Forgetting is a deterioration of learned behavior associated with a retention interval, a period of time during which the organism is denied the opportunity to make the learned response. Forgetting usually means a decrease in the probability of a response, but under certain circumstances, it can mean an increase in response probability.

Forgetting can be measured in various ways, including free recall, prompted recall, recognition (including delayed matching to sample), and relearning (or savings).

Forgetting increases with the length of the retention interval, but the passage of time is not itself a cause of forgetting. The rate of forgetting is controlled by the amount of training, retroactive interference, proactive interference, changes in context (including the internal state of the organism), and other variables.

Forgetting or, rather, *not* forgetting, plays a vital role in survival. Studies of foraging and the retrieval of food caches indicate that even lower animals often have a remarkable talent for retaining learned behavior when it affects survival.

People are also capable of performing complex behavior even after long periods without practice. To some extent people can improve their ability to retain what they learn, mainly by using strategies to improve the initial level of learning. These strategies include overlearning, using mnemonics and mnemonic systems, learning in the appropriate context, distributing practice sessions, and using prompts.

Forgetting seems a pernicious factor in survival. But it should be remembered that even when we forget an experience, we remain changed by it.

REVIEW QUESTIONS

1. Define the following terms:

   overlearning   proactive interference
   paired associate learning   state-dependent learning

2. Why do some teachers ask their students to take the same seat at each class meeting, particularly at the beginning of the year?

3. John was determined to do well on the final exam in biology, so he studied from 10 P.M. to 2 A.M. each night for the two weeks before the test. To keep from falling asleep, he took "uppers." The night before the 8 A.M. exam, John made sure he got a good night's sleep, but he did not do nearly as well on the test as he thought he should. What explanation can you offer? Describe how you could test the accuracy of your explanation.

4. Mary and Hilda each train a cockroach to run a maze. Mary uses an intertrial interval of ten seconds, while Hilda runs one trial every hour. Each animal gets ten training trials

and then runs the maze again 24 hours later. Which cockroach will show the least forgetting?

5. What does Skinner mean when he says we do not remember experiences but are changed by them?

6. Hilda and Ethel work together to train a rat to press a lever. When they are satisfied that the response has been well learned, Hilda suggests that they remove the lever from the cage for a while and then reinstall it to see what happens. Ethel proposes that they leave the lever in place but disconnnect the feeding mechanism. Then they begin to wonder whether they would be studying different phenomena or the same thing. What do you think?

7. In paired associate learning, what is the reinforcer?

8. The amount of forgetting varies directly with the length of the retention interval. Why, then, is time not a cause of forgetting?

9. What is wrong with defining forgetting as the loss of behavior?

10. What is the difference between free recall and prompted recall?

11. Which measure of forgetting discussed in the text is likely to detect the most subtle degrees of forgetting? How could you prove you are right?

12. What is the implication of research on overlearning for your study practices?

13. Which is more likely to be a factor in forgetting what you have learned from this course, retroactive interference or proactive interference?

14. What is the practical significance of the study by Greenspoon and Ranyard (1957)?

15. Some psychologists maintain that spontaneous recovery is a form of forgetting. Explain this.

16. Mary went through a difficult divorce and later found the whole experience seemed a blank; she could remember almost nothing that happened. When she went through a second divorce some years later, she found herself remembering all sorts of things about her first divorce. Explain why.

17. Give an example of both retroactive and proactive interference from your own experience.

18. Invent a mnemonic for remembering techniques for improving recall (overlearn, distribute practice, and so on).

19. What sort of prompts (or self-probes) could you use to remember the name of the sea captain in *Moby-Dick*?

20. Explain why forgetting is not altogether a bad thing.

Suggested Readings

The classic work on forgetting is Hermann Ebbinghaus's *Memory*, first published in German in 1885. An English translation is available and is surprisingly readable. For a fascinating look at someone who had difficulty forgetting, see Luria's *Mind of a Mnemonist* (1968).

For a readable overview of research on memory, see *Your Memory: A User's Guide* by Alan Baddeley or *Memory* by I. M. L. Hunter. You might also try John D. Bransford's *Human Cognition*, or *Memory: Surprising New Insights into How We Remember and Why We Forget* by Elizabeth Loftus.

Answers to Queries

Page 285: Forgetting is the deterioration of learned behavior with the passage of time.

Page 287: In prompted recall there is a cue (a prompt) that helps elicit the previously learned behavior; in free recall such cues are absent (or at least minimal).

Page 292: Paired associate learning is operant learning. A response is followed by either a reinforcing or punishing stimulus (the correct word).

Page 294: Thune and Underwood used the relearning (savings) method of measuring forgetting.

Page 297: Context means the surroundings in which behavior occurs. It therefore refers to stimuli.

Page 306: Answers should include four of the following: overlearn; use mnemonics; use a mnemonic system; make use of context cues; distribute practice; use prompts.

twelve

The Limits of Learning

We cannot command nature except by obeying her.
—Francis Bacon

BACKGROUND

We have seen that learning plays a vital role in the behavior of animals and humans. It is clear, then, that to understand human nature—or the nature of chimpanzees, monkeys, giraffes, rats, pigeons, and many other animals—we must understand how behavior is changed by experience: We must understand learning.

But we must also understand the limits of learning. For while learning contributes to the differences in behavior that distinguish a person from a chimpanzee, and one person from another person, there are limits to what people and chimpanzees can learn. This chapter discusses some of these limitations.

PHYSICAL CHARACTERISTICS

Fish can't jump rope, humans can't breathe underwater, and cows can't coil up like snakes. The very structure of an organism's body makes certain kinds of behavior possible and other kinds of behavior impossible. What an organism can learn to do is therefore limited by what it is physically capable of doing. This is such an obvious fact that one might think it goes without saying. Indeed, it is seldom, if ever, mentioned in learning texts. But obvious generalizations are sometimes worth making because the particulars that lead to the generalization are not always so obvious.

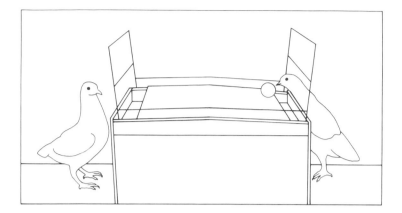

FIGURE 12-1 Physical characteristics and learning. Pigeons can't learn to play Ping-Pong in the usual manner, but these two have learned to play a variation of the game. SOURCE: B. F. Skinner, "Two synthetic social relations," *Journal of the Experimental Analysis of Behavior*, 1962, *5*, p. 531, figure 1. Copyright 1962 by the Society for the Experimental Analysis of Behavior, Inc. Reprinted by permission of the publisher and author.

For instance, a dog's keen sense of smell enables it to find objects hidden from sight. Similarly, a hawk's superb vision allows it to distinguish between heads and tails on a quarter at a great distance, whereas a person would be unable to see the coin at all. Under certain circumstances, then, dogs and hawks would learn faster than people would. All sorts of physical characteristics set limits upon what organisms can learn (see Figure 12-1).

Some years ago, various attempts were made to teach chimpanzees to talk (Hayes, 1951; Kellogg, 1968). These efforts were almost wholly unsuccessful and convinced many people that chimpanzees could not acquire language. It seemed that language was the one difference that set us off from furrier creatures. But then Allen and Beatrice Gardner (1969) began teaching Washoe, a young female chimpanzee, the sign language of the deaf. In less than two years, Washoe had a vocabulary of more than 30 signs, and by the time she was 7, her vocabulary was approaching 200 signs. Since the Gardner's first efforts, a number of other researchers have taught sign language to chimps. Researchers have also attempted to teach sign language to a gorilla (Patterson, 1978; Patterson et al., 1987) and to an orangutan (Shapiro, 1982). Whether any of these animals has learned to communicate in the human sense is subject to debate (see, for example, Petitto & Seidenberg, 1979; Terrace, 1979). The point, however, is not that chimps and other animals are as adept as humans at learning language, but rather that their difficulty in learning to speak is due at least partly to their anatomical structures. People would also have a difficult time learning to speak if they had the kind of vocal structures that chimps have. Thus, the physical characteristics of an organism set important, but not always obvious, limits upon what an organism can learn.

Query: What did the Gardner and Gardner work teach us about animal learning?

NONHERITABILITY OF LEARNED BEHAVIOR

Another obvious limitation of learning is that learned behavior is not inherited. Reflexes and fixed action patterns are passed on from generation to generation, but behavior that is acquired through learning dies with the individual. This places a serious limitation on the ability of a species to benefit from experience because it means that every individual is as ignorant at birth as its parents were when they were born. The lion cub must learn to stalk antelope just as its parents did; the rat must learn to avoid poisonous water; the child must learn to look for traffic before crossing streets.

The idea that learned behavior is not inherited was not always obvious. In fact, it was not so long ago that many people, including a number of scientists, believed that learning experiences might somehow benefit an organism's offspring. The idea grew out of the work of a French naturalist named Jean de Lamarck.

Lamarck tried to account for the peculiarly adaptive physical features of many animals. The crane, for example, finds food by wading into shallow waters. How is it that the crane has such conveniently long legs, legs that ideally suit the bird to its habitat? Or take the giraffe, an animal that lives on the African plains where it feeds on the leaves of trees; were it not for its long neck, the giraffe would not be able to reach the higher leaves. How did the giraffe come by so sensible a physique?

Lamarck, writing in the early 1800s, theorized that these and other physical characteristics were acquired adaptations that were passed on from generation to generation. Consider the giraffe. Suppose the food supply is meager, so that the giraffe must stretch its neck in an effort to reach higher leaves. If the animal had to do this day after day, it might, Lamarck speculated, make a slight difference in the length of the giraffe's neck. If this slight change were inherited by the giraffe's offspring, then over the course of several hundred generations, the giraffe's neck might get longer and longer until it reached its present, very adaptive length. For Lamarck, evolution was the result of a given species' adaptations to its environment. (For an interesting new wrinkle on this idea, see Landman, 1993.)

Query: In what way is Lamarck's theory like Darwin's?

The Lamarckian theory of evolution was replaced by Darwin's theory of natural selection. But some scientists, most notably the eminent psychologist William McDougall, adopted a Lamarckian view of learned behavior. They argued that when experience modifies the behavior of an organism, it also modifies its genes in some way. This did not mean that if a person learned to read Latin his or her offspring would be born knowing how to read Virgil. But McDougall and others did imply that, other things being equal, the offspring might have a slightly easier time mastering Latin than their parents had. And if each successive generation learned Latin, then each child would find the task easier than his or her parents had.

McDougall was no armchair psychologist, and he spent years performing experiments to test his theory. In a typical experiment, McDougall (1927, 1938) would train rats to avoid electric shocks. Then he would train the offspring of these rats on the same task, and then their offspring, and so on for several generations. The idea was that each generation should inherit more and more skill until, after many generations, the offspring would learn to avoid shock much more easily than their progenitors had. McDougall's research convinced him that his hypothesis held true.

Other scientists, though they respected McDougall's integrity, doubted his data. They ran similar experiments with more precise controls than McDougall had used and found no evidence that succeeding generations of animals learned a task any more readily than their forebears (see, for example, Agar et al., 1954).

The nonheritability of learning would seem to be the severest of all limitations on learning. Certainly, anyone who has had a difficult time mastering parallel parking or memorizing the forms of the French verb être will agree that being able to benefit from the learning experiences of one's parents would be helpful.

It is possible, however, that if we did inherit learned behavior, we would not be entirely happy with the results. Had our ancestors been born expert hunters and gatherers, for example, they might never have invented agriculture, probably the most important development in human history. In the past 30 years, there have been dramatic changes in the social roles of men and women in Western societies. It seems unlikely that such changes would have occurred if, over the past million years, men and women had inherited the roles of their parents. Inherited learning might also have slowed the advance of science. Had Copernicus been born *knowing* that the sun revolved about the earth, he might not have been able to develop the view that the earth revolves about the sun.

The value of learning is that it enables us to adapt to changes in our environment. If we inherited learned behavior that was no longer adaptive, learning might be more a hindrance than a help. Yet it must be admitted that the nonheritability of learning severely limits what any individual can learn in a lifetime.

HEREDITY AND LEARNING ABILITY

There is nothing about the gross anatomy of the chimpanzee (for example, the way its arms and legs are put together) that keeps it from

Recipe for Genius

Many of the world's geniuses have had unusually enriched early environments (Albert, 1980; Simonton, 1987). In fact, the childhoods of eminent figures such as Ludwig van Beethoven and Francis Galton are seldom ordinary. Could it be that we could create more geniuses by providing certain kinds of experiences in childhood? No one has performed an experiment that would answer this question with certainty. However, there is some very intriguing evidence to support the idea.

The 19th century British philosopher and historian James Mill could be said to have performed a kind of enrichment experiment with his firstborn son, John Stuart Mill. The boy's father began tutoring him when he was still in the cradle. John was reading by age 3 and routinely answered questions from his father about what he had read. By the time John was 8 years old, he had already read most of the Greek classics (in Greek, incidentally), and as an adult, he went on to outdistance his father as a philosopher. James Mill was unable to devote the same effort to educating his other children, and none of them matched the achievements of their elder brother.

A more recent effort to improve ability by providing an enriched environment came from a man named Aaron Stern (1971). Too ill to work, Stern decided that he would devote his time to educating his daughter. When Edith was still an infant, Stern played classical music for her, showed her cards with numbers on them, read to her, and made a point of speaking to her slowly and in complete sentences. When she was 18 months old, Stern taught Edith math with an abacus, showed her words on cards, and taught her to read street signs. By age 2, Edith was reading books intended for children of 6 and 8; by age 4, she was reading *The New York Times* and playing chess; by age 5, she had read much of the *Encyclopedia Britannica;* by age 6, she was reading Dostoevsky and Tolstoy; and by age 15, Edith had graduated from college and begun graduate work at Michigan State University.

Of course, it is possible that the remarkable achievements of John Stuart Mill and Edith Stern had little to do with the special environments in which they were reared. Nevertheless, these and other cases leave open the possibility that a rich intellectual environment in early childhood can have important effects on the ability to learn.

learning calculus. Yet it seems extremely unlikely that anyone will ever succeed in teaching a chimpanzee, or any other animal, so sophisticated a skill.

Apparently, the principle reason that some people can master calculus, while no chimpanzee can, has to do with inherited differences in learning ability. It is also clear that there are pronounced differences in the learning abilities of individuals within some species, and these differences are also partly due to heredity. Alas, it appears that few of us are born with the learning ability of Albert Einstein.

While the role of heredity in learning ability is controversial, there can be no doubt that it plays a part. Robert Tryon (1940) demonstrated this in animals many years ago. He ran a large number of rats through a maze and recorded the number of errors each rat made on a series of

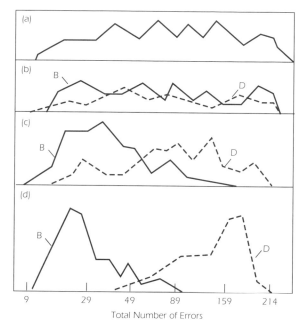

FIGURE 12-2 Heredity and maze learning. Tryon's original sample of rats showed wide variation in maze learning (a). The first generation of selectively bred rats showed considerable overlap (b), but the second generation showed clear differences in maze-learning ability (c). By the seventh generation there was a substantial difference in the average number of errors made by the two groups (d). SOURCE: Robert Tryon, "Genetic Differences in Maze-Learning Ability in Rats," in the Thirty-Ninth Yearbook of the National Society for the Study of Education, *Intelligence: Its Nature and Nurture, Part I: Comparative and Critical Exposition,* G. M. Whipple (Ed.), 1940, p. 113, figure 4. Copyright 1940 by the National Society for the Study of Education. Reprinted by permission of the publisher.

trials. There was a great deal of variability among the rats in the total number of errors made, with some rats making over 20 times as many errors as others. Tryon then bred rats that had made the fewest errors with each other, and those that had made the greatest number of errors with each other. Next, Tryon tested the offspring of these rats on the maze and again bred the brightest of the bright with each other and the dullest of the dull with each other. He continued this procedure for 18 generations, all the while keeping the environments of the two strains as much alike as possible. The average number of errors in maze running for the two groups got further and further apart with each generation (see Figure 12-2), thus suggesting that heredity was having an important impact on learning ability.

There are no comparable data for humans, but there is solid evidence that heredity plays an important role in human intelligence.

Studies of identical twins separated at or soon after birth find that the twins typically have similar IQs, despite being reared in different environments (Newman et al., 1937). And adopted children are more likely to resemble their biological parents in intelligence than their adoptive parents (Skodak & Skeels, 1949).

This is not to say that environment is unimportant in determining learning ability (See "Recipe for Genius" on page 315). But genes do set limits on what we can learn.

NEUROLOGICAL DAMAGE AND LEARNING

The biological equipment with which we learn is not determined solely by heredity. The environment also plays a part.

Prenatal exposure to alcohol and other drugs can interfere with neurological development, resulting in limited learning ability (Hawkins, 1983). Often the damage is not apparent at birth and may be revealed only when the child goes to school. It is even possible that children judged to be perfectly normal have somewhat less learning ability than would have been the case had they never been exposed prenatally to drugs.

Neurotoxins are also a threat to learning ability after birth, particularly in infancy and early childhood. One of the most pervasive neurotoxins is lead, commonly found in old paint and drinking water. Poor children often live in buildings with peeling paint, which they eat. The damage is not usually immediately obvious, but it is cumulative; over a period of months it may make an important difference in the individual's ability to learn.

Head injury can also diminish learning ability (Chance, 1986). This might seem an insignificant factor, but child abuse is fairly widespread and often involves blows to the head or shaking. The punch-drunk boxer provides evidence of the cumulative effects of repeated closed head injuries. Violently shaking a child causes the brain to bounce back and forth within the skull and can cause serious brain injury.

Disease and malnutrition, especially during fetal development, infancy, and early childhood, can also prevent normal neurological development and result in reduced learning ability.

The role of neurological damage in limiting learning is seldom mentioned in learning texts. Although the effects of disease, malnutrition, head trauma, and exposure to neurotoxins on learning are well documented, the assumption seems to be that they are unimportant to our species as a whole. But when such influences are widespread, we have to consider the possibility that human progress is adversely affected.

CRITICAL PERIODS

Sometimes organisms are especially likely to learn a particular kind of behavior at one point in their lives; such stages for optimum learning are referred to as **critical periods.**

For example, many animals are especially likely to form an attachment to their mothers during a critical period soon after birth. If the mother is unavailable, the youngster will become attached to any moving object that happens to pass by, whether another animal of the same species, a mechanical object, or a human being. Konrad Lorenz (1952) was one of the first to study this phenomenon, which he called **imprinting.** He discovered that if you remove a newly hatched goose chick from an incubator, you will have inadvertently become a parent; the chick will follow you about and ignore its mother. "If one quickly places such an orphan amongst a brood which is following its parents in the normal way," writes Lorenz, "the gosling shows not the slightest tendency to regard the old birds as members of its own species. Peeping loudly, it runs away and, should a human being happen to pass, it immediately follows this person; it simply looks upon human beings as its parents" (quoted in Thorpe, 1963, p. 405).

Imprinting has been demonstrated in coots, moorhens, turkeys, ravens, partridges, ducks, chickens, deer, sheep, buffalo, zebras, guinea pigs, baboons, and other animals. Young animals have been imprinted to species different from themselves, including humans, and to objects such as wooden decoys and electric trains. All that is necessary for imprinting to take place is that the young animal be able to view the "mother" and that the mother object move.

Imprinting is not the only evidence for critical periods. John Paul Scott (1958) has shown that social behavior in the dog depends upon its experiences during certain critical periods. He points out, for example, that if a puppy is to become a good house pet, it must have contact with people when it is between 3 and 12 weeks old. Dogs completely deprived of human contact during this period behave like wild animals, ever fearful of humans.

Maternal behavior also may have to be learned during critical periods. Scott (1962) once bottle-fed a lamb for the first ten days of its life and then put the lamb in with a flock of sheep. The lamb cared little for the sheep, preferring to be with people. More important, when this lamb gave birth, it was a poor mother: It allowed its offspring to nurse but took no particular interest in other motherly activities.

Harry and Margaret Harlow (Harlow, 1958; Harlow & Harlow, 1962a, 1962b) obtained similar results when they reared rhesus monkeys in isolation. In the Harlows' experiments, young monkeys were fed by a surrogate mother, a terrycloth-covered object that did nothing but provide food and warmth. The infants became very attached to these cloth mothers and would cling to them for hours. If a monkey were exploring about the cage and became frightened, it would run to "mother" for protection. Later, when these monkeys were placed in cages with normally reared monkeys, they were terrified. They would run to a corner of the cage and roll up into a ball, sometimes sucking on a finger. As adults, these monkeys did not play or mate or rear young the way normally reared monkeys do. While it was possible for these animals to acquire some social skills as adults, they always seemed to be socially retarded. Apparently, the early part of their lives, when they ordinarily would have interacted with their mothers and young monkeys, was a critical period for acquiring social skills.

It is not clear whether there are critical periods for learning in humans. It is possible that there is a critical period in infancy or early childhood for learning to care about others (David et al., 1988). But the evidence for critical periods in people is weak.

Where critical periods do occur, they place severe limits on learning. In most instances, what is not learned on one occasion may be learned on another. Certain opportunities for learning, however, may occur only once in a lifetime.

PREPAREDNESS FOR LEARNING

In the 1960s, researchers began to notice that the ease with which learning occurs varies not only across time, as the critical periods work shows, but across situations. While an animal might learn quite readily in one situation, it might seem downright stupid in a slightly different situation.

Keller and Marion Breland (1961) were among the first to report this phenomenon. They used operant procedures to train hundreds of animals to perform in TV commercials and films and in shopping center promotions. For example, Priscilla the Pig turned on a radio, ate breakfast at a table, picked up dirty clothes and put them in a hamper, ran a vacuum cleaner, and chose the sponsor's brand of animal feed. The Brelands were expert animal trainers, yet they sometimes had great difficulty getting an animal to perform what seemed to be a simple task. In a classic article entitled, "The Misbehavior of Organisms,"[1] published in *The American Psychologist* in 1961, they describe some of the peculiar problems they encountered in their work.

For instance, the Brelands wanted to train a raccoon to pick up some coins and put them in a metal box that served as a bank. The raccoon quickly learned to pick up a coin and carry it to the box, but the animal "seemed to have a great deal of trouble letting go of the coin.

---

[1] The title is a pun on B. F. Skinner's classic work, *The Behavior of Organisms*.

He would rub it up against the inside of the container, pull it back out, and clutch it firmly for several seconds" (p. 682). When the Brelands tried to teach the animal to pick up two coins and put them in the box, the raccoon became even more of a dunce. Instead of dropping the coins into the box, it would rub them together "in a most miserly fashion" (p. 682) and dip them in and out of the box. None of this behavior was reinforced by the trainers.

It might seem reasonable to conclude that the task was simply too difficult for the raccoon to master. But raccoons have no trouble learning other, equally complex tasks, so the idea that their misbehavior was due to stupidity just did not hold up.

Time and again, the Brelands had trouble getting animals to perform acts that should have been easy. In some cases, the Brelands managed to teach an animal to respond as they desired, only to find that the act later broke down. For example, they taught a pig to make bank deposits in a manner similar to that of the raccoon. But after a time, the pig began to behave oddly. Instead of picking up the large wooden coin and carrying it to the bank, the pig would drop the coin to the ground, push at it with its snout, throw it up into the air, and nudge it again with its snout. None of this behavior had been reinforced by the Brelands. In fact, the animal's errant behavior delayed reinforcement.

Why did such "misbehavior" occur? The Brelands theorized that innate behavior interfered with learning. In the wild, raccoons dip their prey into the water and then rub it between their paws, as if washing it. Some biologists speculate that this serves to break away the outer shell of the crayfish that often forms an important part of the raccoon's diet. In any case, it appears that this behavior interfered with teaching the raccoon to drop coins into a bank. Similarly, pigs dig their snouts into the ground to uncover edible roots, and this innate rooting behavior interfered with learning to carry coins to the bank.

Query: Why is the Breland and Breland work important?

The tendency of an animal to revert to a fixed action pattern, a phenomenon called **instinctive drift,** sets limits on learning. If a particular act conflicts with a fixed action pattern, the animal will have trouble learning it. After the Brelands' discoveries, other researchers began to report evidence that animals show talents for learning some things but are resistant toward learning others. The limitations that these oddities place on learning were nicely illustrated in a study of taste aversion in rats.

John Garcia and Robert Koelling (1966) set up four classical conditioning experiments in which they paired water with aversive stimuli. The water was made distinctive by being flavored and by having a light and a clicking noise come on whenever the rat drank. Thus, in one experiment, rats drank water that was bright, noisy, and tasty, and later became sick from exposure to X-radiation. In another experi-

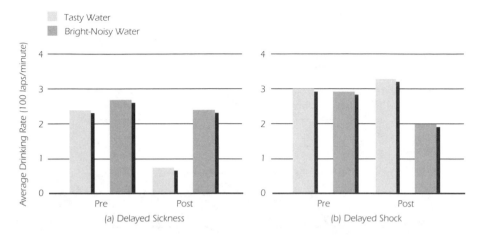

FIGURE 12-3 Preparedness and taste aversion. Rats were given the opportunity to drink bright-noisy and tasty water before and after conditioning. When drinking preceded sickness, rats later tended to avoid tasty water (a); when drinking preceded shock, the rats learned to avoid bright-noisy water (b). Source: John Garcia & Robert Koelling, "Relation of cue to consequence in Avoidance Learning," *Psychonomic Science*, 1966, 4, p. 124, figure 1. Copyright 1966 by the Psychonomic Society. Reprinted by permission of the publisher and authors.

ment, rats drank water that was bright, noisy, and tasty, and later received an electric shock. After training, the experimenters gave the rats a choice between bright-noisy water and water that was tasty. The researchers found that rats that had been made sick were more likely to avoid the *tasty* water; those that had been shocked were more likely to avoid the *bright-noisy* water (see Figure 12-3).

The facility with which animals learn certain responses is illustrated by a classic experiment conducted by Paul Brown and Herbert Jenkins (1968). These researchers put pigeons into Skinner boxes rigged so that periodically a disk would be illuminated. The disk remained lit for eight seconds, and when the light went off a food tray provided the pigeon with grain. As in Skinner's superstition experiment, the bird received food regardless of what it did, but in this experiment the food was preceded by the illumination of the disk. The question was, What sort of superstitious behavior would the birds develop?

What happened was that all of the birds began pecking the disk. The experimenters noted that the birds went through characteristic stages before they pecked the disk. First, there was a general increase in activity level; second, the bird attended more and more to the disk when it was lit; third, the bird began to peck in the general area of the disk; fourth, the bird pecked the disk. These stages are similar to those that one might see in shaping disk pecking through the reinforcement of successive approximations, so the experimenters called the phenomenon **autoshaping** (see Garcia et al., 1973, for a review).

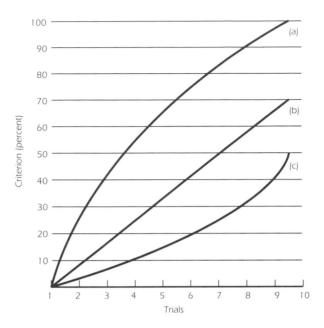

FIGURE 12-4 Preparedness and learning. Hypothetical learning curves for a task an organism is prepared to learn (a), unprepared to learn (b), and contraprepared to learn (c).

Robert Epstein and B. F. Skinner (1980; see also Skinner, 1983a) got similar results with a slightly different procedure. They shone a spot of light on a screen and made it move. When it reached the edge of the screen, the bird received some food. The bird did not have to do anything to receive food, nor did anything it did speed up delivery of the food. Nevertheless, the bird began pecking at the moving spot of light, as if driving it across the screen.

These and other studies show that animals have an inclination to learn some things with great ease while learning other things only with the greatest difficulty. Martin Seligman (1970) proposed that such tendencies can be characterized as a **continuum of preparedness:** An organism comes to a learning situation genetically prepared to learn (in which case learning proceeds quickly), unprepared (in which case learning proceeds steadily but more slowly), or contraprepared (in which case the course of learning is slow and irregular; see Figure 12-4.

According to Seligman's theory, the raccoon's innate tendency to pick up its food and wash it may make it prepared to learn to pick up and carry coins to a bank, but its innate tendency to hold on to food it has dipped into a stream makes it contraprepared to learn to drop coins into a bank. Similarly, Garcia and Koelling's rats are genetically prepared to learn that water with a distinctive taste causes illness, but they are contraprepared to learn that bright and noisy water does so.

Learning and Humanity

A common misconception about evolution is that it is a form of progress, as though each species were aimed at a distant goal and evolution were its means of reaching it. In fact, there is no evolutionary goal. Certain characteristics arise merely because individuals that possess them tend to survive and pass on their genes.

Learning, as we have seen, is a kind of individual evolution: New behavior appears and either survives or dies out. And like evolution, it has no ultimate goal. What we learn depends upon the experiences we have, not upon some scheme of nature.

We forget this. We tend to speak of learning as if it were necessarily a good thing and use the term almost as a synonym for improvement. It is true that love, compassion, tenderness, cooperativeness, sharing, musical composition, and great writing are largely the products of learning. But so are the most despicable acts of which we are capable. Consider this report of one survivor of the concentration camp in Dachau, Germany:

> It was common practice to remove the skin from dead prisoners. . . . It was chemically treated and placed in the sun to dry. After that it was cut into various sizes for use as saddles, riding breeches, gloves, house slippers and ladies' handbags. Tattooed skin was especially valued by SS men. (Blaha, 1946; in Carey, 1988, pp. 557f).

This excerpt reveals that learning does not always mean progress. You may also see the undesirable effects of learning in your own reaction to the foregoing passage. There was a time, not so very long ago, when reading such material would have made many students physically ill. Today's students have viewed so much brutality on television, and sometimes in the streets, that many can read Blaha's account without discomfort.

Learning defines our humanity. For better, and for worse.

And Brown and Jenkins' pigeons pecked a lighted disk, presumably because pigeons are genetically prepared to peck bright objects.

Are people genetically prepared to learn some things more readily than others? Some people think so. Psycholinguist Eric Lenneberg (1967, 1969) points out that language development follows a regular, predictable pattern around the world, which might suggest that people are prepared to learn language in a certain way. In addition, Lenneberg notes that the language skills of retarded children freeze at a primitive stage of development. They learn language in the same way as more intelligent people, though they cannot learn to the same level of complexity.

Query: How does a species become biologically prepared to learn certain things?

Seligman (1970) has proposed that phobias provide additional evidence of human preparedness (see also Ost & Hugdahl, 1985). Certain objects, he points out, are far more likely than others to become phobic stimuli. He adds that "the great majority of phobias are about objects of natural importance to the survival of the species" (p. 320). People are far more likely to fear sharks, spiders, snakes, and dogs than they are lambs, trees, houses, and cars. Seligman and Joanne Hager (1972b) tell the story of a 7-year-old girl who saw a snake while playing in the park. Some time later, the girl accidentally slammed a car door on her hand, after which she developed a fear of snakes. Obviously, the snake did not hurt her hand. The implication is that people are biologically prepared to acquire a fear of snakes but not a fear of cars, yet in this case, a car phobia would have made more sense. Seligman (1970) also observes that people are far more likely to form strong attachments to some objects than to others. As he notes, the cartoon character Linus carries a security blanket, not a security shoe.

It may be that among humans, preparedness is more variable than in other animals. K. S. Kendler and colleagues (1992) studied female twins and found that various social phobias (such as a fear of meeting people) and agoraphobia (fear of open places) have a genetic basis. While not born with such phobias, some people may be genetically prepared to acquire them.

It seems clear that in animals, and probably in humans, learning depends partly upon whether the organism is genetically prepared, unprepared, or contraprepared to learn the task in question. Such genetic preparation sets limits on what is learned from a given experience.

CONCLUSION

We have concluded our introduction to the study of learning and behavior by examining the limits on learning. Those limits make learning appear to be a feeble weapon with which to battle the problems that threaten civilization. The world is faced with war, famine, pollution, crime, disease, unemployment, drug abuse, child abuse, and the grandparent of all problems, overpopulation. What good is a science of learning and behavior in overcoming problems of such magnitude?

The answer becomes obvious once we realize that most of the serious problems confronting us are fundamentally behavior problems. War is a form of conflict. Famine is less the result of bad weather than of mismanaged resources. Pollution is the improper disposal of wastes. Crime is the performance of socially prohibited acts. Most diseases are at least partly the product of unhealthy behavior. And so on.

Once we recognize that the problems are essentially behavioral, not technological or natural, we realize that we can prevent, solve, or at least ameliorate them by changing behavior. A science of behavior change, of learning, then becomes critically important and suggests certain solutions.

Consider, as an example, the problem of teen pregnancy in this country. Each year thousands of babies are born to young teenage girls. These mothers have a tendency to produce low birth-weight babies, and such babies have a tendency to have health problems and learning difficulties. In addition, most teen mothers are ill-equipped to rear children. Many of them neglect their children, and some become abusive parents. Their children tend also to produce children at an early age, so the cycle continues.

Most people probably will agree that it would be a good idea if babies were born to women 18 or older. To reach that goal, we must change the behavior of the people involved, the girls who are getting pregnant and the boys who are impregnating them. How do we change their behavior? So far, we have attempted to change teenage sexual practices primarily with slogans and lectures. The study of learning and behavior suggests that other methods might be more effective.

Early pregnancy is primarily a problem among the poor. For poor teens, producing children may win both the father and mother the admiration of their peers and of adults. It may also be a way to escape an unpleasant home environment, since the girl might be able to move out and receive government assistance. A contingency trap is probably involved, since for many poor teens the positive consequences of becoming pregnant are immediate, while the negative consequences are more remote. Learning research suggests that if we change the consequences of the teen's behavior, the behavior will change. One way to do this would be to provide cash payment to poor teenage girls each year that they do *not* have a baby. Each successive year without a baby would result in a larger cash prize.[2]

There is no way to know in advance whether such a change in consequences would substantially reduce the incidence of teen pregnancy. But there is, as you have seen, good reason to believe it might.

To suggest that we can draw upon behavior science in dealing with societal problems does not mean that the problems will be easily solved. Human behavior is extremely complicated, and solutions to social problems are apt to come slowly. But there is reason to hope that through the application of behavior science, solutions will come.

Indeed, it may be our only hope.

---

[2] The proposal is not new, but I am unable to identify the source.

SUMMARY

An understanding of learning is essential to an understanding of behavior, especially human behavior. There are, however, limits on the ways in which learning can contribute to behavior.

The physical structure of an organism sets limits on what it can learn. For instance, chimpanzees are apparently incapable of speech because of the nature of their vocal equipment.

Learned behavior is not passed on to future generations, which means that each individual must learn many of the same skills acquired by its parents. This limits what any one individual can learn in its lifetime. Heredity does play a role in learning, however, since learning ability is determined partly by genes. Anything that damages the brain, such as head trauma and exposure to neurotoxins, can limit learning ability.

Organisms may be prepared to learn certain things at certain stages in their development. Such critical periods appear to play an important role in imprinting and other forms of social behavior. It is not clear whether there are critical periods for learning in human development.

Another limitation on learning is the extent to which the organism is prepared to acquire some behavior. There seems to be a continuum of preparedness, with organisms being prepared to learn some things, unprepared to learn others, and contraprepared to learn still others. Preparedness has been demonstrated in a number of species, and there is some evidence of preparedness in humans.

While the ability to learn may sometimes work against our own best interests (we may, for example, learn more efficient ways of killing one another), the principles of behavior that derive from the study of learning hold out the best hope of dealing effectively with the many problems that threaten society.

REVIEW QUESTIONS

1. Define the following terms:

   autoshaping   *imprinting*
   critical period   *preparedness*

2. Sally buys a high-frequency whistle at a discount store. She attempts to train her dog to come on command using the whistle as a signal. She follows the correct training procedures but is unsuccessful. What is the likely cause of the failure?

3. Explain why it is sometimes difficult to assess the intelligence of people who suffer from infantile paralysis and similar disorders.

4. Suppose that, because of its superior vision, a falcon can learn a discrimination task faster than a person. Mary believes this means the bird is smarter than the person. What reasons might she have for this idea?

5. Design an experiment that would determine whether there are genetic differences in the learning abilities of men and women.

6. How might preparedness to learn be nonadaptive?

7. Explain the role of evolution in the findings of Garcia and Koelling.

8. In what sense might it be said that autoshaping represents preparedness to acquire a superstition?

9. Some people believe that it is important for a human infant to have intimate contact with the mother during the first few hours after birth (rather than being hurried off to a nursery). How could you determine if there is a critical period for the formation of an adult-infant bond?

10. Design a study to determine the effects of prenatal exposure to tobacco on learning ability.

11. Could variability in learning ability be useful to the survival of our species?

12. Suppose you had inherited everything your parents and grandparents knew. How would you be different?

13. Identify a social problem and explain how it might be dealt with through the application of learning principles you have read about in this text.

14. Many people see nothing wrong with punishing misbehavior, but object to reinforcing desirable behavior. They consider such use of reinforcement manipulative. What is the flaw in their logic?

15. A visitor to New York complained about the noise of the city. Her host replied, "Oh, you get used to it." Does this demonstrate that learning is helpful or harmful?

16. How could you determine whether humans are biologically prepared to learn language?

17. Roger McIntire (1973) recommends that people be required to undergo training in child-rearing before having children. What support for his position can you provide?

18. What would it take to make our judicial system an effective instrument for reducing crime?

19. Explain why it would be desirable to have political leaders who understand basic learning principles.

20. What protection could the public have against the abuse of learning principles by political leaders?

Suggested Readings

Much of the discussion of the limits of learning has to do with biological factors. E. O. Wilson's *On Human Nature* deals with some of these issues. One of the classic works on the limits of learning is *Biological Boundaries of Learning,* edited by Martin Seligman and Joanne Hager.

Answers to Queries

Page 313: Gardner and Gardner showed that what an organism learns depends partly upon its physical structure. While chimps could not learn language in one way (speech), they could learn it in another (sign language).

Page 313: Both assume that organisms evolve as a result of the influence of the environment.

Page 320: The Brelands' work is important because it hinted that genetic factors might facilitate learning in one situation and inhibit it in another.

Page 323: Presumably, preparedness is inherited and is the result of evolution.

Glossary

ABA design A type of single subject research design in which behavior is observed before (A) and after (B) an experimental manipulation, after which the original condition (A) is restored. Also called *ABA reversal design.*

Anecdotal evidence Evidence obtained through casual observation.

Attentional processes In Bandura's theory of observational learning, any activity by an observer that aids in the observation of relevant aspects of a model's behavior and its consequences.

Autoshaping A procedure in which a stimulus is followed by a reinforcer regardless of what the organism does. The procedure often results in the shaping of superstitious behavior.

Aversive control Use of aversive stimuli to modify behavior.

Backward chaining A chaining procedure in which the last response in a response chain is learned first.

Backward conditioning A Pavlovian conditioning procedure in which the US precedes the CS. It is of dubious effectiveness in producing a conditional response.

Baseline period In single-subject research designs, a period of observation during which no attempt is made to modify the behavior under study. The data obtained provide a basis for comparison with data obtained during an experimental manipulation.

Blocking Failure of a stimulus to become a CS when it is part of a compound stimulus that includes an effective CS. The effective CS is said to block the formation of a new CS.

Case study Detailed study and description of a single case. Usually used in clinical settings.

Chaining Use of operant procedures to establish a response chain.

Chain schedule A sequence of reinforcement schedules in which primary reinforcement is delivered only upon completion of the last schedule. A stimulus indicates the schedule in force.

Classical conditioning See *Pavlovian conditioning.*

Compound stimulus   Two or more stimuli presented simultaneously, often as a CS.

Concept   Any class whose members share one or more defining features.

Concurrent schedule   A reinforcement schedule in which two or more schedules are available at once.

Conditional reflex   A reflex acquired through experience. (Cf. *unconditional reflex.*)

Conditional response   The response part of a conditional reflex. The CR is elicited by a CS. Often called *conditioned response.*

Conditional stimulus   The stimulus part of a conditional reflex. The CS elicits a CR. Often called *conditioned stimulus.*

Conditioned reinforcer   See *secondary reinforcer.*

Conditioned suppression   Reduction in the rate of responding due to the appearance of an aversive stimulus. The aversive stimulus is not response contingent.

Contiguity   Nearness of events in time (temporal contiguity) or space (spatial contiguity).

Contingency   Dependency between events. (Cf. *stimulus-contingent, response-contingent.*)

Contingency trap   A response contingency in which a response has immediate consequences that are different from (sometimes the opposite of) delayed consequences. Also called *social trap.*

Continuous reinforcement   A reinforcement schedule in which a particular response is reinforced each time it occurs. Abbreviated *CRF.* (Cf. *intermittent reinforcement.*)

Continuum of preparedness   The hypothetical range in an organism's predisposition to learn various responses. The organism is said to come to a situation biologically prepared to learn, unprepared to learn, or contraprepared to learn.

Control group   In an experiment, those subjects not exposed to the treatment that is expected to affect the dependent variable. The performance of the control group provides a basis for comparison with the experimental group.

Counterconditioning   The use of Pavlovian conditioning to undo the effects of earlier conditioning.

CR   Abbreviation for *conditional response.*

CRF   Abbreviation for *continuous reinforcement.*

Critical period   A period in the development of an organism during which it is especially likely to acquire a particular response.

CS   Abbreviation for *conditional stimulus.*

CS+   In Pavlovian discrimination training, the stimulus that is regularly paired with a US. (Cf. *CS−.*)

CS−   In Pavlovian discrimination training, the stimulus that is regularly appears in the absence of the US. (Cf. *CS+.*)

Cumulative record   A graphic record of responses over time. Changes in the slope of the resulting curve indicate changes in the response rate, which in turn reflect learning.

Cumulative recorder   An apparatus that records every occurrence of a particular response. The record produced is called a cumulative record.

Delayed conditioning   A Pavlovian conditioning procedure in which the CS starts before, and then overlaps with, the US.

Delayed matching to sample   A method of testing for forgetting in which an organism is reinforced for responding to a stimulus that matches a stimulus (the sample) after a predetermined delay period.

Dependent variable   The variable by which the outcome of an experiment is measured. It is expected to vary with (depend upon) the independent variable.

Descriptive study   A study in which the behavior of a number of subjects is observed, often through questionnaires. No effort is made to affect behavior by manipulation of an independent variable.

Differential reinforcement of high rate   A reinforcement schedule in which reinforcement is provided only if at least a given number of responses occurs in a specified interval. Abbreviated *DRH*.

Differential reinforcement of incompatible behavior   A reinforcement schedule in which a response that is incompatible with an undesired response is systematically reinforced. Abbreviated *DRI*.

Differential reinforcement of low rate   A reinforcement schedule in which a response is reinforced only if it occurs after a specified interval since the last occurrence of that response. Abbreviated *DRL*.

Differential reinforcement of other behavior   A reinforcement schedule in which any response other than a specified response is reinforced. Abbreviated *DRO*.

Discrimination   The tendency for learned behavior to occur in the presence of stimuli present during training, but not in the presence of stimuli absent during training. (Cf. *generalization*.)

Discrimination training   A procedure for establishing a discrimination. In Pavlovian conditioning, it consists of presenting the CS+ with the US and presenting a CS− alone. In operant learning, it consists of reinforcing a response when it occurs in the presence of an S^D, but not when it occurs in the presence of an S^Δ.

Discriminative stimulus   In operant learning, any stimulus that indicates either that a response will be reinforced (an S^D) or that a response will be punished or go unreinforced (an S^Δ).

Distributed practice   A learning procedure in which learning trials are spread out over time. (Cf. *massed practice*.)

Drive   In Hull's theory of reinforcement, a motivational state (such as hunger) caused by a period of deprivation (as of food).

Drive-reduction theory   The theory of reinforcement that attributes a reinforcer's effectiveness to the reduction of a drive.

DRH   Abbreviation for *differential reinforcement of high rate*.

DRI   Abbreviation for *differential reinforcement of incompatible behavior*.

DRL   Abbreviation for *differential reinforcement of low rate.*

DRO   Abbreviation for *differential reinforcement of other behavior.*

Errorless discrimination training   A discrimination procedure in which the S^Δ is introduced in very weak form and gradually strengthened. The result is that discrimination is achieved with few or no errors.

Escape-avoidance learning   An aversive learning procedure involving negative reinforcement. The subject first learns to escape aversive stimulation and then to avoid it.

Excitatory gradient   A generalization gradient showing an increased tendency to respond to the S^D or CS+ and stimuli resembling them.

Experiment   A research design in which the researcher notes the effects of one or more independent variables on one or more dependent variables.

Experimental economics   The use of reinforcement schedules to study economic principles.

Experimental group   In an experiment, the group exposed to the treatment condition. (Cf. *control group.*)

Experimental neurosis   Any bizarre or neurotic-like behavior induced through an experimental procedure.

Extinction   The weakening of a response by withholding the reinforcer that normally follows that response.

FI   Abbreviation for *fixed interval schedule.*

Fixed action pattern   Any innate series of relatively invariant, interrelated acts usually elicited by a particular stimulus (the releaser). Formerly called instinct. (Cf. *inherited behavior trait.*)

Fixed interval schedule   A form of intermittent reinforcement in which the first response after a specified interval is reinforced. Abbreviated *FI*. (Cf. *variable interval schedule.*)

Fixed ratio schedule   A form of intermittent reinforcement in which every *n*th response is reinforced. Abbreviated *FR*. (Cf. *variable ratio schedule.*)

Fixed time schedule   A reinforcement schedule in which reinforcement is delivered independent of behavior after a fixed interval. Abbreviated *FT*. (Cf. *variable time schedule.*)

Forgetting   Diminished performance of a learned response following lack of opportunity to perform the response.

Free recall method   Method of measuring forgetting by requiring a subject to produce a response after a retention interval. (Cf. *prompted recall.*)

FR   Abbreviation for *fixed ratio schedule.*

FT   Abbreviation for *fixed time schedule.*

Functional communication training   Training designed to replace inappropriate methods of obtaining reinforcers with appropriate methods. Usually used in the treatment of retarded or psychotic patients.

Generalization   The tendency for a learned response to occur in the presence of stimuli that were not present during training. (Cf. *discrimination.*)

Generalization gradient   Any graphic representation of generalization. The slope of the gradient usually indicates that the more similar a stimulus to the stimulus used in training, the greater the tendency to respond.

Goldiamond's paradox   The principle that in order for bizarre behavior to be reinforced, it must sometimes occur on occasions when it cannot be reinforced. Named after Israel Goldiamond.

Group design   An experimental research design in which some subjects (the experimental group) have a particular experience and other subjects (the control group) do not. Differences between the groups may be attributed to differences in their experiences.

Habituation   A reduction in the strength of a reflex response brought about by repeated exposure to a stimulus that elicits that response.

High-order conditioning   Pavlovian conditioning in which a stimulus is paired with a well-established CS rather than with a US.

Imprinting   The tendency of some animals, particularly birds, to follow the first moving objects they see after birth, usually (but not necessarily) their mothers.

Independent variable   In an experiment, the variable that the researcher controls. The independent variable is what the experimenter believes might affect the dependent variable.

Inherited behavior trait   Any general behavioral tendency that is genetically based. (Cf. *fixed action pattern.*)

Inhibitory gradient   Generalization gradient showing a decreased tendency to respond to the S^Δ or CS− and stimuli resembling them. (Cf. *excitatory gradient.*)

Instinct   See *fixed action pattern.*

Instinctive drift   The tendency for behavior to drift toward innate behavior.

Instrumental learning   See *operant learning.*

Intermittent reinforcement   Reinforcement on any of several schedules in which a response is sometimes reinforced. Also called partial reinforcement. (Cf. *continuous reinforcement.*)

Intertrial interval   The interval separating the trials of any learning procedure.

Latent inhibition   The tendency of a stimulus *not* to become a CS following its repeated appearance in the absence of a US.

Law of Effect   The principle that the probability of a response depends upon its consequences.

Learned helplessness   The failure to escape an aversive stimulus following exposure to an aversive stimulus under circumstances that made escape impossible.

Learning   A change in behavior due to experience.

Massed practice   A learning procedure in which learning trials follow one another with little or no delay. (Cf. *distributed practice.*)

Matched sampling   A technique for reducing extraneous differences among subjects by matching those in the experimental and control groups on specified characteristics, such as age, sex, and weight.

Matching Law   The principle that, given two or more reinforcement schedules, the tendency to respond on each schedule will match the rate of reinforcement on each schedule.

Method of loci   A mnemonic system in which each item to be recalled later is placed in a distinctive spot in an imagined scene, such as a walking path.

Mnemonic   Any technique for improving recall.

Multiple schedule   A sequence of reinforcement schedules in which primary reinforcement occurs at the completion of each schedule. The change from one schedule to the next is signaled by a stimulus.

Mutation   Any change in a gene. When the modified gene occurs in a reproductive cell, the mutation may be passed on to offspring.

Negative reinforcement   A reinforcement procedure in which a response is followed by the removal of, or a decrease in the intensity of, a stimulus. (Cf. *positive reinforcement.*)

Negative reinforcer   The stimulus that reinforces a response in negative reinforcement.

Observational learning   Any procedure in which an organism learns through observation of the behavior of another organism. Also called *vicarious learning.*

One-factor theory   Theory that accounts for negative reinforcement and punishment in terms of one factor, operant learning. (Cf. *two-factor theory.*)

Operant learning   Any procedure by which a response becomes more or less likely to occur, depending upon its consequences. Also called *instrumental learning.*

Overlearning   The continuation of training trials beyond the point required to produce one errless performance.

Overshadowing   Failure of a stimulus that is part of a compound stimulus to become a CS. The stimulus is said to be overshadowed by the stimulus that does become a CS. (Cf. *blocking.*)

Paired associate learning   A learning task involving pairs of words or other stimuli. The subject is presented with the first item of each pair and is expected to produce the second item.

Partial reinforcement   See *intermittent reinforcement.*

Partial reinforcement effect   The tendency of a response to be more resistant to extinction following partial reinforcement than following continuous reinforcement. Abbreviated *PRE.*

Pavlovian conditioning   Any procedure by which a neutral stimulus comes to elicit a reflex response by being paired with a stimulus that regularly elicits that response. Also called *classical conditioning.*

Peak shift   The tendency following discrimination training for the peak of responding in a generalization gradient to shift away from the CS+ or S^D.

Peg word system   A mnemonic system in which each of the first n

integers is associated with a particular image (a "peg"). Each item to be recalled is then "placed" on a peg.

Positive reinforcement A reinforcement procedure in which a response is followed by the presentation of, or an increase in the intensity of, a stimulus. (Cf. *negative reinforcement.*)

Positive reinforcer The stimulus that reinforces a response in positive reinforcement.

Postreinforcement pause A pause in responding following reinforcement; associated primarily with FI and FR schedules.

PRE Abbreviation for *partial reinforcement effect.*

Premack Principle The principle that high-probability behavior will reinforce low-probability behavior. Named after David Premack.

Preparatory response theory Theory of Pavlovian conditioning that proposes that the CR prepares the organism for the occurrence of the US.

Primary reinforcer Any stimulus that is normally reinforcing to all or nearly all members of a species. Examples include food and water. (Cf. *secondary reinforcer.*)

Proactive interference Forgetting caused by learning that occurred prior to the response in question.

Prompted recall Method of measuring forgetting by presenting prompts. (Cf. *free recall.*)

Pseudoconditioning The tendency of a neutral stimulus to elicit a CR when presented after a US has elicited a reflex response. Apparently due to sensitization.

Psychosomatic illness Any organic disorder or symptom due partly or wholly to experience.

Punishment Any procedure that decreases the probability of a response's recurrence. See *punishment, Type 1*, and *punishment, Type 2*; cf. *reinforcement.*

Punishment, Type 1 A punishment procedure in which a response is followed by the presentation of, or an increase in the intensity of, a stimulus. (Cf. *positive reinforcement; punishment, Type 2.*)

Punishment, Type 2 A procedure in which a response is followed by the removal of, or a decrease in the intensity of, a stimulus. Also called *response cost.* (Cf. *negative reinforcement; punishment, Type 1.*)

Ratio strain Disruption of the pattern of responding due to stretching the ratio of reinforcement too abruptly or too far.

Recognition A method of measuring forgetting. It usually consists of requiring the subject to identify from among two or more stimuli the one exposed to earlier.

Reflex A simple relation between a specific stimulus and an innate, involuntary response. Also called *unconditional reflex.* (Cf. *conditional reflex.*)

Reflex arc The anatomical structures through which a reflex is mediated. Consists at a minimum of receptors, sensory neurons, interneurons, motor neurons, and effectors (muscles or glands).

Reinforcement   Any procedure that increases the probability of a response. See positive reinforcement and negative reinforcement. (Cf. *punishment.*)

Relative value theory   Theory of reinforcement that considers reinforcers to be responses rather than stimuli and that attributes a reinforcer's effectiveness to its probability relative to other responses.

Relearning method   A method of measuring forgetting by resuming training after a retention interval. The more training required to achieve an earlier level of performance, the greater the amount of forgetting. Also called *savings method.*

Releaser   Any stimulus that reliably elicits a fixed action pattern.

Response chain   A series of responses that must be performed in sequence.

Response-contingent   Depending upon the occurrence of a response. A response-contingent event occurs if and only if a particular response occurs.

Response cost   See *punishment, Type 2.*

Response deprivation theory   The theory of reinforcement that says a response is reinforcing to the extent that the organism has been deprived of making that response.

Response prevention   A procedure for reducing the rate of unwanted behavior. It consists of restructuring the environment so that the response is difficult or impossible to perform.

Response sampling   A method of obtaining data by periodically observing the performance of randomly selected subjects.

Resurgence   The reappearance of a previously extinguished response during the extinction of a more recently reinforced response.

Retention interval   The time between training and testing for forgetting.

Retentional processes   In Bandura's theory of observational learning, any activity by an observer that aids recall of modeled behavior.

Retroactive interference   Forgetting caused by learning that occurred subsequent to the response in question.

S^D   Any stimulus that indicates that a particular response will be reinforced.

S^Δ   Any stimulus that indicates that a particular response will either be punished or go unreinforced.

SAFMEDS   An acronym for Say All Fast Minute Each Day Shuffle, a system for using flash cards to learn simple factual material.

Savings method   Synonyn for *relearning method.*

Schedule effects   The distinctive rate and pattern of responding associated with a particular reinforcement schedule.

Schedule of reinforcement   The schedule by which a particular response is reinforced.

Secondary reinforcer   Any stimulus that has acquired its reinforcing properties through association with other reinforcers. Also called *conditioned reinforcer.* (Cf. *primary reinforcer.*)

Semantic generalization   Generalization based on the abstract properties of a stimulus rather than its physical properties.

Sensitization   The tendency of a stimulus to elicit a reflex response following the elicitation of that response by a different stimulus.

Sensory preconditioning   A procedure in which two neutral stimuli are paired, after which one is paired with a US. The stimulus that is not paired with the US nevertheless may elicit a CR.

Shaping   An operant learning procedure in which successive approximations of a desired response are reinforced.

Sidman avoidance procedure   An escape-avoidance training procedure in which no stimulus precedes the aversive stimulus.

Simultaneous conditioning   A classical conditioning procedure in which the CS and US occur together in time.

Single subject design   A research design in which a single subject's behavior is observed before and after an experimental treatment. Thus, each subject serves as both an experimental and a control subject.

Social trap   See *contingency trap.*

Spatial contiguity   The distance in space between two events. (Cf. *temporal continguity.*)

Spontaneous recovery   The sudden reappearance of a learned response following extinction.

State-dependent learning   Learning that occurs during a particular state (such as alcoholic intoxication) and is lost when that state passes.

Stimulus   Any event that affects, or is capable of affecting, behavior.

Stimulus-contingent   Depending upon the occurrence of a stimulus. A stimulus-contingent event occurs if and only if a particular stimulus occurs.

Stimulus control   The tendency to respond differentially to different stimuli as the result of discrimination training.

Stimulus substitution theory   In Pavlovian conditioning, the theory that the CS substitutes for the US. Assumes that the CR is essentially the same as the UR. Now largely discredited.

Stretching the ratio   In intermittent reinforcement, the procedure of gradually increasing the number of responses required for reinforcement.

Superstitious behavior   Any response due to adventitious reinforcement.

Symbolic modeling   The modeling of behavior through words or other symbols.

Taste aversion   An aversion, acquired through Pavlovian conditioning, to substances with a particular flavor. Also called *conditioned taste aversion.*

Temporal contiquity   Distance in time separating two events. (Cf. *spatial contiguity.*)

Test trials   In Pavlovian conditioning, the procedure of presenting the CS on some occasions without the US to determine if learning has occurred.

Trace conditioning   A Pavlovian conditioning procedure in which the CS begins and ends before the US is presented.

Transposition   The tendency, following discrimination training, to respond to any stimulus that resembles the S^D in its relationship to S^Δ.

Trial   In learning research, each presentation of the events that constitute the learning procedure. For example, in Pavlovian conditioning, each pairing of CS and US is one trial.

Type 1 punishment   See *punishment, Type 1*.

Type 2 punishment   See *punishment, Type 2*.

Two-factor theory   A theory that accounts for negative reinforcement and punishment in terms of two factors, Pavlovian and operant learning.

Unconditional reflex   A synonym for reflex (see entry for *reflex*); any innate reflex. Often called *unconditioned reflex*. (Cf. *conditional reflex*.)

Unconditional response   The response part of an unconditional reflex. The UR is elicited by a US. Often called unconditioned response. (Cf. *conditional response*.)

Unconditional stimulus   The stimulus part of an unconditional reflex. The US elicits a UR. Often called *unconditioned stimulus*. (Cf. *conditional stimulus*.)

UR   Abbreviation for *unconditional response*.

US   Abbreviation for *unconditional stimulus*.

Variable interval schedule   A form of intermittent reinforcement schedule in which, on average, a specified period of time must elapse between reinforced responses. Abbreviated *VI*. (Cf. *fixed interval schedule*.)

Variable ratio schedule   A form of intermittent schedule in which, on average, every *n*th response is reinforced. Abbreviated *VR*. (Cf. *fixed ratio schedule*.)

Variable time schedule   A reinforcement schedule in which reinforcement is delivered independent of behavior after an interval that varies around a specified average. Abbreviated *VT*. (Cf. *fixed time schedule*.)

VI   Abbreviation for *variable interval*.

Vicarious learning   See *observational learning*.

VR   Abbreviation for *variable ratio*.

VT   Abbreviation for *variable time*.

References

ABRAMOWITZ, A. J., & O'LEARY, S. G. (1990). Effectiveness of delayed punishment in an applied setting. *Behavior Therapy, 21,* 231–239.

ADER, R., & COHEN, N. (1975). Behaviorally conditioned immunosuppression. *Psychosomatic Medicine, 37,* 333–340.

AGAR, W. E., DRUMMOND, F. H., TIEGS, O. W., & GUNSON, M. M. (1954). Fourth (final) report on a test of McDougall's Lamarckian experiment on the training of rats. *Journal of Experimental Biology, 31,* 307–321.

AKIN, O. (1983). *The psychology of architectural design.* London: Pion.

ALBERT, R. S. (1980). Family positions and the attainment of eminence. *Gifted Child Quarterly, 24,* 87–95.

ALBERTS, E., & EHRENFREUND, D. (951). Transposition in children as a function of age. *Journal of Experimental Psychology, 41,* 30–38.

ALESSI, G. (1988). Diagnosis diagnosed: A systematic reaction. *Professional School Psychology, 3,* 145–151.

ALEXANDER, T. (1980, December 1). Economics according to the rats. *Fortune,* pp. 127–130, 132.

ALFORD, B. A. (1986). Behavioral treatment of schizophrenic delusions: A single-case experimental analysis. *Behavior Therapy, 17,* 637–644.

ALLEN, C. T., & MADDEN, T. J. (1985). A closer look at classical conditioning. *Journal of Consumer Research, 12,* 301–315.

American Association for the Advancement of Science (1989). *Science for all Americans.* Washington, DC: Author.

American Heritage Dictionary. (1971). New York: American Heritage and Houghton Mifflin.

American Psychological Association Ethics Committee (1992). Ethical principles of psychologists and code of conduct. *American Psychologist, 47,* 1597–1611.

ANDERSON, K. (1983, April 11). At first I was scared. *Time,* p. 27.

ANDERSON, L. T., & ALPERT, M. (1974). An operant analysis of hallucination frequency in a hospitalized schizophrenic. *Journal of Behavior Therapy and Experimental Psychiatry, 5,* 13–18.

ANGER, D. (1963). The role of temporal discrimination in the reinforcement of Sidman avoidance behavior. *Journal of the Experimental Analysis of Behavior, 6,* 477–506.

ANTHONY, J., & EDELSTEIN, B. A. (1975). Thought-stopping treatment of anxiety attack due to seizure-related obsessive ruminations. *Journal of Behavior Therapy and Experimental Psychiatry, 6,* 343–344.

ARBUCKLE, J. L., & LATTAL, K. A. (1988). Changes in functional response units with briefly delayed reinforcement. *Journal of the Experimental Analysis of Behavior, 49,* 249–263.

ARONFREED, J. (1969). The problem of imitation. In L. P. Lipsitt & H. W. Reese (Eds.), *Advances in child development and behavior.* New York: Academic Press.

AZRIN, N. H., & HOLZ, W. C. (1966). Punishment. In W. K. Honig (Ed.), *Operant behavior: Areas of research and application.* New York: Appleton-Century-Crofts.

AZRIN, N. H., HUTCHINSON, R. R., & HAKE, D. F. (1966). Extinction-induced aggression. *Journal of the Experimental Analysis of Behavior, 9,* 191–204.

AZRIN, N. H., HUTCHINSON, R. R., & McLAUGHLIN, R. (1965). The opportunity for aggression as an operant reinforcer during aversive stimulation. *Journal of the Experimental Analysis of Behavior, 8,* 171–180.

AZZI, R., FIX, D. S. R., KELLER, F. S., & ROCHA, M. I. (1964). Exteroceptive control of response under delayed reinforcement. *Journal of the Experimental Analysis of Behavior, 7,* 159–162.

BACHRACH, A. J. (1962). *Psychological research: An introduction.* New York: Random House.

BACHRACH, A. J., ERWIN, W. J., & MOHR, J. P. (1965). The control of eating behavior in an anorexic by operant conditioning techniques. In L. P. Ullmann & L. Krasner (Eds.), *Case studies in behavior modification* (pp. 153–163). New York: Holt, Rinehart & Winston.

BADDELEY, A. D. (1982). *Your memory: A user's guide.* New York: Macmillan.

BADDELEY, A. D., & LONGMAN, D. J. A. (1978). The influence of length and frequency of training sessions on rate of learning to type. *Ergonomics, 21,* 627–635.

BAENNINGER, R., & ULM, R. R. (1969). Overcoming the effects of prior punishment on inter-species aggression in the rat. *Journal of Comparative and Physiological Psychology, 69,* 628–635.

BAER, D. M., & SHERMAN, J. A. (1967). The development of imitation by reinforcing behavioral similarity to a model. *Journal of the Experimental Analysis of Behavior, 10,* 405–416.

BAHRICK, H. P. (1983). The cognitive map of a city—50 years of learning and memory. In G. H. Bower (Ed.), *Psychology of learning and motivation* (Vol. 17, pp. 125–163). New York: Academic Press.

BAHRICK, H. P. (1984). Semantic memory content in permastore: Fifty years of memory for Spanish learned in school. *Journal of Experimental Psychology: General, 113,* 1–29.

BAHRICK, H. P., & PHELPS, E. (1987). Retention of Spanish vocabulary over eight years. *Journal of Experimental Psychology: Learning, Memory, and Cognition, 13,* 344–349.

BALDA, R. P. (1980). Are seed-caching systems co-evolved? In R. Nohring (Ed.), *Acta 26: Congressus International Ornitologici* (pp. 1185–1191). Berlin: Deutsche Ornitologen-Gesellschaft.

BALSTER, R., et al. (1992, December). In defense of animal research. *APA Monitor,* p. 3.

BANDURA, A. (1962). Social learning through imitation. In M. R. Jones (Ed.),

Nebraska Symposium on Motivation (Vol. 10, pp. 211–269). Lincoln: University of Nebraska Press.

BANDURA, A. (1965). Vicarious processes: A case of no-trial learning. In L. Berkowitz (Ed.), *Advances in experimental social psychology* (Vol. 2, pp. 1–55). New York: Academic Press.

BANDURA, A. (1971a). Analysis of modeling processes. In A. Bandura (Ed.), *Psychological modeling: Conflicting theories.* Chicago: Aldine-Atherton.

BANDURA, A. (Ed.). (1971b). *Psychological modeling: Conflicting theories.* Chicago: Aldine-Atherton.

BANDURA, A. (1971c). *Social learning theory.* New York: General Learning Press.

BANDURA, A. (1973). *Aggression: A social learning analysis.* Englewood Cliffs, NJ: Prentice-Hall.

BANDURA, A. (1977). *Social learning theory.* Englewood Cliffs, NJ: Prentice-Hall.

BANDURA, A., & McDONALD, F. J. (1963). Influence of social reinforcement and the behavior of models in shaping children's moral judgments. *Journal of Abnormal and Social Psychology, 67,* 274–281.

BANDURA, A., & MISCHEL, W. (1965). Modification of self-imposed delay of reward through exposure to live and symbolic models. *Journal of Personality and Social Psychology, 2,* 698–705.

BANDURA, A., ROSS, D., & ROSS, S. A. (1963). Vicarious reinforcement and imitative learning. *Journal of Abnormal and Social Psychology, 67,* 601–607.

BANDURA, A., & WALTERS, R. H. (1959). *Adolescent aggression.* New York: Ronald Press.

BANDURA, A., & WALTERS, R. H. (1963). *Social learning and personality development.* New York: Holt, Rinehart & Winston.

BANNERMAN, D. J., SHELDON, J. B., & SHERMAN, J. A. (1991). Teaching adults with severe and profound retardation to exit their homes upon hearing the fire alarm. *Journal of Applied Behavior Analysis, 24,* 571–577.

BARTLETT, B. (1992, March). Mistaken identity. *Teacher Magazine,* pp. 12–13.

BAUM, W. M. (1975). Time allocation in human vigilance. *Journal of the Experimental Analysis of Behavior, 23,* 43–53.

BELL, S. M., & AINSWORTH, M. D. S. (1972). Infant crying and maternal responsiveness. *Child Development, 43,* 1171–1190.

BERGER, S. M. (1971). Observer perseverance as related to a model's success: A social comparison analysis. *Journal of Personality and Social Psychology, 19,* 341–350.

BERKOWITZ, L. (1964). Aggressive cues in aggressive behavior and hostility catharsis. *Psychological Review, 71,* 104–122.

BERKOWITZ, L. (1968, September). Impulse, aggression and the gun. *Psychology Today,* pp. 18–22.

BERKOWITZ, L. (1983). Aversively stimulated aggression: Some parallels and differences in research with animals and humans. *American Psychologist, 38,* 1135–1144.

BERKOWITZ, L., & DONNERSTEIN, E. (1982). External validity is more than skin deep: Some answers to criticisms of laboratory experiments. *American Psychologist, 37,* 245–257.

BERKOWITZ, L., & LePAGE, A. (1967). Weapons as aggression-eliciting stimuli. *Journal of Personality and Social Psychology, 7,* 202–207.

BERNSTEIN, I. L. (1978). Learned taste aversion in children receiving chemotherapy. *Science, 200,* 1302–1303.

BINMORE, K. (1991). Rational choice theory: Necessary but not sufficient. *American Psychologist, 46,* 797–799.

BIRD, F., PARTRIDGE, P., GROENINGER, M., AND MONIZ, D. (1988, May). Functional communication training to reduce severe self-injurious behavior. Poster submitted at the annual meeting of the Association for Behavior Analysis, Philadelphia, PA.

BITTERMAN, M. E. (1964). Classical conditioning in the goldfish as a function of the CS-US interval. *Journal of Comparative and Physiological Psychology, 58,* 359–366.

BLOUGH, D. S. (1959). Delayed matching in the pigeon. *Journal of the Experimental Analysis of Behavior, 2,* 151–160.

BLOUGH, D. S. (1982). Pigeon perception of letters of the alphabet. *Science, 218,* 397–398.

BOE, E. E., & CHURCH, R. M. (1967). Permanent effects of punishment during extinction. *Journal of Comparative and Physiological Psychology, 63,* 486–492.

BOLTON, P. J. (1983). Drugs of abuse. In D. F. Hawkins (Ed.), *Drugs and pregnancy.* Edinburgh: Churchill Livingston.

BOVBJERG, D. H., REDD, W. H., MAIER, L. A., HOLLAND, J. C., LESKO, L. M., NIEDZWIECKI, D., RUBIN, S. C., HAKES, R. B. (1990). Anticipatory immune suppression and nausea in women receiving cyclic chemotherapy for ovarian cancer. *Journal of Consulting and Clinical Psychology, 58,* 153–157.

BOWER, G. H., MONTEIRO, K. P., & GILLIGAN, S. G. (1978). Emotional mood as a context for learning and recall. *Journal of Verbal Learning and Verbal Behavior, 17,* 573–585.

BOYLE, M. E., & GREER, R. D. (1983). Operant procedures and the comatose patient. *Journal of Applied Behavior Analysis, 16,* 3–12.

BRAGINSKY, B. M., BRAGINSKY, D. D., & RING, K. (1971). *Methods of madness: The mental hospital as a last resort.* New York: Holt, Rinehart & Winston.

BRANSFORD, J. D. (1979). *Human cognition: Learning, understanding and remembering.* Belmont, CA: Wadsworth.

BRAUN, H. W., & GEISELHART, R. (1959). Age differences in the acquisition and extinction of the conditioned eyelid response. *Journal of Experimental Psychology, 57,* 386–388.

BRECHNER, K. C. (1977). An experimental analysis of social traps. *Journal of Experimental Social Psychology, 13,* 52–564.

BRELAND, K., & BRELAND, M. (1961). The misbehavior of organisms. *American Psychologist, 16,* 681–684.

BRIDGER, W. H. (1961). Sensory habituation and discrimination in the human neonate. *American Journal of Psychiatry, 117,* 991–996.

BROADHURST, P. L. (1973). Animal studies bearing on abnormal behavior. In H. J. Eysenck (Ed.), *Handbook of abnormal psychology* (2nd ed.). San Diego, CA: Knapp.

BROGDEN, W. J. (1939). Sensory pre-conditioning. *Journal of Experimental Psychology, 25,* 323–332.

BROWER, L. P. (1971). Prey coloration and predator behavior. In V. Dethier (Ed.), *Topics in animal behavior, topics in the study of life: The BIO source book, part 6.* New York: Harper & Row.

BROWN, J. S. (1942). Factors determining conflict reactions in different discriminations. *Journal of Experimental Psychology, 31,* 272–292.

BROWN, P. L., & JENKINS, H. M. (1968). Auto-shaping of the pigeon's key-peck. *Journal of the Experimental Analysis of Behavior, 11,* 1–8.

BROWN, R. (1965). *Social psychology.* New York: Free Press.

BROWNLEE, J. R., & BAKEMAN, R. (1981). Hitting in toddler-peer interaction. *Child Development, 52,* 1076–1079.

BRUNER, A., & REVUSKY, S. H. (1961). Collateral behavior in humans. *Journal of the Experimental Analysis of Behavior, 4,* 349–350.

BUCHER, R., & FABRICATORE, J. (1970). Use of patient-administered shock to suppress hallucinations. *Behavior Therapy, 1,* 382–385.

BUGELSKI, B. R. (1938). Extinction with and without sub-goal reinforcement. *Journal of Comparative Psychology, 26,* 121–133.

BURDICK, A. (1991, November/December). Spin doctors. *The Sciences,* p. 54.

BURGESS, K. (1968). The behavior and training of a killer whale *(Orcinus orca)* at San Diego Sea World. *International Zoo Yearbook, 8,* 202–205.

BURISH, T. G., & CAREY, M. P. (1986). Conditioned aversive response in cancer chemotherapy patients: Theoretical and developmental analysis. *Journal of Consulting and Clinical Psychology, 54,* 593–600.

CAPEHART, J., VINEY, W., & HULICKA, I. M. (1958). The effect of effort upon extinction. *Journal of Consulting and Clinical Psychology, 51,* 505–507.

CAREY, J. (Ed.). (1988). *Eyewitness to History.* Cambridge, MA: Harvard University Press.

CARR, A. (1967). Adaptive aspects of the scheduled travel of Chelonia. In R. M. Storm (Ed.), *Animal orientation and navigation.* Corvallis: Oregon State University Press.

CARR, E. G. (1977). Motivation of self-injurious behavior: A review of some hypotheses. *Psychological Bulletin, 84,* 800–816.

CARR, E. G. (1985). Behavioral approaches to language and communication. In E. Schopler & G. Mesibov (Eds.), *Current issues in autism: Vol. 3: Communication problems in autism* (pp. 37–57). New York: Plenum.

CARR, E. G. (1988). Functional Equivalence as a mechanism of response generalization. In R. H. Horner, R. L. Koegel, & G. Dunlap (Eds.), *Generalization and maintenance: Lifestyle changes in applied settings.* Baltimore: Brookes.

CARR, E. G., & CARLSON, J. I. (in press). Reduction of severe behavior problems in the community. *Journal of Applied Behavior Analysis.*

CARR, E. G., & DURAND, V. M. (1985). Reducing behavior problems through functional communication training. *Journal of Applied Behavior Analysis, 18,* 111–126.

CARR, E. G., & KEMP, D. C. (1989). Functional equivalence of autistic leading and communicative pointing: Analysis and treatment. *Journal of Autism and Developmental Disorders, 19,* 561–578.

CARR, E. G., & MCDOWELL, J. J. (1980). Social control of self-injurious behavior of organic etiology. *Behavior Therapy, 11,* 402–409.

CARR, E. G., & NEWSOM, C. (1985). Demand-related tantrums: Conceptualizations and treatment. *Behavior Modification, 9,* 403–426.

CARR, E. G., NEWSOM, D. D., AND BINKOFF, J. A. (1976). Stimulus control of self-destructive behavior in a psychotic child. *Journal of Abnormal Child Psychology, 4,* 139–153.

CARR, E. G., NEWSOM, D. D., AND BINKOFF, J. A. (1980). Escape as a factor in the aggressive behavior of two retarded children. *Journal of Applied Behavior Analysis, 13,* 101–117.

CARR, E. G., ROBINSON, S., & PALUMBO, L. W. (1990a). The wrong issue: Aversive versus nonaversive treatment. The right issue: Functional versus nonfunctional treatment. In A. Rapp and N. Singh (Eds.), *Perspectives on the use of nonaversive and aversive interventions for persons with developmental disabilities.* Sycamore, IL: Sycamore Press.

CARR, E. G., ROBINSON, S., TAYLOR, J. C., & CARLSON, J. I. (1990b). Positive approaches to the treatment of severe behavior problems in persons with developmental disabilities: A review and analysis of reinforcement and stimulus-based procedures. *Monograph of the Association for Persons with Severe Handicaps*, No. 4.

CARR, E. G., TAYLOR, J. C., AND ROBINSON, S. (1991). The effects of severe behavior problems in children on the teaching behavior of adults. *Journal of Applied Behavior Analysis, 24*, 523–535.

CARTER, H. D. (1933). Twin similarities in personality traits. *Journal of Genetic Psychology, 43*, 312–321.

CATANIA, A. C. (1966). Concurrent operants. In W. K. Honig (Ed.), *Operant behavior: Areas of research and application*. New York: Appleton-Century-Crofts.

CAUTELA, J. R. (1965). The problem of backward conditioning. *Journal of Psychology, 60*, 135–144.

CHAMBERS, K., GOLDMAN, L., & KOVESDY, P. (1977). Effects of positive reinforcement on creativity. *Perceptual and Motor Skills, 44*, 322.

CHANCE, P. (1986, October). Life after head injury. *Psychology Today*, pp. 62–69.

CHANCE, P. (1987, December). Saving Grace. *Psychology Today*, pp. 42–44.

CHANCE, P. (1992, November). The rewards of learning. *Phi Delta Kappan*, pp. 200–207.

CHARLOP, M. H., KURTZ, P. F., & CASEY, F. G. (1990). Using aberrant behavior as reinforcers for autistic children. *Journal of Applied Behavior Analysis, 23*, 163–181.

CHARNESS, N. (1979). Components of skill in bridge. *Canadian Journal of Psychology, 33*, 1–50.

CHASE, W. G., & SIMON, H. A. (1973). Perception in chess. *Cognitive Psychology, 4*, 55–81.

CHENEY, C. D. (1978, August 21). Personal communication.

CHENEY, C. D. (1991). The source and control of behavior. In W. Ishaq, *Human behavior in today's world*. New York: Praeger.

Chickens of the sea. (1992, May). *Harper's Magazine*, p. 35.

CHRISTOPHER, A. B. (1988). Predisposition versus experiential models of compulsive gambling: An experimental analysis using pigeons. Unpublished Ph.D. thesis, West Virginia University, Morgantown.

COATES, B., & HARTUP, W. (1969). Age and verbalization in observational learning. *Developmental Psychology, 1*, 556–562.

COOLEY, C. H. (1902). *Human nature and the social order*. New York: Scribner's.

COOPER, L. A., & SHEPARD, R. N. (1973). Chronometric studies of the rotation of mental images. In W. G. Chase (Ed.), *Visual information processing*. New York: Academic Press.

COTTON, J. W. (1953). Running time as a function of amount of food deprivation. *Journal of Experimental Psychology, 46*, 188–198.

COWLES, J. T. (1937). Food-tokens as incentives for learning by chimpanzees. *Comparative Psychology Monographs, 14*(No.5).

CRONK, L. (1992, January/February). On human nature: Old dogs, old tricks. *The Sciences*, pp. 13–15.

CROSS, J. G., & GUYER, M. J. (1980). *Social traps*. Ann Arbor: University of Michigan Press.

CUNY, H. (1962). *Ivan Pavlov: The man and his theories* (P. Evans, Trans.). Greenwich, CT: Fawcett World Library.

CUSTER, R. L. (1984). Profile of the pathological gambler. *Journal of Clinical Psychology, 45*, 35–38.

D'AMATO, M. R. (1973). Delayed matching to sample and short-term memory in monkeys. In G. H. Bower (Ed.), *The psychology of learning and motivation: Advances in research and theory* (Vol. 7). New York: Academic Press.

DARWIN, C. (1859). *On the origin of species.* London: J. Murray.

DAVID, H. P., DYTRYCH, Z., MATEJCEK, Z., & SCHULLER, V. (Eds.). (1988). *Born unwanted: Developmental effects of denied abortion.* New York: Springer.

DAVIS, W. M., & SMITH, S. G. (1976). Role of conditioned reinforcers in the initiation, maintenance, and extinction of drug-seeking behavior. *Pavlovian Journal of Biological Science, 11*, 222–236.

DAVISON, M., & MCCARTHY, D. (1988). *The matching law: A research review.* Hillsdale, NJ: Erlbaum.

DAWKINS, R. (1986). *The blind watchmaker.* New York: Norton.

DEANGELIS, T. (1992, May). Senate seeking answers to rising tide of violence. *APA Monitor*, p. 11.

DE GROOT, A. D. (1966). Perception and memory versus thought: Some old ideas and recent findings. In B. Kleinmuntz (Ed.), *Problem solving: Research, method and theory.* New York: Wiley.

DEMPSTER, F. N. (1993). Exposing our students to less should help them learn more. *Phi Delta Kappan, 74*, 432–437.

DENTAN, R. K. (1968). *The Semai: A nonviolent people of Malaya.* New York: Holt, Rinehart & Winston.

DESCARTES, R. (1972). *Treatise of man.* (T. S. Hall., Trans.). Cambridge, MA: Harvard University Press. (Originally published in 1662.)

DEVILLIERS, P. A. (1977). Choice in concurrent schedules and a quantitative formulation of the Law of Effects. In W. K. Honig & J. E. R. Staddon (Eds.), *Handbook of operant behavior.* Englewood Cliffs, NJ: Prentice-Hall.

DEWS, P. B. (1959). Some observations on an operant in the octopus. *Journal of the Experimental Analysis of Behavior, 2*, 57–63.

DICARA, L., & MILLER, N. E. (1968). Instrumental learning of systolic blood pressure responses by curarized rats: Dissociation of cardiac and vascular changes. *Psychonomic Medicine, 30*(5, Pt. 1), 489–494.

DINSMOOR, J. A. (1954). Punishment: I. The avoidance hypothesis. *Psychological Review, 61*, 34–46.

DINSMOOR, J. A. (1955). Punishment: II. An interpretation of empirical findings. *Psychological Review, 62*, 96–105.

DURANT, W. (1926). *The story of philosophy.* Garden City, NY: Garden City.

DURLACH, P. J. (1982). Pavlovian learning and performance when CS and US are uncorrelated. In M. L. Commons, R. J. Herrnstein, & A. R. Wagner (Eds.), *Quantitative analyses of behavior: Vol. 3: Acquisition* (pp. 173–193). Cambridge, MA: Ballinger.

DWORKIN, B. R., & MILLER, N. E. (1986). Failure to replicate visceral learning in the acute curarized rat preparation. *Behavioral Neuroscience, 100*, 299–314.

EATON, G. G. (1976). The social order of Japanese macaques. *Scientific American, 234*, 96–106.

EBBINGHAUS, H. (1913). *Memory, a contribution to experimental psychology.* (H. A. Ruger, Trans.). New York: Columbia University Press. (Originally published in 1885).

EGAN, D. E., & SCHWARTZ, B. J. (1979). Chunking in recall of symbolic drawings. *Memory and Cognition, 7*, 149–158.

EISENBERGER, R., KARPMAN, M., & TRATTNER, J. (1967). What is the necessary and sufficient condition in the contingency situation? *Journal of Experimental Psychology, 74,* 342–350.

EKMAN, P., & PATTERSON, J. (1992). *The day America told the truth.* New York: Prentice-Hall.

EPSTEIN, R. (1983). Resurgence of previously reinforced behavior during extinction. *The Behavior Analyst Letters, 3,* 391–397.

EPSTEIN, R. (1985). Extinction-induced resurgence: Preliminary investigation and possible application. *Psychological Record, 35,* 143–153.

EPSTEIN, R., KIRSHNIT, C., LANZA, R., & RUBIN, L. (1984). Insight in the pigeon: Antecedents and determinants of an intelligent performance. *Nature, 308,* 61–62.

EPSTEIN, R., LANZA, R. P., & SKINNER, B. F. (1981). "Self-awareness" in the pigeon. *Science, 212,* 695–696.

EPSTEIN, R., & SKINNER, B. F. (1980). Resurgence of responding after the cessation of response-independent reinforcement. *Proceedings of the National Academy of Sciences, 77,* 6251–6253.

EPSTEIN, R., & SKINNER, B. F. (1981). The spontaneous use of memoranda by pigeons. *Behavior Analysis Letters, 1,* 241–246.

EPSTEIN, W. (1972). Mechanisms of directed forgetting. In G. H. Bower (Ed.), *The psychology of learning and motivation* (Vol. 6, pp. 147–191). New York: Academic Press.

ERICSSON, K. A., & CHASE, W. G. (1982). Exceptional memory. *American Scientist, 70,* 607–615.

ERICSSON, K. A., & KARAT, J. (1981). Memory for words in sequence. Paper read at meeting of the Psychonomic Society, Philadelphia, PA.

ERIKSON, E. H. (1968). *Identity: Youth & crisis.* New York: Norton.

ESTES, W. K. (1944). An experimental study of punishment. *Psychological Monographs, 57* (whole no. 263).

ESTES, W. K., & SKINNER, B. F. (1941). Some quantitative properties of anxiety. *Journal of Experimental Psychology, 29,* 390–400.

EYSENCK, H. J. (1965). *Fact and fiction in psychology.* Baltimore: Penguin.

EYSENCK, H. J. (1967). *The biological basis of personality.* Springfield, IL: Charles C. Thomas.

EYSENCK, H. J. (1976). *Sex and personality.* Austin: University of Texas Press.

FARBER, S. (1981). *Identical twins reared apart: A reanalysis.* New York: Basic Books.

FERSTER, C. B., & SKINNER, B. F. (1957). *Schedules of reinforcement.* New York: Appleton-Century-Crofts.

FIORITO, G., & SCOTTO, P. (1992). Observational learning in Octopus vulgaris. *Science, 256,* 545–547.

FISHER, J., & HINDE, R. A. (1949). The opening of milk bottles by birds. *British Birds, 42,* 347–357.

FISHER, J. L., & HARRIS, M. B. (1976). The effects of three model characteristics on imitation and learning. *Journal of Social Psychology, 98,* 183–199.

FOXX, R. M., & AZRIN, N. H. (1973). The elimination of autistic self-stimulatory behavior by overcorrection. *Journal of Applied Behavior Analysis, 6,* 1–14.

FRANK, H., & FRANK, M. G. (1982). Comparison of problem-solving performance in six-week-old wolves and dogs. *Animal Behavior, 30,* 95–98.

FREEDMAN, D. G. (1974). *Human infancy: An evolutionary perspective.* Hillsdale, NJ: Erlbaum.

FREUD, S. (1918). *Totem and taboo.* (A. A. Brill, Trans.). New York: Moffat Yard. (Originally published in 1913.)

FUJITA, K. (1983). Acquisition and transfer of a higher-order conditional discrimination performance in the Japanese monkey. *Japanese Psychological Research, 25,* 1–8.

FULLER, J. L., & SCOTT, J. P. (1954). Heredity and learning ability in infrahuman mammals. *Eugenics Quarterly, 1,* 28–43.

FULLER, R. (1991). Behavior analysis and unsafe driving: Warning—learning trap ahead. *Journal of Applied Behavior Analysis, 24,* 73–75.

FYER, A. J., MANNUZZA, S., GALLOPS, M. S., MARTIN, L. Y., AARONSON, C., GORMAN, J. M., LEIBOWITZ, M. R., & KLEIN, D. F. (1990). Familial transmission of simple phobias and fears: A preliminary report. *Archives of General Psychiatry, 47,* 252–256.

GAGNE, R. M. (1941). The retention of a conditioned operant response. *Journal of Experimental Psychology, 29,* 296–305.

GALLUP, A. M., & ELAM, S. M. (1988). The 20th annual Gallup Poll of the public's attitude toward the public schools. *Phi Delta Kappan, 70,* 33–46.

GALLUP, G. G. (1970). Chimpanzees: Self-recognition. *Science, 167,* 86–87.

GALLUP, G. G. (1979). Self-awareness in primates. *American Scientist, 67,* 417–421.

GANTT, W. H. (1941). Introduction. In I. P. Pavlov, *Lectures on conditioned reflexes and psychiatry* (Vol. 2). (W. H. Gantt, Trans.). New York: International.

GANTT, W. H. (1966). Conditional or conditioned, reflex or response. *Conditioned Reflex, 1,* 69–74.

GARB, J. L., & STUNKARD, A. J. (1974). Taste aversion in man. *American Journal of Psychiatry, 131,* 1204–1207.

GARCIA, J. (1981). Tilting at the paper mills of academe. *American Psychologist, 36,* 149–158.

GARCIA, J., CLARKE, J., & HANKINS, W. G. (1973). Natural responses to scheduled rewards. In P. P. G. Bateson & P. Klopfer (Eds.), *Perspectives in ethology.* New York: Plenum.

GARCIA, J., KIMELDORF, D. J., & KOELLING, R. A. (1955). A conditioned aversion towards saccharin resulting from exposure to gamma radiation. *Science, 122,* 157–158.

GARCIA, J., & KOELLING, R. A. (1966). Relation of cue to consequence in avoidance learning. *Psychonomic Science, 4,* 123–124.

GARDNER, R. A., & GARDNER, B. T. (1969). Teaching sign language to a chimpanzee. *Science, 165,* 664–672.

GAUDET, C. L., & FENTON, M. B. (1984). Observational learning in three species of insectivorous bats (chiroptera). *Animal Behavior, 32,* 385–388.

GIRDEN, E., & CULLER, E. A. (1937). Conditioned responses in curarized striate muscle in dogs. *Journal of Comparative Psychology, 23,* 261–274.

GLEESON, S., LATTAL, K. A., & WILLIAMS, K. S. (1989). Superstitious conditioning: A replication and extension of Neuringer (1970). *Psychological Record, 39,* 563–571.

GLEITMAN, H. (1971). Forgetting of long-term memories in animals. In W. K. Honig & P. H. R. James (Eds.), *Animal memory.* New York: Academic Press.

GLEITMAN, H., & BERNHEIM, J. W. (1963). Retention of fixed-interval performance in rats. *Journal of Comparative and Physiological Psychology, 56,* 839–841.

GLOVER, J., & GARY, A. L. (1976). Procedures to increase some aspects of creativity. *Journal of Applied Behavior Analysis, 9,* 79–84.

GODDEN, D. B., & BADDELEY, A. D. (1975). Context-dependent memory in two natural environments: On land and under water. *British Journal of Psychology, 66*, 325–331.

GOETERS, S., BLAKELY, E., & POLING, A. (in press). The differential outcomes effect. *Psychological Record.*

GOETZ, E. M., & BAER, D. M. (1973). Social control of form diversity and the emergence of new forms in children's blockbuilding. *Journal of Applied Behavior Analysis, 6*, 209–217.

GOLDBERG, S. R., SPEALMAN, R. D., AND GOLDBERG, D. M. (1981). Persistent behavior at high rates maintained by intravenous self-administration of nicotine. *Science, 214*, 573–575.

GOLDIAMOND, I. (1975). Insider-outsider problems: A constructional approach. *Rehabilitation Psychology, 22*, 103–116.

GORMEZANO, I., & MOORE, J. W. (1969). Classical conditioning. In M. H. Marx (Ed.), *Learning: Processes.* London: MacMillan.

GORN, G. J. (1982). The effects of music in advertising on choice behavior: A classical conditioning approach. *Journal of Marketing, 46*, 94–101.

GOULD, S. J. (1987). *An urchin in the storm.* New York: Norton.

GREENSPOON, J. (1955). The reinforcing effect of two spoken sounds on the frequency of two responses. *American Journal of Psychology, 68*, 409–416.

GREENSPOON, J., & RANYARD, R. (1957). Stimulus conditions and retroactive inhibition. *Journal of Experimental Psychology, 53*, 55–59.

GREENWOOD, C. R. (1991). A longitudinal analysis of time, engagement, and achievement in at-risk versus non-risk students. *Exceptional Children, 57*, 521–535.

GRETHER, W. H. (1938). Pseudo-conditioning without paired stimulation encountered in attempted backward conditioning. *Journal of Comparative Psychology, 25*, 141–158.

GURSKY, D. (1992, March). The writing life. *Teacher Magazine*, pp. 10–11.

GUTHRIE, E. R. (1960). *The psychology of learning* (rev. ed.). Gloucester, MA: Smith.

GUTTMAN, N. (1963). Laws of behavior and facts of perception. In S. Koch (Ed.), *Psychology: A study of a science* (Vol. 5). New York: McGraw-Hill.

GUTTMAN, N., & KALISH, H. I. (1956). Discriminability and stimulus generalization. *Journal of Experimental Psychology, 51*, 79–88.

HALL, C. S. (1937). Emotional behavior in the rat. *Journal of Comparative Psychology, 24*, 369–375.

HALL, K. R. L. (1968). Social learning in monkeys. In P. C. Jay (Ed.), *Primates: Studies in adaptation and variability.* New York: Holt, Rinehart & Winston.

HANSON, H. M. (1959). Effects of discrimination training on stimulus generalization. *Journal of Experimental Psychology, 58*, 321–334.

HARDIN, G. (1968). The tragedy of the commons. *Science, 162*, 1243–1248.

HARLOW, H. F. (1949). The formation of learning sets. *Psychological Review, 56*, 51–65.

HARLOW, H. F. (1958). The nature of love. *American Psychologist, 13*, 673–685.

HARLOW, H. F., & HARLOW, M. K. (1962a). The effect of rearing conditions on behavior. *Bulletin of the Menninger Clinic, 26*, 213–224.

HARLOW, H. F., & HARLOW, M. K. (1962b). Social deprivation in monkeys. *Scientific American, 207*, 136–146.

HARRIS, B. (1979). Whatever happened to Little Albert? *American Psychologist, 34*, 151–160.

HAWKINS, D. F. (Ed.). (1983). *Drugs and pregnancy.* Edinburgh: Churchill Livingston.

HAYES, C. (1951). *The ape in our house.* New York: Harper & Row.

HAYES, K. J., & HAYES, C. (1952). Imitation in a home-raised chimpanzee. *Journal of Comparative and Physiological Psychology, 45,* 450–459.

HERBERT, M. J., & HARSH, C. M. (1944). Observational learning by cats. *Journal of Comparative Psychology, 37,* 81–95.

HERRNSTEIN, R. J. (1961). Relative and absolute strength of response as a function of frequency of reinforcement. *Journal of the Experimental Analysis of Behavior, 4,* 267–272.

HERRNSTEIN, R. J. (1966). Superstition: A corollary of the principle of operant conditioning. In W. K. Honig (Ed.), *Operant behavior: Areas of research and application.* New York: Appleton-Century-Crofts.

HERRNSTEIN, R. J. (1969). Method and theory in the study of avoidance. *Psychological Review, 76,* 49–69.

HERRNSTEIN, R. J. (1970). On the law of effect. *Journal of the Experimental Analysis of Behavior, 13,* 243–266.

HERRNSTEIN, R. J. (1979). Acquisition, generalization, and discrimination reversal of a natural concept. *Journal of Experimental Psychology: Animal Behavior Processes, 5,* 116–129.

HERRNSTEIN, R. J. (1990). Rational choice theory: Necessary but not sufficient. *American Psychologist, 45,* 356–367.

HERRNSTEIN, R. J. (1991). Reply to Binmore and Staddon. *American Psychologist, 46,* 799–801.

HERRNSTEIN, R. J., & HINELINE, P. N. (1966). Negative reinforcement as shock-frequency reduction. *Journal of the Experimental Analysis of Behavior, 9,* 421–430.

HERRNSTEIN, R. J., LOVELAND, D. H., & CABLE, C. (1976). Natural concepts in pigeons. *Journal of Experimental Psychology: Animal Behavior Processes, 2,* 285–311.

HERRNSTEIN, R. J., & MAZUR, J. E. (1987, November/December). Making up our minds. *The Sciences,* pp. 40–47.

HETH, C. D. (1976). Simultaneous and backward fear conditioning as a function of number of CS-US pairings. *Journal of Experimental Psychology: Animal Behavior Processes, 2,* 117–129.

HICKIS, C., & THOMAS, D. R. (1991). Application: Substance abuse and dependency. In W. Ishaq (Ed.), *Human Behavior in Today's World.* New York: Praeger.

HIGGINS, S. T., MORRIS, E. K., & JOHNSON, L. M. (1989). Social transmission of superstitious behavior in preschool children. *Psychological Record, 39,* 307–323.

HILGARD, E. R. (1936). The nature of the conditioned response: I. The case for and against stimulus substitution. *Psychological Review, 43,* 366–385.

HINDE, R. A., & FISHER, J. (1972). Some comments on the re-publication of two papers on the opening of milk bottles in birds. In P. H. Klopfer & J. P. Hailman (Eds.), *Function and evolution of behavior.* Reading, MA: Addison-Wesley.

HINELINE, P. N. (1984). Aversive control: A separate domain. *Journal of the Experimental Analysis of Behavior, 42,* 495–509.

HIROTO, D. S. (1974). Locus of control and learned helplessness. *Journal of Experimental Psychology, 102,* 187–193.

HO, B. T., RICHARDS, D. W., & CHUTE, D. L. (Eds.). (1978). *Drug discrimination and state dependent learning.* New York: Academic Press.

HOLLAND, J. C. (1978). Behaviorism: Part of the problem or part of the solution? *Journal of Applied Behavior Analysis, 11,* 163–174.

HONIG, W. K., & URCUIOLI, P. J. (1981). The legacy of Guttman and Kalish (1956): Twenty-five years of research on stimulus generalization. *Journal of the Experimental Analysis of Behavior, 36,* 405–445.

HOVLAND, C. I. (1937a). The generalization of conditioned responses: I. The sensory generalization of conditioned responses with varying frequencies of tone. *Journal of General Psychology, 17,* 125–148.

HOVLAND, C. I. (1937b). The generalization of conditioned responses: IV. The effects of varying amounts of reinforcement upon the degree of generalization of conditioned responses. *Journal of Experimental Psychology, 21,* 261–276.

HULL, C. L. (1943). *Principles of behavior.* New York: Appleton-Century-Crofts.

HULL, C. L. (1951). *Essentials of behavior.* New Haven, CT: Yale University Press.

HULL, C. L. (1952). *A behavior system.* New Haven, CT: Yale University Press.

HUMPHREYS, L. G. (1939). The effect of random alternation of reinforcement on the acquisition and extinction of conditioned eyelid reactions. *Journal of Experimental Psychology, 25,* 141–158.

HUNTER, I. M. L. (1964). *Memory* (rev. ed.). Baltimore: Penguin.

HUNTER, W. S. (1913). The delayed reaction in animals and children. *Behavior Monographs, 2,* (whole no. 1), 1–86.

HURSH, S. R. (1980). Economic concepts for the analysis of behavior. *Journal of the Experimental Analysis of Behavior, 34,* 219–238.

HURSH, S. R. (1984). Behavioral economics. *Journal of the Experimental Analysis of Behavior, 42,* 435–452.

JACOBS, L. F. (1992). Memory for cache locations in Merriam's kangaroo rats. *Animal Behavior, 43,* 585–593.

JACOBS, L. F., & LIMAN, E. R. (1991). Grey squirrels remember the locations of buried nuts. *Animal Behavior, 41,* 103–110.

JASON, L. A. (1991). Participating in social change: A fundamental value for our discipline. *American Journal of Community Psychology, 19,* 1–16.

JASON, L. A., JI, P. Y., ANES, M. D., & BIRKHEAD, S. H. (1991). Active enforcement of cigarette control laws in the prevention of cigarette sales to minors. *Journal of the American Medical Association, 266,* 3159–3161.

JENKINS, H. M., & HARRISON, R. H. (1960). Effect of discrimination training on auditory generalization. *Journal of Experimental Psychology, 59,* 246–253.

JENKINS, J. C., & DALLENBACH, K. M. (1924). Obliviscence during sleep and waking. *American Journal of Psychology, 35,* 605–612.

JENKINS, J. H., & MOORE, B. R. (1973). The form of autoshaped response with food and water reinforcers. *Journal of the Experimental Analysis of Behavior, 20,* 163–181.

JOHN, E. R., CHESLER, P., BARTLETT, F., & VICTOR, I. (1968). Observational learning in cats. *Science, 159,* 1489–1491.

JONCICH, G. (1968). *The sane positivist: A biography of Edward L. Thorndike.* Middleton, CT: Wesleyan University Press.

JONES, M. C. (1924a). The elimination of children's fears. *Journal of Experimental Psychology, 7,* 382–390.

JONES, M. C. (1924b). A laboratory study of fear: The case of Peter. *Pedagogical Seminary, 31,* 308–315.

KAGAN, J., & SNIDMAN, N. (1991). Temperamental factors in human development. *American Psychologist, 46,* 856–862.

KALLMANN, F. J. (1953). *Heredity in health and mental disorder.* New York: Norton.

KAMIL, A. C. (1978). Systematic foraging by a nectar-feeding bird, the Amakihi (Loxops virens). *Journal of Comparative and Physiological Psychology, 92,* 388–396.

KAMIL, A. C., & BALDA, R. P. (1985). Cache recovery and spatial memory in Clark's nutcrackers. *Journal of Experimental Psychology: Animal Behavior Processes, 11,* 95–111.

KAMIL, A. C., & BALDA, R. P. (1990a). Spatial memory in seed-caching corvids. In G. H. Bower (Ed.), *Psychology of Learning and Motivation, Vol. 26* (pp. 1–25). New York: Academic Press.

KAMIL, A. C., & BALDA, R. P. (1990b). Differential memory for cache sites in Clark's nutcrackers. *Journal of Experimental Psychology: Animal Behavior Processes, 16,* 162–168.

KAMIN, L. J. (1969). Predictability, surprise, attention and conditioning. In B. A. Campbell & R. M. Church (Eds.), *Punishment and aversive behavior.* New York: Appleton-Century-Crofts.

KAMIN, L. J., BRIMER, C. J., & BLACK, A. H. (1963). Conditioned suppression as a monitor of fear of the CS in the course of avoidance training. *Journal of Comparative and Physiological Psychology, 56,* 497–501.

KAWAMURA, S. (1963). The process of sub-cultural propagation among Japanese macaques. In C. H. Southwick (Ed.), *Primate social behavior.* New York: Van Nostrand.

KEEN, S. (1986). *Faces of the enemy.* New York: Harper & Row.

KEITH-LUCUS, T., & GUTTMAN, N. (1975). Robust single-trial delayed backward conditioning. *Journal of Comparative and Physiological Psychology, 88,* 468–476.

KELLOGG, W. N. (1968). Communication and language in the home-raised chimpanzee. *Science, 162,* 423–427.

KENDALL, S. B. (1987). An animal analogue of gambling. *Psychological Record, 37,* 247–256.

KENDLER, K. S., NEALE, M. C., KESSLER, R. C., HEATH, A. C., et al. (1992). Generalized anxiety disorder in women: A population-based twin study. *Archives of General Psychiatry, 49,* 267–272.

KETTLEWELL, H. B. D. (1959). Darwin's missing evidence. *Scientific American, 200,* 48–53.

KIMBLE, G. A. (1947). Conditioning as a function of the time between conditioned and unconditioned stimuli. *Journal of Experimental Psychology, 37,* 1–15.

KIMBLE, G. A. (1961). *Hilgard and Marquis' conditioning and learning.* New York: Appleton-Century-Crofts.

KOHLER, W. (1939). Simple structural function in the chimpanzee and the chicken. In W. A. Ellis (Ed.), *A sourcebook of Gestalt psychology.* New York: Harcourt Brace.

KOHLER, W. (1973). *The mentality of apes* (2nd ed.). New York: Liveright. (Originally published in 1927.)

KRASNER, L. (1958). Studies of the conditioning of verbal behavior. *Psychological Bulletin, 55,* 148–170.

KRECH, D., & CRUTCHFIELD, R. S. (1961). *Elements of psychology.* New York: Knopf.

KRUEGER, W. C. F. (1929). The effects of overlearning on retention. *Journal of Experimental Psychology, 12,* 71–78.

KUO, Z. Y. (1930). The genesis of the cat's response to the rat. *Journal of Comparative Psychology, 11,* 1–36.

KUSHNER, M. (1968). The operant control of intractable sneezing. In C. D. Spielberger, R. Fox, & D. Masterson (Eds.), *Contributions to general psychology.* New York: Ronald.

KYMISSIS, E., & POULSON, C. L. (1990). The history of imitation in learning theory: The language acquisition process. *Journal of the Experimental Analysis of Behavior, 54,* 113–127.

LACEY, J. I., SMITH, R. L., & GREEN, A. (1955). Use of conditioned autonomic responses in the study of anxiety. *Psychosomatic Medicine, 17,* 208–217.

LANDMAN, O. E. (1993). Inheritance of acquired characteristics. *Scientific American, 266,* 150.

LANE, H. L., & SHINKMAN, P. G. (1963). Methods and findings in an analysis of a vocal operant. *Journal of the Experimental Analysis of Behavior, 6,* 179–188.

LANG, P. J., & MELAMED, B. G. (1969). Case report: Avoidance conditioning therapy of an infant with chronic ruminative vomiting. *Journal of Abnormal Psychology, 74,* 1–8.

LARSEN, O. N., GRAY, L. N., & FORTIS, J. G. (1968). Achieving goals through violence on television. In O. N. Larsen (Ed.), *Violence and the mass media.* New York: Harper & Row.

LASHLEY, K. S. (1930). The mechanism of vision: I. A method of rapid analysis of pattern-vision in the rat. *Journal of Genetic Psychology, 37,* 453–640.

LASHLEY, K. S., & WADE, M. (1946). The Pavlovian theory of generalization. *Psychological Review, 53,* 72–87.

LAVIGNA, G. W., & DONNELLAN, A. M. (1986). *Alternatives to punishment: Solving behavior problems with non-aversive strategies.* New York: Irvington.

LAYNG, T. V. J., & ANDRONIS, P. T. (1984). Toward a functional analysis of delusional speech and hallucinatory behavior. *The Behavior Analyst, 7,* 139–156.

LEANDER, J. D., LIPPMAN, L. G., & MEYER, M. E. (1968). Fixed interval performance as related to subjects' verbalization of the reinforcement contingency. *The Psychological Record, 18,* 469–474.

LENNEBERG, E. (1967). *The biological foundation of language.* New York: Wiley.

LENNEBERG, E. (1969). On explaining language. *Science, 164,* 635–643.

LEVINE, J. M., & MURPHY, G. (1943). The learning and forgetting of controversial material. *Journal of Abnormal and Social Psychology, 38,* 507–517.

LIGHTFOOT, L. O. (1980). Behavioral tolerance to low doses of alcohol in social drinkers. Unpublished doctoral dissertation, Waterloo University.

LINDSAY, P. H., & NORMAN, D. A. (1972) *Human information processing: An introduction to psychology.* New York: Academic Press.

LOCKE, J. (1961). *An essay concerning human understanding.* London: Dent. (Originally published in 1690).

LOFTUS, E. F. (1980). *Memory: Surprising new insights into how we remember and why we forget.* Reading, MA: Addison-Wesley.

LOFTUS, E. F., & PALMER, J. C. (1974). Reconstruction of automobile destruction: An examination of the interaction between language and memory. *Journal of Verbal Learning and Verbal Behavior, 13,* 585–589.

LOGUE, A. W., LOGUE, K. R., & STRAUSS, K. E. (1983). The acquisition of taste aversion in humans with eating and drinking disorders. *Behavior Research and Therapy, 21,* 275–289.

LOGUE, A. W., OPHIR, I., & STRAUSS, K. E. (1981). The acquisition of taste aversion in humans. *Behavior Research and Therapy, 19,* 319–333.

LORENZ, K. (1952). *King Solomon's ring.* New York: Thomas Y. Crowell.

LORGE, I. (1930). Influence of regularly interpolated intervals on subsequent learning. Teachers College, Columbia University.

LOVAAS, O. I. (1987). Behavioral treatment and normal educational and intellectual functioning in young autistic children. *Journal of Consulting and Clinical Psychology, 53,* 3–9.

LOVAAS, O. I., & SIMMONS, J. Q. (1969). Manipulation of self-destruction in three retarded children. *Journal of Applied Behavior Analysis, 2,* 143–157.

LUBOW, R. E. (1965). Latent inhibition: Effects of frequency of nonreinforced preexposure of the CS. *Journal of Comparative and Physiological Psychology, 60,* 454–457.

LUBOW, R. E., & MOORE, A. V. (1959). Latent inhibition: The effect of nonreinforced pre-exposure to the conditional stimulus. *Journal of Consulting and Clinical Psychology, 52,* 415–419.

LUBOW, R. E., RIFKIN, B., & ALEK, M. (1976). The context effect: The relationship between stimulus preexposure and environmental preexposure determines subsequent learning. *Journal of Experimental Psychology: Animal Behavior Processes, 2,* 38–47.

LUISELLI, J. K., MYLES, E., EVANS, T. P., & BOYCE, D. A. (1985). Reinforcement control of severe dysfunctional behavior of blind, multihandicapped students. *American Journal of Mental Deficiency, 90,* 328–334.

LURIA, A. R. (1968). *The mind of a mnemonist: A little book about a vast memory.* (L. Solotaroff, Trans.). New York: Basic Books.

MACKINTOSH, N. J. (1974). *The psychology of animal learning.* New York: Academic Press.

MADSEN, T., SHINE, R., LOMAN, J., & HAKANSSON, T. (1992). Why do female adders copulate so frequently? *Nature, 355,* 440–441.

MALONE, J. C. (1990). *Theories of learning: A historical approach.* Belmont, CA: Wadsworth.

MALCOTT, R. W. (1992). Attack of single-factor theorists. *ABA Newsletter, 14,* 8–9.

MALOTT, R. W., & MALOTT, M. K. (1970). Perception and stimulus generalization. In W. C. Stebbins (Ed.), *Animal psychophysics: The design and conduct of sensory experiments.* New York: Appleton-Century-Crofts.

MANSFIELD, R. J. W., & RACHLIN, H. C. (1970). The effect of punishment, extinction, and satiation on response chains. *Learning and Motivation, 1,* 27–36.

MARLATT, G. A., & GORDON, J. R. (Eds.). (1985). *Relapse prevention: Maintenance strategies in the treatment of addictive behaviors.* New York: Guilford Press.

MARSCHALL, L. A. (1992, January/February). Books in brief. *The Sciences,* p. 52.

MASSERMAN, J. H. (1943). *Behavior and neurosis: An experimental-psychoanalytic approach to psychobiologic principles.* New York: Hafner.

MATTHEWS, B. A., SHIMOFF, E., CATANIA, A. C., & SAGVOLDEN, T. (1977). Uninstructed human responding: Sensitivity to ratio and interval contingencies. *Journal of the Experimental Analysis of Behavior, 27,* 453–467.

MAX, L. W. (1935). An experimental study of the motor theory of consciousness: III. Action—Current responses in deaf-mutes during sleep, sensory stimulation, and dreams. *Journal of Comparative Psychology, 19*, 469–486.

MAZUR, J. E. (1975). The matching law and quantification related to Premack's principle. *Journal of Experimental Psychology: Animal Behavior Processes, 1*, 374–386.

McDOUGALL, W. (1908). *An introduction to social psychology.* London: Methuen.

McDOUGALL, W. (1927). An experiment for the testing of the hypothesis of Lamarck. *British Journal of Psychology, 17*, 267–304.

McDOUGALL, W. (1938). Fourth report on a Lamarckian experiment. *British Journal of Psychology, 28*, 321–345.

McGEOCH, J. A. (1932). Forgetting and the law of disuse. *Psychological Review, 39*, 352–370.

McINTIRE, R. W. (1973, October). Parenthood training or mandatory birth control: Take your choice. *Psychology Today*, p. 34.

MEAD, G. H. (1934). *Mind, self and society.* Chicago: University of Chicago Press.

MERRETT, F., & WHELDALL, K. (1978). "Playing the game": A behavioral approach to classroom management in the junior school. *Educational Review, 30*, 41–50.

MILLER, G. A. (1956). The magical number seven, plus or minus two. *Psychological Review, 63*, 81–97.

MILLER, N. E. (1948). Studies of fear as an acquired drive: I. Fear as a motivation and fear-reduction as reinforcement in learning of new responses. *Journal of Experimental Psychology, 38*, 89–101.

MILLER, N. E. (1960). Learning resistance to pain and fear: Effects of overlearning, exposure, and rewarded exposure in context. *Journal of Experimental Psychology, 60*, 137–145.

Miller, N. E. (1978). Biofeedback and visceral learning. *Annual Review of Psychology, 29*, 373–404.

MILLER, N. E. (1985). The value of behavioral research on animals. *American Psychologist, 40*, 423–440.

MILLER, N. E., & CARMONA, A. (1967). Modification of a visceral response, salivation in thirsty dogs, by instrumental training with water reward. *Journal of Comparative and Physiological Psychology, 63*, 1–6.

MILLER, N. E., & DiCARA, L. (1967). Instrumental learning of heart rate changes in curarized rats: Shaping and specificity to discriminative stimulus. *Journal of Comparative and Physiological Psychology, 63*, 12–19.

MILLER, N. E., & DOLLARD, J. (1941). *Social learning and imitation.* New Haven, CT: Yale University Press.

MILLER, S. J., & SLOANE, H. N. (1976). The generalization effects of parent training across stimulus settings. *Journal of Applied Behavior Analysis, 9*, 355–370.

MINAMI, H., & DALLENBACH, K. M. (1946). The effect of activity upon learning and retention in the cockroach (Periplaneta americana). *American Journal of Psychology, 59*, 1–58.

MINNES, P. M. (1980). Treatment of compulsive hand in mouth behavior in a profoundly retarded child using a sharp pinch as the aversive stimulation. *Australian Journal of Developmental Disabilities, 6*, 5–10.

MOWRER, O. H. (1947). On the dual nature of learning: A reinterpretation of "conditioning" and "problem solving." *Harvard Educational Review, 17*, 102–150.

MOWRER, O. H. (1960). *Learning theory and behavior.* New York: Wiley.

MUIR, J. (1961). *Of men and numbers.* New York: Dell.

NEEDLEMAN, H. L., SCHELL, A., BELLINGER, D., LEVITON, A., et al. (1990). The long-term effects of exposure to low doses of lead in childhood: An 11-year follow-up report. *New England Journal of Medicine, 322,* 83–88.

NEIDERT, G. P., & LINDER, D. E. (1990). Avoiding social traps: Some conditions that maintain adherence to restricted consumption. *Social Behavior, 5,* 261–284.

NEURINGER, A. J. (1970). Superstitious key-pecking after three peck-produced reinforcements. *Journal of the Experimental Analysis of Behavior, 13,* 127–134.

NEWMAN, H., FREEMAN, F. N., & HOLZINGER, K. J. (1937). *Twins: A study of heredity and environment.* Chicago: University of Chicago Press.

NEWSOM, C., FLAVALL, J. E., & RINCOVER, A. (1983). Side effects of punishment. In S. Axelrod & J. Apsche (Eds.), *The effects of punishment on human behavior.* New York: Academic Press.

NICHOLS, J. R., & HSIAO, S. (1967). Addiction liability of albino rats: Breeding for quantitative differences in morphine drinking. *Science, 157,* 561–563.

NISBETT, R. E. (1990). The anticreativity letters: Advice from a senior tempter to a junior tempter. *American Psychologist, 45,* 1078–1082.

NOVAK, M. A. (1991, July). "Psychologists care deeply" about animals. *APA Monitor,* p. 4.

NOVAK, M. A. (1991, July). Rebuttal by Novak: Animal welfare critical. *APA Monitor,* p. 5.

O'BRIEN, J. S., & RAYNES, A. E. (1973). Treatment of compulsive verbal behavior with response-contingent punishment and relaxation. *Journal of Behavior Therapy and Experimental Psychiatry, 4,* 347–352.

O'LEARY, K. D., & BECKER, W. C. (1968–1969). The effects of the intensity of a teacher's reprimands on children's behavior. *Journal of School Psychology, 7,* 8–11.

O'LEARY, K. D., KAUFMAN, K. F., KASS, R. E., & DRABMAN, R. S. (1970). The effects of loud and soft reprimands on disruptive students. *Exceptional Children, 37,* 145–155.

OLIVER, S. D., WEST, R. C., & SLOANE, H. N. (1974). Some effects on human behavior of aversive events. *Behavior Therapy, 5,* 481–493.

OST, L., & HUGDAHL, K. (1985). Acquisition of blood and dental phobia and anxiety response patterns in clinical patients. *Behavior Research and Therapy, 23,* 27–34.

OVERHOLSER, J. C. (1990). Fetal alcohol syndrome: A review of the disorder. *Journal of Contemporary Psychotherapy, 20,* 163–176.

OVERMIER, J. B., & SELIGMAN, M. E. P. (1967). Effects of inescapable shock upon subsequent escape and avoidance learning. *Journal of Comparative and Physiological Psychology, 63,* 23–33.

OVERTON, D. A. (1964). State-dependent or "dissociated" learning produced by pentobarbital. *Journal of Consulting and Clinical Psychology, 57,* 3–12.

PAPINI, M. R., & BITTERMAN, M. E. (1990). The role of contingency in classical conditioning. *Psychological Review, 97,* 396–403.

PARKS, D., CAVANAUGH, J., & SMITH, A. (1986). *Metamemory 2: Memory researchers' knowledge of their own memory abilities.* Washington, DC: American Psychological Association.

PATTERSON, F. P. (1978). The gesture of a gorilla: Language acquisition in another pongid. *Brain and Language, 5,* 72–97.

PATTERSON, F. P., PATTERSON, C. H., & BRENTARI, D. K. (1987). Language in child, chimp and gorilla. *American Psychologist, 42*, 270–272.

PAVLOV, I. P. (1927). *Conditioned reflexes.* (G. V. Anrep, Ed. and Trans.). London: Oxford University Press.

PAVLOV, I. P. (1932). Reply of a physiologist to psychologists. *Psychological Review, 39*, 91–127.

PAVLOV, I. P. (1941). *Lectures on conditioned reflexes (Vol. 2): Conditioned reflexes and psychiatry.* (W. H. Gantt, Ed. and Trans.). New York: International.

PECK, C. P. (1986). A public mental health issue: Risk-taking behavior and compulsive gambling. *American Psychologist, 41*, 461–465.

PECKSTEIN, L. A., & BROWN, F. D. (1939). An experimental analysis of the alleged criteria of insightful learning. *Journal of Educational Psychology, 30*, 38–52.

PEDERSEN, N. L., PLOMIN, R., McCLEARN, G. E., & FRIVERG, L. (1988). Neuroticism, extraversion, and related traits in adult twins reared apart and reared together. *Journal of Personality and Social Psychology, 55*, 950–957.

PERKINS, C. C., JR., & WEYANT, R. G. (1958). The interval between training and test trials as determiner of the slope of generalization gradients. *Journal of Comparative and Physiological Psychology, 51*, 596–600.

PETITTO, L. A., & SEIDENBERG, M. S. (1979). On the the evidence for linguistic abilities in signing apes. *Brain and Language, 8*, 162–183.

PIERCE, W. D., & EPLING, W. F. (1983). Choice, matching, and human behavior: A review of the literature. *The Behavior Analyst, 6*, 57–76.

PIPITONE, A. (1985, April 23). Jury to decide if sex obsession pushed man over edge. *Evening Sun* (Baltimore), pp. D1–D2.

PISACRETA, R., REDWOOD, E., & WITT, K. (1984). Transfer of matching-to-sample figure samples in the pigeon. *Journal of the Experimental Analysis of Behavior, 42*, 223–237.

PLATT, J. (1973). Social traps. *American Psychologist, 28*, 641–651.

POLENCHAR, B. E., ROMANO, A. G., STEINMETZ, J. E., & PATTERSON, M. M. (1984). Effects of US parameters on classical conditioning of cat hindlimb flexion. *Animal Learning and Behavior, 12*, 69–72.

POSTMAN, L., & RAU, L. (1957). Retention as a function of the method of measurement. *University of California Publications in Psychology, 8*, 217–270.

POWELL, D. A., & CREER, T. L. (1969). Interaction of developmental and environmental variables in shock-elicited aggression. *Journal of Consulting and Clinical Psychology, 69*, 219–225.

PREMACK, D. (1959). Toward empirical behavioral laws: I. Positive reinforcement. *Psychological Review, 66*, 219–233.

PREMACK, D. (1962). Reversibility of the reinforcement relation. *Science, 136*, 255–257.

PREMACK, D. (1965). Reinforcement theory. In D. Levine (Ed.), *Nebraska Symposium on Motivation* (Vol. 13). Lincoln: University of Nebraska Press.

PREMACK, D. (1971). Catching up with common sense or two sides of a generalization: Reinforcement and punishment. In R. Glaser (Ed.), *The nature of reinforcement.* New York: Academic Press.

PROKASY, W. F., & WHALEY, F. L. (1963). Inter-trial interval range shift in classical eyelid conditioning. *Psychological Reports, 12*, 55–88.

PRYOR, K. (1991). *Lads before the wind* (2nd ed.). North Bend, WA: Sunshine Books. (Originally published in 1975.)

PRYOR, K., HAAG, R., & O'REILLY, J. (1969). The creative porpoise: Training for novel behavior. *Journal of the Experimental Analysis of Behavior, 12,* 653–661.

QUAY, H. C. (1959). The effect of verbal reinforcement on the recall of early memories. *Journal of Abnormal and Social Psychology, 59,* 254–257.

RACHLIN, H. (1976). *Behavior and learning.* San Francisco: W. H. Freeman.

RACHLIN, H. (1989). *Judgment, decision and choice: A cognitive/behavioral synthesis.* New York: Freeman.

RACHLIN, H., & HERRNSTEIN, R. L. (1969). Hedonism revisited: On the negative law of effect. In B. A. Campbell & R. M. Church (Eds.), *Punishment and aversive behavior.* New York: Appleton-Century-Crofts.

RAINE, A., & DUNKIN, J. J. (1990). The genetic and psychophysiological basis of antisocial behavior: Implications for counseling and therapy. *Journal of Counseling and Development, 68,* 637–644.

RAZRAN, G. (1939). A quantitative study of meaning by a conditioned salivary technique (semantic conditioning). *Science, 90,* 89–90.

RAZRAN, G. (1956). Extinction re-examined and re-analyzed: A new theory. *Psychological Review, 63,* 39–52.

REED, T. (1980). Challenging some "common wisdom" on drug abuse. *International Journal of Addiction, 15,* 359.

RESCORLA, R. A. (1967). Pavlovian conditioning and its proper control procedures. *Psychological Review, 74,* 71–80.

RESCORLA, R. A. (1968). Probability of shock in the presence and absence of CS in fear conditioning. *Journal of Comparative and Physiological Psychology, 66,* 1–5.

RESCORLA, R. A. (1973). Evidence of "unique stimulus" account of configural conditioning. *Journal of Comparative and Physiological Psychology, 85,* 331–338.

RESCORLA, R. A., & WAGNER, A. R. (1972). A theory of Pavlovian conditioning: Variations in the effectiveness of reinforcement and nonreinforcement. In A. H. Black & W. F. Prokasy (Eds.), *Classical conditioning, II: Current research and theory.* New York: Appleton-Century-Crofts.

REVUSKY, S. H., & GARCIA, J. (1970). Learned associations over long delays. In G. H. Bower & J. T. Spence (Eds.), *The psychology of learning and motivation* (Vol. 4). New York: Academic Press.

REYNOLDS, W. F., & PAVLIK, W. B. (1960). Running speed as a function of deprivation period and reward magnitude. *Journal of Comparative and Physiological Psychology, 53,* 615–618.

RIGDEN, J. S., & TOBIAS, S. (1991, January/February). Tune in, turn off, drop out. *The Sciences,* pp. 16–20.

RILLING, M., & CAPLAN, H. J. (1973). Extinction-induced aggression during errorless discrimination learning. *Journal of the Experimental Analysis of Behavior, 20,* 85–91.

RIORDAN, C. A., & TEDESCHI, J. T. (1983). Attraction in aversive environments: Some evidence for classical conditioning and negative reinforcement. *Journal of Personality and Social Psychology, 44,* 683–692.

ROBERT, M. (1990). Observational learning in fish, birds, and mammals: A classified bibliography spanning over 100 years of research. *The Psychological Record, 40,* 289–311.

ROSEKRANS, M. A., & HARTUP, W. W. (1967). Imitative influences of consistent and inconsistent response consequences to a model on aggressive behavior in children. *Journal of Personality and Social Psychology, 7,* 429–434.

ROSENZWEIG, M. R., KRECH, D., BENNETT, E. L., & DIAMOND, M. (1962). Effects of environmental complexity and training on brain chemistry and anatomy: A replication and extension. *Jornal of Comparative and Physiological Psychology, 55,* 429–437.

ROZIN, P., & KALAT, J. W. (1971). Specific hungers and poison avoidance as adaptive specializations of learning. *Psychological Review, 78,* 459–486.

RUDOPH, B. (1986, March 31). Mounting doubts about debt. *Time,* pp. 50–51.

RUNDQUIST, E. A. (1933). Inheritance of spontaneous activity in rats. *Journal of Comparative Psychology, 16,* 415–438.

RUPPELL, G. (1975). *Bird flight.* New York: van Nostrand Reinhold.

RUSHTON, J. P. (1988). Race difference in behavior: A review and evolutionary analysis. *Personality and Individual Differences, 9,* 1009–1024.

RUSSELL, D. E. H. (1986a, March/April). The incest legacy. *The Sciences,* pp. 28–32.

RUSSELL, D. E. H. (1986b). *The secret trauma: Incest in the lives of girls and women.* New York: Basic Books.

RUSSELL, M., DARK, K. A., CUMMINS, R. W., ELLMAN, G., CALLAWAY, E., & PEEKE, H. V. S. (1984). Learned histamine release. *Science, 225,* 733–734.

SAMAAN, M. (1975). Thought-stopping and flooding in a case of hallucinations, obsessions, and homicidal-suicidal behavior. *Journal of Behavior Therapy and Experimental Psychiatry, 6,* 65–67.

SANDS, S. F., & WRIGHT, A. A. (1980). Primate memory: Retention of serial list items by a rhesus monkey. *Science, 209,* 938–940.

SAVORY, T. (1974). *Introduction to arachnology.* London: Muller.

SCHNEIDER, S. (1990). The role of contiguity in free-operant unsignaled delay of positive reinforcement: A brief review. *The Psychological Record, 40,* 239–257.

SCHNEIDER, S. M. (1992). Can this marriage be saved? *American Psychologist, 47,* 1055–1057.

SCHNEIRLA, T. C. (1944). A unique case of circular milling in ants, considered in relation to trail following and the general problem of orientation. *American Museum Novitiates, 1253,* 1–26.

SCHUETT, G. W., CLARK, D. L., & KRAUS, F. (1984). Feeding mimicry in the rattlesnake Sistrurus catenatus, with comments on the evolution of the rattle. *Animal Behavior, 32,* 624–629.

SCHWARTZ, B., & LACEY, H. (1982). *Behaviorism, science, and human nature.* New York: Norton.

SCHWARTZ, B., & REILLY, M. (1985). Long-term retention of a complex operant in pigeons. *Journal of Experimental Psychology: Animal Behavior Processes, 11,* 337–355.

SCHWARTZ, B., SCHULDENFREI, R., & LACEY, H. (1978). Operant psychology as factor psychology. *Behaviorism, 6,* 229–254.

SCOTT, J. P. (1958). *Animal behavior.* Chicago: University of Chicago Press.

SCOTT, J. P. (1962). Critical periods in behavioral development. *Science, 138,* 949–958.

SEARS, R. R., MACCOBY, E. E., & LEVIN, H. (1957). *Patterns of child rearing.* Evanston, IL: Row, Peterson.

SELIGMAN, M. E. P. (1970). On the generality of the laws of learning. *Psychological Review, 77,* 406–418.

SELIGMAN, M. E. P. (1971). Phobias and preparedness. *Behavior Therapy, 2,* 307–320.

SELIGMAN, M. E. P. (1975). *Helplessness: On depression, development, and death.* San Francisco: W. H. Freeman.

SELIGMAN, M. E. P., & HAGER, J. L. (Eds.). (1972a). *Biological boundaries of learning.* New York: Appleton-Century-Crofts.

SELIGMAN, M. E. P., & HAGER, J. L. (1972b, August). Biological boundaries of learning: The sauce-bearnaise syndrome. *Psychology Today,* pp. 59–61, 84–87.

SELIGMAN, M. E. P., & MAIER, S. F. (1967). Failure to escape traumatic shock. *Journal of Experimental Psychology, 74,* 1–9.

SHAPIRO, G. L. (1982). Sign acquisition in a home-reared, free-ranging orangutan: Comparisons with other signing apes. *American Journal of Primatology, 3,* 121–129.

SHAPIRO, K. J. (1991a, July). Rebuttal by Shapiro: Practices must change. *APA Monitor,* p. 4.

SHAPIRO, K. J. (1991b, July). Use morality as a basis for animal treatment. *APA Monitor,* p. 5.

SHARPLESS, S., & JASPER, H. H. (1956). Habituation of the arousal reaction. *Brain, 79,* 655–680.

SHEPHER, J. (1971). Mate selection among second-generation kibbutz adolescents and adults: Incest avoidance and negative imprinting. *Archives of Sexual Behavior, 1,* 293–307.

SHERMAN, R. A. (1991). Aversives, fundamental rights and the courts. *The Behavior Analyst, 14,* 197–206.

SHERRY, D. F., & GALEF, B. G., JR. (1984). Cultural transmission without imitation: milk bottle opening in birds. *Animal Behavior, 32,* 937–938.

SHETTLEWORTH, S. J. (1988). Foraging as operant behavior and operant behavior as foraging: What have we learned? In G. H. Bower (Ed.), *Psychology of learning and motivation.* (Vol. 22, pp. 1–49). New York: Academic Press.

SHIELDS, J. (1973). Heredity and psychological abnormality. In H. J. Eysenck, *Handbook of abnormal psychology* (2nd ed.). San Diego, CA: Knapp.

SHIELDS, J., & SLATER, E. (1960). Heredity and psychological abnormality. In H. J. Eysenck, *Handbook of abnormal psychology.* New York: Basic Books.

SIDMAN, M. (1953). Avoidance conditioning with brief shock and no exteroceptive warning signal. *Science, 118,* 157–158.

SIDMAN, M. (1962), Reduction of shock frequency as reinforcement for avoidance behavior. *Journal of the Experimental Analysis of Behavior, 5,* 247–257.

SIDMAN, M. (1966). Avoidance behavior. In W. K. Honig (Ed.), *Operant behavior.* New York: Appleton-Century-Crofts.

SIDMAN, M. (1989a). Avoidance at Columbia. *The Behavior Analyst, 12,* 191–195.

SIDMAN, M. (1989b). *Coercion and its fallout.* Boston, MA: Authors Cooperative.

SIEGEL, S. (1975). Evidence from rats that morphine tolerance is a learned response. *Journal of Comparative and Physiological Psychology, 89,* 498.

SIEGEL, S. (1976). Morphine analgesic tolerance: Its situation specificity supports a Pavlovian conditioning model. *Science, 193,* 323–325.

SIEGEL, S. (1983). Classical conditioning, drug tolerance, and drug dependence. In R. G. Smart, F. B. Glaser, Y. Israel, H. Kalant, R. E. Popham, & W. Schmidt (Eds.), *Research advances in alcohol and drug problems* (Vol. 7). New York: Plenum.

SIEGEL, S. (1984). Pavlovian conditioning and heroin overdose: Reports by overdose victims. *Bulletin of the Psychonomic Society, 22,* 428–430.

SIEGEL, S., HINSON, R. E., KRANK, M. D., & McCULLY, J. (1982). Heroin "overdose" death: Contribution of drug-associated environmental cues. *Science, 216,* 436–437.

SIMONTON, D. K. (1987). Developmental antecedents of achieved eminence. *Annals of Child Development, 5,* 131–169.

SIQUELAND, E., & DELUCIA, C. A. (1969). Visual reinforcement on non-nutritive sucking in human infants. *Science, 165,* 1144–1146.

SIVY, M. (1987, February). House of credit cards. *Money,* pp. 57–58.

SKINNER, B. F. (1938). *The behavior of organisms: An experimental analysis.* New York: Appleton-Century-Crofts.

SKINNER, B. F. (1948a). Superstition in the pigeon. *Journal of Experimental Psychology, 38,* 168–172.

SKINNER, B. F. (1948b). *Walden two.* New York: Macmillan.

SKINNER, B. F. (1951). How to teach animals. *Scientific American, 185,* 26–29.

SKINNER, B. F. (1953). *Science and human behavior.* New York: Free Press.

SKINNER, B. F. (1956). A case history in scientific method. *American Psychologist, 11,* 221–233.

SKINNER, B. F. (1957). *Verbal behavior.* New York: Appleton-Century-Crofts.

SKINNER, B. F. (1960). Pigeons in a Pelican. *American Psychologist, 15,* 28–37.

SKINNER, B. F. (1968). *The technology of teaching.* Englewood Cliffs, NJ: Prentice-Hall.

SKINNER, B. F. (1969). *Contingencies of reinforcement: A theoretical analysis.* New York: Appleton-Century-Crofts.

SKINNER, B. F. (1971). *Beyond freedom and dignity.* New York: Knopf.

SKINNER, B. F. (1974). *About behaviorism.* New York: Knopf.

SKINNER, B. F. (1975). The shaping of phylogenic behavior. *Journal of the Experimental Analysis of Behavior, 24,* 117–120.

SKINNER, B. F. (1976). *Particulars of my life.* New York: Knopf.

SKINNER, B. F. (1977). *The shaping of a behaviorist.* New York: Knopf.

SKINNER, B. F. (1981). Selection by consequences. *Science, 213,* 501–504.

SKINNER, B. F. (1983a). *A matter of consequences.* New York: Knopf.

SKINNER, B. F. (1983b). Can the experimental analysis of behavior rescue psychology? *The Behavior Analyst, 6,* 9–17.

SKINNER, B. F. (1983c). Intellectual self-management in old age. *American Psychologist, 38,* 239–244.

SKINNER, B. F. (1984). The evolution of behavior. *Journal of the Experimental Analysis of Behavior, 41,* 217–221.

SKODAK, M., & SKEELS, H. M. (1949). A final follow-up study of one hundred adopted children. *Journal of Genetic Psychology, 75,* 85–125.

SLOANE, H. N., ENDO, G. T., & DELLA-PIANA, G. (1980). Creative behavior. *The Behavior Analyst, 3,* 11–22.

SMITH, K. (1984). "Drive": In defence of a concept. *Behaviorism, 12,* 71–114.

SOLOMON, R. L., & WYNNE, L. C. (1953). Traumatic avoidance learning: Acquisition in normal dogs. *Psychological Monographs, 67* (whole no. 354).

SPENCE, K. W. (1936). The nature of discrimination learning in animals. *Psychological Review, 43,* 427–449.

SPENCE, K. W. (1937). The differential response in animals to stimuli varying within a single dimension. *Psychological Review, 44,* 430–444.

SPENCE, K. W. (1953). Learning and performance in eyelid conditioning as a function of intensity of the UCS. *Journal of Experimental Psychology, 45,* 57–63.

SPENCE, K. W. (1960). *Behavior theory and learning.* Englewood Cliffs, NJ: Prentice-Hall.

SPETCH, M. L., WILKIE, D. M., & PINEL, J. P. J. (1981). Backward conditioning: A reevaluation of the empirical evidence. *Psychological Bulletin, 89,* 163–175.

SPIEGLER, M. D., & WEILAND, A. (1976). The effects of written vicarious consequences on observers' willingness to imitate and ability to recall modeling cues. *Journal of Personality, 44,* 260–273.

STAATS, A. W., & STAATS, C. K. (1958). Attitudes established by classical conditioning. *Journal of Abnormal and Social Psychology, 57,* 37–40.

STAATS, C. K., & STAATS, A. W. (1957). Meaning established by classical conditioning. *Journal of Experimental Psychology, 54,* 74–80.

STACHNIK, T. J. (1972). The case against criminal penalties for illicit drug use. *American Psychologist, 27,* 637–642.

STADDON, J. E. R. (1991). Selective choice: A commentary on Herrnstein (1990). *American Psychologist, 46,* 793–797.

STADDON, J. E. R., & SIMMELHAG, V. L. (1971). The "superstition" experiment: A re-examination of its implications for the principles of adaptive behavior. *Psychological Review, 78,* 3–43.

STALLINGS, J. (1980). Allocated academic learning time revisited, or beyond time on task. *Educational Researcher, 9,* 11–16.

STARIN, S. (1991). "Nonaversive" behavior management: A misnomer. *The Behavior Analyst, 14,* 207–209.

STERN, A. (1971). *The making of a genius.* Miami, FL: Hurricane House.

STONE, I, (1980). *The origins.* New York: Doubleday.

STRUM, S. C. (1987). *Almost human: A journey into the world of baboons.* New York: Random House.

STUART, E. W., SHIMP, T. A., & ENGLE, R. W. (1987). Classical conditioning of consumer attitudes: Four experiments in an advertising context. *Journal of Consumer Research, 14,* 334–340.

TARPLEY, H. D., & SCHROEDER, S. R. (1979). Comparison of DRO and DRI on rate of suppression of self-injurious behavior. *American Journal of Mental Deficiency, 84,* 188–194.

TAYLOR, J. A. (1951). The relationship of anxiety to the conditioned eyelid response. *Journal of Experimental Psychology, 41,* 81–92.

TERRACE, H. S. (1963). Discrimination learning with and without "errors." *Journal of the Experimental Analysis of Behavior, 6,* 1–27.

TERRACE, H. S. (1964). Wavelength generalization after discrimination learning with and without errors. *Science, 144,* 78–80.

TERRACE, H. S. (1972). By-products of discrimination learning. In G. H. Bower (Ed.), *The psychology of learning and motivation* (Vol. 5). New York: Academic Press.

TERRACE, H. S. (1979). *Nim.* New York: Knopf.

THOMAS, D. R. (1991). Stimulus control: Principles and procedures. In W. Ishaq (Ed.), *Human behavior in today's world.* New York: Praeger.

THOMAS, D. R., MOOD, K., MORRISON, S. & WIERTELAK, E. (1991). Peak shift revisited: A test of alternative interpretations. *Journal of Experimental Psychology: Animal Behavior Processes, 17,* 130–140.

THOMAS, G. V., LIEBERMAN, D. A., McINTOSH, D. C., & RONALDSON, P. (1983). The role of marking when reward is delayed. *Journal of Experimental Psychology, 9,* 401–411.

THOMPSON, R. F., & SPENCER, W. A. (1966). Habituation: A model phenomenon for the study of neural substrates of behavior. *Psychological Review, 73,* 16–43.

THORNDIKE, E. L. (1898). Animal intelligence. *Psychological Review Monographs, 2*(8).

THORNDIKE, E. L. (1901). The mental life of the monkeys. *Psychological Review Monographs, 3*(15).

THORNDIKE, E. L. (1911). *Animal intelligence: Experimental studies.* New York: Hafner.

THORNDIKE, E. L. (1932). *Fundamentals of learning.* New York: Teachers College Press.

THORNDIKE, E. L. (1936). Autobiography. In C. Murchison (Ed.), *A history of psychology in autobiography* (Vol. 3). Worcester, MA: Clark University Press.

THORNDIKE, E. L. (1968). *Human learning.* Cambridge, MA: MIT Press. (Originally published in 1931.)

THORPE, W. H. (1963). *Learning and instinct in animals.* London: Methuen.

THUNE, L. E., & UNDERWOOD, B. J. (1943). Retroactive inhibition as a function of degree of interpolated learning. *Journal of Experimental Psychology, 32,* 185–200.

THUROW, L. (1992). *Head to Head.* New York: Morrow.

TIMBERLAKE, W. (1980). A molar equilibrium theory of learned performance. In G. H. Bower (Ed.), *The psychology of learning and motivation* (Vol. 14, pp. 1–58). New York: Academic Press.

TIMBERLAKE, W., & ALLISON, J. (1974). Response deprivation: An empirical approach to instrumental performance. *Psychological Review, 81,* 146–164.

TIMBERLAKE, W., & LUCAS, G. A. (1985). The basis of superstitious behavior: Chance contingency, stimulus substitution, or appetitive behavior? *Journal of the Experimental Analysis of Behavior, 44,* 279–299.

TINBERGEN, N. (1951). *The study of instinct.* Oxford: Clarendon Press.

TODD, J. T., & MORRIS, E. K. (1992). Case histories in the great power of steady misrepresentation. *American Psychologist, 47,* 1441–1453.

TODD, J. T., MORRIS, E. K., & FENZA, K. M. (1989). Temporal organization of extinction-induced responding in preschool children. *The Psychological Record, 39,* 117–130.

TODOROV, J. C., HANNA, E. S., & DE SA, M. C. N. B. (1984). Frequency versus magnitude of reinforcement: New data with a different procedure. *Journal of the Experimental Analysis of Behavior, 41,* 157–167.

TRYON, R. C. (1940). Genetic differences in maze-learning ability in rats. In *National Society for the Study of Education Yearbook, Intelligence: Its nature and nurture: I. Comparative and critical exposition.* Bloomington: Public School.

TULVING, E. (1974). Cue-dependent forgetting. *American Scientist, 62,* 74–82.

TUMLINSON, J. H., LEWIS, W. J., & VET, L. E. M. (1993). How parasitic wasps find their hosts. *Scientific American, 266,* 100–106.

TURKKAN, J. S. (1989). Classical conditioning: The new hegemony. *Behavioral and Brain Sciences, 12,* 121–179.

ULRICH, R. E. (1966). Pain as a cause of aggression. *American Zoologist, 6,* 643–662.

ULRICH, R. E., & AZRIN, N. A. (1962). Reflexive fighting in response to aversive stimuli. *Journal of the Experimental Analysis of Behavior, 5,* 511–520.

ULRICH, R. E., HUTCHINSON, R. R., & AZRIN, N. H. (1965). Pain-elicited aggression. *The Psychological Record, 15,* 116–126.

UNDERWOOD, B. J. (1948). Retroactive and proactive inhibition after 5 and 48 hours. *Journal of Experimental Psychology, 38,* 29–38.

UNDERWOOD, B. J. (1949). Proactive inhibition as a function of time and degree of learning. *Journal of Experimental Psychology, 39*, 24–34.

UNDERWOOD, B. J. (1957). Interference and forgetting. *Psychological Review, 64*, 49–60.

UNDERWOOD, B. J., KEPPEL, G., & SCHULZ, R. W. (1962). Studies of distributed practice: XXII. Some conditions which enhance retention. *Journal of Experimental Psychology, 64*, 355–363.

VANDER WALL, S. B. (1982). An experimental analysis of cache recovery by Clark's nutcracker. *Animal Behavior, 30*, 80–94.

VANDER WALL, S. B. (1991). Mechanisms of cache recovery by yellow pine chipmunks. *Animal Behavior, 41*, 851–863.

VERPLANCK, W. S. (1955). The operant, from rat to man: An introduction to some recent experiments on human behavior. *Transactions of the New York Academy of Sciences, 17*, 594–601.

VOLPICELLI, J. R., ULM, R. R., ALTENOR, A., & SELIGMAN, M. E. P. (1983). Learned mastery in the rat. *Learning and Motivation, 14*, 204–222.

VYSE, S. A. (1991). Behavioral variability and rule generation: General, restricted and superstitious contingency statements. *Psychological Record, 41*, 487–506.

VYSE, S. A., & HELTZER, R. A. (1990, August 11). *Intermittent consequences and problem solving: The experimental control of "superstitious" beliefs.* Paper presented at the 98th annual convention, American Psychological Association.

WAGNER, A. R., & RESCORLA, R. A. (1972). Inhibition in Pavlovian conditioning: Application of a theory. In R. A. Boakes & M. S. Halliday (Eds.), *Inhibition and learning.* London: Academic Press.

WAGNER, G. A., & MORRIS, E. K. (1987). "Superstitious" behavior in children. *The Psychological Record, 37*, 471–488.

WALLACE, P. (1976). Animal behavior: The puzzle of flavor aversion. *Science, 193*, 989–991.

WALTERS, R. H., & BROWN, M. (1963). Studies of reinforcement of aggression: III. Transfer of responses to an interpersonal situation. *Child Development, 34*, 563–571.

WARDEN, C. J., & AYLESWORTH, M. (1927). The relative value of reward and punishment in the formation of a visual discrimination habit in the white rat. *Journal of Comparative Psychology, 7*, 117–128.

WARDEN, C. J., FJELD, H. A., & KOCH, A. M. (1940). Imitative behavior in cebus and rhesus monkeys. *Journal of Genetic Psychology 56*, 311–322.

WARDEN, C. J., & JACKSON, T. A. (1935). Imitative behavior in the rhesus monkey. *Journal of Genetic Psychology, 46*, 103–125.

WASSERMAN, E. A. (1989). Pavlovian conditioning: Is temporal contiguity irrelevant? *American Psychologist, 44*, 1550–1551.

WATSON, J. B. (1908). Imitation in monkeys. *Psychological Bulletin, 5*, 169–178.

WATSON, J. B. (1970). *Behaviorism.* New York: Norton. (Originally published in 1930.)

WATSON, J. B., & RAYNER, R. (1920). Conditioned emotional reactions. *Journal of Experimental Psychology, 3*, 1–4.

WEIL, J. L. (1984). The effects of delayed reinforcement on free-operant responding. *Journal of the Experimental Analysis of Behavior, 41*, 143–155.

WEINER, H. (1983). Some thoughts on discrepant human-animal performance under schedules of reinforcement. *The Psychological Record, 33,* 521–532.

WELLS, H. K. (1956). *Pavlov and Freud: I. Toward a scientific psychology and psychiatry.* London: Lawrence and Wishart.

WIDOM, C. S. (1989). Does violence beget violence? A critical examination of the literature. *Psychological Bulletin, 106,* 3–28.

WIEHE, V. R. (1992). Abusive and nonabusive parents: How they were parented. *Journal of Social Services Research, 15,* 81–93.

WILCOXON, H. C., DRAGOIN, W. B., & KRAL, P. A. (1971). Illness-induced aversions in rat and quail: Relative salience of visual and gustatory cues. *Science, 171,* 826–828.

WILLIAMS, C. D. (1959). The elimination of tantrum behavior by extinction procedures. *Journal of Abnormal and Social Psychology, 59,* 269.

WILLIAMS, D. R., & WILLIAMS, H. (1969). Auto-maintenance in the pigeon: Sustained pecking despite contingent nonreinforcement. *Journal of the Experimental Analysis of Behavior, 12,* 511–520.

WILLIAMS, J. E. (1966). Connotations of racial concepts and color names. *Journal of Personality and Social Psychology, 3,* 531–540.

WILLIAMS, J. E., & EDWARDS, C. D. (1969). An exploratory study of the modification of color concepts and racial attitudes in preschool children. *Child Development, 40,* 737–750.

WILLIAMS, S. B. (1938). Resistance to extinction as a function of the number of reinforcements. *Journal of Experimental Psychology, 23,* 506–522.

WILSON, E. O. (1975). *Sociobiology: The new synthesis.* Cambridge, MA: Harvard University Press.

WILSON, E. O. (1978). *On human nature.* Cambridge, MA: Harvard University Press.

WINSTON, A. S., & BAKER, J. E. (1985). Behavior-analytic studies of creativity: A critical review. *The Behavior Analyst, 8,* 191–205.

WOLF, M. M., BRAUKMANN, C. J., & RAMP, K. A. (1987). Serious delinquent behavior as part of a significantly handicapping condition: Cures and supportive environments. *Journal of Applied Behavior Analysis, 20,* 347–359.

WOLF, M. M., RISLEY, T., JOHNSON, M., HARRIS, F., & ALLEN, E. (1967). Application of operant conditioning procedures to the behavior problems of an autistic child: A follow-up and extension. *Behavior Research and Therapy, 5,* 103–111.

WOLFE, J. B. (1936). Effectiveness of token-rewards for chimpanzees. *Comparative Psychology Monographs, 12*(5).

WOLK, R. A. (1992, February). A vision for better schools. *Teacher Magazine,* p. 3.

WRIGHT, A. A., SANTIAGO, H. C., SANDS, S. F., KENDRICK, D. F., & COOK, R. G. (1985). Memory processing of serial lists by pigeons, monkeys and people. *Science, 229,* 287–289.

YANDO, R. M., SEITZ, V., & ZIGLER, E. (1978). *Imitation: A developmental perspective.* Hillsdale, NJ: Erlbaum.

YERKES, R. M. (1912). The intelligence of earthworms. *Journal of Animal Behavior, 2,* 332–352.

ZEILER, M. D. (1984). The sleeping giant: Reinforcement schedules. *Journal of the Experimental Analysis of Behavior, 42,* 485–493.

ZENER, K. (1937). The significance of behavior accompanying conditioned salivary secretion for theories of the conditioned response. *American Journal of Psychology, 50,* 384–403.

Author Index

Subject Index

The terms in **boldface** are defined in the glossary.

A

ABA design, 45–46
Aborigines, Australian, 20
Acquisition, 28
Adaptation
  discrimination and, 208–209
  generalization and, 208–209
  genetic variation and, 2, 4, 15
  learning and, 16–21, 27
  mutation and, 4
  natural selection and, 2–5, 15
Adventitious reinforcement, 151
Advertising, 94
Age, 75, 76
Aggression
  aversive control and, 272–273
  male baboons and, 17–18
  nature versus nurture debate and,
    19–20
  pain and, response to, 19–20
  social, 178–181
Albert B. (infant boy), 89, 90, 111–
    112, 186
Alcohol use, 78
American Psychological Association, 48
Amplitude of response, 37
Anecdotal evidence, 40, 79
Animals
  creativity and, 148–149
  critical period of learning and, 318–
    319
  fixed action pattern and, 8–10

foraging and, 177–178
memory and, 299–300
natural selection and, 2–3
negative reinforcement and, 255–256
nocturnal habits of, 21
operant learning and, 101–106
pecking order and, 28–29
problem solving and, insightful, 146–
    147
rights of, 48–50
selective breeding and, 2, 13
self-awareness and, 137–138
shaping and, 112–113
as subjects in research, 48–51
supernormal psychology of, 101–102
superstitious behavior and, 150–
    152, 153
Anorexia, 187
Attentional processes, 173–174
Autism, 49
Autoshaping, 321–322
Aversive control. *See also* Negative rein-
    forcement; Punishment
  aggression and, 272–273
  alternatives to, 275–278
  noncontingent aversives and, 252–255
  price of aversives and, 271–274
  suffering and, 251–252
Aversive event, 12
Aversives
  noncontingent, 252–255
  price of, 271–274

TO THE OWNER OF THIS BOOK:

I hope that you have found *Learning and Behavior,* 3rd Edition, useful. So that this book can be improved in a future edition, would you take the time to complete this sheet and return it? Thank you.

School and address: _____

Department: _____

Instructor's name: _____

1. What I like most about this book is: _____

_____

2. What I like least about this book is: _____

_____

3. My general reaction to this book is: _____

_____

4. The name of the course in which I used this book is: _____

_____

5. Were all of the chapters of the book assigned for you to read? _____

   If not, which ones weren't? _____

_____

6. In the space below, or on a separate sheet of paper, please write specific suggestions for improving this book and anything else you'd care to share about your experience in using the book.

_____

_____

_____

_____

_____

_____

Optional:

Your name: _____ Date: _____

May Brooks/Cole quote you either in promotion for *Learning and Behavior*, 3rd Edition, or in future publishing ventures?

Yes: _____ No: _____

Sincerely,

Paul Chance